States versus Markets

The Emergence of a Global Economy

Third Edition

Herman M. Schwartz

palgrave
macmillan

First edition 1994
Second edition 2000
Third edition 2010

Published by
PALGRAVE MACMILLAN

Palgrave Macmillan in the UK is an imprint of Macmillan Publishers Limited,
registered in England, company number 785998, of Houndmills, Basingstoke,
Hampshire RG21 6XS.

Palgrave Macmillan in the US is a division of St Martin's Press LLC,
175 Fifth Avenue, New York, NY 10010.

Palgrave Macmillan is the global academic imprint of the above companies
and has companies and representatives throughout the world.

Palgrave® and Macmillan® are registered trademarks in the United States,
the United Kingdom, Europe and other countries

ISBN 978–0–230–52133–9 hardback
ISBN 978–0–230–52128–5 paperback

This book is printed on paper suitable for recycling and made from fully
managed and sustained forest sources. Logging, pulping and manufacturing
processes are expected to conform to the environmental regulations of the
country of origin.

A catalogue record for this book is available from the British Library.

A catalog record for this book is available from the Library of Congress.

7
12

Printed and bound in Great Britain by
CPI Antony Rowe, Chippenham and Eastbourne

For RLS and in memory of KMS

Contents

List of Tables

List of Figures

List of Abbreviations

ACP	African Caribbean Pacific system
BEM	Big Emerging Markets
CDO	Collaterized Debt Obligations
EMS	European Monetary System
EOI	Export Oriented Industrialization
FDI	Foreign Direct Investment
FIE	Foreign Invested Firms
GATT	General Agreement on Trade and Tariffs
IBRD	International Bank for Reconstruction and Development [World Bank]
ICOR	Incremental Capital Output Ratio
IMF	International Monetary Fund
ISI	Import Substitution Industrialization
ITO	International Trade Organization
LDC	Less Developed Countries
MBS	Mortgage Backed Securities
MEW	Mortgage Equity Withdrawal
MFA	Multi Fiber Agreement
MFN	Most Favored Nation
MITI	Ministry for International Trade and Industry
NAC	New Agricultural Countries
NAFTA	North American Free Trade Agreement
NCE	Neoclassical economic explanations
NFA	Non-Food Agricultural
NIC	Newly Industrialized Countries
OECD	Organisation for Economic Co-operation and Development
OPEC	Organization of Petroleum Exporting Countries
RTAA	Reciprocal Trade Agreements Act
RULC	Relative Unit Labor Costs
TNC	Transnational Corporations
TRIM	Trade Related Investment Measures
VER	Voluntary Export Restraint
WST	World Systems theory
WTO	World Trade Organization

Preface

Fifteen years ago when the first edition of this book was published, the debates about globalization had just started. Those debates were largely simple, polarized debates about the impending triumph of markets as states withered away, or claims that some vaguely defined masses would rise up against markets and restore the world to the golden age of Bretton Woods regulation. These debates pitted those who claimed that globalization represented an intrinsically new, irresistible force against those who claimed that globalization was nothing new and certainly incapable of effecting much displacement of the immoveable, local constellations of political power that states represent. Over the years, more nuanced analyses of specific global commodity chains, social movements, state efforts at regulation, and human migration replaced those old debates.

The debate has thus shifted towards the position this book first elaborated in 1994: Globalization was the re-emergence of markets that states had temporarily suppressed in the aftermath of the Great Depression and World War II. These markets are as old as the international system of states, as are states' efforts to use those markets for their own purposes. Markets create winners and losers, and conflict between states is generally zero-sum, so non-uniform outcomes are always likely. Moreover, states and social groups often transform state institutions precisely in order to take advantage of market opportunities or resist market pressures.

The third edition of this book makes these points more pointedly, showing how the industrialization of Asia required the same kinds of state policies as the industrialization of Western Europe in the nineteenth century, and how the global financial crises of the 1990s and 2000s closely resemble similar market-driven phenomena in the nineteenth century. It also shows how the United States, unlike Britain, tried to renovate its hegemony in the late twentieth century precisely by continuing the centuries-old process by which states have forcefully created markets. In this case, the United States deliberately created markets in the service sector, which had been closely regulated by states after the Depression.

When the second edition of *States versus Markets* was published in 2000, it was already obvious that China had been reintegrated into world markets. American consumers could not enter a store for clothing, toys or kitchen tools without encountering Chinese-made goods. In the eight years since 2000, China has become even more important in the global economy, translating its dominance of labor-intense manufacturing into a substantial share of medium technology industry, and both of these into the world's largest hoard of foreign exchange – mostly US dollars. China's rise has also helped developing country raw materials exporters, like Brazil, dig their way out of much of their indebtedness to the developed countries by temporarily reversing a decades-long decline in raw materials prices. This third edition thus considers how China does and does not fit into the analytic pattern laid down in the 1994 edition.

This edition also argues that the sudden collapse of global financial markets and trade in the crisis that started in 2007 closes a chapter – but not the final chapter – on globalization as a process. The current crisis has brought states back to center stage to manage markets, particularly financial markets. But even if these states retain ownership of financial firms – and I think this unlikely – most large firms and their supply chains are and will remain globally oriented. Oil-based transport costs will continue to rise on a secular basis dampening trade in goods. But the economy of the future is an economy dominated by services, where communications costs matter more. These costs will continue to fall on a secular basis, encouraging further investment and sales offshore. Just as with agriculture and manufacturing in the past, markets will disperse some activities geographically and concentrate others, dislocating employment patterns and state revenues. And just as with agriculture and manufacturing, states will compete to retain or capture these activities. States went to extraordinary lengths to save global capitalism in 2008–9. But they did so intending to prevent a cataclysmic de-globalization, not to accelerate it.

This book was revised at the Miller Center of the University of Virginia, which kindly provided me with a quiet space to think about what had changed over nearly a decade. Charlottesville is anything but a featureless plain extending in all directions. Yet the US housing boom of the 2000s caused a relentless horizontal and vertical expansion of Charlottesville housing and businesses that displaced local farming and older housing. As always, I learned as much from wandering around with my eyes open as from various documents. But I learned even more from my colleagues, so I thank Gerard Alexander, Dale Copeland, John Echeverri-Gent, Robert Fatton, Jeff Legro, Allen Lynch, John Owen, Bruce Reynolds, Jim Savage, Leonard Schoppa, David Waldner, and Brantly Womack for various interesting conversations that one way or another, wittingly or unwittingly helped make this book better. Peter Breiner, Robert Denemark, Shelley Hurt, Alethia Jones, Greg Nowell, Louis Pauly, Andrew Schrank and Dimitris Stevis also helped with comment and criticism of various parts of the second edition. Special thanks to Randall Germain, Henk Overbeek and Geoffrey Underhill for encouraging Palgrave and me to pursue a third edition, and for providing much useful criticism. All errors remain mine, at least until I find a ratings agency that will slap an investment grade label on them.

HERMAN M. SCHWARTZ

Introduction

Imagine a very large town, at the center of a fertile plain which is crossed by no navigable river or canal. ... There are no other towns on the plain. The central town must therefore supply the rural areas with all manufactured products, and in return it will obtain all its provisions from the surrounding countryside.

Johann von Thünen (1826)

Globalization or globaloney? This book's third edition reiterates earlier editions' major point: globalization – pervasive global price pressures on all market actors – is nothing new, but neither are pervasive and often successful efforts by states to contain and structure those price pressures. Moreover, extremists on both sides of this debate are wrong not simply because they overstate their arguments, but also because they misstate the symbiosis between markets and states, and because they misunderstand some of the ironies inherent in the global expansion of both phenomena over the past half-millennium. Modern states and modern markets cannot exist without each other: states selectively create and enforce the property rights that maintain markets; property rights sustain the accumulation of capital and growth of incomes that create the regular and substantial sources of revenues which sustain states. States encouraged and shaped the penetration of global market pressures into territory formerly insulated from those pressures, and this has enabled an even faster redistribution of economic activity over a global space. But states' very success in monetizing and 'marketizing' their territories means that more and more market activity becomes domestically oriented, exposing state revenue streams to changes in market activity. This dynamic tension is why the book is titled states *versus* markets rather than states *and* markets.

It's hardly accidental that mainstream economics, exemplified by Paul Krugman's publication of three books on economic geography in the 1990s, rediscovered that the market distributes and redistributes economic activity over space. Krugman notes:

About a year ago I more or less suddenly realized that I have spent my whole professional life as an international economist thinking and writing about economic geography, without being aware of it.

(1991)

But Krugman comes late to this enterprise. Nearly two centuries before Krugman awoke, the German economist-farmer Johann von Thünen (1966 [1826]) had already shown that market-based agricultural activity will organize itself into rings of specific crops centered on a city. A short logical step takes us from Thünen's abstraction to the largely agricultural world economy, integrated by waterborne transport and centered on emerging agglomerations of industry that existed well into the twentieth century.

1

The rediscovery that markets shape the location of global economic activity occurred precisely when states' ability to control markets began breaking down, most visibly with the collapse of the post-World War II Bretton Woods system. This allowed global market pressures to re-emerge. But globalization in this sense, rather than in its buzzword sense, has been around for a long time. What we see today is a re-emergence of patterns that existed in the pre-World War II world economy. The best way to understand what is new or not about globalization, and how globalization matters or not, is not to look at the period most analyses of international political economy take as their lodestone – the Bretton Woods era – but rather at the period before Bretton Woods. Bretton Woods, Keynesian regulation of the economy, and the regulation of the service sector are the unusual phenomena here, not globalization.

The problem

At its most basic level, the international political economy is about how market pressures cause actors to constantly relocate productive activities in a global space, about how states try to bend those market forces when it hurts them and allow them to work when it helps, and about the essential unity of modern states and capitalist markets. Market pressures on individuals and firms motivate them to relocate production and consumption. States intervene to help or hinder this market-driven redistribution, but often with unintended results. States' ability to intervene and dictate market outcomes during most of the postwar period leads most people to cast the current problem as one of intervention versus its absence and to pose states as natural antagonists to markets. But the essential issues are the kind of intervention, not its quantity, and the ways in which states and markets both need each other and are in a dynamic tension. Focusing on the quantity of intervention obscures what is most essential about the modern world economy, because, in its most fundamental respects, the world economy is becoming much more like the kind of world economy that existed in the late nineteenth century when states encouraged and coped with the expansion of two different kinds of market forces.

The first was a *secular* trend towards greater movement of people, capital, commodities, and firms in a global market. Entering the market before 1914 meant entering the world market. Trade grew rapidly before 1914, based on complementary flows of goods between exporters of agricultural goods and exporters of manufactured goods. Roughly 120 million people moved overseas, either voluntarily or involuntarily, and large numbers also migrated inside Europe and Asia. And billions of dollars of investment facilitated the ecological transformation of entire continents by migrants and colonial governments trying to produce more food and raw materials. Market forces dictated the general location of these new agricultural zones. Competent or lucky states in those areas seized these opportunities; incompetent ones fumbled the future. At the same time, the British industrial revolution threatened to displace industrial production from Continental Europe and turn much of Europe into an agricultural supply region for Great Britain. Again, competent or lucky states blocked this threat and helped local firms defend themselves from the British; incompetent ones ruled economies relegated to being raw materials suppliers for Britain. Yet, in all this activity states rarely blocked the effects of market forces. Instead, they deflected market pressures in the directions they preferred.

The Great Depression and World War II stopped growth of this global economy; trade and other flows actually shrank. This period presents a great rupture with past centuries. Relative to total economic activity, global trade did not regain its 1914 levels until roughly 1980. The diminished importance of world trade and controls on the movement of capital created a space in which states could impose a remarkable, if temporary, stability on their domestic economies by controlling the allocation of investment capital and by dictating market outcomes. This may seem a peculiar statement, since the 1930s are generally regarded as a period in which markets ran wild, harming many people. However, precisely in reaction to the calamities of the 1930s, states gained the legal and institutional power to determine market outcomes using controls over capital movements, foreign exchange, interest rates, labor markets, and prices and outputs in the agricultural, industrial and especially service sectors. In short, they invaded and regulated local markets to a considerable extent, while sheltering those markets from what became the old international economy.

But today's world is more like the world before 1914, when global market pressures induced capital movements, trade, and migration, and when global prices increasingly dictated local prices. Like then, some states, in their own interest and acting at the behest of local social groups, have actively promoted the intrusion of global price pressures into their own and other's economies. Like then, other states find it impossible to set exchange rates or conduct an independent monetary policy in the face of international capital flows that can exceed their entire money supply. Like then, states struggled to shape the global economy for their own ends and to satisfy local material and normative interests.

The second trend is *cyclic*: recurrent – but not automatic – upswings and downswings in the economy linked to the emergence of new leading sectors. The innovations embodied in these leading sectors usually combine different kinds of scientific/engineering technologies with new management technologies. These dramatically reduce the energy costs of physically transforming and transporting goods, and the costs of monitoring labor so as to assure adequate profit rates during the transformation of goods into saleable commodities. In today's economy, this means energy saved by using electronic rather than physical processes to move information, real-time monitoring of sales, prices, and workers' output, and, of course, an astounding variety of new products. Simply using these new tools or making these new products is no guarantee of success, however; they also have to be used more efficiently. 'Soft' management technologies like team work, total quality management, and just-in-time inventory systems, combined with new organizational structures such as so-called virtual or networked corporations, matter just as much as and perhaps more than the hard scientific technologies themselves.

These hard and soft innovations have tended to cluster in time and in space, and, as Joseph Schumpeter noted, these 'gales of creative destruction' threaten extant industrial dinosaurs with extinction. Because they cluster, the core of industrial activity has shifted, much to the chagrin of states whose political and economic domination of world markets rested on older technologies. For example, Britain's nineteenth-century industrial supremacy wilted before challenges from the United States and Germany, and US postwar industrial supremacy was partially eroded by Japan and Germany. The renaissance of US hegemony in the 1990s was inextricably linked to the success of US firms that incorporated the latest cluster of new technologies into service sector activities. A further revival hinges on control over the next wave of technologies.

What this book is about

This book looks at how markets created distinct spatial patterns in what was produced and at how states attempted to influence that distribution of production. Part I describes the coincident emergence of a world economy and the modern state. The modern state emerged at a time when the international economy was the only real market economy. Use of 'international' here is actually an abuse of the term, for nations did not exist: a waterborne economy is perhaps closer to the truth. Chapter 1 shows that national economies did not exist as such, because a set of largely self-sufficient microeconomies comprised the interior of what became most nations. In the guise of mercantilism, emerging states actively and often violently 'marketized' those microeconomies, linking them to each other and the global economy. At first, this process involved the creation of a homogeneous internal legal space in which self-regulating markets could function. Later, state-sponsored railroad building physically integrated the interior, creating national markets. In this process, states sought stable internal sources of revenue. Ironically, however, they also exposed these markets, and thus their revenue sources, to enormous external competitive and monetary pressures.

This created an enduring set of problems for the state. Chapter 2 focuses on the most important of these, the way that markets unevenly distribute economic activity and growth, and considers state responses to that problem. Market pressures caused agricultural production to move outward from areas of increasingly concentrated manufacturing activity, producing distinct zones ranging from core to periphery. States responded two different ways. *Ricardian* strategies, based on comparative advantage, used exports of raw materials to generate economic growth. *Kaldorian* strategies tried to use Verdoorn effects – the increased rates of productivity growth created by increasing rates of output, increasing returns to scale, learning by doing, and rapid technological innovation – to generate economic growth and ultimately *competitive* advantage. The easier Ricardian strategy predominated in the nineteenth century. The Kaldorian strategies at the heart of successful industrialization are more difficult, which is why development is relatively rare.

Chapter 3 examines the recurrent emergence of new paradigms for manufacturing, and thus the constant relocation of core manufacturing activities. It also discusses the emergence of new paradigms for organizing the world economy politically, that is, the creation of hegemony. Chapters 4 through 6 expand on this discussion by looking at the symbiotic expansion of European industry and agriculture globally in the nineteenth-century. Chapter 4 discusses the British industrial revolution and late development. Britain's extraordinary, if temporary, industrial competitiveness threatened Continental European and Asian states with deindustrialization. British industry's appetite for agricultural raw materials and foods induced or forced much of the world to begin supplying it with those things.

States responded to the British industrial revolution with a combination of Ricardian and Kaldorian strategies. They mobilized capital for investment, created disciplined labor forces, acquired foreign technology, and secured their domestic markets for local firms. One of the most important points made in Chapter 4, therefore, is that European and Asian states could not take industrialization for granted. Britain's new paradigm for 'best practice manufacturing' threatened to sweep away those states' own industrial bases. Nineteenth-century industrialization in Western Europe and Japan was just as problematical as industrialization is in China and the periphery today. It was neither automatic nor fully spontaneous. Like today's late industrializers, European states and Japan systematically intervened in the market, sheltering local industry from external competitors and cultivating leading sectors.

Fears that external competition might sweep away local industry were not confined to the nineteenth century. Early (or earlier) industrialization did not guarantee continued competitiveness for European economies. Every few generations a cluster of innovations threatened established producers with Schumpeter's creative destruction. Thus, the mortality and morbidity among US and European firms confronting new Asian producers in the 1990s was nothing new. The same thing happened when US firms invaded Europe and when Britain exported to the world. Chapters 7, 10, and 13 look at this process of competition among developed industrial economies. Later, Chapters 11 and 12 pick up the discussion of late industrialization begun in Chapter 4 and extend it to the modern Developing World, particularly Asia.

Chapters 5 and 6 discuss the consequences of British industrialization for the parts of the world opting or forced to opt for Ricardian strategies. Western Europe's industrialization both depended on and energized a vast ecological transformation inside and outside Europe. Any discussion of the international political economy that ignores agriculture minimizes the forces that created today's periphery. Millions of acres of forest and plain were turned into fields for production of grain, fibers, stimulants, and sugar. Millions of foreign animals spread into relatively empty ecological niches in the Southern Hemisphere. If kangaroos could pass immigration laws, there would not be over 100 million sheep in Australia today. Food and agriculturally derived raw materials accounted for over half of international trade as late as 1929.

Transportation costs and the availability of land ruled the global dispersion of European agriculture.

This ecological transformation caused a vast demographic transformation. Traditionally, the international political economy's holy trinity has been money, trade, and investment. A better trinity might be commodities, capital, and people. Over the centuries people have also entered into international exchange as commodities – slaves and indentured labor – and as willing migrants. Slavery is largely a thing of the past now, but the reasons why Salvadorans migrate today are fairly similar to the reasons why the Irish migrated in the nineteenth century. Chapter 5 considers migration and the role of political force in creating labor supplies in the world economy. Chapter 6 considers states' efforts to use Ricardian strategies for growth and development, global capital flows, most of which revolved around the creation of these agricultural supply regions, and the recurrent problem of overcapacity and falling prices that plagues most Ricardian development.

Part I comes to a close with a consideration of the international trade and monetary systems. Here, too, the past is a good guide to the future. The international trading system has been drifting away from the guarded liberalism of the Bretton Woods era to the more extensive and eclectic kind of protectionism present in the nineteenth century. This protection mixed political concerns about noncompetitive sectors with a desire to promote leading sectors. Nineteenth-century trade was not 'managed,' but that reflected a paucity of instruments, not of desire. The international financial system has seen an increasing number of ever more severe financial crises. The most recent of these, in 2007–9, prompted state intervention in financial markets at levels unseen since the 1930s Depression.

Chapter 7 considers this issue by focusing on the decline of British competitiveness as the United States and Germany pursued successful Kaldorian industrialization strategies. The international monetary system today also increasingly resembles the securities (stocks and bonds)-based money system of the late nineteenth century. The only major difference is the absence of gold backing for money, which predisposes the system to inflation. By World War I railroads had constituted national markets in many states' territories, and exposed those territories to world markets. But the vast pool of international money held as overseas assets and the weakness of central banking meant that any independent monetary policy in defense of those markets was impossible, even though the rise of new manufacturing and agricultural economies exposed established producers to extreme competitive pressures. The end of Chapter 7 focuses on these issues, then closes with a discussion of declining British hegemony and the origins of the Great Depression.

Part II continues these themes, looking at the political and economic basis for the temporary suppression of markets. Chapter 8 discusses the rise of a new paradigm for best practice manufacturing based on the production of consumer durables on assembly lines by semiskilled, unionized workers in the United States. A tightly regulated macroeconomy best served the needs of firms in this cluster of leading sectors, but it took both the disruptions of the

Depression and the local and global institution building that occurred before and after World War II to make that regulated macroeconomy possible. Chapter 8 shows how US domestic politics contributed to the creation of multilateral institutions to regulate the world economy after World War II, and how this helped states temporarily to control their economies. Two crucial features of this regulation were controls on the international flow of capital and on international trade in services. Together these permitted states to direct their local economies to an unprecedented degree, creating rapid rates of economic growth.

Chapter 9 discusses how the international monetary system changed from a handmaiden for this economic regulation to a housewrecker. Unlike the first half of the book, which subordinates its discussion of international money to deeper processes, money deserves a full and early chapter here because states' (temporary) postwar control over monetary flows constrained the market flow of goods and capital.

The constraints on global capital flows discussed in Chapter 9 in turn generated an enormous surge of investment by mostly US transnational corporations. Chapter 10 examines this, and particularly the conflicts created first by US firms' intrusions in European markets, and then Japanese firms' intrusions in US markets.

Chapter 11 picks up the discussion of late development started in Chapter 4, but shows that 'Third World' industrialization today has been an on-going phenomenon that started in the nineteenth century, and that it closely resembles the processes observed in Europe in Chapter 4. Rich countries' regulation of domestic agriculture forced much of the Third World to abandon Ricardian strategies based on agriculture. Some, but by no means all, of states successfully industrialized. Among them, China stands out for its size and swiftness.

Chapter 12 provides the trade and systemic sides of the discussion started in Chapters 9 and 11. It adapts arguments made in Chapters 6 and 7 about the rise of new agricultural supply regions to the rise of low-wage labor zones for the manufacture of simple commodities, particularly in Asia. It shows how trade continues largely to be regionalized, and it reveals how trade frictions are related to the adoption of Kaldorian strategies by late industrializers.

Chapters 13 and 14 continue the discussions started in Chapter 7, explaining how successful Kaldorian industrialization strategies in Japan undermined US competitiveness. In turn, US firms partially revived the US manufacturing base by learning from Japan, while the US state made an all-out effort to make new global markets for US service exports. The 1990s saw US revival, with above OECD average levels of GDP and productivity growth. Chapter 14 argues that the United States ran a huge system of international financial arbitrage akin to Britain's in the nineteenth century. By borrowing short term at low interest rates from the world and then lending back to the world long term at higher returns, the United States was able to energize its economy. Housing finance led the United States to above-average but unsustainable rates of growth, with an excess of mortgage debt triggering the 2007–9 financial crisis. And as in the nineteenth century, and before, conflicts among powerful states had little to do with economic efficiency and much to do with diverging normative visions and material interests.

In sum, then, this book is about globalization. It links the production of goods and services to markets for those goods, and to conflicts among states trying to create, enhance, or subdue those markets. It shows how markets and states fed off of each other long before Bretton Woods collapsed and the world rediscovered global markets. And, as the book is meant to provide food for thought, it begins with a discussion of states, markets and agriculture.

Part I

States, Agriculture, and Globalization

Chapter 1

The Rise of the Modern State

From Street Gangs to Mafias

> At present we [Europeans] ceaselessly imitate ourselves. ... Have some made use of new kinds of weapons? Everyone else soon will try them. Does one state increase its troops? Or levy a new tax? It is an advertisement for the others to do the same.
>
> *Montesquieu*

States and markets in the 1500s

The modern state and the modern global market emerged together and are inextricably intertwined. Efforts by emerging absolutist states in Europe to subordinate their local nobilities and achieve an unmediated relationship with peasants and merchants unintentionally created 'globalization.' The failure of these states to subordinate each other also contributed to globalization. These absolutist states needed money to transform a state based on personal ties to the nobility into one with a paid, loyal bureaucracy. As Gabriel Ardant (1975: 164) observed, 'The history of the state seems ... to be inseparable from the history of taxation.' But the global economy provided much more cash than largely subsistence-oriented local economies, so absolutist states forced those economies into the emerging global market. As Karl Polanyi (1957: 68) argued, 'The territorial state ... [was] the instrument of the "nationalization" of the market and the creator of internal commerce.' Thus, the origins of the modern globalized political economy lie in the origins of the European state and state system and its related global markets around the fifteenth century. And neither can be understood without looking at agriculture and at the limits placed on the division of labor by the miserable transportation systems of the time.

One of the great peculiarities of history is that an economically marginal, technologically backward set of religiously fractionalized and fanatic peoples 'governed' by elites with virtually no administrative apparatus managed to conquer most of the world in about 300 years. European states achieved this because they combined lawyers, guns, money and god – routinized dispute resolution, organized violence, revenue extraction, and legitimation – in a particularly potent and violent way that enabled them to subordinate much larger economies and empires (Mann, 1986). Circa 1500, the total population of Europe, let alone its individual states, was barely two-thirds of China's; per capita GDP was at best the same (Maddison, 2007; see Broadberry and Gupta, 2006 for a dissenting view). European states' 'comparative advantage' initially lay only in the use of organized violence. Europe's peculiar states emerged from a three-sided conflict among kings, nobles, and merchants for control of the resources that could be extracted from the peasant-based, agricultural economy of fifteenth-century Europe. States where one side won completely tended to have long-run weaknesses relative to states in which the three sides worked out durable compromises that constituted and funded well-armed states capable of suppressing the local peasantry, fending off rapacious neighbors, and aligning nobles' interests with those of the central state. By contrast, Qin Shi Huang's successful conquest of his rivals enabled the Qin dynasty to harness commercial life to the Chinese state's needs.

The modern national state is a well-defined organization with a legitimate and continuous monopoly of violence over a defined territory. This monopoly of violence gives the state its ability to subordinate other organizations and groups within that territory to its rules, its laws. Creating and maintaining a monopoly of violence requires resources. In the short run, states can steal from outside their territory. In the long run perpetuating a monopoly of violence requires a stable internal supply of resources. Stability can come from time and tolerance, as Frederic Lane describes: 'A plunderer could become in effect the chief of police as soon as he regularized his "take," adapted it to the capacity to pay, defended his preserve against other plunderers, and maintained his territorial monopoly long enough for custom to make it legitimate' (Lane, 1958: 403; Levi, 1988). But the active support created by compelling national or religious identities is even stronger.

Because agriculture constituted about 80 percent of economic activity, it ultimately provided the resources supporting all states at that time. However, the nature of premodern agriculture limited the amount of surplus available for extraction, as one unit of seed yielded only four units of harvested grain (Abel, 1980). The poor transport systems meant that even if surplus could be extracted it was hard to concentrate in the hands of the state. The nature of agriculture thus set limits on the forms state organization potentially could take in the fifteenth century. This was true everywhere, not just in Europe. The most successful empires were successfully precisely because they found ways to overcome this limit, usually by increasing output, monetizing the economy, and creating roads and canals. China's emperors brought yields up to 10:1 by systemically spreading technical knowledge to the peasantry, and then concentrated those larger harvests into a system of regional granaries or moved it on the Grand Canal to its northern capital (Maddison, 2007: 35).

Because of the difficulties involved in extracting resources from agriculture, most European states pursued a policy known as mercantilism. Mercantilism is usually described as an externally oriented policy by which states tried to create inflows of bullion (specie or metallic money). Actually, mercantilism's external policy was also a means to an internal end: the creation of a homogeneous, monetized internal economy, dominated by a central authority capable of defining property rights. This homogeneous and monetized economy provided the stable internal resources states needed. Reciprocally, internal funds mean a more stable and homogeneous internal administration and law. Thus, the distinctive compromise worked out in successful European states between lawyers, guns, money and god also emerged from struggles over the implementation of mercantilist policies.

This chapter first examines the nature of fifteenth-century agriculture, the limits it imposed on European state-building, and the ways agriculture shaped the social groups contending for power in Europe. Then it discusses the trajectory of state-building in three European states to show how conflicts within and among those states forced them to develop novel and powerful combinations of lawyers, guns, money and god. Mercantilism, with its sometimes complementary and sometimes conflicting goals, is a key part of that story. Finally, the chapter surveys the early period of European expansion to show how a handful of primitive and puny European states began to dominate the entire world, reshaping ecologies and economies as they went. The patterns and problems established in this early period persist today. States' relative power continues to rest on their ability to extract resources from society without damaging long-term growth in the economy, to transform those resources into organized violence, and to manage the interface between their internal economy and the world economy. Meanwhile, the diffusion of the institutional outcomes of the European compromise – professional militaries, extensive bureaucratic systems for domestic taxation, regularized justice, and unifying national myths – to the rest of the world has steadily eroded European dominance of the world economy, as the re-emergence of Japan and especially China demonstrates.

Agricultural limits on state formation

From the fifteenth to the end of the nineteenth century, agriculture lay at the heart of the global economy (and naturally most 'local' economies as well). As late as 1929, primary products, mostly agricultural goods, made up three-fifths of internationally traded goods. The common challenge of extracting resources from agriculture to fund armies and administration shaped all efforts to construct states. And all those efforts ran into one overwhelming difficulty: before mechanically powered transport, hardly anyone ever transported grain overland for more than 20 miles.

All economies involve the transformation of energy into life and goods. In pre-railroad agricultural economies, virtually all energy came from grain, and was processed through human and animal muscle power into goods. Using grain as the primary source of energy set the outer limits of exchange through both barter and, to a certain extent, even monetized markets. For humans – particularly the peasants who constituted 80 to 90 percent of the population in the world in the fifteenth century – 20 miles represented about the longest possible one-day walk to a market, with 10 miles a more practical limit (Skinner, 1964; Abel 1980: 7). But what if our peasant had some horses and a wagon?

A nineteenth-century German economist, Johann von Thünen, conducted an experiment on this question. He determined that theoretically a standard wagon load of grain, drawn by two horses and driven by two farm workers, could go about 230 miles on a flat road before the humans and animals consumed all the grain, which was their only source of energy (Thünen, 1966). Practically, however, the real limit to *profitable* overland wagon transport approximated transport on someone's back: 20 miles. First, a shipper would want his wagon, horses, and farmhands back, so some grain had to be reserved as 'fuel' for the trip back. Second, Europe's scarce roads and hilly terrain increased grain consumption en route to market. Finally, once the wagon reached its destination, it had to have enough grain left to sell to make it economically worthwhile to ship grain in the first place.

Consequently, virtually all economic, social, and political life took place in *microeconomies* centered on market towns surrounded by an agricultural hinterland of about 20 miles. Adam Smith argued that the greater the division of labor, the greater productivity and thus incomes would be. The relatively small area and population of the microeconomy meant that the Smithian division of labor was quite low, because few people could afford to specialize even if they had the capital to do so. In microeconomies a vicious cycle thus limited economic growth and income: a small division of labor limited productivity; low productivity limited economic growth; and low economic growth kept the division of labor low. Even China's highly commercialized economy largely failed to break out of its local limits after two large, once-only jumps upwards under the Sung and Ch'ing (Arrighi, Hui, Hung and Selden, 2003; Maddison, 2007).

This 20-mile limit persisted well into the modern period. As late as 1835, France consumed about 173 million tons of goods, of which only 15 million moved via water transport. About 127 million tons, or 73 percent, were consumed at the place of production. The remaining 46 million tons were consumed an average of 37 miles away, indicating that only about 13 percent of production was consumed more than 20 miles from its production site. The 15 million tons moved by water transport probably made up the bulk of long-distance consumption. Transport barriers led to huge regional variation in prices. In 1800 wheat prices varied by as much as 400 percent in different regions; in 1817 by 200 percent; and as late as 1847 by 70 percent (Price, 1981: 19–20, 72–3).

Although microeconomies all lay nestled together, they traded only a little with their neighboring microeconomies and virtually nothing with more distant ones. (The obvious exceptions, microeconomies with access to water transport, are dealt with later in this chapter.) *Until the era of canals and railroads, and indeed well into that era, no such thing as a 'national economy' existed.* The global economy – that is, a complex division of labor linking economic areas located in different political units – existed long before transportation improvements brought all microeconomies into close economic contact within most political units.

Since virtually all forms of social organization larger than a village need to extract surplus energy (meaning money or food) from the agricultural economy, the 20-mile limit meant that it was hard, but not impossible, to construct 'states' on a large geographical or administrative scale. Peasant economies usually do produce a surplus well above their subsistence needs, allowing a state to pay and feed armies and bureaucrats. However, even if the agents or builders of a would-be state could extract that surplus from those peasants, they could not move it very far in the form of physical grain. The difficulty in moving bulk goods overland obstructed any attempt to extract and move more than a minimal amount of revenue from those microeconomics. Michael Mann notes that it was extremely difficult to consistently project military power more than 55 miles before the railroad; Charles Tilly notes that in 1490 the average radius of most European political units was about 50 miles, meaning about two microeconomies in any given direction, or the distance a band of men on horse could travel in one day in order to supervise a noble's peasants or to patrol 'borders' (Mann, 1986: 136; Tilly, 1990: 45).

How did these limits manifest themselves? Tilly (1990: 5) observes that the average European state occupied about 9500 square miles, fewer than El Salvador, and contained about 300 000 people, fewer than Wyoming. Given typical European agricultural yields in 1500, Tilly's 300 000 people needed 3300 square miles to feed themselves (Abel, 1980: 5). The diversion of land into animal pasture, forests for fuel and timber, peasants' own consumption, and fallow and non-arable land, accounts for the other 6200 square miles. The typical Chinese county under various dynasties approximated these population and areal limits, suggesting that the practical limits to local control were the same everywhere, given that seven microeconomies – a central one, plus the six contiguous microeconomies – amount to roughly 8800 square miles.

Nevertheless, large social organizations and states spanning multiple microeconomics could emerge, because the overland transport of grain was not the only way to move energy. Ancient empires exhibited regular patterns of conflict and oscillation in their span of control until the industrial revolution. Central authorities struggled against locally based authorities for control over the physical grain surplus. These struggles reflect the difficulties of finding durable political and administrative solutions to the limits set by premodern agriculture.

The three exceptions to this limit defined both the possibilities for building larger social organizations and the three groups that ultimately contended for control of the European state in the fifteenth century. First, water and wind power could be directly harnessed through mills. Second, grain and other commodities could be transported by water, using the free energy wind provided, although capturing this energy required a large fixed investment in ships. Finally, money and other precious items (that is, goods with a very high value-to-weight ratio) could be moved long distances, freeing travelers or shippers from hauling their food/energy with them by allowing them to purchase grain where it was produced. Information is, of course, the classic high-value but low-volume, low-weight commodity.

Each of the three social groups contending for control of territory and economic activity in Europe tried to construct different networks to mobilize and move surplus food/energy using one of these exceptions. The melding of these groups in uneven ways created variations on the distinctive European state. And each group's strategy overlapped and came into conflict in the market town at the heart of each microeconomy. By contrast, in dynastic China, the center established a relatively durable control over market towns and eliminated an independent nobility with control over land.

The nobility and the acceptance of limits

Nobles controlled the first exception – wind and water mills. They solved the problem of resource extraction by moving themselves, not grain; they went to where the grain was, and they used direct coercion to extract surplus grain. In most of premodern Europe, a collection of brigands turned nobles controlled the local economy. These nobles were a kind of dispersed biker gang: armor, horses, and their propensity to resort to violence elevated them above the rest of the population in the same way that leather and Harleys elevate movie bikers in situations where state authority is absent. Nobles had made themselves into the state when the Roman empire collapsed, removing most legal constraints on the behavior of people who happened to have weapons. Similarly, in a European variation on the typical dispersal of nomadic conquerors in premodern economies, Charlemagne deliberately dispersed his soldiers across the countryside so they could find grain to feed their horses.

Nobles extracted a surplus from peasants through a mixture of custom and coercion. They directly appropriated grain and other products as rents and payments for the use of mills where peasants ground grain for bread. They also forced peasants to work on noble-owned land. Nobles had little need directly to monetize their local economy, that is, to shift from a barter economy with the direct exchange of goods to a commercial economy in which money served as a universal medium of exchange and prices reflected the cost of production. Virtually everything they needed was at hand through direct exchange or as rents in kind. Nobles and peasants lived in a delicate balance of terror, with the peasantry's propensity and ability to revolt limiting how much nobles could extract.

The nobility constructed a society based on mobile people controlling an immobile surplus. Nobles linked themselves together through a network of hospitality that allowed nobles to travel without carrying grain, since invariably another manor was located one day's horse ride away. Once they arrived they could 'refuel' their horses and themselves, gossip, annoy each other, and then move on to the next manor. Nobles moved themselves, and through marriage their children, rather than the economic surplus.

What nobles lacked was anything that could not be locally produced. So, by definition, they lacked luxuries. Nobles could buy these luxuries from merchants if they had either money or commodities that the merchants wanted. Inland nobles usually had to exchange money, while nobles on coasts or navigable rivers often could exchange bulk commodities directly for luxury goods. Nobles resisted the monetization of their local economies above and beyond this minimum amount of money. Although monetization might help them attack and conquer their neighbors, it exposed them to the possibility that the rents they charged peasants could be fixed in money terms. Then inflation might erode the real value of those rents. Inflation was a real problem for the nobility after 1500, because the great inflow of silver and gold from the newly conquered Americas increased the European money supply by about half (Vilar, 1976; Kriedte, 1983). In this respect the nobility struggled with a contradiction between their desire to control the peasantry and the purposes of that control. The nobility needed inflows of American silver to finance their purchases of Baltic and Asian luxuries, but these inflows threatened to undermine their control over peasants.

Nobles' reluctance to monetize the economy beyond the point needed for them to acquire luxuries brought them into conflict with kings, the second social force attempting to control the microeconomies. Kings and would-be kings sought to monetize their microeconomies in order to shift part of the peasants' surplus away from nobles and towards themselves. But nobles and monarchs also had a common interest in keeping the peasantry under control and fending off other predatory states. During the sixteenth and seventeenth centuries, the nobility faced nearly constant internal and external threats, forcing them to calculate finely how much of the surplus they needed to relinquish to their king in order to get collective protection (Anderson, 1979).

Absolutist monarchs, internal markets, and external enemies

Europe's kings were really 'wannabe' kings, who faced considerable internal and external obstacles to their desires to centralize power over lawyers, guns, money and god. Kings' authority was weakened by the nobility's legal claims to land, by the nobility's autonomous military power, and by the web of mutual obligation linking king to vassal. Because nobles controlled considerable military force, they could actively resist royal authority with violence. Sovereignty – legal authority – was dispersed in feudal society and varied from one locality to the next, with the nobility controlling the local administration of justice. And the web of obligations binding kings and nobles legitimated the nobility's independent existence.

Europe's would-be kings sought to subordinate the nobility by connecting all the microeconomies via and under a single administrative hierarchy. Nobles linked discrete microeconomies through a horizontal, primarily social network. Kings wanted to link microeconomies together with a vertical bureaucracy, using easily transported flows of information (orders down to bureaucrats and reports back up to the king's cabinet) and money (salaries down to bureaucrats and taxes up to the king). In this respect, Europe's would-be absolutist monarchs (including the Papacy) did not differ in intent from emperors in the Ottoman lands, India and China. Europe's kings differed in their relative degree of success. The Chinese emperors successfully converted local nobilities into 'prebends,' paid servants of the imperial state, prevented prebends from acquiring ownership of local land and transferring it to their children, and maintained control over the armies they had to deploy on distant borders.

European kings' weakness reflected Europe's considerable administrative backwardness relative to empires elsewhere. Kings were originally nominated leaders of the bands of brigands from which the nobility emerged, merely princes *(principes),* or first among the equal society of nobles. Having conquered some region, these princes dispersed their gangs into the country-side, because these bands were too large to be fed off any single microecon-omy, and because, as Ghenghis Khan reputedly said, 'An empire cannot be ruled on horseback' (Mann, 1986: 142). Instead, kings dispersed their brig-ands into fiefs where they could find enough peasants whose rents (grain) could support those brigands, their horses, and their ancillary thugs. Kings tried to retain control over this new nobility by retaining the right to confirm the inheritance of fiefs. Technically, kings retained landownership but exchanged use of the land for the nobility's loyal military service. But once they dispersed their armies, kings both lost their ability to subdue rivals and created a host of new rivals. Nobles' own interest in extracting rent from their serfs and passing a fief on to their children overrode residual loyalties to the king. Nobles represented the real locus of government, justice, and taxation in each microeconomy, because they were there and the would-be monarch's hired representative was not. Unlike China, where emperors successfully split control of civil administration and the military over two people, European kings confronted nobles with militaries rivaling that of the wannabe kings.

Kings could increase their internal authority only to the extent that they could, first, replace nobles' local monopoly of violence with police forces controlled from the center, and second, shift control over law and taxation from the nobility to their own hired hands, that is, bureaucrats with no inde-pendent source of power. Shifting control over law, policing, and resource extraction to bureaucrats took enormous amounts of money, for kings had to pay their agents enough to prevent them from being suborned by the local nobility. This gave kings two strong reasons to monetize microeconomies as much as possible. First, monetization gave them access to a greater volume of resources in any given area. Second, it allowed kings to extract resources without having to go through the nobility. Ideally, kings would use the tolls charged for access to market towns to pay their agents' salaries. By purchas-ing microeconomy-produced goods to sustain themselves, those agents then put money back into the local economy, closing the local financial loop.

To monetize the microeconomies over which they sought control, kings also had to find some source of real money – gold, silver, or copper – to put into circulation in the microeconomies. This led them to look to merchants for support against nobles, for merchants, naturally, had money.

The kings' external problem likewise forced them to look to merchants, but, paradoxically, it also forced them to look back to nobles for support. Externally, kings faced a second threat to their authority: other would-be kings. Kings could only increase their wealth (the minimal flow of monetized resources flowing out of the microeconomies and into their hands) by taking

Table 1.1 *Warfare costs for Britain, 1689–1784*

War	Duration (years)	Average annual expenditure (£ million)[a]	Increase in public debt (£ million)[a]
Nine Years' War (1689–97)	9	5.5	16.7
War of Spanish Succession (1702–13)	11	7.1	22.1
War of Austrian Succession (1739–48)	9	8.8	29.2
Seven Years' War (1756–63)	7	18.0	48.0
American Revolutionary War (1775–84)	9	20.3	115.6

Note: [a] £2 would buy a year's supply of grain for one person.

Source: Based on data from Brewer (1988: 30).

away land from other kings and nobles. Therefore, would-be kings were in constant conflict with other would-be kings over turf. Wars with other kings forced kings to deploy increasingly larger and better organized armies, raising the amount of cash needed for success (Howard, 1976: 35–48). Most medieval armies started as a reaggregation of the brigand gangs and their ancillary thugs. Their disloyalty, insubordination, and erratic individualism all undermined a king's ability to fight other kings. In response, kings tried to professionalize their armies, replacing undisciplined gang members with hired mercenaries. But mercenary and later professional armies had to be paid. Table 1.1 shows the ratcheting-up of British war costs in the 1700s.

Conflict with other kings also limited kings' efforts to subordinate nobles. No king could long risk fighting both internally and externally. Therefore, where kings could not subdue local nobles or the reverse, both often entered into pacts in which nobles permitted kings enough revenue to defend everyone against external threats and restive peasants. But nobles were often cheap about funding a king's ability to project power outward, because armies could be used in either direction. Therefore, kings' need to pay for war also forced them to borrow from merchants.

Merchants and the wider maritime world

Merchants constitute the last group struggling to control the resources available from the microeconomies. Merchants fall into two categories depending on whether they were oriented more towards long-distance trade, usually over water, or local, usually overland trade. This distinction is not the traditional one between trade in luxuries and trade in daily necessities. Trade in luxuries inevitably occurred alongside trade in much more mundane commodities like grains, wool, timber, and pitch. Merchants often needed these commodities simply to build and to ballast their ships. Trade in mundane commodities also provided a kind of cheap money for merchants involved in the long haul of luxury goods. If they simply loaded their ships with luxuries, they would have to parcel out these goods along the way in order to buy food and water. By ballasting with bulk commodities, they could exploit local differences in prices between points A, B, and C to earn enough to provision their ships at each of those points. They thus preserved their luxury cargo for resale at the end of their journey, where it would fetch the highest possible price.

One group of merchants controlled inland trade and in particular the trade of the market towns in each microeconomy. To the extent that they dealt in commodities produced outside the microeconomy, they dealt largely in luxuries, for the high cost of transport hindered overland movement of bulk commodities. These merchants got involved in the production and transportation of bulk goods after kings established centralized law and order.

The other group of merchants conducted long-distance trade. They constituted a third network, based not on social obligation or sovereign authority backed by violence, but on contractual obligation (ideally, anyway, as many merchant communities were tied together by ethnicity or religion). Merchants linked communities on the coast and navigable rivers through flows of money and goods; kings linked mostly inland microeconomies through flows of information, money, and violence. Thus, they were not completely in opposition, except where waterborne and inland trade overlapped. This group of merchants benefited from the fact that water transportation undid the limits on the division of labor imposed by local food supplies. Because waterborne food from other microeconomies augmented local supplies, the urban population could grow and more labor could be devoted to industrial activities.

These merchants wanted to be left alone to make money unhampered by either nobles or kings, both of whom had an annoying habit of stealing from merchants. The best way to gain this independence was to construct a network of armed trading cities. Because these cities had much higher productivity and incomes than any given microeconomy, they often could assemble and pay for substantial military forces. Genoa raised revenues three times those of the 'King' of France, for example (Anderson, 1974: 193).

The presence of external and internal threats created overlapping interests between merchants and kings, and merchants and nobles. Merchants possessed relatively enormous amounts of money. Kings' intermittent efforts to seize this money typically only worked a few times, for merchants could and always did move elsewhere in a politically fragmented Europe. Erratic ripoffs yielded to regular borrowing from merchants. Merchants liked this since it provided an outlet for surplus funds. And since kings in effect used this money to monetize microeconomies, they increased the markets available to merchants by integrating them into the network of waterborne trade and removing the internal tolls nobles threw up along trade routes. Finally, merchants benefited from the kings' ability to deploy violence on their behalf against competing merchants and predatory nobles and kings (Lane, 1958). Meanwhile, merchants and the nobility had a common interest in seeing that kings did not become too powerful. Since it was never clear which would-be king would actually triumph, prudence dictated diversifying loans among many different nobles.

State-building: lawyers, guns, money, and god

Kings, nobles, and merchants each possessed a preferred vision for the world, respectively absolutist states, hyperfragmented entities like the Holy Roman Empire or Poland, and networks of mercantile cities like the Hanse or Italian city-states. (Peasants, of course, preferred none of the above.) To different degrees, each of the large-scale societies outside of Europe took one of these forms. But in Europe the respective weaknesses of each group and their mutual vulnerability to external competitors combined with their occasionally overlapping interests to produce the peculiar amalgam of lawyers, guns, money, and god characterizing the modern state. Compromises brokered among all three parties were regularized into constitutions that defined property rights and political obligations (lawyers). These states rested on territorially defined monopolies over violence, deployed against internal and external threats (guns). The bureaucracy running this monopoly of violence depended on a parallel bureaucracy for revenue extraction (money). And national myths unified the population behind and justified states' actions (god).

States' constitutions developed at the intersection of conflicts and common interests among kings and nobles. The medieval revival of Roman law provided principles facilitating a deal over property rights (Anderson, 1979; Reynolds, 1994). Roman law contained two absolute but conflicting principles. First, it guaranteed an absolute right to private property, unlike the multitude of weak rights and mutual obligations that feudal law placed on property and persons. The nobility seized on this principle to guarantee their rights to landownership and the rents thereof, in the face of centralizing kings and rebellious peasants who also claimed landownership. Second, Roman law implied that the sovereign's will was law, in contrast with limits feudal obligations placed on kings. Would-be kings seized on this principle to justify imposing taxes and reducing the privileges of the nobles.

The clash of these two principles and the common fear of internal and external enemies led to the formation of parliaments that regularized the king's ability to raise and finance a central military, while also affirming new property rights. In these constitutional compromises, kings reduced the nobility's privileges and power (that is, exemptions from taxation and their right to private armies) but not to the point where nobles would revolt and seek aid from other kings against their own. Although the nobles submitted to regular taxes, they limited the king's ability to impose them without the permission of the assemblies of nobles. They also permitted the king to raise his own army, but only if they were allowed to staff that army. Regular taxes allowed kings to generate the steady flow of money that their new bureaucracies of violence (police and armies) and administration required. Kings destroyed common property rights in land (primarily peasants') to create new rights for the nobility, but in doing so they made it possible to identify specific, individual property owners who could be subjected to taxation, unlike the collective owners of the past.

The intersection between kings and merchants produced the public debt as an institution. As specialists in organized violence, kings enticed merchants to support them in return for protection from other kings and merchants. Merchants supported kings' efforts to build more powerful militaries with loans and, sometimes, taxes. Merchants benefited from this protection insofar as it opened otherwise closed markets and reduced the risks of long-distance trade (Lane, 1958; Steensgaard, 1974; Tilly, 1990).

The intersection of nobles' and merchants' conflicting and common interests produced lawyers. Both groups wanted absolute private property rights, and both groups had an interest in limiting kings' ability to tax them. At the same time, both had an interest in colonizing the king's bureaucracy so as to seize control of the revenues it generated. Absolute private property rights and regular taxation created a legal framework in which mercantile activity could flourish.

The intersection of different kings' conflicting and common interests produced formidable armies but also grudging agreement to respect one another's control of specific turfs. In other words, it produced a belief in absolute sovereignty that replaced prior feudal practices of divided and partial sovereignty – a noble could theoretically owe allegiance to multiple lords – with the notion that loyalty had to be undivided.

Charles Tilly (1985) has provided a perfect metaphor for this process of compromise: state-building was at first a form of organized crime. Just like the modern-day mafias, would-be absolutist monarchs tried to establish monopolies of violence over specific turfs, promising protection to nobles and especially merchants on that turf. Kings were would-be godfathers seeking to transform a multitude of small neighborhood gangs run by nobles into one larger gang. Merchants benefited from protection, as long as conquest opened new markets, piracy hurt only competing merchants, and trade barriers kept out competing merchants enough to offset taxes and the occasional defaulted loan. The merchants' and nobles' acquiescence gave legitimacy to the violence that states deployed inward; the violence they deployed outwards won grudging respect from other, competing godfathers.

Mercantilism as the hinge: internal and external state-building projects

The characteristic policy of these 'mafias' en route to statehood was the messy agglomeration of practices later called mercantilism. Mercantilism is traditionally viewed as the use of state power (organized violence) in the pursuit of plenty (economic wealth). Mercantilist states tried to boost their exports and limit their imports so as to accumulate specie – metallic money. Most analyses concentrate on this external aspect of the mercantilist project, the better to condemn it as irrational from the point of view of neoclassical economic theories.

When we consider mercantilism as a two-sided project with both an external and an internal impulse, a compelling and rational political logic reveals itself: trade surpluses and the accumulation of metallic money were the most practical way for kings to monetize their realms. Because of limits on overland grain transport, a unified global market emerged far sooner than 'national' markets almost anywhere. The waterborne economy contained more movable resources than did any given king's collection of microeconomies. Given this situation, states consciously tried to use external resources to provide immediate revenues while cultivating long-term and dependable internal revenues. Running trade surpluses allowed a king to exchange the many diverse commodities created by his many otherwise worthless subjects in the microeconomies for the one crucial commodity needed to build a state: money. This money accumulated directly in royal companies and indirectly in local merchants' hands.

Internally, kings removed barriers to the movement of goods imposed by the nobility and tried to make noble wealth taxable by homogenizing the legal status of all of the king's subjects. The elimination of barriers to trade reduced the sources of revenue the nobility controlled. Thus, the global economy and state system grew simultaneously. Mercantilism funded and consolidated some states while impoverishing others; meanwhile mercantilist imperialism created new and broad markets abroad. As Michael Mann (1986) notes, European kings' long-standing inability to tap internal resources intensively led them to tap external sources extensively, and this ironically helped merchants expand their own power and become indispensable to wannabe monarchs. The last two sections of this chapter will look at this process for several European states.

Each of the European states that survived and thrived from the fifteenth to the nineteenth century – and over 300 potential states did not – worked out its own version of the lawyers, guns, money, and god compromise. To steal Tilly's phrase, if states made war and war made states, war also *unmade* many states. States that evolved ever better, ever cleverer, and ever more efficient means for extracting revenue, deploying armies and winning internal consent through submission rather than coercion were more likely to survive (Parker, 1972, 1988; Spruyt, 1994). These advances in the social technologies for funding and deploying organized violence ultimately allowed relatively backward states to invade and transform societies that were often demographically larger and more advanced technologically and administratively. A quick survey of areas outside Europe shows why the absence of the compromise blocked a ratcheting-up of states' war-making and revenue-raising capacities.

State-building outside Europe

A brief look at Imperial China, where in effect the monarchy triumphed completely over its other two adversaries and created an absolutism more absolute than any found in Europe, and at the Indian Ocean trading economy, where merchants largely triumphed and created a trade-based world, provides a useful comparison with the European experience (Abu-Lughod, 1990; Reid, 1990).

As William Skinner (1964) has shown, China had a highly commercialized (monetized) economy in which most microeconomies were linked to a complex hierarchy of towns and cities. At the top of this hierarchy sat walled administrative cities which collected rice destined for the capital via one of the two great rivers or the Grand Canal connecting them. Because this economy was highly monetized, the monarchy could acquire a fairly large proportion of peasant surplus as money and then use this to pay a dedicated corps of civil servants, selected by examination, to rule each county, rather than having to delegate authority to nobles 'paid' in kind as in Western Europe.

As in Europe, external and internal enemies threatened central authority in China. When these enemies triumphed, however, they tended to restore central authority. The very administrative superiority of China's bureaucracies made it easier to restore the old system than to invent better ways to use violence in the pursuit of money. Invading 'barbarians' assimilated themselves into the administrative elite. Internally, China's highly commercialized economy – much more advanced than Europe's in the 1400s and 1500s – made it easy for central authority to gather the resources needed to crush challenges from would-be nobles. But the high level of monetization did not help merchants constitute a capitalist market economy with secure property rights. Many prices appear to have been set administratively, by power brokers, and the Chinese state did not tolerate the fusion of mercantile power with military might that characterized European incursions into the New World and Asia (Mann, 1986: 297; Pomeranz, 2000: 203–5; Arrighi *et al.*, 2003: 276–81). Nor was there any brokering of compromises that might establish the basis for higher levels of taxation, because merchants were unimportant to efforts to seize or maintain central power. Most mercantile activity was inward-oriented, focusing on day-to-day life or the network of canals in southern China. And most surplus extraction went towards sustaining both the capital and the canals that fed it. Emperors enveloped external trade in their own bureaucracy to pre-empt or shut down potential threats (Dunstan, 2006). Merchants fleeing to more congenial locations in Southeast Asia could not construct viable threats to the empire.

In contrast, the Indian Ocean and its neighboring Southeast Asian archipelagos harbored a complex network of trading communities whose power and autonomy most European merchants could only envy. These communities were insulated from the various inland empires by the same means that insulated Europe's merchants from would-be kings. Therefore, inland rulers were content to buy what they needed and usually left merchants alone. Among themselves, the different merchant communities had reasonably peaceful relations. Most merchants were small, privately organized traders plying between independent emporium ports organized as city-states. These ports sometimes exploited their up-river hinterlands, as in Sumatra, but just as frequently merchants simply 'rented' space in a city nominally controlled by a local noble.

While piracy did exist, it was not the state-organized, tax-funded piracy that developed in Europe. None of the merchant or pirate communities possessed the capacity for organized conquest at sea, or generated durable state-organized and militarized merchants akin to those of Venice. Consequently, no one tried to monopolize the sea-lanes. Unlike Europe's Mediterranean coasts, where Muslim and Christian fought with considerable hostility, Muslims, Hindus, and a score of other groups cohabited the Indian Ocean's coasts with a minimum of conflict.

These two descriptions reveal extremes that were rare in Europe. China made real what European monarchs dreamed: parallel civil and military bureaucracies controlled by the king, barred from direct landownership, and paid by a king able to extract revenue from an extensive, highly monetized economy populated by pragmatic peasants. The Southeast Asian archipelago and littoral embodied merchants' dreams: a multitude of ports and coastal economies unfettered by imperial authorities, linked by a dense network of financial and commercial ties, sharing enough common Hindu and Islamic culture to interact, and hungering for the multitude of goods sea-trade offered.

These two outcomes were much harder to achieve in *medieval* Europe. Europe's geography presented a much higher ratio of economies on coasts and navigable river to inland microeconomies than did China's (perhaps excepting southeast China). This created much greater opportunities for European merchants to generate cash by trading long distance. Thus, Europe's mercantile community was stronger relative to the monarchy than China's. Yet if merchants were more powerful relative to wannabe monarchs than they were in China, many of them were located inland, where they were much more vulnerable to land-based powers than Indian Ocean and Southeast Asian merchants. Merchant cash represented the only easily accessible source of finance for centralizing kings and for nobles resisting centralization. Meanwhile merchants possessed more advanced administrative and sometimes military technologies than did wannabe monarchs, who usually had to rely on a mixture of their few literate household servants and the occasional trustworthy priest. Among the European states, France's administrative centralization best approximates China's. However, the French nobility retained considerable independent power and privilege. Furthermore, overseas commerce provided many cities on the periphery of France with the resources to stand away from Paris (Fox, 1966).

Still, even if European monarchs lacked administrators and money, they did possess enough guns to prevent merchants from creating Indian Ocean-style safe havens in insular city-states. The many merchant city-states in the Rhine corridor, Italy, and on France's coast that were absorbed into larger, microeconomic-based political units reveal the fragility of merchant cities that cannot easily move their capital. In contrast, geography shielded mercantile states like the United Provinces (Holland), and England. These mercantile states contained large hinterlands enabling them to raise armies formidable enough to dissuade their neighbors from attacking and absorbing them.

Those European states that survived essentially constant warfare from 1500 to 1814 developed various uneasy combinations of and equilibria among lawyers, guns, money, and god. Europe's specific geographic balance of coastal and inland areas combined with its relative backwardness in administrative technologies to block exclusive dominance by any single state. Continuous war meant continuous pressure on states and their merchant communities to develop better forms of organized violence. This evolutionary pressure ratcheted-up European states' ability to use violence 'productively,' as the successful European incursions into the Indian Ocean littoral show. The next two sections first sketch the development of compromises and military ability in Spain, France, and England, and then examine Portuguese, Dutch, and English incursions into the Indian Ocean.

From mafias to states: mercantilism's internal project

Constant struggle among European kings, nobles, and merchants from the 1500s to the 1800s produced states out of the multitude of small 'mafias' then present in Europe. These mafias preyed on their immediate neighbors as well as on the Americas and Indian Ocean economies. Both efforts show a decisive trend towards more bureaucratic forms of control and an oscillation between commercial and state interests. During these two centuries, Europe's wannabe kings tried to establish absolutist states, subordinate both nobles and merchants, and swallow up competitor states in Europe.

Internally, expanding conflict meant raising taxes, provoking an unusually high number of peasant revolts against nobles, and noble and mercantile revolts against would-be monarchs. The European states that prospered after 1650 survived because they steered a course between the external Charybdis of war and the internal Scylla of revolt. Somewhat accidentally, they generated a law-governed compromise among the kings' guns, the nobles' guns, and the merchants' money that was blessed by nationalist myths.

Externally, as German historian Ludwig Dehio and other have noted, these struggles often pitted commercialized coastal states against more coercive land-based powers (Strayer, 1970; Thompson, 1993). While these land-based powers often were able to cripple the leading commercial state, they never permanently dominated either Continental Europe or the wider global economy. Drawing resources largely from microeconomies, the continental powers lacked the financial resources to do so. In contrast, the commercialized sea-power states could use the relatively inexhaustible wealth the maritime economy generated to hammer hostile continental powers against the anvil of the apparently inexhaustible manpower resources of relatively poor neighbors further east.

Thus France and Holland subsidized Ottoman and Swedish attacks on the Habsburg empire, Britain subsidized Russian and Prussian attacks on France, and eventually Britain and the United States subsidized Russian attacks on Germany. Had any of these various continental powers succeeded, it would have created a dominant land power much like China, indifferent to the scattering of mercantile communities on its periphery. Instead, the sea-power states fended off land powers while commercializing more and more of the globe. Ultimately, Britain contained the continentally based France and Spain, while subordinating commercial Portugal and Holland.

English superiority seems predictable only in hindsight, of course. Looking forward from 1500 to 1700, most contemporary observers would probably have said that Spain and the Habsburgs were more likely to become the dominant continental power, while France was more likely to work out a viable law-governed compromise between king and nobles. Spain had the largest and most potent combination of guns and money. At its peak the combined Spanish-Habsburg empire combined all the wealth of the Americas, Portugal's Indian Ocean holdings, the Netherlands (then meaning both Holland and Belgium), much of southern Italy, and Austria's Central European holdings, including mineral-rich Silesia and silver- and food-rich Bohemia (now the western part of the Czech Republic). These resources financed armies on a then unprecedented scale. France, meanwhile, had established forms of representation for nobles and towns that should have facilitated a brokered deal between them and the monarchy.

England, by contrast, was a relatively poor, backward economy on the fringe of Europe, with a fairly centralized, powerful monarchy that seemed to preclude any need to deal with noble or mercantile interests. England's geography also seemed to insulate it from the kind of pressures that forced would-be kings to create military and civil bureaucracies. So England seemed to lack guns and money, as well as any pressure to find some brokered compromise among merchants, nobles, and the monarch.

Spain and the Habsburgs and then France made the only serious efforts to eliminate all potential continental rivals. Both of these projects came to grief, however. The Spanish state could not balance the competing claims of 'guns and money' through any formal legal deal. Its apparent homogenization of the Iberian peninsula through expulsion and inquisition concealed a crazy quilt of nationalities, religions and motives in the actual operation of its overseas empire (Kamen, 2003). The French king brokered deals giving too much away to the nobility, despite the apparent centralization of power into Paris. Why did England come to work out a viable compromise and dominate the world economy? In the cases of Spain and France, initial advantages turned out to be disadvantages. In England, meanwhile, initial disadvantages turned out to be long-term advantages. (The same process occurred in the Indian Ocean.) Meanwhile Britain possessed an advantage neither Holland nor the continental powers possessed, namely the lack of any serious landward threat from the east.

Spain

Spain's large initial financial and military advantages turned into long-term disadvantages. Its initial military advantage accrued from Castile's and Aragon's long wars to expel the Muslim Umayyad Caliphate from southern Iberia. At first, the nobility subordinated itself to the monarchy's military simply to withstand Muslim expansion and then to grab Muslim land during the Caliphate's long retreat back to Africa. However, the deal which united Castile and Aragon against the Muslims prevented any true center from emerging in Spain. Aragon, Catalonia, and Valencia remained free from central taxation, and the central state did not have the right to send troops into these areas (Anderson, 1979: 64–7). A modern, bureaucratic tax apparatus emerged only in Castile. The Spanish crown bridged this gap in its tax capacity with American gold and silver. The easy availability of this silver deterred the crown from trying to find more durable internal sources of revenue.

The crown actually went out of its way to destroy internal sources. Muslims and Jews had controlled most mercantile activity in the Iberian peninsula before 1492, but the *reconquista* and subsequent Inquisition drove both sets of merchants either out of Spain and Portugal or underground. This one-off windfall deprived the crown of access to mercantile wealth on a continuing basis. Meanwhile, massive silver inflows led to inflation, which priced Spanish and Portuguese producers first out of export markets and then out of their own domestic markets, and reduced the potential mercantile tax base. Finally, American silver freed the crown from the necessity of coming to terms with its own nobility. The seemingly enormous and secure source of American revenue made it irrational for the crown to reduce its power voluntarily in order to convince nobles to submit to taxation.

American silver created a continuing reliance on itself. Imported silver was an inflexible and ultimately inadequate source of revenue vulnerable to piracy, which the English practiced and perfected at Spain's expense. Spain's continental-scale military adventures created a need for continental-scale revenues. Beginning in 1519, Spain and the Habsburg empire tried to conquer most of the lands lying between Madrid and Vienna while also holding off the manpower-rich Ottoman empire in the Balkans. In that century, Spain's military expanded from about 20 000 to 100 000. Spain's budget grew by 80 percent from 1520 to 1600, with military spending accounting for 80 percent of total spending (Kriedte, 1983: 47). Unable to tax either its (now nonexistent) domestic merchants or the kingdom of Aragon, the crown declared bankruptcy in 1557. Then it tried to tax the rich Spanish Netherlands, leading nobles there to demand lower taxes and an end to military occupation, and finally to rebel in 1557–58.

Paradoxically, Spanish efforts to raise revenue ended up not only depriving Spain of revenue, but also requiring it to find more money to try to retake the Netherlands. With Spain severed from Habsburg Austria after the abdication of Charles V (1556), fiscal pressure increased. The Spanish crown turned to tax-exempt and more commercially oriented Portugal and Catalonia, both of which revolted in 1640 rather than bear the cost of Spanish wars. Spain's early military and fiscal advantages pre-empted the need to forge a balance among lawyers, guns, and money. Spain relied too heavily on parasitic and despotic sources of revenue rather than more reliable and sustainable commercial sources, and never developed a durable national myth. Having lived by the sword, Spain died by the sword when England cut its lifeline to the wealth derived from American mines.

France

France, which launched the second effort to create a dominant inland empire in Europe, seemed better positioned to forge a compromise. First, the agricultural revolution, which increased the revenues that could be extracted from peasants, started in Île de France, the king's turf. Second, the king had already won the right to place his administrative agents in each province. However, he had not won the right to impose the king's law in these provinces. Third, a large number of representative institutions already linked the Valois kings and the nobility in France. But this proliferation of regional parliaments preempted any central institution for brokering deals between nobles and king. Threatened by the rampaging English during the Hundred Years' War (1337–1453), the Valois made one mediocre deal with the nobility and then tried to overcome its consequences. In this relatively early deal, the nobility agreed to a countrywide tax, or *taille royale,* to support a central army. In return, the king exempted the nobility from the tax and accepted limits on the size of the central army, and thus his power.

Lacking Spanish-scale external resources, the monarchy naturally sought to use both merchants and peasants as its tax base. To compensate merchants for increased taxation, the king allowed them to become 'tax-farmers,' creating and selling offices in his fiscal bureaucracy to merchants. Tax-farmers were responsible for collecting taxes from a given region and were allowed to keep a fixed percentage of what they collected. Inland merchants began investing in tax-farming rather than production, essentially shifting the tax burden onto the peasantry and overseas-oriented merchants. Consequently, many coastal mercantile towns remained in overt or covert rebellion through the 1500s and 1600s. Tax-farming was an inefficient, venal, and corrupt form of taxation; why transfer revenues to the central state until it came looking for them?

This weak fiscal and administrative base forced the king to grind peasants and coastal merchants into the ground during the conflicts of the 1500s. The Habsburgs attacked France from all sides and conquered northern Italy, and religious and regional schisms erupted into a long civil war. The *taille* rose from an estimated 6.5 percent of gross agricultural product in 1515 to 8.0 percent in 1607. Cardinal Richelieu's decision to have France enter the Thirty Years' War, and to expand the army from 15 000 to 100 000 men and thoroughly modernize it, entailed even greater increases in taxation. Taxes rose 250 percent between 1610 and 1640, provoking rebellions in six of France's great port cities and many peasant areas. The *taille* on the peasants rose to 14.6 percent of gross agricultural product by 1641 and then to 19 percent by 1675 as Louis XIV expanded the army to around 400 000 (Kriedte, 1983: 93).

These taxes prompted continual peasant revolts from 1625 to 1675, forcing the king to turn again to the expedient of selling offices. This short-run cure for the revenue problem stifled the development of a loyal, professional bureaucracy. Once more the inland mercantile community invested in offices rather than in productive activity. By the 1640s the sale of offices generated about 35 percent of royal revenues. To compensate for this fragmentation of authority (bought offices were only partly loyal to the king, since the buyers saw them as a source of revenue for themselves), the king actually had to construct a parallel system of administration.

Meanwhile subduing the revolting port cities gutted the vitality of that part of France's mercantile community which was oriented towards the dynamic overseas economy. With inland merchants still diverting their investment into offices, the state was forced to create purely state-run commercial operations to compensate for the absence of a dynamic merchant community. Jean-Baptiste Colbert (1619–83) set up a range of state-run factories and overseas ventures. Then and now these seemed the purest expression of mercantilism, but in fact they express the earlier failure of the emerging French state to come to terms with its mercantile community. The defeated coastal mercantile community could finance ventures in Caribbean sugar and tobacco, the fur trade in Canada, and a limited Indian Ocean operation, but these did not approach the comprehensive and global scale of Dutch and English operations. Like Spain, France was hemmed in between relatively wealthy Dutch and British on the one side, and manpower-rich enemies on the other.

Just as Spain was fatally hindered by its seeming advantage in centrally controlled revenues from the Americas, France's initial advantage in representative institutions turned into a disadvantage. The very range of institutions cemented regional particularism in place and shielded the nobility from the center. The king debased his own administrative apparatus to raise funds, inventing offices and undoing the centralization and bureaucratization that underpinned an effective absolutism. A truly unified and uniform professional central bureaucracy awaited France's last great king, Napoleon Bonaparte.

England

Relative to Spain/Portugal or France, England seemed an unlikely candidate for world power or for a viable compromise among merchants, nobles, and kings. It was economically and militarily weak, and dwarfed in area and population by both the French and Spanish/Habsburg empires. Even so, it had a number of strengths. Because of the Norman Conquest (1066), England's kings had already constructed a central and systematic administrative apparatus free of local particularisms. The Exchequer (Treasury) had a reasonably professional staff for its time, and the king's right to tax was fairly well established. Neighboring Scotland and Wales were too weak to require an expensive English army.

Geographic peculiarities enhanced the relative power of England's mercantile community. Aside from Holland, England alone among the large and medium powers had a very high ratio of coastal and riverine land to inaccessible interior land. Proportionately many more trade-oriented towns and nobles emerged than in Spain or France. In 1500, 10 percent of the English population was already living in towns with a population of over 400, and by 1700 the figure had risen to 25 percent, with London as Europe's largest city.

Overseas trade apparently grew twice as fast as 'national' income 1500–1700 (Braudel, 1981: 483–4; Mann, 1986: 472).

As for the English nobility, in 1400 they still resembled a typical brigand gang controlling traditional, cheap, feudal levies. A series of clever princes had led them on rampages through France for most of the past 100 years, but once France responded to these rampages with a professional army and the *taille*, English military power waned rapidly, and France retook England's major continental holdings. Unable to rampage in France, the nobility turned their violence inward and killed first their kings and then one another in the Wars of the Roses (1455–85), strengthening the monarchy's relative power.

The English state's need for funds was never tested by a real war, despite the crown's seeming administrative centralization. The Tudor monarchs' military ventures were financed on the cheap and through expedient. For example, Henry VIII sold off the church land he had seized to finance his (failed) invasion of France, and both he and Elizabeth I turned to a voracious and vicious pirating of silver from Spanish America to finance naval operations. But even under Elizabeth I (1558–1603), England never assembled an army over 10 000 men. England's puny military effort required puny fiscal resources; therefore, unlike France's, its monarchs could resist the temptation to exempt the nobility from taxes or to sell offices on a large scale.

After 1603 the Stuarts continued this pattern of ignoring the nobility and Parliament and, in Charles I's case, alienating them. Charles I (1625–49) tried an accommodation with the nobility in 1628, when he promised not to levy taxes without parliamentary approval. Thereafter, however, he resorted to forced taxes. As in Spain, this expedient created a crisis for the state when it really needed funds. Revolts in Scotland and Ireland (1639–41) forced Charles to call Parliament, which refused to grant taxes and eventually sponsored a rebellion against him. Unlike noble revolts on the continent, however, which centered around nobles' efforts to win or retain *immunity* from taxes, the English Civil War revolved around efforts to obtain *consent* for taxes, because substantial parts of the rebellious nobility in England had become commercialized.

This conflict mostly pitted those nobles within 15 miles of a coast or navigable river (and thus capable of participating in a commercial economy based on water transport) against those more than 15 miles inland (who thus were more oriented towards subsistence and rent in kind from the microeconomy they controlled) (Hochberg, 1984). By 1640, many landowners produced for the London market and wanted the kind of absolute property rights guaranteed in Roman law; others benefited from the state's ability to project violence into overseas markets. The fusion of noble and mercantile interests created a potential community of interests between a commercial nobility interested in 'protection' for its overseas ventures and the emerging central state. The Civil War fatally weakened the ability of the monarchy to rule without consent. The subsequent Glorious Revolution of 1688 confirmed this development when the incoming King William III accepted parliamentary control of spending in the Bill of Rights. Unlike France or Spain, no manpower-rich eastern power could easily project force into England.

Like Spain's monarchs, England's precociously powerful kings and queens tried to rule without forging a durable consensus with the nobility over taxation. Like Spain's monarchs, they found themselves faced with revolt when they did tax nobles. Unlike Spain's nobility, England's commercialized nobility had the financial resources to fund their own army. Unlike France's nobility, England's was gathered in one central parliament. England's nobles could survive their monarch's onslaught and forge a durable compromise over how and from whom to fund the level of military activity England needed to survive in a world of competing powers. And, unlike these three countries, England drew its tax revenue mainly from regularized exactions from a productive base, not a parasitic collection of other people's treasure. Therefore, England alone had the durable fiscal base needed to sustain global operations. This was the domestic counterpart and basis for its successes in the Indian Ocean, to which we now turn.

Mafias abroad: the external side of state-building

States struggling for survival and mastery in Atlantic Europe used mercantilist policies to acquire metallic money (specie) so as to widen their tax base and pay for loyal military and civil bureaucracies. All of these states faced two problems. First, the isolation of most microeconomies kept the division of labor and thus the potential level of revenue available to each state small. Second, Western Europe's backwardness meant that it consistently ran trade deficits with the Baltic, the Mideast, and Asia (see Table 1.2). Because the rising European states produced few goods desirable to exporters in those areas, exporters there demanded specie for payment. The constant eastward drain of money conflicted with monarchs' need to monetize their internal economies and drove them to search for specie overseas. Their overseas ventures generated specie in four ways. First, Spanish conquest of the Americas and pillage of Spanish specie shipments from the Americas directly

Table 1.2   *Specie outflow from Western Europe, 1600–1750, selected years (annual average in millions of guilders[a])*

Region	1600	1650	1700	1750
Baltic	1.85	2.65	2.65	2.65
Mideast	1.0	2.0	2.0	2.0
Asia	1.0	1.7	3.3	5.7
Total	3.85	6.35	7.95	10.35

Note: [a]20 guilders would buy a year's supply of grain for one person.

Source: Based on data from Johansen (1986: 127).

provided states with specie. Second, successful mercantilists reduced over- seas specie shipments by violently taking control of trade with Asia. Third, domestically, states generated enormous revenues by controlling and taxing imports of Indian Ocean goods. Fourth, externally, any state that successfully monopolized the flow of goods from the Indian Ocean could re-export those goods to other European states, helping to draw money out of its competitors' economies.

[handwritten margin note: 4 reasons]

The Spanish and Portuguese pillage of the Americas, from 1492 to about 1650, ultimately found the most raw specie. According to official figures, the Spanish and Portuguese stole or mined – at an incredible cost to human lives – about 180 tons of gold and 16 000 tons of silver, an amount roughly equal to half of Europe's money stock (Braudel, 1981: 466–7). The almost purely mili- tary enterprises of the Spanish and Portuguese were not self-sustaining, however. Having emptied the hoards of the local civilizations and worked the natives to death in the mines, Europe again faced the problem of specie flow- ing east. The production of drugs, foods, and raw materials soon replaced mining as the chief activity in the Americas (see Chapter 5). Meanwhile, real wealth lay eastward, in the Indian Ocean region. European incursions there reveal more about the new European state than Iberia's pillage of the Americas. Just as Spain's reliance on American silver prevented it from devel- oping the institutional forms needed to compete inside Europe, so a European reliance only on American silver to fund its trade deficit with Asia would have permitted only a glorious period of overconsumption rather than centuries of dominance. While the Baltic initially was the largest drain on European specie, the Dutch soon dominated this trade to their own advantage.

Three European powers in the Indian Ocean

Virtually all maritime European states eventually entered the Indian Ocean, but three dominated it, in succession, from 1500 to 1800: Portugal, Holland, and England. The Indian Ocean region contained a large, sophisticated, and highly articulated maritime economy. This economy had three natural circuits of trade defined by wind and water currents, composed of short coastal hops, and organized by a multitude of traders of different religious and ethnic back- grounds (Chaudhuri, 1985, 1990) (see Figure 1.1). The first circuit centered on the western Indian Ocean, linking the Arabian peninsula (and from there the Mediterranean and Europe), the eastern coast of Africa, and the Indian west coast. The second centered on the eastern Indian Ocean, linking the Indian east coast and the Southeast Asian peninsula and archipelago. The last centered on the China Sea, linking the Southeast Asian archipelagos, China and, occasion- ally, Japan. These circuits met at choke-points defined by geography and prevailing winds: Hormuz and Aden, which, respectively, controlled trade between the Indian Ocean and the Persian Gulf and Red Sea; Surat, which sat in the middle of the west coast circuit; Jaffna and Colombo, which controlled trade between the eastern and western Indian Ocean; and Malacca and Aceh, which controlled access from the Indian Ocean to the South China Sea.

34

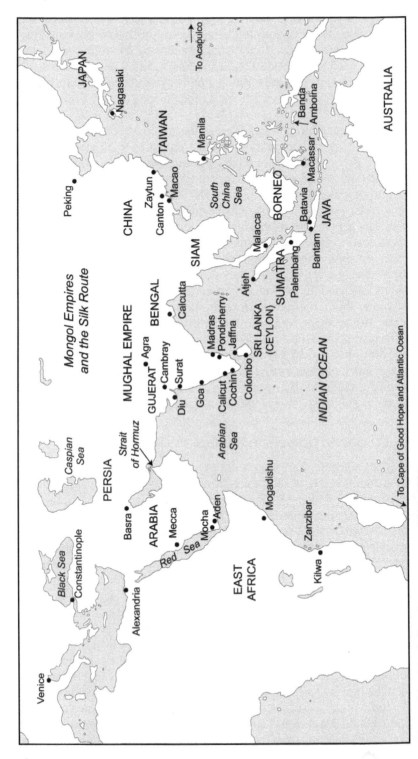

Figure 1.1 *The Indian Ocean economy, 1500–1750*

Both bulk and luxury goods entered trade, with textiles and fine spices the most important. Each culture and cuisine on the ocean prized goods and spices it could not produce: Hindus and Arabs valued Southeast Asian cinnamon, cloves, and nutmeg; Arabs desired Indian rice and cottons; Chinese wanted Indian pepper; and the archipelagos favored fine Chinese silks and Indian cottons. Everyone liked Arabian coffee, an addictive drug. Each group of merchants brought one of these goods to the table to be exchanged for the goods desired back 'home,' so all had to coexist.

The Indian Ocean economy had a twofold attraction for the European states. First, its large supply of goods with potentially high levels of price-insensitive demand in Europe meant that control over those goods could be used to generate revenue for the state (O'Rourke and Williamson, 2002). The various spices that added variety to an otherwise monotonous diet of bread and porridge were culturally addicting. Sugar, caffeinated drinks like tea and coffee, and, of course, opiates produced varying degrees of physical addiction. Like today's mafias, the European states and their merchants found these goods irresistibly tempting. Second, by going directly to the Indian Ocean, emerging European states hoped to reverse the outflow of specie from their societies.

The Europeans were able to fasten themselves, leechlike, to the Indian Ocean economy because they violated the rules of the Indian Ocean mercantile communities. First, the Portuguese claimed exclusive jurisdiction over the entire ocean and backed this claim up by seizing all the important trade choke-points. Second, the Dutch attempted to monopolize production of critical commodities and thus remove the necessity for cooperation. Finally, the English integrated European and Indian Ocean societies through trade in bulk commodities.

Portugal

The Portuguese were the first Europeans propelled in large numbers by economic motives into the Indian Ocean. They sought gold, and they sought African slaves for the production of sugar and tobacco. They also sought to challenge the Venetian monopoly on Indian Ocean pepper with pepper from West Africa. Once in the Indian Ocean, the Portuguese essentially created a gigantic protection racket. Portugal's 'comparative advantage' lay in the use of organized violence, not in trading *per se*, particularly because most Indian Ocean merchants were not armed. The organizational structure of the Portuguese venture into the Indian Ocean reflects their military orientation. The Portuguese armed ships for defensive and offensive purposes. They traded out of *feitorias*, which combined a fort and trading post and excluded traders other than those associated with their own monopoly. The Carreira da India, a state-owned military organization that monopolized the transport of Indian Ocean goods back to Portugal, and the Estado da India, a military organization running the *feitorias*, were Portugal's instruments for extracting protection money and spices.

Beginning in 1505, the Portuguese systematically set about seizing Diu, Goa, Malacca, Hormuz, and Colombo, which allowed them to blockade the Red Sea and the Persian Gulf, and to control access from the Indian Ocean to the China Sea and shipping from one side of the Indian Ocean to the other. Continuing the *reconquista*'s religious battles, they destroyed their only plausible and mostly Muslim maritime rivals in 1509. This also allowed them to defeat their rivals in Europe, for Genoa supported Portugal financially, while Venice's alliance with Muslim Mamluk Egypt reflected its reliance on pepper and spices shipped through the Red Sea and the Persian Gulf. The Portuguese used a divide-and-conquer strategy against the Muslims, for many Hindus were smarting from the recent conquest of inland India by the Muslim Mughals.

Portuguese innovations – forts, armed ships, and control of the choke-points – allowed them to force merchants to buy a *cartaze*, a safe-conduct pass. The *cartaze* was purely and simply a form of protection. Passage through the choke-points required a *cartaze*; if a shipper lacked one, the Portuguese would seize the ship and cargo. The Portuguese used *cartaze*-generated revenues to support their network of outposts in the Indian Ocean, to buy pepper for resale in Europe, and to provide revenue for the Portuguese crown. In the years for which data are available, over 80 percent of Portuguese imports from Asia by weight were pepper, and nearly 100 percent were some sort of spice. In the 1500s Indian Ocean pepper production is estimated to have doubled. This meant steadily rising revenues for the Portuguese crown, whose external revenues soon exceeded those from its very small domestic demographic base of about 1.5 to 2 million Portuguese. Roughly half of the Portuguese crown's revenues in the 1500s came from various imperial sources, of which the Estado da India consistently provided a quarter (Subrahmanyam and Thomaz, 1991: 309, 328).

The Portuguese shaped Indian Ocean trading patterns for half a century with blockade, fort, and *cartaze*. Their monopoly began to unravel after 1550, when the Dutch successfully displaced them. Portuguese decline stemmed first from its almost purely military character. What the sword could do, other, better swords surely could also undo. The Portuguese military edge dulled fairly rapidly as local merchants and states adopted European cannon and methods of warfare. One of the major Portuguese technological edges came from its combination of the Arab triangular lateen sail with traditional European square-rigged ships to produce fast, highly maneuverable ships capable of carrying many cannon. This allowed the Portuguese to destroy much larger fleets. However, Indian Ocean shipbuilders rapidly assimilated both changes and soon built armed ships rivaling those of the Portuguese.

Second, the Estado da India was an inefficient revenue-extractor. As a purely predatory military operation, it had no way to increase revenues on its own; in fact, the more it extracted from Indian Ocean merchants, the less likely they were to cooperate and pay for 'protection.' The Portuguese responded to this inefficiency by trying to establish more commercial ventures in the Indian Ocean. Consistent with their domestic absolutism, which rested on royal monopolies over salt, slaves and soap, they auctioned off the right to organize voyages to well-connected individual nobles and soldiers after 1564. 'Entrepreneurs' who only completed one voyage had no incentive to continuously invest in an efficient and permanent commercial organization capable of exploiting the Indian Ocean economies. Indeed, these entrepreneurs had every incentive to underinvest in the forts and ships that were the basis for Portuguese supremacy; they could not take these home with them.

Third, just as the Portuguese did not control the production of spice in the Indian Ocean, they did not control wholesaling in Europe. This was centered in two places – Antwerp, in the Spanish Netherlands, and Amsterdam, in the United Provinces (Holland). When Spanish depredations of Jewish merchants drove the Antwerp merchant community to Amsterdam, control over the spice trade shifted to merchants domiciled in a state hostile to Portugal.

Portugal's dominance began to unravel almost immediately after its consolidation, as Muslims organized a concerted counter-attack, and as Spain began absorbing metropolitan Portugal. By 1530 the Turks were challenging Portuguese control of the western side of the Indian Ocean. Meanwhile, Malacca, key to trade between the eastern Indian Ocean and the rich China Sea, remained dependent for food on Muslim sultanates in Java and Sumatra. These sultanates became quite proficient with cannon and began to sail directly across the Indian Ocean to Aden, thus bypassing Portuguese chokepoints. The *cartaze*, estimated to have affected only 20 percent of trade, began to slip, and by 1630 Portugal also controlled only about 20 percent of the pepper coming from the Indian Ocean. The old Muslim-Venetian pepper trade through the Mideast revived after 1560, and about 60–80 percent of spices again flowed to Europe through overland routes. As the Portuguese declined, the Dutch entered with innovations that overcame the deficiencies of the Portuguese military operation.

Holland

Holland did everything the Portuguese did, but better. Holland used a bureaucratic, commercial organization – at the time the world's largest joint stock corporation – not only to organize trade, but also to control the production and sale of the spice. By controlling spice production, the Dutch directly controlled trade, rather than simply taxing it like the Portuguese.

Dutch supremacy over the Portuguese rested on five factors. First, the Dutch had more, better, and cheaper ships. Because the Dutch literally lived off grain exports from the Baltic and fishing, they pioneered the production of standardized shipping. While these ships were smaller than the Portuguese galleon, they also had better-designed and -controlled sails, and so used a much smaller crew (Braudel, 1984: 190). More and cheaper ships with smaller (and thus cheaper) crews permitted the Dutch to dominate North Sea fishing. About 1500 ships and 20 000 sailors fished for herring alone. Fish proteins meant Dutch sailors tended to be less debilitated than their rivals.

Second, cheap fish, cheap ships, and cheap crews lowered transport costs, allowing the Dutch to undercut their rivals in trade with the Baltic, which then was the source of most inputs for the production of ships: pitch, timber, linen, hemp, and iron. The Dutch got the first cut at all of these crucial inputs and thus were able to dominate European waters. By 1570 Amsterdam alone could deploy about 232 000 tons of shipping, and a century later about 568 000 tons, more shipping than all the other Atlantic states combined. (To put this in perspective, the 1600s Dutch fleet carried annually what nine 'Panamax' container ships carry in one voyage today.)

To superior naval might – and thus a much more efficient enforcement of the *cartaze* – the Dutch added a sophisticated private trading corporation, the Dutch East India Company, or VOC (its Dutch initials). The VOC was organized as a joint stock corporation, with a capital roughly ten times the size of its closest foreign rival, the English East India Company (EIC). Its owners' liability was limited to the money that they had invested in the VOC's stock shares, so the company could raise money through impersonal capital markets and permanently staff its Indian Ocean operations. By 1690 the VOC deployed about 100–160 ships, 8000 sailors, and about 10 000 settlers in garrisons in the Indian Ocean area.

Fourth, the whole strategic orientation of the VOC differed from that of the Estado da India. Unlike the parasitic Portuguese, the VOC used its dominance over spice production to control all Indian Ocean exchange. Simultaneously with its efforts to capture or destroy Portuguese *feitorias* at the geographical choke-points, the VOC also captured islands in the Southeast Asian archipelago (modern Indonesia) that produced the four fine spices crucial to Indian Ocean trade patterns: cinnamon, cloves, nutmeg, and mace. Beginning with Amboina in 1605 and ending in the 1660s with the fall of the clove-producing islands and of the pepper-producing coast in India, the VOC systematically eliminated rival producers of spices. It first tried to assure itself a monopoly via exclusive contracts with each island's leadership, but when this approach failed to control trade it turned to violent methods. Starting in 1621 with nutmeg-producing Banda, it began killing and relocating island populations as slaves on Dutch-controlled spice production islands.

Finally, by controlling the flow of the four fine spices into Indian Ocean commerce, the Dutch could control both the prices and quantities of goods flowing around all three Indian Ocean trade circuits. By linking the entire coastal trade of Asia under one company, they could systematically exploit opportunities for arbitrage. Arbitrage occurs when a middleman can exploit buyers and sellers who lack knowledge of each other's costs and prices. The Dutch could convert the profits spun out of this arbitrage into goods for export back to Europe.

Whereas the Portuguese exported protection money back to Europe in the form of spices, the Dutch exported their profits in a wider variety of goods: spices (about 60 percent of Dutch exports back to Europe by value in the 1600s, of which about half to two-thirds was pepper), sugar (5 percent), drugs (about 5 percent), and textiles (about 20 percent). By the 1700s trade shifted decisively in favor of tea and coffee (about 25 percent) and textiles (30 percent) (Steensgaard, 1991: 114–17). The VOC's control of both production and wholesaling allowed it to shift among goods as demand changed, because it was positioned inside rather than primarily outside trade circuits.

Like the Portuguese, however, the Dutch had to yield supremacy in the Indian Ocean to another contender, although the VOC and a Dutch colonial presence in the Indian Ocean managed to survive in various guises until 1947. The VOC had fewer weaknesses than Portugal's Estado. The purely commercial orientation of the VOC and its owners meant that they were loath to engage in military operations and to sustain the levels of violence necessary to control Indian Ocean trade. During the period when the VOC was consolidating Dutch supremacy in relation to the Portuguese, the VOC's directors in Holland constantly hectored their on-site proconsul to spend less on forts and campaigns. In the same way, the commercialism of the VOC's directors led them to help fund and provision Portuguese campaigns in the 1650s in order to retake Brazil from the VOC's rival, the Dutch West Indies Company! Dutch purchases of English public debt also served to enhance their competitor's position. Meanwhile, back in Europe, the manpower-rich French continually hammered at Holland, trying to gain enough resources to challenge England.

The VOC preserved its position as English strength waxed by cutting a deal with the English, whose East India Company (EIC) had entered the Indian Ocean in the early 1600s. The EIC agreed to help fund part of the cost of maintaining VOC forts in return for a guaranteed quota of spices. When the VOC seemed at the point of dominating the Indian Ocean and used its control of spice prices to rip off the EIC, the EIC became openly hostile. The VOC and EIC struggled from 1650 to 1700, with the VOC eventually ceding hegemony to the English. None the less, the Dutch remained the largest shippers in the Indian Ocean and dominated Baltic trade until well into the 1700s. *strictly interested in commerce*

England

Like the Dutch before them, the English triumphed because they both assimilated all their predecessors' strengths while also generating a few institutional innovations of their own. Like the Dutch they excelled in shipbuilding, and like the Portuguese they divided and conquered their enemies. To these methods they added long-distance trade in bulk goods rather than luxuries. In the short run, they probably would have preferred to muscle into the Dutch spice trade, but in the long run, being forced to take the second-best alternative, textiles, proved more lucrative.

The English state used a variety of judicious industrial policies to propel its merchants into a more competitive position. In 1609 King James I (1603–25) reserved all English fishing grounds to English ships in an effort to displace Dutch fishing fleets. Oliver Cromwell's Navigation Acts in 1651, which restricted all English trade to English ships, created a demand for new ships. English shipwrights rapidly reverse-engineered Dutch ships, assimilated their techniques, and tripled the size of the United Kingdom's fleet during 1600–89. Eventually, they were able to outgun the VOC in the Indian Ocean.

The English also revived Portugal's divide, conquer, and coopt techniques. The EIC's strategy produced two condominia – agreements on shared owner- ship – in the Indian Ocean, one over trade with the VOC and one inside India with local rulers. The EIC first allied with the Dutch against the Portuguese, and then reversed this alliance, using the shift to consolidate control over Portuguese exports back to Europe. With Portugal coopted and the Dutch weakened, the English then cut a new deal with the VOC in order to be free to confront the French. Under this deal, the VOC retained control both of the production of spices and of the coastal trade. The EIC took over control of long-distance trade in drugs, particularly tea, and, equally important, of bulk goods such as textiles.

The EIC's condominium with the VOC dovetailed with its early involve- ment on the mainland; it helped to push the EIC into a condominium with mainland rulers, particularly in Bengal. The EIC turned to Bengal and the east- ern coast in general because the Dutch and Portuguese had ignored this rela- tively poor area. This move involved the EIC in local politics, however. As it had with the European powers, the EIC played various Indian powers off one another. The Mughal empire's control over southern India, always tenuous, began to disintegrate as a result of internal power struggles after 1707. The EIC offered coastal principalities military advisers and equipment in return for trade concessions; the EIC also wrested the legal right to collect taxes from the Mughals, in effect tax-farming for their long-term enemy.

These two condominia both permitted and forced the EIC to deal in bulk goods. The EIC had always specialized in the shipment of second-best bulk goods like textiles and tea to Europe. From 1650 to 1700 roughly three-quar- ters of the EIC's exports to Europe consisted of cotton textiles and silks, compared to the VOC's 20 percent; absolutely, the EIC exported twice as much fabric as the VOC. At first, this distribution reflected necessity: the VOC controlled the lucrative spice trade while the EIC lived off less valuable commodities. However, the EIC's onshore condominium eased EIC develop- ment of the trade in bulk goods by allowing it unmediated access to local producers; earlier, most European merchants had to deal with powerful Indian middlemen.

As it turned out, the spice trade had inherent limitations: it was geared primarily to a well-to-do but limited Continental European market. Pepper sales stagnated at around 7 million pounds annually from the mid-1600s on (Furber, 1976: 263). In contrast, cotton textiles had a large mass market, and even if the average person could afford to buy only one shirt a year, that still meant millions of potential consumers, especially in England.

To the trade in textiles the EIC added tea and coffee. Both proved more durable long-term profit makers than spices. Tea sales enjoyed explosive rates of growth in the 1700s, doubling from the 1720s to the 1740s, and then nearly doubling again to the 1750s; by then, tea constituted nearly half of all Asian exports to Europe. During the 1800s, when tea production shifted from China to EIC-controlled plantations in India and segments of the British working class experienced rising real incomes, tea sales would rise astronomically,

Balances rivals
against eachother
via condominium.

hitting 96 000 tons in 1900 (Steensgaard, 1991: 131). Along with sugar and tobacco, American products that other English companies controlled, tea and coffee enjoyed the fantastic sales that addictive substances generate. These substances, particularly tobacco, were the crack cocaine of their time. Equally important, opium and other commodities that were produced for and by the British in Bengal could be sold in China, thus reducing the outflow of specie from European-controlled economies to the east. As late as the mid-1700s, three-quarters of the EIC's exports to Asia were still specie, but by the end of the century only one-fifth were, lower than the European average of one-third (Kriedte, 1983: 121–5; Pearson, 1991: 108). The English thus created and dominated a new circuit of intra-Asian trade to which the Dutch could not gain access. During 1752–54, years for which relatively complete data are available, the EIC exported 17 percent more by value from the Indian Ocean than did the VOC, mostly because larger textile and tea exports offset the VOC's larger spice exports (Steensgaard, 1991: 148–9).

In the long run, the EIC's involvement on the Indian mainland allowed it to extract enormous revenues from a highly monetized set of microeconomies that it then incorporated into overseas commerce. Before 1800, the EIC took its spoils in money as taxes and land rent; after 1850, the railroad allowed the cheap inland transport of goods taken as taxes in kind. The EIC in effect became the 'king' of the Indian microeconomies, squeezing taxes out of a massive peasant population. In the nineteenth century this revenue source would help stabilize the English pound sterling, helping to constitute British financial hegemony as British industrial might declined.

'Money for nothing'

European efforts to extract resources from the Indian Ocean economy both mirrored and enhanced the European states' ability to deploy and use organized violence back in Europe. The entire Indian Ocean economy was probably larger and certainly more sophisticated than the European economy, even relative to its rich northwest corner. The relatively small European states that attached themselves to this enormous economy were able to draw enormous resources out of it without 'killing the goose that laid the golden eggs.' Even though the Europeans took only a small percentage of the surplus available from these economies, this had enormous consequences for European state-building.

Mercantilism and state-building required money. Despite its predatory activity, Europe overall continued to lose specie to the Indian Ocean economies through 1800, a loss offset only by the specie coming out of the Americas. But this outflow had differential effects. The states that fastened onto the Indian Ocean accumulated specie to monetize their economies. These states reduced the outward drain of specie caused by their own society's consumption of Indian Ocean commodities, by paying for those imports with the profits of their own Indian Ocean mercantile (and protection-racket) activity. Simultaneously, the three most successful dominators of the Indian Ocean were able to re-export Indian Ocean commodities to other states and areas, thus offsetting potential deficits with those areas. For England and Holland, this re-export was particularly important in offsetting imports of irreplaceable Baltic commodities used for shipbuilding. Northwestern Europe's deficit with the Baltic almost equaled deficits elsewhere in the world in 1600 and was still significant as late as 1750. But the volume of colonial produce shipped by northwest European countries into the Baltic increased from 3.1 million pounds in 1700 to 33.8 million pounds by 1780 (Johansen, 1986: 128–38). Britain's re-exports were a consistent third of its total exports in the 1700s, and more significantly its re-exports to Europe rivaled its domestically produced exports. Eighty percent of those re-exports came from Asia or America, and their prices were typically marked up 100 percent before being resold (Kriedte, 1983: 124). Later, Britain would offset its tea-created deficit with China by exporting Indian opium to China in exactly the same way. The primarily Continental European states without access to the Indian Ocean lagged economically behind those that could monetize their economies, making it harder for a dominant continental empire to emerge.

Domestic and overseas success worked together to create durable states capable of deploying organized violence in a systemic, sustained way. Yet at the same time, the compromises needed to create regular revenue extraction at home, as well as the competitive pressures facing states in their adventures abroad, guaranteed that states would not dominate economic activity. At home, law assured merchants protection in return for specified payments. Abroad, the increasing costs of financing protection rackets in an Indian Ocean full of rapidly arming peoples forced a shift from purely predatory activities to a more business-oriented approach using monopoly control of commodities. States moved from simply threatening to toss rocks through windows to actually having to help run the enterprises. England's and Holland's experiences in the Indian Ocean created enormous institutional centers of financial power, linking the external and the internal world and balancing the state's ability to project violence inward and outward. Both state and economy simultaneously reached inward and outward, and both literally grew up in the interface between the internal, territorial base of the state and the world market based on water transport. The growth of states and the global economy reshaped both their internal economies and those of other states, which is the topic of the next chapter.

Chapter 2

States, Markets, and the Origins of International Inequality

> Division of labor is limited by the extent of the market.
>
> *Adam Smith*

Markets and the rise of spatial inequality

The last chapter looked at the rise of predatory European states and their use of organized violence to exploit other parts of the world. Did the economic inequality this predation created rest only on political or non-economic mechanisms like predation? Or did the rise of a global economy initially centered on Europe also cause inequality through *economic* mechanisms? Specifically, did the market forces unleashed by Europe's agricultural and industrial revolutions necessarily create inequality elsewhere by generating an unequal global distribution of production? Were these revolutions dependent on the creation of absolute poverty elsewhere? And finally, could this inequality be overcome? These questions lie at the heart of earlier assertions that what we now call 'globalization' has been a persistent and defining feature of the world economy since 1500.

Each question centers on the fact that a novel kind of economic inequality emerged after 1400, and even more strongly after 1800: enormous disparities of income across societies. Economic inequality, after all, had always existed. But the kind of inequality found in premodern Europe and other agrarian societies reflected stratification *within* societies: peasants versus landlords and warriors; impure versus pure castes; the damned versus the saved; slaves versus the free. What was novel about inequality consequent to the expansion of the northwestern European maritime economy was its spatial aspect: inequality existed and persisted not just inside societies but also among regions and nations. Did this inequality originate from the workings of the global economy itself?

As late as 1800, Asian per capita income was roughly equal to that in Europe and North America as a bloc, with the richest country having no more than twice the per capita income of the poorest (Bairoch, 1976, 1982; Pomeranz, 2000). By the end of the 1800s, however, Britain and settler societies like the United States, Australia, Canada, and Argentina had per capita incomes 10 *times* those in Asia and India. By 2005, on a per capita basis, the developed countries were about 20 times richer than the non-oil exporting Third World, even after adjusting for purchasing power parity, and despite rapid industrialization in China (World Bank, 2008: 4).

Do market forces alone explain this new kind of inequality? If the coercion associated with colonization is more important, then the sovereignty attained by virtually all Third World countries should lead to a lessening of inequality. However, if markets alone can create spatial inequality, what options do states/economies have for altering the global distribution of production in their favor? We can re-cast these questions in the following, more analytically tractable ways: how does the division of labor expand? what are the consequences of its expansion? how does an expanding division of labor bear on the (im)possibility of technological diffusion and development? Looking at how the market shapes the spatial distribution of production provides a key to understanding the emergence of unequal rates of growth, innovation, and development.

Roughly speaking, we can give three possible answers to the question of whether European *economic* growth alone, or the world market alone, caused poverty and backwardness elsewhere: no, yes, and maybe. Theories based in neoclassical economics (NCE) claim that economic growth produced a relative inequality, but that economic growth in one place does not cause poverty elsewhere or require exploitation of those other areas. Participation in the world market should lead to growth. In short, the international market and international trade are benign forces – they affect all economies the same way, and any success or deficiency in growth is due to unit-level (local) institutional successes and failures.

A set of quasi-Marxist theories going by the name of world systems theory (WST) or dependency theory argues the reverse: European growth created poverty and could not have occurred without economic exploitation of other regions. Poverty is relational rather than simply being relative, because participation in the world market *underdevelops* many countries. In short, the international economy and international trade are malign forces that sort different areas into a 'core,' 'semiperiphery,' and 'periphery.' This is a system-level argument, in which the units merely express forces playing out at a global level. Local institutions matter very little.

Finally, there is an intermediate position. It argues that global markets create a hierarchy of potential production sites globally. These sites potentially have different income levels – thus the hierarchy. But the kinds of state institutions and policies that emerge from local political struggles determine in part which particular outcome will emerge from the set of possibilities revealed by an area's position in the world market. These struggles are not fully independent of the global market, because state revenues and thus competence ultimately rest on the revenue available in the local economy. While this view is more agnostic than the pure unit-level or pure system-level arguments, this does not mean it lacks a set of mechanisms and a specific set of theoretical claims.

The intermediate view blends two models from economic geography. (A full analysis can be found in Schwartz, 2007). One is Johann von Thünen's (1966) agricultural location model, and the other is Paul Krugman's (1991a, 1991b; Krugman and Venables, 1995) model for spatial agglomeration of industrial activity (see also Weber, 1929[1909]). Thünen explains the uneven distribution of agricultural production on the basis of the interaction of land costs and intensity of production. Krugman explains why manufacturing is distributed unevenly spatially, using the interaction of transportation costs and economies of scale. These analyses reveal that markets powerfully shape the kinds of economic opportunities available to discrete regions, distributing productive activity in a hierarchical pattern of zones producing goods with diminishing degrees of value added. In other words, the *normal operation of the global market* certainly can produce an inequality that is not simply a relative inequality but a relational inequality.

State institutions and social coalitions determine whether a given region either adapts to those forces or tries to overcome them. We can label these generic strategies *Ricardian* and *Kaldorian*, after the economists most closely associated with the ideas presented under those names. This chapter will focus mostly on a static consideration of the question of inequality (i.e., the spatial distribution of production), and will end with a look at the two different strategies for development. Later chapters provide a dynamic and empirical consideration of the forces described here.

Neoclassical economic explanations

Neoclassical economics (NCE) argues that differences in local governance institutions typically do produce global economic spatial inequality but reject any argument for automatic inequality or exploitation. Backwardness is relative, not relational: rising incomes in industrial societies make nonindustrial societies look backward. However, external poverty only hampers growth in industrialized countries by reducing total demand, and the natural diffusion of production technologies means that backward societies will rarely lose ground absolutely, if their local institutions enable them to adapt and adopt those technologies. Thus international trade only helps economies, by maximizing allocative efficiency, that is, by allowing them to produce whatever they make most efficiently and to exchange it for goods they are less efficient at producing. In principle, the market might produce equality if everyone had the same governance institutions.

NCE argues that strong institutions protecting discrete, absolute property rights led to rapid innovation and the agricultural and industrial revolutions in northwestern Europe, particularly Holland and Britain (North and Thomas, 1973; Pollard, 1981; Reynolds, 1985). Consequently, their incomes per capita rose above the level prevailing in the rest of the world, where parcellized property rights and premodern forms of agriculture set lower income levels. But as agricultural and industrial innovations diffused outward, productivity and income rose elsewhere (see Broadberry and Gupta, 2006 on different wage levels). The major impediments to the adoption of technology were social and political, not economic. Weak states incapable of enforcing property rights deter investment. The diffusion of innovation and of an increasingly complex division of labor thus produces spatial inequality because not all areas take up innovations or continue innovating at the same rate. NCE argues that the diffusion of innovation produces only relative inequality: while laggards may never catch up, they usually do not regress either. Similarly, since innovation is *endogenous*, it obviously cannot be true that development (i.e., rising productivity and incomes) in one place causes regression (not simply a *relative* decline) in another, or that this decline is necessary for innovation to take place in areas with high or rising income. Thus, NCE sees trade links between rich and poor areas as desirable, for these links will speed technological diffusion.

NCE arguments derive from Adam Smith and David Ricardo. Smith argued that economic growth came from an increase in the division of labor. Increasing economic specialization increased productivity and incomes. Smith assumed that people's natural inclination to 'barter and truck' would create markets, and that markets in turn would force producers to innovate and increase the division of labor. He thus offered both mechanisms for the origin and maintenance of capitalist growth as trade led to innovation and increased specialization in a virtuous circle.

David Ricardo amplified this argument with his insights into static comparative advantage. Obviously, if Country A produces wheat with fewer inputs of capital and labor than Country B, but Country B produces MP3 players with fewer inputs than Country A, both countries will gain by exchanging wheat and players and concentrating on the production of what they do best. This is *absolute advantage*, because A is absolutely better at making wheat and B better at producing players. Ricardo showed that even when absolute advantage did not exist, *comparative advantage* made trade worthwhile. Even when Country A produced both wheat and players more efficiently than Country B, if A used more inputs to produce players than wheat when it made both, while B used relatively more inputs to produce wheat than players when it produced both, it made sense for A to shift its resources into the production of wheat and for B to shift resources into the production of players. Then both countries gained from exchanging A's wheat for B's players. Specialized production and exports increased income and consumption in both countries.

World systems theory and Marxist explanations

World systems theory (WST) makes a system-level argument diametrically opposed to NCE's unit-level argument. It argues that the development of capitalism in northwest Europe both required and caused not just relative but also *absolute* backwardness elsewhere, as trade generated and exacerbated spatial inequalities (Emmanuel, 1972; Wallerstein, 1974–89). WST makes a categorical distinction between world empires and world economies. A world empire contains the division of labor within one political system. A world economy by contrast has a single division of labor but multiple polities. For WST, capitalism is unlikely to emerge within a world empire. In our terms, WST argues that in world empires dominant kings tend to squeeze out both nobles and merchants, as in China. Because nobles are turned into salaried officials, kings can absorb virtually all of the peasants' surplus. The absence of internal and external enemies removes merchants' leverage over kings. In contrast, financial and military competition among states in a world economy creates a space in which accumulation can occur. Kings need merchants to fund their public debts, and offer property rights in return.

WST argues that participation in the world economy determines domestic class structures, the structure of export production, and ultimately state power. The spatial expansion of the world economy differentiates national economies into core and periphery areas, but this specialization benefits only core areas. Trade forces peripheral areas into the production of low-value-added goods that do not lead to more economic development. Wages and national income there stagnate, while the core benefits from low-cost inputs that raise its rate of capital accumulation. This 'unequal exchange' occurs because low wages in peripheral areas mean that peripheral areas in general have to exchange many more hours of labor with core economies to buy goods embodying a given hour of high-wage work (Emmanuel, 1972). Unequal exchange is a significant part of the WST argument. Mere looting of colonial areas would not necessarily have impeded long-term development. Unequal exchange provides a mechanism – albeit implausible – through which market pressures *alone* cause underdevelopment.

WST is loyal to its Marxist origins: the analysis of core and periphery mirrors Marx's analysis of the dialectical relationship between capital and labor. Core and periphery could not exist without each other. Core implies periphery in the same way that capital – private ownership of the means of production by a limited group of people – implies labor – a larger group separated from the means of production. The core's growth depends on exploitation of the periphery. Moreover, in contrast to NCE, which sees only a relative poverty, WST claims that absolute regression not only can occur but often is also the norm in the periphery, because unequal exchange can cause capital declines there.

Because observed reality confronts WST with a gradient of incomes, market power, and state power rather than a sharp polarization, WST inserts an intermediate zone called semiperiphery between core and periphery. WST defines the semiperiphery in relation to the core and periphery. The semiperiphery trades high-value-added goods to the periphery and low-value-added goods to the core in exchange for low- and high-value-added goods, respectively. The semiperiphery suffers from unequal exchange with the core but exploits the periphery through unequal exchange.

While NCE makes no claims about how things will be produced, WST asserts that the world market also structures the kinds of classes and production systems in each type of economy. Core economies combine skilled labor and highly capitalized production systems without overt extraeconomic coercion. Peripheral economies typically use unskilled labor and low levels of capitalization, and often coerce labor through methods ranging from slavery

to state-enforced violence. Once more, semiperipheral areas occupy an intermediate position with systems that mix market and political coercion. By shutting their economies off from market pressures emanating from the world
economy, states can move their economies up in this hierarchy of economic
zones.

Intermediate explanations

The intermediate explanation does not simply say that system and unit explanations both matter, and mix them unsystematically. Instead it has a genetic
component and a logical relationship between systemic and unit-level forces,
albeit with a lower degree of determinacy for those unit-level forces. The genetic
component – an argument about how a capitalist system emerged – comes from
Robert Brenner (1977, 1985). Systemic models elucidating clear mechanisms
for how that system produces global inequalities come from Thünen and
Krugman. And Alexander Gerschenkron (1966) provides us with a way to
understand the relationship between systemic forces and institutional structure
in various units, as well as which local institutions matter. Collectively these
allow us to understand the general pattern of inequality we can observe, as well
as the causes for changes in the position of specific countries.

Brenner looked at struggles between landlords and peasants/serfs in
seventeenth-century Poland, England, and France, to understand why they
emerged as WST's paradigmatic peripheral, core, and semiperipheral areas.
WST claims that Poland's participation in world grain markets led to the
underdevelopment of its economy, whereas England and Holland developed
by virtue of manufactured exports to Poland. Brenner instead argues that the
absence of towns in Poland and Eastern Europe in general weakened the position of the peasants relative to landowners. Recently settled peasant villages
in Poland and Eastern Europe lacked the internal solidarity necessary to
confront and contain rapacious landlords who sought greater income through
grain exports (Wunde, 1985 and Anderson, 1974 disagree). Landowners
deployed state violence to fix peasants in place, making them serfs who
worked on nobles' estates. The reinforcement of feudalism prevented investment so Poland stagnated.

In France, meanwhile, peasants had relatively greater power *vis-à-vis*
nobles than did English or Polish peasants. They asserted their ownership
rights to the land they farmed and restricted nobles' ability to extract grain
rents. French nobles who could not clear peasants off the land also could not
assemble the kind of landholdings that would make agricultural investment
rational. Peasants also could not and would not consolidate holdings. They
could ignore market pressures to increase production or productivity continuously; competition did not affect their ability to survive. Only in England,
where towns existed but landlords were able to dispossess peasants, did a classic capitalist investment dynamic emerge. There the replacement of peasants
by tenant farmers created a group of actors whose long-term survival did

depend on their ability to cope with competitive pressures by investing and increasing productivity. Tenants risked losing their lease to higher bidders if they fell behind in the competitive struggle.

While Brenner argues that trade was a relatively minor part of economic activity in this period, trade clearly motivated nobles' pursuit of greater power over both peasants and land. And opting to participate in trade meant that producers had to accommodate themselves to what the world market demanded. Much as NCE expects, this permitted some societies to expand output and productivity via specialization. We need to detour into an analysis of this before proceeding to the Thünen and Krugman models. But this detour reconnects the argument to issues raised in the prior chapter.

Agriculture and the division of labor

As Chapter 1 noted, limits on agricultural productivity and the transportation of staple (bulk) agricultural products set profound limits on an increased division of labor in Europe and China. The agricultural surplus left over after peasants, nobles, and their draft animals have been fed determines the size of the urban population available for nonagricultural but productive activities. Low productivity in premodern European agriculture limited this surplus, and in turn limited the urban population. Until about 1600, European agriculture yielded three or four units of grain for every one unit sown; this condition persisted outside northwestern Europe until the 1800s even as China's state pushed and trained peasants to attain 10:1 yields (see Table 2.1). The division of labor in an ideal typical microeconomy was limited by the relatively small population that could be fed on the relatively small surplus produced within the effective 20-mile transport limit to its market town. Moreover, most 'manufacturing' involved the transformation of agriculturally derived raw materials, setting yet another limit on expansion of the division of labor inside microeconomies. Food and agricultural raw materials (nonfood agriculturals, or NFAs) competed for land in most microeconomies; expanding one meant shrinking the other.

Fifteenth-century European agriculture thus was caught in a vicious circle in which a limited surplus (often consumed unproductively by the nobility) in

Table 2.1   *Average harvest-to-seed yield ratios in Europe, 1500–1820*

Years	England, Netherlands	France, Spain, Italy	Central Europe	Eastern Europe
1500s	7.4	6.7	4.2	4.1
1600s	8.0	6.2	4.3	3.9
1700s	10.1	6.7	4.6	4.1
1800–20	11.1	6.2	5.4	–

Source: Based on data from Kriedte (1983: 22).

turn limited both the ability to invest in agriculture and the utility of investment in agriculture. This meant that the majority of towns in 1500 held between 400 and 1000 people; in all of Europe only 100 had populations over 10 000. China similarly had about 110 large cities but many more medium-sized ones (Maddison, 2007: 39). As a result, specialization in Smith's sense stayed very low, limiting productivity and income. Towns that could not find additional economical sources of food or NFAs faced a 'Malthusian' future, in which inefficient local production limited the town's expansion and development.

Fernand Braudel succinctly states towns' two ways out of the Malthusian trap: 'Thousands of towns were founded [in the 11th century], but few of them went on to brilliant futures. ... The destinies of these very special cities were linked not only to the progress of the surrounding countryside but [also] to international trade' (Braudel, 1981: 482, 511). Braudel's 'progress of the surrounding countryside' could be called the Brennerite path, as it involves the continuous market-based pressure for innovation Brenner identified in Britain (and also present in Holland). Squeezing more production in a sustainable way from a microeconomy's land allowed the town population and the division of labor to grow. The agricultural revolution of the 1500s in Holland and England did generate new crop rotations that substantially increased productivity per acre and reduced fallow (Slicher van Bath, 1963). Much as NCE expects, these Dutch and English techniques diffused, but slowly. Techniques innovated in 1500 did not reach Poland and Hungary – a distance of only 700 miles (1100 km), or about the distance from New York to Chicago – until 1825.

New crops from the Americas after 1600 supplemented these new crop rotations in Europe and China. The potato was perhaps the single most important 'innovation,' because it generated three times as many calories out of a given area as did grain production. Planting potatoes on one-third of a microeconomy potentially freed up the other two-thirds for use in producing animal protein, more urban food, or industrial raw materials. The potato thus 'created' new land in Europe. By 1800, potatoes provided 40 percent of calories in highly urban Belgium (Salaman, 1949; Braudel, 1981: 170). Turnips had the same consequences for livestock; in the nineteenth century, palm oils, which generate ten times as many calories per acre as wheat, fed the expanding urban proletariat.

Adopting the new technologies was not simple. Multiple rotations required relatively large parcels of land and more inputs of labor and manufactured goods (such as seed drills). This was easiest when markets for land and labor already existed or when peasants, for whatever reason, were responsive to market signals. Brenner correctly notes that the slow diffusion of convertible husbandry equaled capitalist development, and occurred only where the state and landlords displaced peasants and consolidated property rights in land. And, as we will see in Chapter 5, this was also true in Europe's colonies. Meanwhile, the Chinese state's internal technology transfer also produced an 'industrious revolution' if not an industrial one (Bin Wong, 1998; Pomeranz, 2000). Crucially, though, the mass of peasants never lost their direct access to land. Commercialization expanded and stabilized their incomes. As in

Brenner's France, this commercialization did not produce capitalism in the absence of a large landless labor force dependent on wages.

Braudel's second, 'international trade' path might be called the Wallersteinian path. This required towns to extend their agricultural supply zones into new areas via water transport, in effect creating new land through a global division of labor. The mercantile cities of northwest Europe pioneered this path. They turned to overseas sources of grain, fish, and NFAs as they outgrew their own microeconomies. By the 1600s the Baltic was shipping enough grain to feed about 750 000 people yearly (roughly twice as much as the Chinese Grand Canal apparently carried), allowing Holland to import about 15 percent of its food (Glamann, 1974: 454–67). Holland and then England also drew their industrial supplies – flax, timber, hemp, and wool – from new agricultural zones extending into the Baltic and up its major rivers, as well as up the Rhine River. Dutch and English cities would have faced a severe trade-off between raw materials and food production without access to these zones.

The emergence of the modern global capitalism thus required the combination of capitalism with an expanding global market. Diffuse global mercantile networks had always existed without being dynamic. Dynamic but localized capitalist production without access to external sources of foods and NFAs would have hit its Malthusian limits. *The creation and expansion of an industrial capitalist world economy of the sort WST describes thus rested on the core's ability to find and generate an expanded supply of foods and NFAs.* At this minimal level, WST is correct about the reciprocal interaction of core and periphery: because food and NFA production could not be increased within the confines of the microeconomies surrounding most towns, the core could not have developed without the periphery. But was this periphery doomed to poverty?

The international division of labor and spatial inequality

Johann von Thünen and Paul Krugman provide us with systemic mechanisms that predict global inequality as a natural outcome of the market. Von Thünen's major contribution to economics, *Der isolierte Staat*, or *The Isolated State*, was a thought experiment that asks how agricultural activity distributes itself around a single town constituting the largest source of monetized demand. (Krugman makes problematic the number and size of urban manufacturing centers.) Thünen posited a flat, featureless plain of uniform fertility with a single town at its center, and *capitalist* markets for land, labor, and commodities. Thünen's town provides all manufactured inputs to agriculture; agricultural areas provide all foods and raw materials for the town. Thünen assumes that transportation costs rise linearly with distance from town. Marginal urban demand determines the volume of production for all agricultural commodities, while the intersection of urban demand with the combination of production costs and marginal transport costs sets final prices.

Thünen argued that agricultural activity would distribute itself in regular, concentric rings around the town, with each ring devoted to a particular type of product, and, more importantly, using *different production systems*. These different production systems implied that this spatial division of labor could create sharp disparities in income.

Why did specialization and income disparities emerge? Assume wheat is the only crop grown. Since we assume uniform fertility and knowledge, wheat costs the same to produce everywhere, and total demand for wheat is set by urban demand for food. The final price for grain in the town is equal to the cost of production (P) and transportation (T) for wheat coming in from the outermost farm supplying the last urban customer, since the market sets prices at the margin. This implies that wheat producers located next to the town will be able to capture extra profits equivalent to the cost of transporting grain from the outermost farm, while farms at intermediate locations will capture a similar but smaller profit net of their own transportation costs to town. The area *R* in Figure 2.1 represents that extra profit, which in strict economic terms is actually a *rent*. In our one-commodity world, rents will be highest nearest the town, and zero at the point where the last unit of wheat is produced. For analytic clarity, Thünen presumed that landowners and farmers were different actors. Landowners actually captured this extra profit as rent. Landowners closer to town would charge higher rents than those further away; landowners located at the same distance from town would charge the same rent.

Even in a one-commodity world, Thünen's model predicts that production technology will shift from capital-intense choices to labor-intense choices at a specific distance from town. Where rents are high, farmers need to produce more intensively (get higher yields per acre), so as to be able to afford those rents. At some point further out, rents drop to the points where a less intensive production technique becomes more profitable. This general rule underlies the processes in a more complicated multi-crop world.

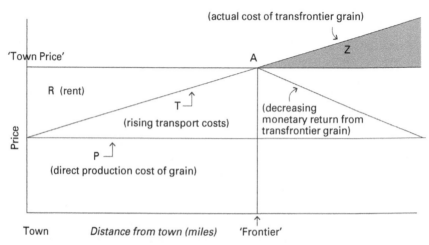

Figure 2.1   *Relationship between transportation costs and rent*

If we now free ourselves from the assumption that only grain is produced, we can see why differences in rents (the market cost of land) cause different production zones to emerge. In a two-commodity world (e.g., wheat plus cattle), the crop capable of generating the highest revenue per acre will bid rents nearer to town up to the point where the lower yielding crop becomes unprofitable at that rent level. This crop thus moves further away from town in search of cheaper rents. As rents fall with distance (because transport costs rise), the lower yielding crop eventually becomes profitable, and locates itself there. In a two-crop world, agricultural production will arrange itself in two concentric rings around the town, with the crop yielding higher revenue per acre closer to town. More crops (or more accurately, more distinct commodities with different revenue yields) mean there will be more rings, each devoted to a specific crop or set of crops. With a fully functioning land market, farmers who invested in the economically 'wrong' product for their zone would tend to be bid off the land by savvier farmers growing the higher profit product and able to pay higher rents. Actors, responding rationally to market signals, will create a spatially organized hierarchy of wage levels, skills, and probably wage systems. *Rational market behavior thus produces production zones differentiated by commodity and production technique.* The Thünen model thus has a micro-foundation for the behaviors that produce a more variegated (but also more precisely delineated) set of production zones than the WST core, semiperiphery, and periphery trio.

Thünen predicted and observed six general production zones around his town, which we will see again in Chapters 5 and 6. The first ring around the town produced fresh milk, vegetables, and other high-value crops, using large amounts of labor, big capital investments, and no fallow land. The next two rings use complicated five- to seven-crop rotations, the convertible husbandry referred to above. These crop rotation systems also wasted no land in fallow and had large labor inputs to feed animals in stalls and work the soil. Ring four used simpler rotations involving fallow and less labor. More fallow land meant that revenue per acre is lower, and the demand for labor per acre is lower because land is used less intensively. Ring five produced only grain, leaving even more land fallow to restore its fertility. It thus has even lower revenue per acre, while monocultural grain production reduces labor demand, except at planting and harvest. Finally, ring six featured extensively grazed animals. Grazing uses such enormous amounts of land that it can be profitable only where land is cheap, that is, carrying a low-rent cost. Grazing uses very little labor and capital per acre, and produces corresponding low per acre revenues per acre.

Going from ring one to ring six takes one from high-value-added per acre to low-value-added per acre. The decline in value-added per acre going outward from the town reflects not only the kind of crop being grown, but also the way it *is* grown. Put simply, when one is going from ring one to ring six, the volume of labor inputs per acre decreases, but the proportion of labor costs in total cost rises. Thus, from the economist's viewpoint, labor intensity of production rises going further out, whereas capital intensity rises coming in towards town. In addition, the intensity with which land is used also rises coming back towards town, which means there is more total demand for labor, even though production is capital intensive. Higher productivity per acre and per worker closer in to town means higher incomes there; low-value-added per acre and lower capital intensity further out from town means low incomes *per acre* there. The first important implication of this pattern is that the standard NCE marginalist techniques behind Thünen's model confirm WST's assertions about zonal differentiation and inequality. Inequality can emerge directly from a market for reasons that have nothing to do with the uneven diffusion of technology or 'nonrational' behaviors.

The second important implication concerns peripheralization. The Thünen analysis also shows why Brenner is right that underdevelopment is a possible but not a *necessary* outcome of trade. The declining demand for labor produced by the shift to simpler forms of crop production further away from the town *potentially* implies declining living standards. Clearly the total social product available for distribution among landowners, tenants, and laborers in the outermost rings will be small. First, while the price of grain in the town is set by grain brought in from the outermost ring, this does not imply high grain prices in the outer ring. Quite the opposite is true: the actual production cost of grain sets grain prices in the outer ring. The town price of grain reflects both production costs *and* the cost of transport. In the outer ring, grain is available without transportation costs, and thus its price simply reflects its production cost, including the normal rate of profit. In the sixteenth century, grain prices in Danzig (modern Gdansk) were about half those in Amsterdam (Kriedte, 1983: 26–7). Lower grain prices imply lower nominal wages, but not necessarily a lower standard of living.

Second, the higher percentage of peripheral land left fallow means that the average volume of food/NFA produced per acre is smaller than that closer to town. Therefore, a larger land area is necessary to maintain the same level of value produced per worker, and less income is available to distribute in that society. Finally, the simpler production systems imply lower Smithian specialization and thus lower productivity per worker, which in turn implies lower incomes. Outer rings (that is, the periphery) most likely will have lower incomes than the core, and precisely because they are engaged in commerce with the core. Market pressures emanating from the town/core force production into an extensive, low-value-added, mold, as noted above.

These three conditions will not *necessarily* produce lower living standards or underdevelopment in this outermost ring. If the number of workers is small relative to the production area (that is, if the ratio of available labor to land is low), then the total value produced per worker may be high enough to sustain high living standards, even though the value produced per acre is still low. Second, in the face of labor shortages and high wages, rational producers substitute capital for labor, increasing productivity and again resulting in high incomes per producer, despite low prices for what they produce. In both cases, the increased volume produced per worker overcomes low prices and profit margins. The very areas WST finds most nettlesome for its tripartite scheme –

for example, high-income agricultural exporters like Australasia – are precisely those areas where highly capitalized, highly productive forms of agriculture offset the lower value produced per acre characteristic of the outer-most rings. We look more closely at this in Chapters 5 and 6. On the other hand, peripheral areas with high labor-to-land ratios and low capital invest-ment do exhibit the low living standards WST predicts. When labor is scarce relative to land but there is no incentive to increase productivity via invest-ment, the value-added per worker remains low.

What about the issue of regression? Thünen's model, like NCE, does not predict declining income in his peripheries. If the income from trade is lower than the income from subsistence production, then rational peasants will avoid commercial production. But peasants can be forced into the market against their interests. Coercion is the more direct cause for underdevelopment and regression in places like Brenner's Poland than the market *per se*. Return to Figure 2.1 and consider what happens when a landowner lies over the 'frontier' set by transportation costs and the prevailing price of grain in the town (see point *A* in Figure 2.1). This landowner loses money because of the additional transport costs (the shaded area Z) needed to deliver grain to the town at the prevailing price. However, if that landowner could shift the cost of that loss or subsidy onto his labor force, then he could still ship grain to the town and make a profit.

This is what happened in the sixteenth- and seventeenth-century Vistula River grain trade. Certainly, landowners proximate to the river could trade profitably with Holland, but those further inland also wanted to trade. Their desire for the consumption that trade bought moved them to exploit their peas-ants by squeezing additional labor time out of them – time that those peasants needed for their own subsistence production. It also motivated landlords to edge out as many middlemen as possible – destroying Polish towns – because the narrowness of the surplus generated by this system meant that few could share it.

Increasing Polish involvement in trade was paralleled by increased compulsory labor for peasants (Denemark and Thomas, 1988). From 1460 to 1560, Polish grain exports via Danzig increased from 12 500 bushels, a negli-gible quantity, to 300 000 bushels, and then doubled again over the next century to 600 000 bushels, an amount capable of feeding about 750 000 people per year. Beginning in 1493, nobles legislated increasing restrictions on peasant freedoms and compulsory labor on nobles' land. (Poland's elected king remained a pawn of the nobility.) Compulsory labor was set at one day per week in 1520 and reached six days per week by 1600.

In Poland this coerced labor came at the expense of peasants' ability to feed themselves, and thus led to falling incomes and demographic collapse. This kind of trade could occur only when landlords were maximizing personal consumption and indifferent to the gradual depreciation of their 'capital stock,' that is the peasantry, and when landlords could prevent peasant flight. So the regression WST observes at the fringes of the periphery is a function of inte-gration with the world market, but not a product of market rational behavior.

Outright slavery, however, is an outcome of the market, as we will see in Chapter 5, and the market alone would never have induced large areas of the world to enter global markets. Elites almost everywhere had to use violence to push land and labor into the market. Once the market started operating, though, the dynamics above also began to operate.

What about industry?

Thünen's model explains only agriculture. Krugman offers a parallel model for manufacturing 'in which there are no inherent [initial] differences among national economies, yet in which an international division of labor can nonetheless spontaneously emerge, and in which some nations fare better under this division than others. That is, we offer a model in which the world economy may organize itself into a core-periphery pattern' (Krugman and Venables, 1995: 858).

Krugman's model adds production of manufactured and intermediate goods to Thünen's basic agricultural model, again assuming essentially immobile labor. Manufacturers enjoy economies of scale; agricultural producers cannot. In this model, transportation costs interact with economies of scale to determine whether manufacturers will agglomerate. Assume a totally homogenous world in which manufacturing activity is evenly distributed alongside agriculture (like a peasant economy with dispersed artisanal production). As long as the economies of scale from agglomeration are *lower* than transportation costs, manufacturing remains evenly dispersed, because manufacturers save more money by dispersing production to locations near their markets than they sacrifice from losing agglomeration economies.

Yet if transportation costs decline, manufacturing will agglomerate geographically once the gains from economies of scale become greater than the now lower cost of transportation. By co-locating, manufacturers reduce the transportation costs for the intermediate goods that they consume, while also enjoying economies of scale. The agglomeration of manufacturing causes new manufacturing towns to emerge, creating purely agricultural regions. Each new firm that joins a given town causes other firms to concentrate production in that town to take advantage of higher demand for its goods. If collocation causes economies of scale to rise enough to fully offset transportation costs even to the most distant market, then all firms end up in one place (Krugman and Venables, 1995: 868). The nineteenth-century world economy resembled this, with manufacturing concentrated in two very small zones in northwestern Europe and the northeast United States.

Does this agglomeration of manufacturing and creation of purely agricultural economic zones produce underdevelopment? Krugman argues that a large enough manufacturing sector can drive up the demand for labor and thus wages in the industrializing region, while the deindustrialization of the other region leads to falling labor demand and thus wages (Krugman and Venables, 1995: 861). The market – falling labor demand and lower wages – in turn implies permanently lower aggregate demand in agricultural regions, which both deters manufacturing firms from locating in those regions and implies underdevelopment.

The well-known product cycle model (discussed in Chapter 10) reinforces the effects of agglomeration in Krugman's model. The product cycle model assumes that new industries emerge in areas with high incomes, high wages, and high skills. These new products command high prices and generate technological or monopoly rents for innovators. As new products become standardized, competition tends to center more on price and rents disappear. At the same time standardization permits the hiring of workers with lower skills and thus lower wages. Competitive pressures thus tend to force at least some firms to seek areas with lower wages (to lower costs) and adapt production to lower skills. In the product cycle model this occurs in the last two phases of the model, when firms invest overseas, away from high-skill, high-wage areas. Thus, as with agriculture, when peripheral areas get industry it tends to be lower-value-added, standardized processes, devoid of rents. As with agriculture, industrial incomes thus tend to be low and stay low in the periphery. Once again, the natural working of the market produces global income

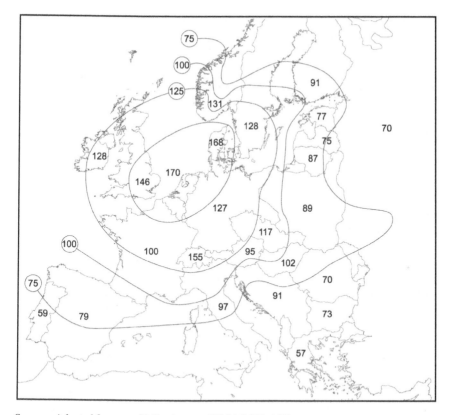

Source: Adapted from van Valkenburg and Held (1952: 102).

Figure 2.2 *European agricultural productivity zones, 1937 (100 = average for eight crops)*

inequality and large differences in what gets produced where and how it is produced.

Spatial dispersion and a Europe-centered world economy

The Thünen and Krugman models of the structuring effects of what we call globalization are not simply lovely thought experiments. Empirical confirmations of the reality of Thünen zones at both a local and a global scale abound (for the Atlantic economies, see: Schlebecker, 1960; Peet, 1969; Grotewold, 1971; in Europe, see Christaller, 1966 [1933]; Abel, 1980; Braudel, 1982; for the United States, see Muller, 1973; for Japan, see Yokeno, 1956). These zones persisted well into the modern period. Figure 2.2 presents a map of the average level of productivity for the eight major crops in European agriculture in 1937, before the distorting effects of the European Union's Common Agricultural Policy (CAP). This map shows concentric rings of decreasing productivity centered on northwestern Europe's urban center. The world economy that grew up around Holland during the early period of state-building is the beginning of the system of agriculture zones which Figure 2.2 illustrates. (We will revisit the same phenomenon in relation to British industrialization in Chapters 5 and 6.

International trade: two responsive strategies

What can be done about the peripheralizing pressures inherent in world markets? NCE and WST respectively err in expecting the world market not to produce any kind of pattern of rich and poor areas and in expecting the market to determine both the kinds of goods and the kinds of *production systems* that emerge. Market pressure from rents and agglomeration economies do distribute economic activity, including industry, into definite zones (which are not, however, always contiguous with specific states!) But these pressures do not necessarily determine development, its absence, or its opposite. Peripheral areas may be fated to produce low-value-added goods by virtue of their location in terms of transportation cost, but even so, development – rising productivity and incomes – is possible, because local political responses to those pressures can produce institutions designed to ameliorate or reverse the effects of those pressures. As noted above, states can adopt two generic strategies in the face of globalization: *Ricardian* and *Kaldorian* strategies. These represent the extremes of a continuum of responses to world market pressures, and most real-world responses mix elements of both. Ricardian strategies represent acquiescence to the peripheralizing tendencies Thünen and Krugman highlight. Kaldorian strategies represent an effort to mitigate or reverse those tendencies.

Adoption requires the right institutions, which is why Chapter 4 will consider Alexander Gerschenkron's (1966) analysis of late development in more detail. For now it suffices to note that Gerschenkron focused on the role of the state and state institutions as midwives of economic development. Consistent with our Thünen and Krugman models, Gerschenkron argues that the world market sets up substantial obstacles to the emergence of modern industry in backward countries. But he does not see these as insuperable. Instead, Gerschenkron invests the state with a much wider role in and ability to correct market failure in backward economies than does NCE or WST. Brenner and Gerschenkron come together in their insistence that local institutions profoundly shape economic development.

Acquiescing to the market – a Ricardian strategy – would produce peripheralization, but still required adequate state institutions. Attempting to catch-up – a Kaldorian strategy – required the state to create novel institutional frameworks that facilitated successful productive investment. Without these new institutions, market forces emanating from existing producers selling world markets would dissuade local entrepreneurs from investing. In effect, Gerschenkron argued that states had to take positive action to create a 'town' in their own economy. This would induce local agriculture to redistribute itself around that town, and encourage high-value-added agriculture to emerge. It would also prevent agglomeration economies from sucking manufacturing to the core. Both actions in turn would increase incomes and productivity. How do these strategies work?

Ricardian strategies

The first strategy relies on comparative or factor advantages along the lines presented earlier in the section on NCE. I will call this a *Ricardian strategy* after David Ricardo (1772–1823). Ricardian strategies typically use agricultural or other primary product exports to drive economic development, but they can also be based on low-value industrial activities, like garment assembly and export. These strategies try to maximize the economic gains from the efficient allocation of the various factors of production present in the society in question, and so are necessarily export-oriented.

Ricardian strategies do not emerge spontaneously. Successful Ricardian strategies rely on a resolution of what David Waldner (1999: 167–70) calls Gerschenkronian collective action problems. That is, Ricardian strategies require state mobilization of capital for social overhead capital (such as the provision of the transportation networks needed to get exports to market), for the provision of capital to producers, and for the creation of a labor supply, as we will see in Chapters 5 and 6.

The long-term success of Ricardian strategies is limited because Ricardian exports are subject to constant or to decreasing returns, and only indirectly generate increasing returns to scale. At best, an increase in the factors of production (land, labor, and capital) yields a proportional increase in output. At worst, an increase in those factors may yield a lower output than it used to – as, for example, production is pushed onto more marginal land, or less able workers are taken on for garment assembly. Ricardian exports can only create increasing returns *indirectly*, as increasing export volumes and values permit growing economies of scale for the massive infrastructural investments – like railroad networks – that characterize new Ricardian exporters, and by inducing investment in manufacturing activities that are characterized by increasing returns. Long-term Ricardian success thus rests on the ability (1) to find new agricultural (or mineral) exports when the old one runs out or suffers from declining returns, or (2) to link other industries to the export sector and use export growth to create growth in those other industries. Raw materials exports can induce investment in industry that produces inputs for agriculture or for processing agricultural outputs. Thus, for example, in the nineteenth century in the United States and in Hungary milling of flour for export became a large, sophisticated industry that induced industrialization in other sectors.

But the positive effects of rising exports are linked to the rate of growth of export volumes. As these exports taper off, so do industrial growth and increases in industrial productivity. Consequently, long-term Ricardian growth depends on the ability of the state both to organize the flow of exports outward and to connect the rest of the local economy to this external engine of growth while exports are booming. It also rests on the propensity of those local groups who are actually doing export production to invest. Ricardian strategies based only on raw material exports are the most exposed to the dangers of constant returns, but even exports of simple industrial goods are vulnerable. Ultimately, Ricardian strategies can create self-sustaining growth only by shifting over to the second type of strategy.

Kaldorian strategies

The second strategy relies on a set of interrelated phenomena like increasing returns to scale, learning by doing, imperfect competition, and economies of speed to generate growth. I will call it a *Kaldorian strategy,* after Nicholas Kaldor (1908–86), the economist who first presented a relatively coherent model of industrial growth. Kaldorian strategies attempt to take advantage of so-called Verdoorn effects, namely, that the greater the rate of increase of output inside a firm, the greater the increase in that firm's productivity. The more a firm produces of any one good, the more experience it gets and the more efficient it becomes at producing not only that good but other, similar goods. Verdoorn effects are the general case of the learning curve.

Kaldorian strategies are thus investment driven and partly ignore any existing factor disadvantages or advantages. Even though a country may not be competitive in the production of, say, microwave ovens at time A, by investing in additional capacity, selling at a loss, and increasing production volumes, it may learn enough about the production process to become more efficient and thus competitive at time B, just as South Korean firms did. By increasing skills, experience, and the division of labor, investment and production themselves change the nature of the factors available in the production mix, and so can override any initial factor disadvantages. Investment in an initially loss-producing activity is rational because many activities have increasing returns. That is, a given investment calls forth a disproportionate increase in output. Greater levels of output create greater specialization in the provision and processing of inputs and also induce process innovations as firms try to cope with increased throughput (economies of speed). Rising output thus can induce investment in other, related industrial activities providing inputs for a growing sector.

Kaldorian growth is thus much more likely with manufacturing. Because investment yields disproportionate increases in output, Kaldorian strategies are also necessarily export oriented. As the local economy grows, income is diverted into imports. The size of the local economy, and thus of effective demand for manufactured goods, is ultimately constrained by its ability to pay for its imports with exports. All Kaldorian strategies thus rely at least initially on Ricardian exports to fund imports of capital goods. But the best possible Kaldorian strategy soon shifts to industrial exports to maximize Verdoorn effects and increasing returns.

Like Ricardian strategies, Kaldorian strategies require the state to overcome Gerschenkronian collective action problems, and concentrate capital for investment, organize labor markets, reduce the risk of investment, and promote exports. However, Kaldorian strategies carry an additional and different kind of risk than Ricardian strategies. While Ricardian strategies are exposed to the risk that demand will eventually taper off for a given raw material, Ricardian exports are by definition competitive in world markets. States pursuing a Ricardian strategy can invest in social overhead capital, knowing that local firms (or farms) already have a comparative advantage.

Kaldorian exports, by contrast, at least initially are not competitive. Investments are made in the expectation that productivity will rise with output, making exports competitive. Kaldorian strategies thus are exposed to the risk that Verdoorn effects and learning by doing may not occur. After all, ultimately, firms and not states produce and export goods. Verdoorn effects and learning by doing are social processes; both emerge from the interaction of managers and workers on the factory floor. Management may be incompetent and fail to recognize ways to increase throughput or cut costs. Moreover, because Kaldorian strategies at least initially require protection of local firms from world market competition, managers have no incentive to seek productivity increases. Similarly, workers may resist the reorganization of work processes or attempt to use tariff protection to claim wages that exceed their productivity. In either case, firms producing at a loss in order to increase production volumes may just make big losses and go bankrupt; states subsidizing exports may just run up big debts, while subsidized firms fail to learn. Kaldorian strategies thus require the state not only to resolve Gerschenkronian collective action problems – that is, collective problems surrounding investment – but also to resolve Kaldorian collective action problems – that is, collective problems surrounding the growth of productivity (Waldner, 1999: 192–6).

States and growth strategies

Kaldorian growth strategies attempt to construct a new town somewhere in the agricultural or low-value industrial supply zones surrounding a larger town.

These strategies try to reorient production around this new town and eventually generate sufficient demand to contain or displace the pressures emanating from that larger town. Ricardian strategies accept a region's position in the international division of labor created by some other urban center, and try to maximize the gains from accepting that position. Because most state formation occurred when agriculture was the predominant form of economic activity, particularly in the periphery, it makes sense to ask if the Thünen model tells us anything about whether states will have the bureaucratic capacity to execute these strategies.

The unit-level characteristics NCE points to obviously matter when explaining state formation and behavior, but NCE cannot explain the origins of these characteristics. By contrast, the Thünen model has an immediate connection to later versions of staples theories (Baldwin, 1956; Watkins, 1963) that argued for a one-to-one correspondence between export profile (in Thünen's world, a specific zone) and the kind of state that emerged. In staples theory, wheat exports caused family farms and democracy; sugar caused slave plantations and authoritarianism. But just as our two models above predicted falling production intensity as one moved towards the periphery but not automatic poverty, they also don't predict specific governmental forms, capacities, or social classes. Nevertheless, these models allow two very strong probabilistic statements about states.

First, states are machines for extracting revenue, monopolizing internal violence, and supplying protection and contract services to a defined territory. *Ceteris paribus*, the greater the per capita revenue base available to a state, the more it will be able to do this job, the better it will be able to do this job, and the more specialized the services it may offer in that territory. Building the coherent, loyal, and effective Weberian bureaucracies needed to execute a Ricardian or even more so Kaldorian strategy requires cash for training and salaries. But by definition, Thünen and Krugman peripheries will enjoy less intensive production per acre. This necessarily limits the state revenue available to construct dedicated bureaucracies. Even in some of the successful cases examined later, like Brazil or Korea, the state had to concentrate its scarce resources into special bureaux, segregate them from the rest of the bureaucracy, and rely on large infusions of external financial and technical assistance to help build a few modern Weberian bureaucracies.

Second, again *ceteris paribus*, states with more revenue are more likely to win wars against similarly sized but economically weaker opponents. Security and economic inequalities tend to reinforce each other. Peripheries generally will lose wars with core states; by losing wars they remain peripheries. Moreover, the effort to match core state spending levels using a smaller resource base predictably will decrease the volume of resources available for investment (Janos, 1989).

Finally, the geographic expansion of the modern system of capitalist production usually involved the violent creation of new frontier zones. Would-be producers of the extensively produced goods found at the periphery typically acquired both land and labor coercively. Many peripheral commodities

were associated with concentrated landholding and labor-repressive production systems. This concentrated landownership reduced state autonomy in the
periphery. The next chapter provides a dynamic picture of the Thünen town's
growth and Krugman's industries in order to structure the discussion of the
real-world experiences with Ricardian and Kaldorian strategies discussed in
Chapters 4 through 7, and again in Chapter 12.

Chapter 3

Economic and Hegemonic Cycles

> The idea that the dynamics of economic life in the capitalist social order is not of a simple and linear but rather of a complex and cyclical character is nowadays generally recognized.
>
> *Nikolai Kondratieff, 1935*

Chapters 1 and 2 presented relatively static pictures of the interaction of states and markets. In Chapter 1 states transformed themselves from mafias into modern bureaucratic states by deploying increasingly more organized forms of violence internationally and internally. Much of the funding for this organized violence initially came from the use of violence to secure monopolies over global trade, but over time regularized forms of internal extraction proved more secure. Meanwhile, the growth of industrial activity inside some specific regions within those emerging nations created or enforced opportunities for other nations/regions to specialize in the production of agricultural goods. We saw in Chapter 2 how the market pressures generated by a Thünen or Krugman metropolis will structure global economic activity around itself in persistently unequal ways. This chapter instead looks at a critical internal dynamic of that metropolis, namely economic cycling driven by the emergence of new leading sectors. This cycling conditions the stability of the global economy, can shift the location of that metropolis, and can generate new metropoli. William R. Thompson succinctly summarizes the issues here:

> The governance of global politics, focusing primarily on the management of long distance trade, is intermittent and dependent on the concentration of capabilities of global reach. One state ... emerges from periods of global war in a position of preeminence and with a commanding lead in these global reach capabilities. The ability to pay for these capabilities is predicated in large part on leadership in a pre-war wave of economic innovation. Winning the global war and controlling a high proportion of the most valuable capabilities then enables the world power to develop policies for the management of the world's political economy.
>
> (1993: 143–4)

Many analysts perceive fairly regular economic cycles of 50–60 years, alternating periods of relatively rapid growth and slower growth (Goldstein, 1988). Consistent with the literature I will call these economic cycles Kondratieff cycles, after Nikolai Kondratieff (1892–1938), the Soviet economist given most credit for the original insight into cycling (Kondratieff,

1935). No convincing data are available to project Kondratieff cycles back before the French Revolution. The historical data suggest, at best, Frank Spooner's or Fernand Braudel's logistical price cycles in Europe lasting 150 years, not the faster 50-year-long Kondratieffs. During the nineteenth century, sufficient statistical evidence becomes available to discern economic cycles. Kondratieff and others have suggested that 1789, 1849, 1896, and 1940 all marked the end of downswings in economic activity, whereas 1815, 1873, 1920, and 1973 signified the end of upswings. Perhaps 2007–9 does also.

Is there a parallel political cycle, reflecting the establishment of a hege-monic position by one state and its eventual disintegration in the face of chal-lenges by other states? Immanuel Wallerstein and Giovanni Arrighi (1994) see 150-year-long cycles matching the Spooner/Braudel logistic cycle, with the Dutch dominant from 1618 to 1815, the British from 1815 to 1945, and the United States after that. Arrighi does not believe in automatic cycles though. George Modelski, who has tried to document these most systematically, sees five more automatic periods of hegemony in the emerging Europe-centered world economy, punctuated by convulsive wars involving all major powers (Modelski, 1987; Modelski and Thompson, 1990). According to Modelski, the Portuguese were dominant from 1494 to 1580, but their position disinte-grated during the wars of 1572–1609, which pitted the Portuguese, as part of the Habsburg empire, against the Dutch, the French, the English, and the Ottoman empire. Holland replaced Portugal as the hegemonic power from 1580 to 1688. England and France repeatedly attacked Holland, until the hostilities culminated in the wars of Louis XIV during 1684–1713. Britain emerged from conflicts in 1688–1792 as hegemon. The French Revolution and the subsequent Napoleonic wars of 1789 to 1814 again pitted all of Europe against France, and again Britain emerged as hegemon from 1815 to 1914. The United States replaced Britain as hegemon after 1914; Modelski dates the decline of US hegemony as beginning circa 1973 but (wisely as it turned out) did not provide a terminal date.

Typically hegemony is defined as a situation in which one country domi-nates the world economy intellectually, economically, and militarily. Charles Maier provides a succinct example:

> Empire is a form of political organization in which the social elements that rule in the dominant state create a network of allied elites in regions abroad who accept subordination in international affairs in return for the security of their position in the own administrative unit. ... [Those allied elites] intertwine their economic resources with the dominant power, and they accept and even celebrate a set of values and tastes that privilege or defer to the culture of the metropole.

> (2006: 7)

However, this definition is too sociological to really understand the emer-gence, persistence and erosion of hegemony. Consistent with Chapters 1 and 2, this chapter distinguishes between a dominant power's relatively unstable use of predation and the relatively more stable situation of hegemony, as well as looking at the 'bottom up' sources of hegemony. These 'bottom up' sources of power come from the emergence of what Schumpeter called new leading sectors. They are the content that fills in the more abstract models presented in Chapter 2. New leading sectors can create an economy whose sheer size (understood as purchasing power) and dynamism causes other economies to orient themselves towards the production of goods for that large economy. This creates social groups in those supply zones whose prosperity depends on a continuation of demand from and integration with the leading economy (Hirschman, 1980).

A metropolis possessing the passive advantages that flow from a large economy dynamized by new leading sectors necessarily has an interest in imposing hegemony from the 'top down.' While all firms or capitalists desire well-defined and stable property rights, different industrial sectors need different types of governance structures. Different sectors need different forms and levels of access to finance, need different kinds of work forces, and flourish best under different kinds of macroeconomic regimes. We will revisit these issues in Chapters 4, 10 and 14. For now it suffices to note that one way in which hegemony can be understood is 'Making the world safe' for the specific kind of business organization that populates the leading sector.

The profits generated by a new leading sector enable – Marxists would argue *compel* – the metropolis to reshape the global economic environment in ways that favor its leading sector. These profits can be loaned at relatively cheap interest rates to purchasers of goods from those leading sectors, and enable the metropolis to buy imported inputs cheaply. The leading economy then must politically and economically maintain an international financial system to secure this lending and the flow of goods. However, the stability of this financial system is not assured. First, the ability of borrowers in Ricardian supply zones to absorb imports and repay loans ultimately depends on the prices they get for their exports. As we will see in Chapter 6, there is a persistent tendency towards speculation and oversupply of basic raw materials. Second, states whose elites – for either military or economic reasons – are not interested in simply pursuing Ricardian growth strategies will attempt to use Kaldorian strategies to reproduce those leading sectors themselves. This ultimately creates overcapacity in leading sector industrial goods as well. Overcapacity and falling prices threaten to devalue the loans initially advanced by the leading economy, as we will see in Chapters 6, 7, 11, and 14. However, before we can understand those issues, we need to understand economic cycles.

Economic cycles

Kondratieff waves

Competitive pressure causing the constant improvement of productivity is perhaps the defining feature of capitalist economies. But why should this produce long waves rather than a gradual change in productive techniques (Berry, 1991)? Kondratieff first proposed the existence of a long economic cycle in prices lasting 50 to 60 years. Using five-year moving averages, Kondratieff charted periods of rising and declining prices for a variety of commodities, including labor, from the French Revolution to the Great Depression. His cycles were composed of a period of stagnation (downswings) in which bad economic years outweighed good economic years and a period of expansion (upswings) in which the reverse was true. Kondratieff provided description of rather than a compelling causal analysis for his price cycles. Other economists have tried to link these price movements causally to the underlying real economy. In each case, we will use the *locus classicus* of these arguments, adding more modern commentary when this is useful.

Kondratieff noted a correlation between agricultural depressions and periods of stagnation. Economists W. Arthur Lewis and W.W. Rostow thus argued that long cycles only characterize agricultural and raw materials output. Kondratieff also observed that innovation clustered at the end of a downswing. Joseph Schumpeter thus argued that entrepreneurial promotion of scientific innovations – what we will call hard innovations – caused long waves. Finally, Kondratieff proposed that cusp points – the turning points between downswings and upswings and vice versa – were characterized by wars, social upheaval, and the reorganization of economic life. A Marxist, Ernest Mandel, thus argued that workers' resistance to exploitation forced capitalists to reorganize production processes in fundamental ways that established the basis for a new period of exploitation and later resistance. We will call these managerial innovations soft innovations in contrast to hard, scientific innovations.

Raw materials cycles

Lewis made the most limited set of claims. But the pre-twentieth-century global economy was agriculturally centered, so these claims merit sustained consideration (Lewis, 1978). Lewis argued that price cycles emerged from inverse relationships between agricultural and industrial prices. Agricultural production (and raw materials production in general) was inherently inelastic, because of a fairly tight connection between human life cycles and the formation of agricultural production units. Lewis noted that while global grain acreage quadrupled in uneven spurts from 1870 to 1914, most of the expansion came outside Europe in areas characterized by family-based farming, like Australia, Argentina, and the United States. Rising grain prices in the 1860s and 1870s triggered new family farms in the United States; a second phase of high prices renewed high prices in the 1890s and 1900s and triggered more farms in Canada, the US Midwest, Argentina, and Australasia. Price cycles emerged from the interaction of discontinuous farm formation with relatively more continuous industrial expansion.

Families tended to start farms in response to periods of high agricultural prices created by booming industrial demand. Rising industrial profits, and thus investment, generated rising industrial demand for raw materials and industrial workers' demand for food. Rising demand for nonfood agriculturals (NFAs) and foods in turn drove up agricultural prices. But families did not start farms monotonically as prices rose. Instead, a prolonged period of high prices induced a wave of new farms. Increased output from these farms was also not instantaneous, as producing it took time to make the land productive. But as these farms came 'on line,' agricultural production expanded and caught up with industrial demand for agricultural goods, driving agricultural prices down. As prices fell from overproduction, family farms did not exit the market. Thus, low prices continued, depressing the rate of growth of agricultural output and deterring new farm formation.

Meanwhile, low raw materials prices in these depressions increased urban real wages and reduced raw materials costs for industrial economies. Higher urban real wages reduced emigration to new farming zones. Lower raw materials costs meant higher profits in industrial activity, so less capital was lent to new agricultural lands while industrial investment increased. This development pushed the rate of growth of industrial output, and thus industrial demand for agricultural raw materials, up above the rate of growth of agricultural goods, causing agricultural prices to rise again. The rate of growth of industrial demand outstripped the rate of growth of agricultural supply. Rising agricultural prices then reversed these relationships: metropolitan real wages fell, encouraging emigration, and industrial profits fell, encouraging investment in overseas agricultural areas. As new farms came on line, agricultural prices fell once more, starting the cycle all over again. Lewis's argument could be strengthened by noting that the infrastructural costs of opening up new land for agricultural production also created discontinuous entry into the market and discouraged easy exit. Thus, the Lewis cycles reflect the spasmodic expansion of Thünen's agricultural rings in response to growing urban demand for agricultural goods.

Lewis's argument dovetails with the arguments advanced by economists Simon Kuznets (1967) and Thomas Brinley (1973) to describe 20–25-year cycles in the United States and British economies in the late nineteenth century. They argued that waves of immigration to the United States caused reciprocal waves of city-building in both economies, because both economies relied on the same pool of capital. Immigration to the United States led to building booms there; when those waves subsided, city-building boomed in Great Britain.

Lewis did not believe that industry *per se* generated cycles. Rather, because agriculture tended to dominate economic life before 1914, agricultural price cycles propagated through the general economy much more strongly than they do today. Lewis thus argues that Kondratieff cycles exist only in the long nineteenth century. Thus, Lewis also implicitly argues that hegemony is irrelevant to any explanation of economic cycles, and vice versa.

More recent formulations of Lewis's argument encompass all raw materials. W.W. Rostow (1978; Volland, 1987) argues that each growth cycle rests on specific and inelastic supplies of energy and characteristic raw materials. Like family farms, new sources of supply generally require large, infungible, and illiquid investments. The cost of extracting raw materials tends to rise as better and more easily extracted sources are exhausted. Rising extraction costs deter more investment and in turn create the kind of price cycles Lewis described. Because the driving force in all these analyses is urban demand, they all complement and provide a bridge to the leading-sector perspective of Joseph Schumpeter. This perspective looks at industrial investment as the driving force in economic cycles and argues that cycles reflect not only price movements but also underlying changes in the rate of growth of production volumes.

Schumpeterian leading sectors

In contrast to analyses based on raw materials, Schumpeter saw long waves in industrial production itself (Schumpeter, 1939, 1942). He argued that understanding these waves was the central problem in economics: 'The problem that is usually being [investigated by economists] is how capitalism administers existing structures, whereas the relevant problem is how it creates and destroys them' (Schumpeer, 1942: 84). Schumpeter thought that the emergence of new leading sectors caused Kondratieff upswings. The innovations embodied in new leading sectors forced changes in the process of production and the objects produced across all industries, by threatening those industries and production systems with 'creative destruction.' Dynamic growth in new leading sectors propels the whole economy forward.

Schumpeter was interested primarily in the relationship between entrepreneurship and innovation. He viewed most economic activity as routine, providing daily necessities. Routine activity yielded a steady-state economy in which a growing population forced an extensive expansion of total GDP but never materially changed per capita GDP. Investment covered depreciation but did not change products, production systems or capital-to-labor ratios. Conservative administrators, not energetic innovators, ran enterprises. For Schumpeter, intensive growth came only when entrepreneurs created new leading sectors and re-energized capitalism by raising the rate of profit above the level that simply covered depreciation and interest payments.

For Schumpeter a leading sector is a cluster of innovations that create new products with high demand, made with newer, cheaper forms of energy and distributed via newer, cheaper modes of transportation. Schumpeter nominated as leading sectors the cluster of cotton textiles, iron, and water power (canals and mills) from the 1780s to the 1820s; steel, steam engines, and railroads from the 1840s to the 1870s; industrial chemicals, electricity, and intra-urban trams from the 1890s to the 1920s; and the internal combustion engine, petroleum, and motor vehicles from the 1940s to the 1970s. To this, we can certainly add digitalization (a new form of transportation that conserves energy – think of how faxes and e-mail replace the physical movement of paper, while shopping on the web substitutes one delivery vehicle for multiple personal car trips); microelectronics and embedded intelligence (now a pervasive enhancement in many products); and 'information' as a product, from the late 1980s until …?

Bringing new leading sectors on line both required and forced massive new investments. New leading sectors force new investment because they immediately threaten existing ways of doing business. Railroads undercut the vitality of canals, and long-haul trucking undercut railroads; electricity and oil were cheaper than coal. Older firms had to adapt to these new technologies or go out of business. Leading sectors also require massive new investment to establish themselves because the leading cluster itself is a complex of interrelated innovations. New transport systems are worthless without their accompanying energy sources; both are worthless unless they carry the new goods that will make them profitable ventures. The infrastructure for transportation systems and energy distribution has to be created from scratch. So, too, do new production systems using the new energy source and producing the new good. From our perspective as well, the drop in transportation and energy costs significantly expands the potential division of labor by increasing the market open to profitable transportation of bulk commodities. The huge risks involved in simultaneously making large fixed investments usually require government intervention to overcome Gerschenkronian collective action problems, which we will discuss in detail in Chapter 4.

Leading sectors therefore can energize the economy through new, highly profitable investments. Their massive investment spurts cause rising economic growth, pulling existing firms along as they get reorganized and demand for their product increases. Think of the internet boom and its associated investments in fiberoptic cable for broadband access. The growth rates of leading sectors display a clear S-type logistic curve of innovation, explosive growth, maturity, and stagnation or decline. (See Figure 10.1 on the product cycle.) In the first phase, uncertainty about the extent of the market, the profitability and utility of existing production processes, and the reliability of new technologies keeps output low and prices high. As producers gain more experience, falling prices help the market expand. Increasing certainty and experience combine with falling prices to create rapid growth; producers settle on an accepted production technique. At the level of individual products, more consumers can now afford to buy the new good. At the level of the economy, more and more producers find they must adapt production processes to the new technologies, relocate near new transportation nodes, and reconfigure products to be compatible with new sources of energy. All this activity creates a surge in investment. However, as new transport and energy networks are completed, as new production complexes relocate near them, and as consumers' closets, houses, or driveways become clogged with the new product, growth rates level off. Instead of producing for new consumers, producers find they are merely replacing the existing stock of goods as they wear out. Producers depreciate their investments rather than investing for more output. With new infrastructures and factories built, investment slows, and economic growth grinds to a halt. Schumpeter's innovators become conservative administrators of large fixed investments, whose very size deters new investments.

Consider the car. For about 30 years cars were expensive toys for the rich, built by hand, with few interchangeable parts, and in limited numbers – about 4000 in 1900. Then Ford combined the assembly line with interchangeable parts and sophisticated logistics. Car prices fell, the government constructed roads and highways, stabilized the price of petroleum and regulated the construction of national pipelines, and, after World War II, made credit freely available. The number of standardized cars produced rocketed from 200 000 in 1910 to almost 4.5 million in 1929. By 1970 nearly everyone who needed a car had one, and once-innovative US car firms became sleepy bureaucracies, competing only over the size of tailfins. We could easily tell the same story about computers, with the development of the microprocessor and PC as the decisive hard innovation, and internet-based build-to-order firms as the soft innovation. But this discussion has already signaled the degree to which managerial innovations (for example, the assembly line and logistics) are as important as scientific or technological ones (for example, the internal combustion engine).

The organization of the firm and work

Ernest Mandel's (1975, 1980) analysis closely parallels Schumpeter's. But as a Marxist, Mandel emphasizes the way work is organized rather than entrepreneurs' catalytic role. Mandel focuses on the soft organizational technologies that constitute the actual process of production: how is work organized, who works, and on what? Mandel argues that the labor process has undergone four major shifts, breaking the postindustrial revolution world into five periods. The first period, from roughly 1789 to 1848, was characterized by craft workers operating water- and steam-powered machinery in small factories. Craft workers fabricated unique machinery tailored to the idiosyncratic needs of the factory owner, on-site. The archetypical machines of this period were spinning and weaving machines made of wood but using iron fittings, and driven mostly by water. The iconic worker here is a British textile worker, organized in movements like Owenite unionism and Chartism.

These movements lead into the second period, from the European upheavals and rebellions of 1848 until the 1890s. The industrial production of machines by specialist firms and the emergence of specialist machine operators mark this period. The archetypical machines of this period were steam engines used in locomotives, steamships, and factories. The iconic worker is the master craftsman with a practical knowledge of how engines or machines work, but not the degreed engineer's theoretical training. This skilled worker controlled the flow of production and often acted as a subcontractor, hiring labor to work some capitalist's machinery. These workers attempted to form skill-based unions, whose violent mass strikes in the 1890s terminated this period.

Taylorist methods of production characterize the third period, from the 1890s to the 1930s. Taylorism (from the industrial engineer Frederick Winslow Taylor) shifted control of the production process from master craftsmen to university educated engineers, permitting limited kinds of continuous-flow production to emerge. Engineers organized the production of goods developed from systematic research; workers mutely followed orders. Foremen replaced skilled workers as the immediate overseers of the lowest workers. These work conditions triggered a revival of mass unionism in the 1930s, electorally successful left-wing parties, and the dissemination of the assembly line.

The fourth period, the post-Depression era, was characterized by the grouping of electrically powered product-specific machines into assembly lines for the production of cars and other consumer durables. The iconic worker is the assembly-line worker doing one repetitive task, organized into state-sanctioned mass unions. Mandel claims that this period came to an end in the great strike wave of the 1960s–70s.

The current form of labor organization is based on continuous-flow production systems built from smart machines, run by self-supervising, multi-skilled workers who service customer orders on a just-in-time basis, and whose pay and benefits are individuated and linked to share (equity) prices. A high-skill white collar variant in research-based firms parallels this. This fifth period corresponds to the new cluster of energy-saving technologies, micro-processors, and telecommunications.

Mandel and Schumpeter overlap in their analysis of the firm, which is an institutional arrangement for organizing investment in innovative labor processes making innovative goods. Firms successfully producing new leading-sector products usually do so in a new and characteristic institutional form: mills owned by individual capitalists; factories owned by small groups of capitalists; corporately owned multiplant firms; vertically and horizontally integrated firms producing everything they need for their assembly lines; and networked alliances of specialist firms, or Japanese-style *keiretsu* (Chandler, 1962, 1977, 1990; Williamson, 1985; Lazonick, 1991). Like the hard technologies in leading-sector clusters, innovative institutional forms also threaten old-style firms with 'gales of creative destruction.' Old-style firms must adopt these new forms or die.

The chronological overlap between Schumpeter's leading-sector clusters and Mandel's new organizational forms should not surprise us. The sheer scale of investment needed to utilize new technologies usually mandates both new organizational forms and new work practices. Neither innovation can stand alone: new work practices and management systems make little sense unless changes in machinery and power systems accompany them; new machinery cannot be used to its fullest potential without changes in work practices and the management of production. Following business language, we will call the combination of new leading-sector technology and new institutional forms 'best practice manufacturing.'

Schumpeter and Mandel diverge from Lewis, who saw a regular, if temporary, cycling in the world economy. Neither Schumpeter nor Mandel saw cycling as inevitable. The advantages of new institutional forms and new leading sectors always exhaust themselves, leading to stagnation. But renewed growth is not automatic. Without new entrepreneurs, without political tolerance of massive new credit creation, or facing entrenched worker resistance, a new cycle might not start again. Each analyst, however, saw enormous incentives for actors to innovate and thus restart the economy. Schumpeter believed that stagnation would send entrepreneurs in search of profitable innovations and thus higher profits, though he feared governments might stifle innovation. Mandel believed that worker resistance to exploitation would force capitalists to search for new organizational forms to restore profitability, though he hoped for worker resilience. In anticipation of the next chapter, we can introduce a third factor forcing new cycles, namely states' fears that strategic rivals might outgrow them and thus threaten their survival. Both economic and security competition drove states and their industrialists to generate new organizational forms and adopt new technologies more rapidly than they might otherwise have done. As these late developers attempted to imitate best practice manufacturing, they adapted it to local circumstances and created new organizational forms and spurred locally appropriate technological advances that in turn threatened existing producers.

Economic cycles and hegemony

Leading-sector clusters are discontinuous over space as well as time. Not surprisingly, the emergence of new institutional forms and leading sectors is closely tied to the emergence or revival of hegemonic states. The British created the first mills and mill towns. US and German entrepreneurs proliferated joint stock companies controlling multiple plants in the late nineteenth century. US firms created the assembly line and conglomerate. And US firms appear to have assimilated and reorganized around information technology better than European and perhaps Japanese firms (Bloom and Van Reenen, 2006; Bloom, Sadun and Van Reenen, 2007).

Leading sectors usually emerge inside one country and then spread unevenly to others. This observation allows us to begin to link economic cycles and hegemony: in all cases new leading-sector clusters first emerged either in an existing hegemon or in the country that became hegemonic soon after. While all hard and soft technologies do inevitably diffuse, the new hegemon has a period of unchallenged technological superiority, so the emergence of new leading sectors creates the military and economic basis for hegemony. Chapter 1 discussed successive phases of domination in the Indian Ocean by contrasting the advantages in hard and soft technologies for the Portuguese, Dutch, and British.

Hegemony has a simple military side. Businesses need security and stability – the assurance that goods shipped will arrive, that contracts will be enforced, and that the world in general is predictable. As we saw in Chapter 1, states replaced the internal anarchy and multiple sovereignties of the nobility with one law, Hobbes's *Leviathan*, in exchange for taxes. Internationally, anarchy, in the sense of a Hobbesian state of nature in which contract is difficult or impossible, prevailed until 1815, if only because warfare was almost constant from 1500 to 1815. Because most commerce even after World War II was maritime in nature, the relevant index of a hegemon's military power thus has to be overwhelming naval power. Modelski and Thompson (1990) have shown that the powers that everyone agrees were hegemonic – Holland, Britain, and the United States – as well as Portugal, all apparently controlled roughly half the warships available during their period of domination. Moreover, those warships incorporated technologies drawn from the new leading sectors. The connection between control of the maritime economy and military security is relatively clear. As Chapter 1 showed, the maritime economy generated a greater and more easily harvested social surplus than an economy composed predominantly of microeconomies. Maritime powers could fund successful military action against intrinsically poorer continental powers by calling on resources present in the world economy (Thompson, 1993). But military security or domination is a necessary condition for hegemony, not a sufficient one.

Military domination alone is fragile. Pre-modern China abjured conquest yet exercised considerable influence over its neighbors via trade and scores of Chinese settled port-polities scattered in the Southeast Asian archipelago. In the modern world, a new cluster of leading sectors also creates an economic basis for hegemony more durable than pure military dominance, because it is anchored firmly in the material self-interest of social groups outside the hegemonic power. The purchasing power created by the emergence of a new leading sector leads, among other things, to growing imports of raw materials and low-value-added manufactured goods as capital and labor is redeployed into the new leading sector. These imports create a durable link between the states occupying supply zones and the (emergent) hegemonic power occupying the new 'town.'

Why would a hegemon trade freely though? Until the diffusion of best practice manufacturing associated with the new leading sector occurs, a hegemon's productive and financial advantages should incline it to pursue free trade. After all, in most competitive battles its firms are likely to prevail. Open markets benefit the strong (that is, the economically competitive) and punish the weak. By drawing on a much wider source of agricultural and other primary inputs, hegemons could then expand their internal division of labor, lowering costs for the new leading sector even further. Logically, strong coalitions favoring at least a limited free trade would be expected to emerge in a hegemon as its dominance of the new leading sector became clear. In practice, however, creating such a coalition might be difficult.

On the other hand, why will other states and economic regions cooperate with this hegemon? Hegemonic countries' high levels of productivity and income mean that they usually constitute a sizeable portion of world import markets. Britain's share of world imports, for example, fluctuated between the 33 percent of 1850 and the 25 percent of 1870. The US share in 1950 was about 18 percent, and after falling to about 15.4 percent by 1990 had recovered to 20 percent by 1997 and then floated down to about 18 percent again by 2005. (Japan's 2005 share was 4.7 percent, down from 7.5 in 1997; the

European Union's share, net of intra-EU trade, was 13 percent, down from 18 in 1997.) Markets this size present subordinate countries with a huge potential export market. This market could well exceed their own internal market. Certainly the pre-1914 or pre-railroad era markets largely composed of micro-economies had relatively low levels of purchasing power.

Would-be hegemons necessarily have to have economies that are relatively large compared to the global economy. Some of the arguments rejecting a hegemonic position for Portugal, Holland, and the early period of English hegemony misunderstand this point. Looking at only the small *absolute* size of these economies suggests each lacked the economic weight to shape other economies in its environment. However, at that time the global economy was a thin coastal crust surrounding a vast number of microeconomies that were not effectively integrated into the world market. Relative to this thin crust, the Dutch and English economies may well have been sufficiently large, although the Spanish and Portuguese certainly were not. While China's inexorable demand for silver certainly shaped European trade patterns, China was too distant to affect European security and political arrangements (Bin Wong, 1998).

The more a hegemon is capable of importing, the bigger the groups else-where who make a living by exporting to it, and thus the more states will tend to align around the hegemon. This is because of the way in which 'national interests' are constituted. All states naturally pursue their own interests, but with the significant exception of physical security, the constitution of those interests is a politically contested activity. Without fully accepting purely factor-based models like that of Ron Rogowski (1991), it is clear that the creation of a Thünen hinterland around an emerging hegemon will generate groups/classes with strong and compelling interests in accepting a hegemon's preferred financial and institutional arrangements in order to pursue a Ricardian strategy.

What makes a Ricardian strategy so attractive to dominant social classes in a Thünen hinterland? The outward expansion of agricultural production potentially creates new wealth for landholders in Ricardian economies. Recall that as the 'town's' demand increases, agricultural raw materials come from further and further away in transportation cost terms and nonagricultural raw materials are produced from deposits of lower and lower quality. In each case the potential rent available to 'nearby' producers (or higher-quality deposits) increases. The revenue stream attached to that nearby land thus also increases. Because the capital value of any asset, including land, is a positive function of the revenue stream it generates, an increase in the value of that revenue stream also increases the value of that asset. Social groups controlling land could reap enormous capital gains from cooperation with a hegemonic power importing goods from their economy.

Once those groups invested in durable (or specific) assets producing goods for the hegemon, the cost of breaking the trade relationship rose considerably. The same is also true for social groups and firms in the hegemonic economy that benefit directly or indirectly from inflows of cheaper goods. But as Albert

Hirschman (1980) showed, economic interdependence is strongly asymmetrical, because hegemonic economies typically represent a much larger proportion of trade for smaller economies than the reverse. Finally, as Robert Cox (1988) argued, international hegemony also has Gramscian aspects. The convergence of interests among those groups that have managed to define a state's nonstrategic interests and groups in other states with similar interests generates a strong sense of mutual identity and common discourses. The emergence of 'free trade' blocs around hegemons is thus no surprise.

Before the twentieth century, hegemony rested on the complementarity of hegemonic Thünen towns, like industrial Britain, and their agricultural supply zones. Demand from a Thünen town showered wealth on producers willing to orient agricultural activity towards that town (or on colonists forcing natives to produce), and they thus constituted a powerful interest bloc favoring accommodation with the hegemon. The British, for example, were oriented towards free trade in areas where it really counted from their point of view, namely, in the import of foods and other agricultural raw materials. Most food and nonfood agricultural raw materials entered Britain tariff free (McKeown, 1983; Nye, 1991). Britain's selective free trade policy created a trade empire substantially larger than its formal empire. In the twentieth century, access to industrial markets looms larger.

What about countries that for strategic reasons reject a purely Ricardian strategy in order to industrialize their own economies? A hegemon's enormous open markets might tempt locals to export there. But what to export? Since the hegemon by definition likely possesses a competitive advantage in the leading sectors, this means that exporters are selling raw materials, intermediate goods, or finished goods from other, nonleading sectors to the hegemon. This would probably lock the exporting country into slower growth or low profit sectors. Would-be challengers need to develop their own industry in order to compete militarily and eventually economically.

So countries pursuing Kaldorian industrialization strategies might temporarily opt for free trade so as to use exports into the hegemonic market to finance imports of the capital goods they needed to adopt/adapt the current leading sector. Here interests converge at the level of means, not ends. Thus, in the nineteenth century France's and Britain's coordinated reduction of tariffs in the Cobden-Chevalier Treaty occurred when France needed to import iron rails and railroad equipment for its first phase of industrialization (Kindleberger, 1975). Prussia and the US also freely imported British rails and locomotives in the early stages of their industrialization. France, Prussia and the US exported primary products (wine, grain, and meat), fine products with stagnant local markets (woolens and linens), and low-value manufactured goods (German toys) into Britain. Once these countries were capable of building their rail networks with local resources, they turned to protectionist policies to develop their own industry. All three then flooded world markets, driving down prices for manufactured goods and igniting what contemporaries called the Great Depression of 1873–96. This period of intense competition and falling prices and profits eroded Britain's dominant position from the bottom up. Britain failed to renovate or innovate in the face of this challenge (Gilpin, 1975).

What about hegemony from the top down? Dominant economies typically also have both the capacity and the incentive to organize the provision of credit globally and maintain the global credit system (Germain, 1998). The productivity advantages inhering to a leading sector generate a large volume of profits that make a hegemon the center of international credit and money markets. Amsterdam, London, and New York (and briefly Tokyo) in turn have provided a pool of relatively cheap credit to finance international trade. Each of these cities drew this credit from the enormous pool of savings available in their economies. (China so far lacks an appropriate financial infrastructure to play this role, despite its huge pool of savings. Chapter 14 looks at this issue.)

High domestic productivity rooted in best practice manufacturing generates too much profit for local reinvestment, particularly because part of the competitive potential of new leading sectors comes from the introduction of capital-saving technologies that reduce the cost of fixed and circulating capital. This pool of savings drove down local interest rates, giving the hegemon's banks enough of a cost advantage to dominate world lending. As with trade, once non-hegemonic economies begin borrowing they become inextricably enmeshed with the hegemonic economy. First, local elites usually need foreign loans in order to realize the capital gains from land used for export production. Second, routine trade transactions rely on commercial finance from the hegemon. This, of course, redounds to the advantage of the hegemonic economy: its currency is used for global transactions, allowing it to generate purchasing power at will; interest on global loans pays for imports; its economy gets a piece of the action whenever another economy grows (Palloix, 1977).

Dutch domination of the Baltic trade displays all the advantages of arbitrage based on lower domestic interest rates (Israel, 1989). The Dutch used their abundant cash to buy up Baltic grain exports in advance of the harvest at large discounts. Grain sellers willingly sold at a steep discount because the interest rate in the Baltic was quite high, and the present value of money they received was thus very high. Dutch traders in turn were financing grain purchases with money borrowed at low interest rates in Amsterdam. From their point of view, they obtained a deeper discount for the grain than they would have if Baltic sellers had access to equally cheap credit.

Lending internationally, however, is a risky business. Ultimately borrowers' ability to repay loans rests on their ability to export goods at prices that are sufficiently high to enable the borrower to both repay the loan and reinvest for future production. Because uncoordinated private actors provide the bulk of international lending, the potential for individually rational but collectively irrational behavior is high. Private lenders typically overlend, creating more export capacity than the hegemon's domestic market can absorb. Once prices begin to fall, lenders overreact and abruptly cut off lending, driving debtors into bankruptcy. At that point the evolution of the crisis depends on the ability of the hegemonic state to function as a lender of last resort, by absorbing more imports and thus stabilizing prices, by imposing discipline on flighty creditors, or by providing emergency loans to illiquid borrowers.

All of these activities carry the risk of eroding hegemony from the 'top down.' Absorbing unusually large quantities of imports can hollow out the domestic economy. At the same time it sustains growth in non-hegemonic economies, reducing the relative share of the hegemon's import market in world markets. And if states pursuing Kaldorian strategies can tap into that growth in non-hegemonic markets, this further undermines the hegemon's position of relative strength.

The next four chapters detail the diffusion of the industrial revolution from Britain to the European continent and Britain's construction, in cooperation with local elites, of new zones of specialized, export-oriented agricultural production financed with British loans. European efforts to cope with Britain's economic pre-eminence created a variety of new institutional forms for organizing industrial activity. The evolution of British hegemony revolved around both of these developments. Just as the British benefited from apparent disadvantages in the Indian Ocean, the advantages of adversity allowed some European states to catch up with and surpass Britain by the end of the nineteenth century. In this process, they opted first for free trade – for a Ricardian strategy – and then for protection – a Kaldorian strategy. British promotion of free trade primarily concerned its new agricultural suppliers. The flood of exports the successful countries released created a challenge paralleling that of Britain's industrial revolution, and undermined British hegemony.

Chapter 4

The Industrial Revolution and Late Development

> The statesman who should attempt to direct private people in what manner they ought to employ their capital would not only load himself with a most unnecessary attention, but assume an authority which could [not] safely be trusted ... and which would nowhere be so dangerous as in the hands of a man who had folly and presumption enough to fancy himself fit to exercise it.
>
> *Adam Smith*

The British and then European industrial revolution did not change the fundamental workings of the world economy described above. Instead it accelerated processes already under way, decentering the existing pattern of world trade from China and recentering it on Europe and particularly Britain. The industrial revolution made this recentering more abrupt and more transformative than in prior epochs. The industrial revolution, a clustering of innovations in cotton textile production, the systematic application of water and – to a much lesser extent – coal-fired steam power to manufacturing, and the gathering of previously dispersed manufacturing operations under one factory roof, had three major consequences. First, Britain's exploding demand for raw materials and rising industrial population pushed agricultural production outward from Europe, generating a global set of agricultural production rings based on Ricardian growth strategies orchestrated by independent states. By contrast, the older China-centered world economy did not reorient entire economies globally.

Second, the industrial revolution in Britain threatened industry in other regions and countries with a gale of Schumpeterian creative destruction. If non-British manufacturers could not assimilate the hard and soft technologies of the industrial revolution, they faced extinction. The market pressures associated with the industrial revolution added Krugman's centralizing processes to the existing Thünen-type pressures for peripheralization in northwest Europe and the Atlantic economy. Only the wretched transportation systems of the period sheltered existing handicraft producers. In the older China-centered world economy, trade expanded local manufacturing based on handicrafts rather than obliterating it.

Finally, the economic growth generated by the industrial revolution underpinned Britain's rise to global hegemony after 1814. Britain's dominance in coal, metallurgy, and steam gave its navy the material basis for control of the seas, and thus control of a world economy that still largely moved goods over water. The British market for raw materials consolidated a profound hegemony over most export-oriented economies. A few states resisted this lure and continued the mercantilist policies of the pre-Napoleonic wars period. They tried to extend central state power into their own microeconomies, homogenizing and routinizing the administration of law and taxation, and they aggressively promoted local industrialization. States did this because the malign strategic consequences of industrial backwardness were more visible than ever by the 1840s, when Britain passed into the second stage of the industrial revolution, with an economy based on iron, steam engines, and the railroad. At that point, British hegemony extended not only into China's periphery, but also China itself.

The industrial revolution thus presented a dilemma for these states. States' efforts to drag their economies forward involved generating Ricardian exports to pay for the imported capital goods they needed to start a Kaldorian strategy. Paradoxically, however, Ricardian exports created domestic social groups hostile to the import restraints and tariffs implied by a Kaldorian strategy. Equally paradoxically, transportation improvements tended to link microeconomies together and create a unified internal market. This advanced efforts at internal security. But it also exposed the domestic economy to shocks emanating from the international market and to British competition. Since most economies could not compete with Britain in basic manufactured goods, states risked the displacement of entire industrial sectors when they opened their economies to the world market (Senghaas, 1985). If their firms succeeded in catching up with British firms, then better transport meant a bigger market. If their firms did not catch up, better transport meant easier pickings for foreign competition.

Finally, states' tools for a Kaldorian strategy of industrial promotion – tariff and border protection, subsidies, public enterprise – were vulnerable to a contradiction between their economic and political purposes. States wanted these subsidies to induce and validate investment, but they were also used to generate political support for incumbent politicians. Would subsidies be withdrawn if investment created uncompetitive industries (Waldner, 1999)? Late industrialization can thus be viewed as a difficult gamble in which success reinforced success, and failure, failure, and in which the outcome was determined partly by timing and partly by the state's autonomy from the demands of social groups controlling Ricardian exports as well as incompetent industrialists.

Internationally, Kaldorian strategies typically created trade frictions. Successful late industrialization relied on rapidly increasing output to stimulate rapid increases in productivity. Part of this rapid increase in output had to be exported. The sudden streams of exports generated by successful late industrializers tended to overflow the canals of international commerce, threatening to inundate other, less successful late industrializers and eroding the market share of existing industrial powers. Both of these resorted to protection to dam the flow of goods from a successful late industrializer.

This chapter looks at efforts to industrialize in response to the industrial revolution. State intervention to promote industry tended to intensify the later industrialization occurred, with states in Asia and Latin America more

interventionist than earlier industrializers in Western Europe. In
successful industrialization was rare, even in Europe. Among suc
European industrializers, the first response was often increased spec
tion in agricultural production, not industrialization. The successful
created new institutions that aided and encouraged their firms to assimilate
British technologies creatively. This chapter also sets up arguments that will
be used in Chapters 7, 10, 11, and 13, because the problem of late industrialization recurred every time a new leading sector emerged. Chapter 11
studies late industrialization in the old agricultural periphery. Chapter 7
takes the story of Germany and the United States begun in this chapter
forward to the point where these late industrializers were capable of challenging Britain's global dominance. Chapters 10 and 13 retell the story in
Chapter 7, looking at the infiltration of transnational firms into local
economies, and the Japanese and Chinese challenges to post-World War II
US industrial supremacy.

Before that, however, come two chapters (5 and 6) examining responses to
the industrial revolution in agricultural supply areas. Putting Chapter 4 first
seems to give priority to industrialization as a causal factor, but this priority
should not be overstated. European industrialization and the global spread of
European agriculture were self-reinforcing sides of a growing division of
labor. Industrialization required growing volumes of cheaper raw materials;
agricultural suppliers provided a market for industrial goods. Like late industrialization, however, export agriculture did not automatically come into being
in areas with the proper climate. States organized and often imposed Ricardian
growth strategies. Like late industrialization, export agriculture-led growth
required and generated a range of new state institutions supporting production. Furthermore, continual industrial growth in Europe confronted Ricardian
developers with problems akin to those faced by late industrializers.

As our focus is international, we do not discuss the internal causes of the
industrial revolution; instead, the discussion begins with two questions
about external aspects of the revolution. Did predatory empire and the
industrial revolution interact, and if so, how? What role did international
competitive pressures play in the development of the British textile industry? Then the chapter turns to state promotion of late industrialization. The
chapter ends with a discussion of the international consequences of successful late industrialization.

International origins of the industrial revolution

The interaction between empire and industry revolves around two questions
(Hobsbawm, 1969; Pomeranz, 2000). Marxists have argued, first, that imperial depredations provided the investment capital for the industrial revolution,
and second, that imperial markets were places to dump exports. Liberal histo-
rians maintain that colonial revenues at most constituted a very small part of
capital investment and that domestic markets were more important. The truth

seems to lie somewhere in the middle. While imperial profits could not have funded the industrial revolution, they did contribute to widespread wealth in British society, and this in turn created ready markets for the investments that capitalized the industrial revolution.

During the eighteenth century, 'colonial' markets steadily replaced 'European' markets for British exports. But many of those so-called 'colonial' markets had higher per capita incomes than the European ones; contrast North America with France. During the nineteenth century, 'Third World' imperial markets took at most about 10 to 15 percent of all manufactured exports from developed countries; the bulk of exports went to self-governing, rich colonial markets, like North America or Australia (Bairoch, 1982: 279). Colonial Third World markets were important only for particular industries at particular times. Britain's declining cotton textile industry relied heavily on Third World markets by 1900. Finally captive colonial markets arguably allowed some producers with high fixed capital costs to expand production runs, thus lowering the average cost per unit produced and creating additional profits. However, this argument presupposes that producers could take for granted markets in the areas absorbing the bulk of their production. Colonial markets actually had a more important supply-side contribution. Their exports expanded the food and nonfood agricultural (NFA) supplies available for European industrializers, thus overcoming the limits imposed by micro-economies on Europe's division of labor. Consider the supply-side contribution of slave-produced cotton for the textile boom.

Oddly enough, it may be that international competitive pressures on the British textile industry mattered more for the industrial revolution. Before the industrial revolution, low-wage Indian producers threatened to displace this British industry. Even at subsistence levels, eighteenth-century British wages were about 50 percent higher than those in India; unlike inland continental producers, British producers could not rely on high transportation costs to provide some kind of protection. As late as 1780, Indian producers of calico and muslin fabrics had a 60 percent cost advantage over British producers, transport included (Kawakatsu, 1986: 636). The British government actually embargoed the import of Indian cottons in the early 1700s in order to protect local producers. Porous borders were doomed by this effort. Unable to compete on wages or close their market, British producers had to innovate, reducing their production costs by applying mechanical power to production. This increased productivity by 300 to 400 percent. Similarly, the inability to find exports cheap and attractive enough to Chinese consumers – who still accounted for about one-third of world output in 1820 – spurred the search for gold and silver in colonial Latin America, which in turn helped monetize Western European economies. So parts of the industrial revolution's causes and consequences were the same: international competitive pressures causing innovation. The existence of a world market both facilitated and forced British innovation.

Late development as a response to the threat of displacement

How did some regions and states cope successfully with the flood of hyper-competitive British goods, despite responding to the siren call of British demand for foods and NFAs? Three issues matter: how the British challenge differed from prior competitive threats; the kind of local state institutions available for overcoming Gerschenkronian and Kaldorian collective problems; and how local social groups supported or opposed those state policies. Social groups benefiting from agricultural export production had huge incentives to resist state efforts at industrialization. At the same time, British demand for agricultural exports helped create rising local incomes that in turn almost always induced new local manufacturing. But aside from goods with natural forms of protection (for example, high transport costs), most of this manufacturing produced low-value-added, commodity type goods.

Industrialization beyond that point depended on whether the interaction of local state institutions and social groups could overcome two collective action problems: creating and concentrating capital for investment, and inducing productivity growth and innovation. Solutions depended on the kinds of state institutions already present or which could be constructed at the time industrialization started, and the kinds of policies either social groups permitted the state to conduct or that the state could impose on social groups. From a policy point of view, the issue can be put rather simply: if states could use agricultural or low-value manufactured exports to stimulate growing demand and thus Verdoorn effects for local industrial goods, and if they could then concentrate capital for investment in those nascent industries, they generally succeeded in at least extensive forms of industrialization. If not, they failed. Progressing to intensive industrialization based on local innovation and rapid productivity growth then depended on how the state shaped the outcomes of factory floor struggles.

British first mover advantages …

The British industrial revolution constituted a profound rupture with prior economic patterns and thus presented a major threat to everyone else. Britain's cotton textiles industry, the leading sector, generated productivity gains of 3.4 percent per annum. Although there has been a recent tendency to relabel the industrial revolution the industrial *evolution* and to downplay the role of cotton textiles, this growth rate was absolutely unprecedented in a largely agrarian world. Compare this to the fifteenth-century agricultural revolution that underlay industrialization in northwest Europe. This revolution used a variety of new crops, new crop rotations, new and more fertilizer, and new implements to increase productivity by about 0.25 percent per year. It took the English and Dutch 150 years to raise the ratio of seed to yield from 1:3 to 1:6, and another 100 years to get to the 1:10 ratio the Chinese had attained already by 1100. These innovations spread slowly, given the inherent risk-averseness of peasants and their limited exposure to market pressures.

The 'industrious revolution' in East Asia, which absorbed China's and Japan's rising populations into massive handicrafts industry and high-yielding agriculture, produced similarly low levels of productivity growth (Sugihara, 2003: 88–92). Rural China and Japan were already quite 'industrial' by the 1800s, in that over one-third of the rural population worked nearly full time at handicrafts. But the much higher rates of manufacturing productivity growth in the industrial revolution, and the fact that it largely affected producers who were already in the world market, meant that those producers could not afford this kind of passivity.

The (relatively) explosive growth of British production during the industrial revolution meant British producers could satisfy domestic demand and still export a sizeable volume of goods to those parts of Europe accessible by water transport. British cotton textile production doubled every ten years from 40 million yards of fabric equivalent in 1785 to over 2 billion yards in 1850 (unless noted, all statistics come from Mitchell (1992), and all tons used here are metric tons, or 2200 pounds). British iron production doubled every 13 years, rising from 68 000 tons in 1788 to 250 000 tons in 1806 and 678 000 tons in 1830. Production of pottery, glassware, alcohols, kitchen goods, soap, and other household goods followed similar growth curves. Increased production flowed into British exports. In 1800 these exports had constituted about 18 percent of British gross domestic product (GDP); by 1830 they were 35 percent of a much larger GDP. This flood of exports put enormous competitive pressure on producers in Europe and elsewhere, particularly because the British were supplying familiar commodities ever more efficiently.

Britain's rising share of world manufacturing output rose correspondingly. In 1750 Britain had a little more than 1 percent of world population and produced less than 2 percent of manufacturing output, while China accounted for about one-third of each, and was growing somewhat faster than Europe (Maddison, 2007: 44). By 1860, Britain had approximately 2 percent of the world's population but produced about 20 percent of world manufacturing output. British per capita industrial production was about twice that of its nearest competitor, Belgium, and four to six times that in Central Europe (Bairoch, 1982: 275, 281). Table 4.1 provides illustrative comparisons, based on the best estimates of nineteenth-century industrial productivity.

This level of productivity enabled Britain to close in on China's estimated share of global industrial output even though China's population was roughly ten times Britain's (data in this section are from Pomeranz, 2000). While China was still growing, and indeed added about 200 million people to its total population, output per capita stagnated in the eighteenth century. Some regions of China, particularly the lower Yangzi, had per capita levels of industrial output comparable to Britain circa 1800. But these areas could not overcome transportation costs and resource shortages to leap into dynamic growth. The Chinese empire's internal logic was the extensive reproduction of similar production units westward into Asia, and the intensive development

Table 4.1 *British industrial dominance, 1800, 1860, and 1913 (per capita level of industrialization; Britain in 1900 = 100)*

1800		1860		1913	
Britain	16	Britain	64	United States	126
Belgium	10	Belgium	28	Britain	115
Switzerland	10	Switzerland	26	Belgium	88
France	9	United States	21	Switzerland	87
Netherlands	9	France	20	Germany	85
Norway	9	Germany	15	Sweden	67
United States	9	Sweden	15	France	59
Germany	8	Norway	11	Canada	46
Sweden	8	Netherlands	11	Denmark	33
Denmark	8	Austria-Hungary	11	Austria-Hungary	32
Austria-Hungary	7	Denmark	10	Norway	31
Japan	(7)	Japan	(7)	Japan	20

Note: Numbers in parentheses are best-guess estimates.

Source: Based on data from Bairoch (1982: 281, 286, 330).

of agriculture inside those units to feed their ever growing population. By contrast, Britain and then Europe developed the complementary Thünen zones described in Chapter 2.

British and European consumption of imported raw cotton thus provides a good proxy measurement of the growing size of their cotton textile industries. It thus highlights both dynamic British growth, and its displacement effects on European producers. As late as the 1770s, European firms' raw cotton consumption exceeded British firms' consumption, reflecting relatively equal productivity levels and Europe's much larger population. After the industrial revolution, however, total European consumption lagged behind the British until the 1880s, indicating that British exports displaced potential European production (Ellsworth, 1950: 421–2).

Outside Europe, European colonial governments often impeded industrialization. Colonized and soon to be colonized areas' share of world manufacturing fell steadily in both relative and absolute terms. In 1750, at the beginning of the industrial revolution, productivity was relatively equal around the world, and about three-quarters of world manufacturing took place outside northwest Europe and North America (Bairoch, 1982: 275; Pomeranz, 2000). By 1830, largely because of British industrialization, this share had fallen to about three-fifths; by 1880, with the United States and northwest Europe substantially industrialized, it was down to one-tenth. Third World manufacturing output seems to have fallen in absolute terms until 1900, producing an inverse Verdoorn effect in which declining production led to declining productivity per unit labor. This effect was particularly marked in British India and China, which lost considerable relative share. Figure 4.1 shows how the global distribution of total GDP changed.

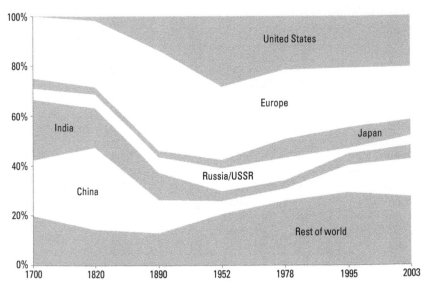

Source: Data from Maddison (2007: 44).

Figure 4.1   *Distribution of world GDP, 1700–2003*

... are every late-comer's disadvantages

The British enjoyed what we would today call first-mover advantages and Verdoorn effects. British success in cotton textiles rested not just on the application of power to the spinning of fibers and weaving of cloth. As the first to enter the market with industrially produced goods, the British acquired the expertise that comes from 'learning by doing.' They developed a workforce with the skills needed to run the new machines and a large pool of practical engineering talent to build those machines. Fairly specialized firms emerged for particular fabrics, giving each firm some economies of scale, as in Krugman's model. British success also reflected expertise in dyeing and the production of natural dyes, in the production of textile machinery, in marketing into a staggering variety of global markets, and in access to, control over, and transportation of colonial sources of raw cotton. Technological innovation in supporting industries also spurred innovation in related industries, because innovation in one particular industry forced innovation on its users or suppliers by revealing new production bottlenecks. All the advantages listed above involve market imperfections that impede the technology diffusion, and permit first movers to enjoy technological rents.

The industrial revolution did diffuse to Europe, but a generation behind Britain, and quite unevenly. François Crouzet (1996) provides a succinct description of the difficulties French firms faced in trying to assimilate the new technologies:

The main trouble was that the [French] imitation was not a good one: it was smaller than the [British] original, its equipment less up-to-date, its mills and works tinier; and its growth slower, at least up to 1850. These short-comings [are explained by] market forces and comparative 'disadvantages'. ... For the textile industries ... and some others, the brake on growth was on the demand side; they were ... prevented from exporting by the competition of cheaper British goods. ... They depended on the French home market, where incomes per capita were lower – roughly by 30 percent – than in England. The home market was also heterogenous, fragmented and did not expand fast.

(1996: 58)

Unlike Britain, industrial latecomers lacked labor settled into factory disciplines and skilled on the new machines; lacked managers with factory experience; had smaller, more fragmented and more costly capital markets; did not have firms capable of supplying inputs and finishing off outputs from the main industrial branches; lacked a distribution network; and by definition possessed backward technologies. All of these presented collective dilemmas to would-be industrialists and their states (Hall and Soskice, 2001). Obviously the owners of firms would benefit from an expansion of, say, the basic transportation infrastructure or the development of a trained labor force or investment in complementary industries. But equally obviously, each individual factory owner would benefit from avoiding the cost of supplying these collective goods and letting someone else bear the costs or the risks involved. Ultimately, only states or private actors backed by the state could overcome these collective dilemmas. In Chapter 2 we adopted Waldner's (1999) label 'Gerschenkronian collective action problems' for this process, because Alexander Gerschenkron (1966) argued that successful late industrialization is marked by the development of institutional innovations that overcome each of these problems.

Gerschenkron and syndromes of late development

Gerschenkron's argument about how late developers became competitive is deceptively simple: the later any given country's industrialization started after Britain's, the greater the degree of state intervention needed to make industrialization successful. Late industrializers could not replicate Britain's experience and institutions. Instead, they had to follow different institutional paths to industrialization because new institutional forms were needed to overcome the barriers that markets – Krugman's agglomeration pressures – threw up to late industrialization. No new institutions, then no, or limited, industrialization. British industrialization rested on a mixture of individual entrepreneurs using their own savings and retained earnings to capitalize small-scale industry, while a large stock market helped to capitalize big industry. In this institutional model, most banks concentrated on short-term commercial finance, while investment banks concentrated on overseas lending and the floating of new shares on the stock market. Only Holland's and Switzerland's states imitated Britain's. Everywhere else in Europe states intervened to support local industry, sometimes successfully, sometimes not.

Gerschenkron (1966) argued that four syndromes co-varied with the lateness of industrialization. The later successful industrialization occurred:

1. the more the state needed to support industry through special institutions to create, concentrate, and lend capital, and to control labor unrest;
2. the more concentrated the pattern of industrial ownership and the larger the institutional form of ownership would be;
3. the faster the rate of growth of output – usually faster than that in the current dominant economy – would be once industrialization started;
4. the more likely that agriculture would remain undeveloped relative to local industry, hindering later expansion of the domestic market.

Each syndrome reflected the consequences of efforts to overcome competitive disadvantages relative to earlier industrializers.

Late developers' single biggest internal problem was their relatively backward agriculture, which limited the capital and labor available for investment in new industry. Capital first. Here two problems hinder late developers: they absolutely lack capital, and they lack an efficient means to link savers and investors institutionally. In the nineteenth century, 'savings' in one year ultimately equaled grain left over from the preceding year's consumption, either as grain itself, as livestock fed with that grain, or as cash earned by exporting/selling that grain somewhere else. 'Fixed capital' or 'investment' equaled the structures or machines built by the workers fed with that extra grain. *A region's agricultural efficiency or ability to import foods thus set the upper limit on potential investment.* The amount of grain that landlords (and later the state) could squeeze out of peasants represented the practical limit on investment. This was true even where money capital existed: if peasants would or could not surrender extra food, then investment could not occur unless foreign capital was available. In these regards, it is noteworthy that British agricultural productivity permitted Britain to be a net exporter of grain in the 1700s, despite a rapidly rising population. Similarly, high levels of agricultural productivity in Japan and China as compared with much of Europe enabled their 'industrious revolutions,' even if these did not generate dynamic growth.

Agricultural inefficiency also set a second limit on capital formation and thus industrialization. Late industrializers usually financed their initial imports of modern physical capital goods (such as machinery or rails) by exporting part of the local agricultural surplus – that is, they pursued a Ricardian strategy first. However, agricultural modernization also required investment, that is, access to surplus agricultural production. If states siphoned off too much of the agricultural surplus for industrial investment, they risked permanently crippling agriculture, making it useless as a source of investment funds, and depriving the economy of labor supplies. Naturally, local landowners often resisted the diversion of the agricultural surplus away from their consumption and towards investment.

Finally, the earliest stages of industrialization could be accomplished with quite limited resources: textile production is within the resources of an extended family, and rapid turnover permits an easy liquidation of their investment. But canals, not to speak of railroads, steel mills, or production of bulk chemicals, require long-term capital on a larger order of magnitude. The capital for 'lumpy' projects like these has to be gathered from many individual investors and concentrated in one institution, be it a firm drawing on equity markets, or a bank, or the state. This problem of intermediation between savers and investors did not exist, for example, for family-owned textile mills; they were both saver and investor. The only practical way to capitalize and manage large firms was through joint stock companies, which institutionalized the raising and investment of capital. But no rational financial intermediary would want to take on short-term deposits and then relend the money for long-term industrial projects. The absence of banks oriented towards long-term investment, or of stock and bond markets to facilitate the floating of company shares (stock), inhibited the creation of joint stock companies. Firms also faced internal organizational difficulties because they lacked a reliable legal system for regulating corporate enterprise and assuring that shareholders would not be abused.

Gerschenkron identified two stylized constellations of institutional deviations from the British model that overcame all or many of these problems through the provision of collective goods. In successful late industrializers, either banks (supported by the state) or the state itself resolved the problem of generating capital and channeling it to nascent industrial firms. In addition to the form, the intensity of intervention also steadily increased as economies industrialized later and later and thus faced greater and greater difficulties. Bank-led development characterized countries industrializing one to two generations (20 to 40 years) later than Britain; state-led development characterized countries industrializing three to four generations (40 to 80 years) later. For Gerschenkron, Germany presented the ideal type of the first novel institutional solution. Germany's banks concentrated local capital for long-term industrial investment and tended to control clusters of industrial firms. Most capital came from long-term loans rather than sale of stock shares (equity). The state used tariffs and purchasing policy to induce local production of industrial goods it wanted.

Russia presented a case of state-led development. The novel institutional form here was state ownership of financial and industrial companies across a range of industrial sectors. The Russian state concentrated capital for investment in a mix of privately and publicly owned enterprises. The state raised capital by taxing its relatively primitive agriculture and borrowing abroad. Lacking local entrepreneurs, the state used state-owned firms to ensure production of goods, occasionally privatizing these firms. As with bank-led development, the state used tariffs and purchasing policy to secure the local market for domestic producers. Even so, the shortage of entrepreneurs and skilled labor meant that foreign investors and entrepreneurs assumed a major role in industrialization. Foreign investors apparently owned 41 percent of Russian joint stock industrial companies in 1914 (Falkus, 1972a: 63–71).

In either case, the state (or banks guided by the state) induced investment that otherwise would not occur. For example, a coal mining firm might resist an expansion of output until a steel mill was built that would absorb the additional coal output; but the steel firm might reasonably also refuse to invest until it was assured that sufficient coal would be available. State-directed banks, however, could simultaneously advance loans to each. Meanwhile the state reduced the risk of concentrating short-term deposits into intermediaries (banks in one syndrome, itself on the other) which then invested this capital in ventures with an inherently long-term payoff. It reduced the risks of investment by assuring that investment would take place simultaneously in the whole range of upstream and downstream industries needed to make any one discrete industrial venture successful. And using tariff and other forms of border protection it could guarantee that new production would find a market.

What about labor markets? Here, too, agriculture set limits on late industrialization. The more efficient agriculture was, the more labor that could be freed (or expelled) from agriculture for industrial employment. Workers also lacked skills that we take for granted, as well as more obvious technologically based skills. In agrarian economies around 1800, most workers lacked 'skills' such as showing up for work regularly. The nature and intensity of males' agricultural labor varied enormously depending on the season. It took several generations of urban life to get them to come to factory work every day and to work at a constant rhythm throughout the year (Thompson, 1966). Unsurprisingly, most industrial workers in the 1800s were women and children, who could be spared from the field and who were accustomed to the more constant rhythms of domestic work.

Late developers also have problems creating labor discipline. Models of worker resistance, including unionization, traveled as fast as technological imports. Thus, while it took almost two generations for British workers to develop durable unions, similar unions emerged simultaneously with industrialization in Scandinavia and Germany. These unions could impede efforts to raise productivity to the point where low wages were actually a competitive advantage rather than a reflection of poor skills. One of the late developers' few competitive advantages is relatively low wages, expressed in money terms. However, relatively low wages are an advantage only when productivity is as high as that of one's competitors. Late developers try to increase productivity by using the most modern technology available, but the lack of skilled labor makes this difficult, and even when skilled labor is available they often lack specific experience with this technology.

A parallel deficiency of managerial ability mirrors workers' technological naivety. Late developers lack a trained pool of managers. Most European and Asian firms were family firms. The absence of professional managers and engineers hindered the successful management of large-scale enterprise. Jurgen Kocka (1978: 553) puts this point bluntly regarding German industrialization: 'It was difficult for German factory owners around 1850 to find qualified and reliable officials and office staff to perform those tasks which the entrepreneur could not closely control himself.' Only the state had experience running large-scale organizations like armies, bureaucracies, and their related colonial administrations and enterprises. In late developing countries, the military consequently played an important role in creating professional management cadres.

Gerschenkron's states also intervened to create the largest possible market for local producers. State efforts to maximize local producers' control of the market dovetailed with their strategic concerns. In the nineteenth century nonindustrial states seemed likely to lose wars, and outside Europe they risked incorporation into someone else's empire. Therefore, states usually tried to build up a railroad network along with its supporting industries. Railroads helped unify the microeconomies over which the state ruled. Railroad development also helped important industries linked to the railroads, such as engineering, metals production, and mining, to enjoy rising sales and output. States used tariffs, contracts to buy output, and sometimes state ownership to ensure that local firms emerged or made a successful transition to modern production methods. From the firm's point of view, investing in high-productivity, high-volume production often was rational only if it could be sure of having at least the domestic market to fall back on. Otherwise, firms would not be able to gain economies of scale and scope by running their factories at full capacity.

Concentrated ownership and the use of the most modern production methods also reflected the positive effects of concentrating output and thus Verdoorn effects into a handful of firms. As Alice Amsden (1989) argues, late development requires the development of permanent managerial structures that can generate and retain production knowledge. Putting scarce resources such as skilled labor, management, and capital in one place concentrated profits and learning effects. Geographic concentration also fostered faster learning by doing, because it permitted interaction among different producers in the same area.

The rapid growth of Gerschenkron's successful industrializers reflects the fact that successful late industrialization required a shift to a Kaldorian growth strategy. In other words, they involved conscious efforts to create Verdoorn effects in order to bring local industry's productivity up to a level that would enable them to compete with earlier industrializers. Most of the gain in Verdoorn effects comes from learning by doing, as workers and management gain experience at producing a particular good and at overcoming temporary bottlenecks in production. The faster production grows – that is, the bigger the Gerschenkronian spurt – the more workers and management are forced to think up creative ways to expand production, and the greater the economies of speed as they reduce the amount of time it takes to actually produce something. Meanwhile, established competitors facing stagnant demand will be tempted to routinize production and in doing so are less likely to innovate more efficient production methods.

Because Verdoorn effects require the mobilization of tacit knowledge – knowledge carried around in people's heads rather than knowledge which has been codified and written down – the state also often was involved in overcoming Kaldorian collective dilemmas on the shop floor. Workers quite reasonably enough rarely voluntarily offered employers the secrets of their trade or of production; they feared owners would appropriate the knowledge and use it to lower wages or reduce employment. Notably, in the most spectacular cases of late development, Japan, Korea and Taiwan, the state overcame workers' reticence by structuring the labor market to assure lifetime employment for core industrial workers.

Finally, because of the need to maximize Verdoorn effects, the later industrialization occurred the more likely it was that agricultural growth would lag behind industrial demand for capital. Generally, the later industrialization took place, the greater the need for capital relative to the local supply. This forced the state to squeeze as much as possible from agriculture in the shortest amount of time using taxes and other coercive mechanisms. States appropriated this surplus food in kind or as money taxes and used it to fund initial investment in heavy industry. When Stalin starved the Ukrainian peasantry to industrialize the Soviet Union in the 1930s, he merely continued, albeit in an extremely violent and telescoped way, nineteenth-century processes in Western Europe (Ellman, 1975).

This kind of rushed extraction typically diverted investment funds from agriculture, leaving agricultural production unmodernized and thus less useful in the long run as a source of investment funds. Slower rural income growth also hampered the expansion of the market for locally produced industrial goods and the expansion of agriculture as a source of exports. Late industrializers thus walked a fine line between too little extraction to fund industry on a competitive scale and so much extraction that investment in agriculture collapsed. A weak or decaying agriculture often forced reliance on foreign borrowing, which in turn brought its own danger of foreign control over industry or the state's own financial apparatus. Earlier industrializers could exploit agriculture more slowly, until industry became self-financing. Though Gerschenkron did not comment on this, in most late industrializers the state also helps large industry extract rents from smaller firms, which tends to stunt the service sector and weaken small and medium-sized industry.

'Early' late industrializers: the United States

A quick survey of European and Asian industrialization demonstrates these points. Even in the first two countries to industrialize after Britain, Belgium and the northeastern United States, banks and state intervention played a much greater role than in Britain.

We will concentrate on the United States, where, contrary to received wisdom, the states and banks played a major role in the initial stages of industrialization (Callender, 1902). Alexander Hamilton's views on the importance of a protective tariff for infant industry are well known. But the various American states also created and financed, often with foreign capital, most of the early canals and railroads. In the southern states, the state usually helped planters capitalize cotton plantations and other export-oriented agriculture by backing their efforts to secure mortgages with state bonds. In the emerging

Midwest, federal land policies supported another export-oriented agricultural complex centered on grain and pork. These policies culminated in the four great policies that built the Midwest: land grant railroads; homesteading; the land grant college; and the extension service of the US Department of Agriculture. In the North, states provided about 40 percent of all railroad capital in the 1830s (Dunlavy, 1991: 12). By 1850, the United States already had 50 percent more miles of railroad than Britain; more important, the extensive use of steamships on internal rivers and canals helped create and expand sophisticated machine tool and engineering industries from firms initially providing simple manufactures to farmers. (Chapter 6 provides more information on the agricultural side of this story.)

Second-generation late industrializers: Germany

The states that Prussia welded into Germany were the most successful late industrializers in Europe. Initially, Germany was even more backward than France, experiencing virtually no urban growth from 1815 to 1848 (see Table 4.2). Ninety percent of the labor force in textile mills in the early 1800s came

Table 4.2 *Relative industrial backwardness in nineteenth-century Europe, selected years*

	Britain	France	German States	Russia
	Iron production (thousands of tons)			
1818	330	113	85[a]	127
1828	714	221	105	178
1847	2000	592	230	195
1860	3888	898	529	298
	Mechanical Energy (thousand horsepower)			
Year	*1839*	*1842*	*1860*	*1860*
Steam engines	1641	243	100	–
Water mills	674	462	–	5
	Railroad mileage (kilometers)			
1830	157	31	0	0
1840	2390	410	469	27[b]
1850	9797	2915	5856	501
1860	14603	9167	11089	1626

Notes: [a] 1823 for German states.
[b] 1837 for Russia.

Source: Based on data from Mitchell (1978: 215–16, 315–16).

from peasant households supplementing subsistence farming with part-time work, and 60 percent of their mills were worked by hand. Even in highly industrialized areas like Saxony, steam power seems to have been a rarity in the first half of the 1800s, and just as in China handlooms outnumbered powerlooms in both cotton and wool until after 1873 (Borchardt, 1972–77: 104; Crouzet, 1996: 48). The famous Zollverein toll was more of a revenue tariff than any protection, so in the 1830s and 1840s cheap imported British textiles drove many peasants out of textile production. Meanwhile (see Chapter 5), Prussia was one of Britain's largest suppliers of grain.

Germany's pathway out of the periphery revolved around a handful of banks that came to own most heavy industry and coordinated its development. This development occurred in two big waves. One centered on railroads and created basic iron and engineering capacity. The other centered on the new leading-sector cluster of electricity and chemistry, but ran in tandem with a further expansion of steel making on the basis of new smelting and casting technologies and new ways of organizing the flow of production. The three largest firms in Germany during the late 1800s were also the three largest banks.

After a series of private efforts failed, the state intervened to promote rail-roadization (Dunlavy, 1991). Railroad construction then acted as a leading sector, pulling the German engineering industry and the economy forward into modernity in Germany's first big industrial spurt. The state-subsidized rail-road construction with cheap loans, guaranteed the profits of rail firms, and, when necessary, purchased shares in rail companies to assure their flotation. The state used a state corporation, the Seehandlung, to create new exports and, equally important, to demonstrate new technologies to local entrepreneurs. The Seehandlung established model factories in textiles, chemicals, mining, and luxury goods production, often in collaboration with expatriate British engineer/entrepreneurs and skilled workers. Grain exports to Britain initially financed capital goods imports. Later, low-value manufactured goods like toys and similar trinkets made up a surprising share of German exports. All of this anticipated late-twentieth-century Asian development, where ministries of trade and industry would actively acquire technology, coordinate export drives through state trading companies, and flood world markets with the low-value-added manufactured goods I will call 'textiles, toys and trash,' or the three Ts.

German rail construction benefited from German backwardness and distance from the British town. Despite their later start, by the middle of the 1800s the Germans had managed to build roughly twice as many miles of rail as France. Cheaper land, lower wages, and planning that took roads around difficult terrain rather than through it meant that German rail construction costs per mile were roughly one-third those in Britain (on average £11 000 per mile versus £30 000 to £40 000 in Britain). Railroad investment averaged over 20 percent of total investment in Germany from 1855 to 1870, dwarfing any other single sector. The demand for locomotives also helped promote local engineering. Until 1842, all locomotives came from Britain. Tariffs and state contracts induced local production, and by 1854 all locomotives came from Central European sources. Germany imported British and Belgian skilled workers to speed this process. Rising output led to rising productivity, and by the 1860s Germany became a net exporter of rails and locomotives.

The second wave of industrialization centered on steel and chemicals, with banks playing an even more active role than before. Industrial production grew an average 3.7 percent per year during 1870–1914 (Kocka, 1978: 555). Reflecting a relative scarcity of capital, the big banks promoted high levels of concentration in Germany. The banks fostered cartels and vertical and horizontal integration in order to reduce competition and thus the risk of overinvestment, to exercise more control over raw materials prices, and to coordinate export efforts. Protectionist tariffs also shifted rents from small firms towards larger ones, speeding growth by the latter at the expense of the former (Gourevitch, 1985). By the 1870s the German iron and steel industry was already more concentrated than its British rivals. This pattern obtained in other growth sectors as well. By 1896 banks had founded 39 firms in electrical goods. The banks then rationalized the industry into two great firms – an enlarged AEG and Siemens. In 1904 the same thing happened in the chemicals industry with the creation of Farben-Cassella and Bayer-Agfa-BASF.

The state, particularly under Bismarck, actively pre-empted unionization and outlawed the Socialist party. Bismarck developed a state system of health insurance and old-age pensions to break the working class into a series of occupational and income strata. Even so, Germany had one of the most radical working classes west of St Petersburg during the last quarter of the nineteenth century.

German late industrialization was highly successful. Per capita industrial production went from about one-quarter of British levels in 1860 to about three-quarters in 1913 (see Table 4.1). Germany's larger population meant it actually out produced Britain in gross terms that year (Bairoch, 1982: 292, 294). Austria and northern Italy, industrializing about one generation later than Germany, replicated the institutional features of the German model, albeit less successfully. Countries industrializing after this period had much greater state involvement, particularly direct involvement in financing and running industrial enterprises.

Squeezing peasants in Asia: late industrialization in Russia, Japan, and China

Gerschenkron's classic case of state-led industrialization is Russia. However, Japan and China illustrate much better Gerschenkron's state-led syndrome. Japan is closer to what Gerschenkron imagined because it had high levels of state intervention, despite possessing a highly commercialized economy with a vibrant mercantile class, and low levels of foreign penetration as compared to Russia. Japan also set a normative model for later Asian industrialization. China was also highly commercialized on the eve of industrialization, but relied more on foreign entrepreneurship than Japan. The post-1949 Chinese state went even further in terms of state-owned industry, and retained control over much of the economy even after Deng Xiaoping's gradual liberalization of the economy after 1979.

Two key differences marked late industrialization outside Western Europe and North America. First, where the state largely aided private entrepreneurs in Western Europe, in Russia and Asia the state tended to create (state-owned) industry itself in the early stages of industrialization, particularly in Russia. Second, the more successful the state was in eliminating landlords and seizing control of the agricultural surplus, the more likely it would succeed in sponsoring industrialization, because this provided the state both with the means to finance industrialization and lessened political opposition to industrialization. Agriculture was more important because the European market for true handicrafts (which Germany, for example, exploited) had largely evaporated by the end of the nineteenth century.

Russia

In Russia the Ministry of Finance played a key role in raising and allocating capital. The Russian state established a series of state banks, subordinated to the Ministry of Finance, to lend to industry, matching each bank to one particular industrial sector. These banks steered borrowed foreign capital into the sectors they were trying to promote. The state built most of the early railroads, a factory to produce rolling stock, and an iron mill for rails. Very high tariffs protected these new firms. Industrial growth averaged roughly 8 percent per annum during this first industrial spurt. Despite these efforts, by 1914 European Russia had less than 20 percent of the railroad trackage of the comparably sized United States, and the typical Russian industrial worker employed one-third the mechanical horsepower used by the average American worker (Gregory, 1994).

Russia's efforts ultimately failed because of the grim choices imposed by its backwardness. Its backward agriculture (Siberia aside) yielded a very small surplus, and the relative absence of rivers, canals, and railroads meant that most agriculture took place in microeconomies, making extraction of that surplus difficult. Moreover, the state, which was largely staffed by landlords, could never displace those landlords and reallocate the agricultural surplus to industry. Rising rents led to peasant unrest and the abortive 1905 revolt. While the state suppressed this revolt, Russian peasants successfully defended their communal ownership against Stolypin's post-1905 efforts to expose more peasants to market pressures and so make more surplus available to the state. This forced the state to rely on borrowed foreign capital, which created a conflict between debt service and agricultural modernization. Russia relied on grain exports to finance its foreign debt payments. As international grain prices fell, peasants came under more and more pressure to deliver more grain without having any way to increase productivity.

The great peasant uprising of 1917 ushered a new round of state-led industrialization that exaggerated all these tendencies under the new communist regime. The state assumed ownership of all industry, and used its control over collective agriculture to fund that industry with grain exports. By prioritizing grain exports over peasants' survival, Stalin did successfully create a substantial heavy industrial sector. But these policies permanently crippled Russian agriculture (as well as starving approximately 20 million Ukrainians).

Japan

The Japanese state, in contrast, proved highly successful at repressing landlords, capturing the agricultural surplus, and channeling it on a discretionary basis to industrialists. Japan also made a fairly rapid transition away from agricultural exports. Instead, Japan took advantage of the structure of markets in Asia to export low-value-added, low-quality manufactured goods. Later Asian industrializers also deliberately pursued this strategy. In Europe, 'early' late industrializers typically funded capital goods imports with a mix of agricultural and handicraft exports, and then modernized those handicraft sectors as new technologies appeared. France and Belgium, for example, were able to jump into modern woolen production when woolens production was mechanized in the mid-nineteenth century. In Asia and Japan (and parts of Latin America), manufacturers initially targeted markets for low-quality, low-price goods ignored by European producers, and then, under state pressure to do so, they inched their way up into markets for higher-quality goods through continuous innovation and improvement. Asians' prior industrious revolutions enabled them to industrialize from the bottom up. Both the conscious appropriation of rural surplus and bottom-up industrialization also reflect efforts to cope with adverse circumstances created by European commercial and military dominance of the world. The external political and economic environment for Asian industrialization was much harsher than for European industrialization.

Japan avoided being hobbled by the agricultural problems that tripped up Russia by carefully cultivating the agricultural sector as a source of surplus for investment. Thus Japan was able to industrialize without substantial foreign debt. Japanese agricultural reforms in the early Meiji period (1867–90) removed nominal samurai landlords and established capitalist relations of production in the countryside (Norman, 1975). The state systematically helped those peasants increase their yields above their already high levels in order to increase its own ability to tax peasants. As in Russia, peasants (and ex-landlords) frequently revolted, but, in the absence of any external shocks, the Japanese state easily quelled these revolts. (In contrast, Japan's defeat of Russia, 1904–5, triggered Russia's 1905 peasant revolt.) Because the Meiji state taxed land values, not the harvest, peasants had an incentive to increase productivity, while the tax structure pushed marginal farmers off the land and replaced them with more productive farmers. Land taxes extracted about 30 to 40 percent of the value of agricultural production for the state, providing between 60 and 70 percent of state revenue (Norman, 1975: 250–8). The state then invested this money in railroads, in generic heavy industries critical for military security, and in its military *per se*. These investments secured Japan from the colonization typical of the rest of Asia.

The Japanese state also channeled capital extracted from agriculture to the large family-owned merchant companies that had emerged during Japan's long self-imposed isolation under the Tokugawa shogunate. These merchants transformed themselves into banks, which, as in Russia and Germany, controlled much industrial investment and fostered considerable centralization. Japan also adopted joint stock company institutions right from the start of its industrialization. The combination of bank control and joint stock organization led to an early form of conglomerate that the Japanese called *zaibatsu*, or financial clique, in which banks controlled and coordinated a group of firms. Many of these industrial firms had been started by the state and then sold off to the *zaibatsu* banks.

Meanwhile, Japan also benefited from Europe's colonization of Asia. After 1842 the British and other Europeans opened Asia to more Western trade via colonization and unequal treaties. The Europeans integrated Asia into their world economy as exporters of primary products to Europe and importers of manufactures from Europe just as they did colonial areas in Latin America and Africa. (See Tables 4.3 and 4.4.) This created demand for industrial goods inside Asia that Japanese industry satisfied. By 1909 Japan was a net textile exporter, primarily to China (Abe, 2005: 76).

Table 4.3   *Composition of Asian trade with Europe, c. 1912*

Country	Exports (%)		Imports (%)	
	Primary	Manufactures	Primary	Manufactures
Japan	69	31	34	66
India	92	8	8	92

Source: Based on data from Sugihara (1986: 711–13).

Table 4.4   *Distribution of Asian trade, c. 1913[a]*

Country	Exports (%)		Imports (%)	
	Asia	'The West'	Asia	'The West'
China	48	50	16	83
Japan	47	50	44	53
India	27	63	22	75

Note: [a] Rows do not add up to 100 because of exports to/imports from other regions.
Source: Based on data from Sugihara (1986: 711–13).

China

Unlike Japan and Russia, China could not maintain its territorial integrity in the nineteenth century, hampering late industrialization. As in Japan and Russia, the state pioneered munitions factories and armories, but there was little technology transfer. Instead, a mixture of private domestic and foreign entrepreneurs developed a cotton textile industry centered on Shanghai, using fibers from China and India. This industry was capable of supplying China's domestic needs, but unlike Japan's was not able to earn enough foreign exchange to capitalize other industries (Hamilton and Chang, 2003: 199–202). China's tenuous sovereignty and recurrent civil wars hampered nationalist efforts at industrialization by limiting the use of tariffs and state contracting. Instead, China participated in a newly expanded division of labor inside greater Asia.

The integration of the Asian economies in the late nineteenth century differed in two respects from that in Africa and Latin America. First, strong local state structures survived the European incursions, particularly in Japan, but also in Siam (Thailand) and China. Even in India and what became Malaysia much European rule was indirect. Second, as noted in Chapter 1, Asia possessed a deep and vibrant economy based on intra-Asian trade. This intra-Asian trade provided the market that supported Asian industrialization once European demand for raw materials dynamized this existing trade. Total exports by Asian countries rose from about £82 million in 1883 to £214 million in 1913. However, the intra-Asian component of this trade rose from £31 million to £149 million during the same period, a rate of growth of 5.4 percent per annum compared to the 3.2 percent growth for exports to Europe (Sugihara, 1986: 712–13). Asian consumers, flush with cash from exports to Europe, created much of the increased demand for intra-Asian exports of locally produced industrial goods.

The same leading sectors that produced the expansion of the European economies also drove expansion of Asian industry via European demand for Asian raw materials. European demand rose in two waves. The first was linked to the diffusion of the initial industrial revolution cotton textiles leading-sector cluster to Continental Europe and the simultaneous railroad cluster in Britain. The second, much larger wave was linked to the chemistry and electricity cluster, and centered on demand for rubber (for insulation and bicycle tires), tin and palm oils (for canned and processed foods for an enlarged urban working class), and petroleum (for the emerging motor industry). These exports came from plants introduced to or transplanted within Asia. Rubber in Malaya, tea in northeast India (Assam) and Sri Lanka (Ceylon), and systematically cultivated palm and coconuts almost always occurred in new monocultural production zones. Labor for these new production zones came from displaced peasants turned into indentured or migrant labor (see Chapter 5). These ex-peasants now worked full time for money incomes and turned to the market to buy food and manufactures which they had previously made for themselves or in isolated microeconomies. In turn, this additional demand for food called forth new rice export production zones in Siam, Vietnam, and Bengal, adding to demand for manufactures by enlarging incomes there.

Parts of this expanding Asian market remained the preserve of European firms: rail and oceanic transport, electrification, colonialists' consumption. None the less, a huge Asian market segment remained untouched by European producers. Local producers, particularly the Japanese, jumped into this market segment. One Japanese scholar precisely marks the divide between the European and Asian textile markets as cotton textiles with thread counts above about 25 and those below (Kawakatsu, 1986: 626–31). Thread count is a measure of fineness and quality, with higher thread counts denoting finer fabrics. European, especially British textile producers in search of higher profits, systematically moved upmarket into higher thread counts at the end of the nineteenth century. They abandoned the lower ranges of the market to Asian producers in textiles and other household goods. When 'European' firms competed in this product range, they did so by locating production in what we would now think of as 'export processing zones' in India (especially Bombay) or China (especially Shanghai).

Low-wage Asian producers could compete in these low-priced goods. Japanese manufacturers particularly introduced a wide range of knockoffs of European goods into local Asian markets. Verdoorn's law held in Asia as in Europe, and rising output for the Asian part of their market helped the Japanese increase their productivity to the point where they could begin to compete with European producers at the bottom of the market for higher-quality goods. Japan's successful creation of a textile industry allowed it to become a kind of Britain within Asia, exporting finished textiles to India and China while importing raw cotton from India and rice from Taiwan, which it colonized after 1895. Japan's large agricultural surplus, its successful exports, and its colonies allowed it to industrialize without the need for significant amounts of borrowed foreign capital – perhaps the last real instance of this.

Finally, the Japanese state also intervened in factor markets. Japan actively sought out skills. It sent students overseas to acquire technical knowledge and imported Western academics and professionals to teach local students. As in Germany, the military was a key training ground for management personnel. The state ruthlessly suppressed labor movements, but also innovated and diffused lifetime employment in a bid to generate and retain skilled labor (Weiss, 1993). Japanese per capita industrial production rose from about one-tenth the British level in 1860 to one-fifth that level in 1913, reflecting a growth rate about 50 percent higher than Britain's (Bairoch, 1982: 292, 294). Later Asian industrializers like Taiwan, South Korea, and China would imitate the Japanese model, squeezing agriculture to fund their initial round of industrial investment and then using low-grade consumer nondurable exports to fund industrial deepening. Textiles continued to play a crucial role in this process, amounting to roughly 30 percent of Japanese exports 1912–39, Korean exports 1964–78, and Taiwanese exports 1971–78 (Anderson, 1990: 143).

Late development succeeded only in economies where the state intervened

to provide investment capital by squeezing agriculture, concentrate and redeploy that capital, protect local producers, and control labor. Among European
countries with failed or stunted industrialization, the Iberian states failed to
protect local industry, the Italian state did not come into being until the late
nineteenth century, and the Balkans lacked stable states, literacy, and even the
most rudimentary transportation systems. Eastern Europe's generally impov-
erished agriculture proved a weak base for investment in manufacturing and
later marketing. The segmentation of the Asian market between high-cost,
high-quality and low-cost, low-quality goods allowed certain Asian countries
to industrialize, even though Asian industrializers and Asia overall remained
exporters of raw materials to Europe. Colonized nonindustrializers, failed
industrializers, and deindustrializers in the nineteenth century had two other
options: Ricardian strategies using agricultural or other raw materials exports
as a prerequisite to industrialization, or even more extreme state involvement
to create successful Kaldorian growth in industry in the twentieth century. The
next two chapters deal with the agricultural option. Chapter 11 picks up the
second option for late industrializers in Latin America and East Asia.

International consequences of late development

What were the international consequences of late industrialization? Late
industrialization created pressures for increased trade protection. The late
industrializers' drive for wider markets usually led to trade frictions, particularly with the dominant or hegemonic economy, which after all was usually
the world's largest market.

Because late industrialization rested on Kaldorian growth – rapid increases
in output to stimulate rapid increases in productivity – it inevitably stimulated
conflicts among countries for domestic and foreign market share. Late industrializers generated two kinds of export streams. The first usually consisted of
some kind of raw material or traditional manufactured goods. Late industrializers exported these in order to finance their initial imports of the capital goods
needed for industry. These exports often threatened agricultural producers in
the dominant economy – a Thünen town – who naturally had higher implicit
rental costs than producers in late industrializers. The second export stream
consisted of new industrial goods.

Consequently, the opportunities for reciprocity through, for example, tariff
reductions between the existing hegemonic economy and would-be late industrializers usually shrank. As noted earlier, late industrializers needed to maximize local firms' share of the domestic market in order to run their plants at
full capacity and to maximize overall output. Late industrializers had a strong
temptation to free ride on the hegemonic economy's openness to international
trade (Lake, 1988).

In one sense, then, late industrialization occurred at the sufferance of the
hegemonic economy. Almost always the largest market in the world, the hegemonic economy was a logical target for late industrializers trying to expand

output. If the hegemonic economy chose to protect its market from the export streams of late industrializers, those late industrializers would have a more difficult time starting and sustaining a virtuous circle of rising output–rising productivity–rising competitiveness–rising sales. On the other hand, if late industrializers produced products that firms in the hegemonic economy were abandoning, then the hegemonic economy could benefit from cheaper low-value-added industrial goods. In effect, the hegemonic economy could shed industries along the lines of comparative advantage, allowing low-value-added agriculture and low-value-added labor-intensive industry to shift location, while hoping that higher real incomes at home would stimulate more output in local high-value-added industries. This is why protectionism in the nineteenth and twentieth centuries seems to be very closely related to the business cycle (Strange and Tooze, 1981; McKeown, 1983). During upswings, as new leading sectors emerged in the hegemonic economy, older sectors could be abandoned at relatively low political and economic cost. Capital and labor could redeploy into new sectors with higher returns via profits or wages. In periods of relatively slow growth, however, the political and economic costs would be higher.

In another sense, successful late industrialization also occurred at the expense of other would-be late industrializers. To the extent that one late industrializer's export stream spilled over into third-party markets, then firms in that and other third-party markets lost the ability to generate a virtuous Kaldorian circle. Nineteenth-century German success in heavy industry implied slower growth in French, Austrian, and Russian heavy industry, and blocked the emergence of heavy industry elsewhere, as the Krugman model would predict.

Paradoxically, then, the hegemonic economy's efforts to take advantage of its economic superiority by opening up its markets creates pressures to close markets. The hegemonic economy's structural power comes from the pressures its enormous market generates, inducing producers everywhere to reorient their production towards that market. The only way to resist that pressure is to close off the local market and force local producers to look inward, until the demand generated by local industry is large enough to draw in those producers on its own. The next chapter looks at pressure to adopt a Ricardian strategy.

Chapter 5

Agricultural Exporters and the Search for Labor

> It is not the land that we want, but the use of it. The use of land may be got ... by means of exchange.
>
> *Edward Gibbon Wakefield*

The opportunity for Ricardian development and the problem of labor supplies

Chapter 4 discussed states that opted for Kaldorian strategies in response to Britain's industrial revolution. What about those areas that opted for or were forced into a Ricardian strategy? The industrial revolution's voracious appetite for agricultural goods created a system of agricultural production rings, like those described in Chapter 2, around industrializing northwestern Europe. The expansion of those Thünen rings created two distinct dynamics.

First, states everywhere began using or supporting the use of violence in order to create labor supplies for these new production zones and then to enforce property rights in them. While the 'market,' or more precisely rising prices, meant these areas potentially could become production zones for supplying Europe, that potential meant nothing without workers and enforceable property rights. Efforts to expand agricultural production zones encountered two paradoxical limits: where there were potential workers, they often were hostile to work in the market; where there was easily available land, there usually was no labor. The solution favored by the market – that is, the relatively cheaper one – was to seize land and use some form of coerced labor. Though new owners in these new rings did not intend this outcome, their exports eventually triggered successive waves of more or less voluntary international migration. The enforcement of property rights in land and/or the presence of newly freed labor forces prevent most immigrants from exiting the labor market. Ironically, the successful creation of new production zones helped create the voluntary migration that eventually allowed those new zones to dispense with coerced labor.

Second, the continuous expansion of industrial demand for nonfood agriculturals (NFAs) and of urban demand for foods forced most of the areas supplying northwestern Europe and later the industrial United States to transform their economies roughly every 50 years. Each expansion forced existing supply peripheries to shift to higher-value agricultural exports – to become inner rings – or risk being priced out of the market by suppliers further out who had cheaper land costs. Most Ricardian developers did not initially respond to falling prices by discarding their Ricardian strategy in favor of a Kaldorian strategy. Instead, they shifted away from producing the agricultural good experiencing falling prices and began producing different agricultural goods with stable or rising prices. This shift was automatic nowhere; everywhere it was fraught with political conflict as existing owners fought to protect fixed assets and peasants or workers fought to avoid being displaced from settled lifestyles. So here too states intervened to reconstruct economies.

This second effort at Ricardian development was also vulnerable to falling prices, creating a second crisis in the 1930s. This crisis forced countries to shift from Ricardian to Kaldorian development strategies. Again most countries missed the boat (or, in the case of colonies, were denied a boarding pass) when they tried to use changing European demand to develop and perhaps industrialize on the basis of new or increased agricultural exports back to the European 'town.' All the lessons observed in the late industrialization of European regions apply to these supply regions, as we will see in Chapters 6 and 11. Both chapters look at the process of Ricardian development from the inside out.

This chapter, however, focuses on the first dynamic listed above. It examines the process from the outside in, asking how states created these areas and how they generated labor forces for them. The first section looks at the general expansion, outward from Europe, of the production zones Thünen predicted. Rising European demand for food and NFAs in effect turned industrial Britain and then the industrial triangle in northwestern Europe (defined by Hamburg–Paris–Frankfurt) into a gigantic Thünen town; this town drew commodities from a global agricultural supply zone. Paradoxically, the more successful European industrialization was, the greater the competitive pressures on European agriculture. It had either to adapt or to die, shifting millions of peasants and agricultural workers into local industry or the new production zones.

The second section examines Irish agriculture, in order to provide a sort of experimental control for the later sections. Irish agriculture exhibits the successive expansion of Thünen's agrizones through a fixed geographic space. The Irish case is useful because, unlike most new agricultural supply areas elsewhere, Ireland already had a labor supply and a state. Finally Ireland's colonial status meant that the local state could not resort to protection as a way of slowing the passage of Thünen rings through the geographic space Ireland occupied. Ireland thus provides us with a sort of natural experiment in which market pressures forced a region to transform its economy as a variety of agricultural supply zones rolled over its space unimpeded. This unmasks the unnatural processes by which states created themselves, labor supplies, and production systems in new zones. The conflicts generated in Ireland also show us why new production zones tended to be located in areas with low population densities.

The final sections concentrate on states' creation of labor supplies in the agricultural periphery and on the shift from slavery to non-slave forms of labor. It contrasts economic models of high- and low-density populations with the reality of new agricultural zones in the Caribbean, Southern Hemisphere, and Asia. As we will see, states had to create markets by force. Production flowed most easily into relatively unpopulated lands lacking complex local state or political structures. In particular, this meant the Southern Hemisphere's temperate zones and temperate North America, which were well suited to grow foods and NFAs already familiar in Europe. But the ease of conquest in these relatively unpopulated areas came at a price: the absence of settled populations and states meant that, once acquired, the land had little or no productive value until a labor force (or the combine harvester) could be created. Most colonists chose not to wait one to three centuries for the marriage of McCormick's reaper and the petrol engine. Nor could they wait for the market to provide a flow of labor to these empty places. So at first the rise of wage labor and industrial capitalism in Britain and Europe created slavery and coercion virtually everywhere in the agricultural periphery.

The rise of global agricultural production zones

Most industrial activity up to World War I transformed agricultural raw materials into some finished or intermediate good, so the industrial revolution's explosive increases in output implied proportionately increasing demand for agricultural inputs. Increased demand rapidly outpaced local production capacity. By 1871 over 90 percent of Britain's imports by value were foods and NFAs. While the share of foods and NFAs declined to about 80 percent by 1913, the absolute value grew from £234 million to £436 (Mitchell and Deane, 1962: 298–301). Specific commodities linked to leading sectors experienced exponential growth in demand, rising more rapidly than population. In 1759 Britain consumed about 1000 tons of raw cotton per year, enough to make one shirt for every Briton. By 1787 Britain consumed roughly 10 000 tons. Demand doubled every twelve years in the early 1800s, reaching nearly 1 million tons in 1913. Demand for wool, after mechanization of production in the 1830s, also doubled about every thirteen years, from 4400 tons in 1820 to 214 000 tons in 1913. By 1900 Britain imported 80 percent of its wool consumption (Mitchell, 1992). Demand for wood (to produce machinery), for leather (to bind machinery and connect it to rotary power sources), and for tallow (to grease machines) rose similarly. In the 1890s expansion of the electrical industries and of bicycling caused a similar explosion in rubber imports.

Like its machines, the industrial revolution's growing urban proletariat also had to be fed. Despite massive emigration, Britain's population quadrupled from 10.2 million people in 1801 to 37 million in 1901. Local food production increasingly lagged behind demand, forcing Britain to import vast quantities of food. By 1900 Britain imported 84 percent of its wheat, 37 percent of its beef and 47 percent of its mutton, and 53 percent of its dairy and poultry (Peet, 1969: 297). About 17 percent of Britain's caloric needs came from sugar, virtually all of which was imported, and roughly 60 percent of its total calories were imported (Mintz, 1985: 113). As northwest Europe industrialized, it increasingly consumed like Britain. Continental Europe's population (excluding Russia) also doubled in the 1800s, creating rings south and eastward from Europe. By 1914 Germany imported about one-fifth of its calories, concentrated mostly in meats and fats (Offer, 1989: 25, 81). Expanding urban demand caused a 50 percent expansion in world crop production from 1840 to 1880, of which half was in North America and Australia. World wheat acreage experienced even greater expansion: from 1885 to 1929 it grew 78 percent, with virtually all of this growth occurring outside Western Europe (Friedmann, 1978: 546).

Increased demand for agricultural raw materials and food created Thünen-style agrizones on a global scale, with industrial Britain/Europe becoming a gigantic Thünen town surrounded by a plethora of roughly concentric production zones. At the beginning of the 1800s, Britain imported only about 10 percent of its consumption of temperate agricultural products. Britain's supply zones essentially ended in Ireland (for grain). Nontemperate products came from the most distant semitropical US South (cotton) and the West Indies (sugar), but with water transport these areas were 'closer' than their distance in miles might indicate. The European economies were largely self-sufficient, excepting sugar and cotton. As Britain's population grew, it drew first on Holland, Denmark, and Prussia for grain. But industrialization in northwestern Europe increased total demand, causing Britain to import grain from the Ukraine, the United States, and eventually Argentina. By 1900 the growing population and diminishing local supply capacity of the British and European economies had pushed these production rings outward as far as Australasia. (Figures 5.1 and 5.2 show the changing origins and volumes of British wheat

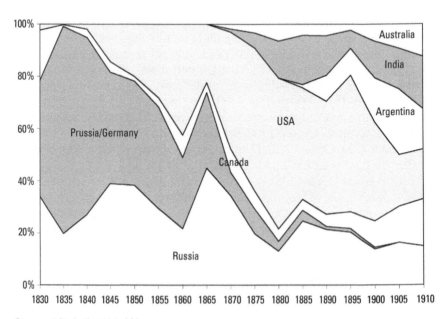

Source: Mitchell (1988: 229).

Figure 5.1 *British wheat imports by source, 1830–1913*

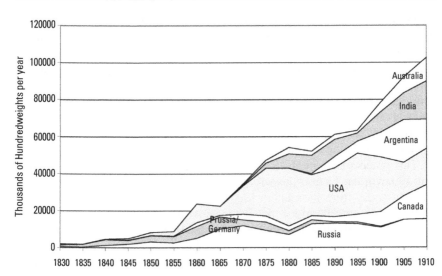

Source: Mitchell (1988: 229).

Figure 5.2 *Volume of British wheat imports by source, 1830–1913*

imports.) In the 1830s, Britain imported negligible quantities of fruit, vegetables, and live animals – all products of the innermost rings. By 1900 these imports traveled an average distance of 1880 miles to London. Similarly, wool and hides, products of the outermost ring, traveled an average distance of 2330 miles in 1830 but 10 900 by 1910 (see Table 5.1) (Peet, 1969: 295, 297).

This global playing out of the Thünen model caused enormous ecological changes around the globe, for only a few of the foods and raw materials grown for Britain and, later, Europe naturally occurred in the areas Europeans came to control. Even where they occurred naturally, their geographic range was

Table 5.1 *Expansion of agricultural production rings around Britain, 1831–1909, selected years[a]*

	1831–5	*1856–60*	*1871–5*	*1891–5*	*1909*
Ring 1 Fruit and vegetables	0	324	535	1150	1880
Ring 2 Butter, cheese, eggs	262	530	1340	1610	3120
Live animals	0	630	870	3530	4500
Ring 3 Feed grains	860	2030	2430	3240	4830
Flax, linseed	1520	3250	2770	4080	3900
Ring 4 Wheat and flour	2430	2170	4200	5250	5950
Ring 5 Meat and tallow	2000	2900	3740	5050	6250
Wool and hides	2330	8830	10 000	11 010	10 900
Weighted average	1820	3650	4300	5050	5880

Note: [a] Average distance traveled by agricultural imports in miles.

Source: Based on data from Peet (1969: 295).

fairly limited. We tend to perceive places like Australia, Malaya, Brazil, or Iowa as having a natural comparative advantage, but the ecology in virtually all of today's agricultural areas with obvious comparative advantage was in fact conquered and transformed by transplanted animals, weeds, pests, predators, and pathogens. In the temperate zones of the Americas (Argentina, Chile, Uruguay, the Rio Grande do Sol region of Brazil, the United States, and Canada) and some of its tropics (the Caribbean littoral and most of Brazil), in Australasia, and in southern Africa, European incursions quickly eliminated the local population, thus also eliminating local sources of labor.

This process also involved a great swap of plants and animals by the new and old worlds. In exchange for the potato and maize (corn), Europeans brought sugar from the eastern Mediterranean to the West Indies; released cattle, sheep, and horses in the Pampas, Australasia, and temperate North America; sowed wheat everywhere; and deforested enormous swaths of the Americas and Australasia (Crosby, 1986). Europeans also deliberately transplanted species in order to create new supply areas, particularly in the tropics and Southern Hemisphere. For example Brazil, the source of rubber, became a coffee producer, while the British made Malaya into a rubber plantation. American plants also transformed Asia, with corn (maize), potatoes, sweet potatoes, and peanuts becoming widespread in China and Japan.

The constantly changing production profile of these areas also reveals how artificial the notion of natural comparative advantage is. Comparative advantage changed as population growth in the European town turned former outlying zones into inner zones, making it profitable, rational, and necessary to produce higher-value-added goods. These shifts involved enormous changes in established production practices and thus the demand for labor. Changes in Irish agriculture clearly show this process. Ireland's proximity to industrial Britain meant that every Thünen zone passed through its geographic space as Britain's population grew between 1600 and 1900. Ireland shows the expansion of Thünen rings without bringing in the problem of labor supply and state-building, which will be discussed later. The Irish case allows us to isolate – relatively speaking – more purely economic processes so that we can later introduce the effects of explicitly political processes.

Zonal shifts in Irish agriculture

Ireland originally stood outside the frontier of the stock-raising ring but ended up as an inner zone of Britain's economy. As transportation links improved and as Britain's population grew, pushing agrizones offshore, Irish agricultural production processes, population, and exports changed. Each transportation improvement and increase in British demand brought Ireland one ring closer in to the English town, changing production and increasing the value-added per acre. The Irish story thus reflects a complex interplay between market opportunities and local action.

English colonization did not begin in earnest until the 1600s. Until then,

Ireland had supplied very small amounts of money rent, wood, and iron for England. At that time, Ireland was over the frontier from the point of view of the English economy. It could only supply goods with either extremely low transportation costs (e.g., money) or quasi-luxuries. Because England was deforested, both wood and iron (a disguised export of wood via the consumption of charcoal) could be profitably exported. Because Ireland exported wood products to England, trade left unchanged the peasantry's basic diet, which consisted largely of oats, milk, and beef (providing peasants had managed to keep English colonists from stealing their cattle).

During the seventeenth century, all this changed as London's population grew. Ireland became part of the outermost grazing ring, supplying range-fed cattle to England. Cattle exports, averaging 60 000 head in the mid-1600s, accounted for 75 percent of Irish exports (Peet, 1972: 5). Meat began to disappear from the peasantry's diet at this point, and the specter of a year-round Lent ignited a rural Catholic rebellion. Oliver Cromwell restored English rule, driving the population down to 900 000 by slaughtering thousands of Irish and exporting others as slaves to British sugar and tobacco plantations in the Caribbean. With order restored, Anglo-Irish landlords expanded their production of low-quality beef to the point where they posed a competitive challenge for English producers. Consequently, in a response later imitated in Europe, the English closed their market to nonmainland producers, including their Anglo-Irish kin, in 1666. This action diverted Irish beef exports, as salt beef, to the Royal Navy and to the West Indian colonies.

From 1700 on, the number of cattle increased rapidly as these markets grew. The Irish peasantry found its diet shifting from oats to potatoes as 'cattle ate men' in the Irish version of the enclosures. Landlords pushed peasants off oat-producing land and onto wastelands so that the landlords could graze their cattle on former oat fields. Peasants unsuccessfully resisted this displacement, and those arrested were again shipped off to the West Indies to eat salt beef and make sugar and tobacco. The rest converted former wastelands to potato fields. As in Europe's urban-centered microeconomies, the introduction of the potato permitted the compression of the population. The potato's higher calorific yield per acre allowed the peasantry to subsist on a smaller area while freeing up land for other uses. The population increased slowly, reaching 1.7 million by 1739. At that point, potatoes constituted half of local food consumption, and virtually all meat was exported.

The British population doubled during the 1700s and Britain became a consistent net grain importer by the end of the century. Politics and location made Ireland the major supplier of these grain imports, and grain soon displaced beef as Ireland's major export. Foster's Corn Law in 1784 and the British Corn Laws (1815–1846) helped increase the area tilled for grain sixfold from 1784 to 1805. Grain acreage peaked at 301 000 hectares in 1847. In the 1780s Ireland had been a marginal net exporter of grain; by the 1800s it exported ten times more grain than it imported and provided half of British grain imports. Where low-quality cattle had displaced peasants in the 1700s, grain now displaced both in the early 1800s.

Rising grain exports presented Anglo-Irish landlords with a dilemma. In order to grow more grain, they had to push cattle and peasants off the land, but to harvest that grain they needed more seasonal labor. Landlords resolved the dilemma by compressing the peasantry's smallholdings, forcing them into an increasing, almost exclusive reliance on the potato. These displacements provoked a century-long guerrilla war against landlords. About 1 million Protestant cottagers began migrating to the North American colonies. Despite rising emigration, the population rose from 5.4 million in 1805 to nearly 8 million by the 1840s. So Irish grain exports and potato production rose steadily in tandem.

The interaction between rising grain production and rising potato consumption on a shrinking area reached its natural limits in the 1840s during the Famine. Although the potato blight (1845–49) triggered the Famine, the population was already debilitated and any further increase in grain production would have created a demographic catastrophe. Roughly 1 million peasants starved while grain exports to England increased. Another 4.3 million people emigrated between 1851 and 1918. Why were landlords indifferent to this sudden shrinkage in their labor force?

The doubling of the British population in the early 1800s had pushed its agricultural supply zones outward once again, creating both a threat and an opportunity for Anglo-Irish landlords. The repeal of the Corn Law in 1846 confronted Irish producers with world market competition from Prussia, Denmark, and Russia, which had more extensive acreage and cheaper, more docile labor. However, by 1846 Ireland was positioned to export higher-quality live cattle for fresh slaughter and fresh cream, so landlords switched from wheat production to these goods. This shift caused the landlords' harvest labor requirements to drop so precipitously that emigration slightly outpaced the rate of natural increase. Meanwhile, grain acreage fell from its 1847 peak of 301 000 hectares to 60 000 hectares in 1880, while cattle increased from 1.9 million in 1841 to 3.8 million by 1870.

This outcome had been foreshadowed in 1824 with the first regular steamship connection to Britain. This induced Protestant colonists in Northern Ireland and some farmers around Dublin to export eggs and butter. The landlords' continuous conversion of production from wheat to cattle grazing during 1848–1914 eliminated thousands of Irish smallholders, provoking Ireland's last, longest, and greatest rebellion against the English, as well as continued migration. Roughly six million Irish emigrated, 1848–1950. Irish agriculture still sits in the innermost ring, supplying fresh meat and dairy goods for Britain, but with a family farmer-based agriculture that reflects the diminishing power of Anglo-Irish landlords.

Agricultural production zones and the problem of labor

European industrialization re-created Ireland's experience around the world, as agricultural production rings rippled outward, but with one key difference:

the best places for production of temperate agricultural goods lacked an existing population to serve as a labor force, and the second-best places lacked a willing labor force. The absence of labor slowed the transformation of available agricultural land into supply zones for Europe. Although the industrial revolution triggered enormous population movements, prior to 1800 few people moved overseas voluntarily. Of an estimated 9 million to 15 million transatlantic migrants before 1800, fewer than 10 percent were free. Most of the unfree were slaves from Africa, but prisoners and indentured servants also flowed to the US east coast, New France, and, eventually, Australia. Only about 20 percent of indentured servants lived to see the end of their term of bound labor (Wolf, 1986: 202).

Most Europeans still lived in microeconomies, where their direct access to land gave them a secure existence. Getting to the Americas, and later Australasia, required an enormous amount of money and also had huge social and emotional costs. Most voluntary migrants were religious fanatics, suggesting that the economic motivation to migrate was fairly small before 1800.

Only about 1 million to 2 million Europeans voluntarily migrated to the Americas before 1800. Even that minimal number did not create much of a labor force. Many dropped out of the labor market voluntarily. They crossed the frontier and went native, intermarrying with indigenous peoples and melting into the countryside. They and their descendants served as intermediaries between surviving indigenous peoples and the markets for some of the goods those people hunted and gathered. Métis in Québec/Canada, gauchos in the Argentine/Uruguayan Pampas, llaneros in Colombia, vaqueros in northern Mexico, griqua in southern Africa, cossacks in the eastern Ukraine, all facilitated a trade in beaver, hides, jerked meat, and the like (Denoon, 1983). Yet these people did not constitute a stable, disciplined workforce capable of producing the consistent, continuous, and sizeable flow of raw materials England's industry demanded. Moreover, because weapons were an essential part of their means of production, these intermediary populations also undercut any local state's monopoly of violence and thus its stability and ability to enforce property rights.

After 1800 coerced labor played a declining but still significant role, particularly for non-Europeans. Most of the roughly 50 million European migrants during the nineteenth century went voluntarily, that is, not as indentured servants. In contrast, most of the 50 million Asian migrants went as indentured labor and an additional 3 million Africans as slaves. Because labor represented the great limiting factor to agricultural transformation, most production in the New World and Asia relied on some form of involuntary labor: slaves, indentured servants, convicts, or peasant production compelled by imperial authority. Why was there a labor shortage, why use coerced labor, and why did coercion give way to nominally free labor later in the 1800s?

Frontiers, workers, and coercion

A political economy of violence answers these questions. It was relatively expensive to subdue native populations and states in areas with high-density populations as compared with Europe. But until states could reliably enforce European-style property rights over land in areas with lower population densities, it was cheaper to use coerced labor than it was to pay free labor to migrate. We can see this by comparing what it costs to draw people out of subsistence production and into the market economy under conditions of high and low land-to-labor ratios (Lewis, 1954; Thünen, 1966). These two situations correspond to frontier areas and to 'Ireland,' understanding Ireland as a region with a densely settled population. Like Thünen, let's assume the existence of an active, commercialized economy centered on an urban area. The high cost of transportation to the town from beyond the frontier makes production for the urban market uneconomical. Only subsistence production will take place in the transfrontier area. What wage do commercial farmers have to pay to induce someone to cross the frontier and voluntarily take up paid employment?

In the extreme high land-to-labor situation, workers can simply migrate over the frontier and establish a self-sufficient existence on the free land just outside the outermost production ring. In order for a commercial farmer inside the frontier to pull workers back into the system of agrizones, the farmer must offer those transfrontier workers a wage greater than the implied value of production possible on their own subsistence farm. The availability of open land makes that wage very high.

In the extreme low land-to-labor situation, high population density means we can assume there is no open land over the frontier. Instead, absolute overpopulation characterizes the subsistence sector. Because there are too many workers relative to available land, the marginal productivity of labor in the subsistence sector is so low that any subtraction from the labor supply does not decrease production in the subsistence sector. Here the wage needed to induce someone out of subsistence production into the capitalist economy still equals the implied value of subsistence production, but that implied value is quite low, since the last worker essentially produces nothing.

Both models assume that the actors they describe are pure economic beings for whom a positive wage differential suffices to impel greater effort. In the language of economics, they assume forward-leaning labor curves. Suppose, however, that those actors have backward-leaning labor curves. Then higher wages lead to fewer hours of work. Actors simply maintain their desired level of consumption by working fewer but better-paid hours. In a frontier situation, only extremely high wages would induce transfrontier labor to participate in labor markets inside the frontier. And even in the low land-to-labor, 'Irish' situation, even moderately high wages might not induce labor market participation. Peasants might be happy producing just enough to feed themselves and buy goods they cannot produce locally. Why work harder?

Would-be agricultural capitalists thus faced a dilemma. Empty places, places without a rooted peasantry, landlords, and a state, were the cheapest places for production. There, capitalists did not have to pay rent to a nobility that had locked up most land; there, capitalists did not have to worry about provoking violent resistance from settled peasant communities; and there, capitalists did not have to replace existing states with one of their own. As it happened, most of the empty places were in temperate climate zones in the Americas, Australasia, and southern Africa suited for the bulk of the foods and NFAs that Europeans devoured. They were empty because the local population either died out or was killed off. But open frontiers in those empty lands meant that labor could simply disappear over the frontier and take land. Inducing them back into the labor market was quite expensive. Owners thus had to use bound labor to prevent their workforce from walking over the frontier. Things were not much better in the tropics. In most cases even the great tropical agricultural supply zones came into being in relatively empty areas because settled peasants resisted change. The great tea plantations of Assam and Ceylon, the rubber plantations of Malaya, the coffee plantations of Africa, the rice farms of the Mekong Delta, and the palm and coconut oil plantations everywhere started in relatively empty lands with imported workers.

In full places, with their high population density, would-be capitalists had access to labor. But they faced the considerable political, social, and police costs of controlling the peasantry and acquiring land. Squeezing peasants out of the subsistence economy was difficult and expensive, as Ireland shows. Economically it only made sense in Ireland because the far larger British economy bore the tax costs of subduing periodic peasant uprisings and policing quite high daily levels of violence. Most of the areas with settled populations that did engage in extensive commerce had been doing so for hundreds of years. Peasants were already responsive to market or landlord pressures to boost production. But those landlords were unwilling to simply move out of the way just because Europeans wanted them to do so. Moreover, few of these areas before the 1800s really approximated the extreme low land-to-labor situation. Ireland was one of the few, and even there, mass migration did not begin until after 300 years of steady population growth and compression of the area available to the peasantry. In most places, peasants did not have to rely on the market for their survival, and wage work generally was discretionary. Colonial governments often had to go to extreme lengths to force peasants into the market (see, e.g., Arrighi, 1970).

Consequently the market selected in favor of would-be producers who went to empty places and who were willing to use coercion to supply those places with labor. Over time, however, as frontier states became strong enough to police their transfrontier areas and keep workers from crossing the frontier, and as populations filled in those empty areas, it became possible to relax coercion and shift to a wage labor system. At the same time, the use of violence – colonial authorities' tax and land tenure policies – in settled areas, especially tropical Asia and Africa, made them more closely resemble the 'Irish,' low land-to-labor case. This then induced an outward flow of migrants at wages low enough to permit would-be farmers to profitably employ that labor.

We will consider these transitions by looking at increasingly complicated cases. The Caribbean began as an open frontier, using slave labor to produce sugar. Once the islands were (re-)populated the frontier became the water's edge, and slavery gave way to a situation more closely resembling European serfdom. Australia and Argentina began as open frontiers, using coerced (prisoner) labor to grow wool. Once the state was able to close the frontier by enforcing property rights over land, coerced labor gave way to voluntary migration and more effective wage labor. In tropical Asia British colonial policy in India created a low land-to-labor frontier in which parts of India served as subsistence zones in relation to commercial production located inside and outside India.

Markets alone could not constitute labor supplies in the agricultural production zones Europe's growing industry needed. Instead, states used violence to constitute labor forces until markets could generate both labor and land (as commodities). Slavery and disguised forms of slavery like convict labor and indentured servitude characterized all the new production areas feeding Europe. But all in all slavery was a last-resort kind of labor, carrying high purchase and supervision costs. Would-be producers used it mainly because of the utter insufficiency of any other kind of labor.

Slavery as a last-resort labor supply: Caribbean sugar

Because slavery was very expensive, slaves were used almost exclusively to produce high-profit agricultural commodities in capitalist economies. Only highly productive agricultures growing very valuable crops could afford it for long periods of time. In the Americas, slavery is associated with sugar, a mildly addictive food; tobacco, a highly addictive drug; and cotton, the raw material for the industrial revolution's leading sector. High demand in Europe for these assured high prices. Sugar is the most interesting of these crops, because slavery and sugar have been linked from the eastern Mediterranean in the 1200s to Cuban manumission in 1886.

Sugar is valuable as a crop because of its high productivity in terms of calories created per acre. One acre of subtropical land under sugar yields about 8 million calories; to produce the same amount with potatoes requires four acres, with wheat nine to 12 acres, and with beef about 135 acres (Mintz, 1985: 190–1). Its high productivity made it profitable to pay for the kidnapping of humans and their shipment, with extraordinary wastage, to distant areas. There was nothing unusual about the use of slavery in sugar production. The Venetians had been using Slavs as slaves to make sugar on Mediterranean islands ever since the Crusades. Portugal itself already had a large slave population acquired during the reconquest of Iberia from the Muslims. For the Portuguese, Africa was a convenient source of bodies. It already had an established, though small, slave trade. The introduction of American crops like the potato and corn (maize) facilitated the expansion of African slavery by helping to double the West and Central African populations (despite slaving) from 1500 to 1800 (Wolf, 1986: 240). Hence, the peculiar aspect of modern slavery was not its existence, but its scale.

The Portuguese landed in Madeira in 1402, in the Azores in 1430, and in Sao Tomé (off present-day Cameroon) in 1470. Disease, slaughter, and

Portuguese efforts to use them as slaves killed off the indigenous population on these islands. Emigration from Portugal itself was very low, totaling perhaps 40 000 people in the 1500s and 1600s combined. This barely provided a minimal administrative and military presence for a Portuguese empire stretching from Brazil to Malacca. Thus the Portuguese resorted to slavery to man (almost literally) their sugar plantations. The Portuguese experience with slaves on islands near Africa naturally led them to repeat this scenario in Brazil after 1520. From 1450 to 1600, Portuguese sugar planters in Brazil and Dutch, French, and English imitators in the West Indies bought about 275 000 African slaves. As the imitators caught up with and surpassed the Portuguese, the flow of slaves from Africa increased rapidly. From 1600 to 1700 about 1.3 million slaves were sent to the greater West Indies. During the 1700s demand for sugar and then tobacco boomed. British North America and the British and French sugar islands split another 6 million or so slaves. Finally, despite British efforts to stamp out the slave trade after 1807, Cuban and Brazilian sugar and coffee production absorbed another 2 million slaves until 1870 (Wolf, 1986: 200–1; Zolberg, 1987).

The Dutch, French, and British established sugar production with slaves in a two-stage process. First, each set up the slave-sugar system on a small island, respectively, Curaçao, Martinique, and Barbados. These small islands served as test beds for plantation systems that were deployed on a larger scale after 1750. When improved transportation made it possible to exploit part of the interior of the larger Caribbean islands, they shifted production, respectively, to Surinam, Haiti (then known as St Domingue), and Jamaica.

On each island, slavery evolved away from a pure slavery into a situation resembling that of Eastern European serfdom. Eventually, after manumission, indentured labor replaced slaves. Dale Tomich's (1990: 271–8) fine-grained study of Martinique details this transition nicely (see also Vilar, 1976: 112–44). Labor demand in sugar production varied considerably over the course of a year. Harvesting and processing had to be done quickly and required massive amounts of labor. Sowing and routine maintenance required much less labor. Plantation owners permitted their slaves to work their own gardens, thus freeing themselves from feeding their slaves during off-peak periods. Over time and with considerable struggle, the slaves' rights to both free time and land increased. By the 1800s masters had to pay slaves when they wanted to absorb slaves' plots into cane production, and slaves could inherit plots. So slaves essentially had property rights in their plots. Increased property rights and built-in free time meant that masters could in effect extract a labor rent of only 5 to 5.5 days per week for their land, much like the Polish landlords in the 1500s. Hence, slaves had become serfs.

Manumission (or, in Haiti's case, revolution) simply changed this *de facto* status to a *de jure* status, reinforcing this situation of quasi-serfdom. Despite legal freedom, most ex-slaves continued to work on plantations as part-time, part-year workers, who now truly had to fend for themselves in the off season. Manumission threw all ex-slaves into the nascent subsistence economy on the periphery of the plantation. While plantation owners still needed labor, they could buy labor in discrete amounts that corresponded to their need for labor.

From the point of view of ex-masters, this situation worked best on the smaller islands. The smaller islands had no frontier between cultivated and wild land; the ocean stopped slave-serfs from running away. On the larger islands and continental coastal areas like Surinam, however, the availability of unused but arable land in the interior made it possible for some ex-slaves simply to walk across the frontier and create a subsistence life, often joining existing communities of runaway slaves. In Jamaica, for example, ex-slaves walked up the mountainside, grew dreadlocks and ganja, and glared red-eyed at labor recruiters coming up from the coastal plantations. They were useless as a labor force for the plantations, but their presence made it possible for plantation owners to import *non-slave* labor for the first time.

Manumission made it physically possible to use indentured labor, because it closed the frontier on the larger West Indian islands and the Caribbean littoral. With ex-slaves covering all the transfrontier land available for subsistence, incoming indentured workers had no option but to continue working for wages once they arrived. With successive waves of voluntary and involuntary migrants to the area unable to escape over the frontier, slavery yielded to this cheaper and more elastic form of workforce. The sources of this new indentured labor force will be examined in the section on tropical Asia.

'Covert' slavery? Wakefieldism in the temperate colonies

European transformation of the tropics generally gets more attention than its transformation of temperate zones. However, the temperate zones were more important than the tropics in terms of global investment flows and the supply of agricultural raw materials, particularly during Europe's nineteenth-century industrial revolution. European settlements in temperate areas also began as open frontiers, and production started with various forms of involuntary labor: indentured servants and convicts in North America, convicts in Australia, slaves and forced labor in Latin America's southern cone. As in the West Indies sugar zones, these coerced labor regimes gave way to open labor markets. What explains the transition? Australia and Argentina are the most interesting examples.

Like early America, Australia enjoyed little voluntarily migration at first. When the American Revolution closed off their usual dumping ground, the British started shipping convicts to Botany Bay. The convict labor regime initially passed through a period in which production was clubbed out of the labor force, as in tropical slavery. Like the tropics, this shifted to a less malign regime in which owners conceded considerable autonomy to their convict workforce in order to increase production. With the rise of sheep grazing for wool, the prison administration (that is, the state) began to rent convicts to graziers (sheep raisers) for use as shepherds. The difference between this and West Indian slavery was at best a matter of two degrees: ownership rested in the state, not in individuals, and in principle convicts were freed once they had served their term. Otherwise, workers were essentially chattels.

Argentina also relied on slave and coerced labor in the early 1800s. The various areas that became Argentina utilized overt African slavery well into the middle of the 1800s, with Africans constituting up to one-third of the population by some estimates. After independence, the state (such as it was – Argentina's great misfortune was perhaps not to have been run from London) in Buenos Aires imposed a system of coerced labor. Workers without papers could be automatically impressed into the army.

The mechanization of wool textile manufacturing in the 1830s created intense demands for wool which rapidly outran Europe's own supply capacity. Western Europe's internal raw wool production peaked in the mid-1800s at around 200 000 tons. By 1895, however, British production alone consumed almost that amount. From 1840 to 1860 demand doubled. Rising prices spurred Australian and Argentine producers to increase output, but they found that convict and impressed workers did not make good shepherds. Argentine landowners began importing Irish shepherds displaced by British cattle; Australian graziers began political agitation to end shipments of convicts (Lynch, 1981; McMichael, 1984). However, both were still living on an open frontier. How could they be sure that immigrants and freed labor would not walk away?

Edward Wakefield, the English advocate of systematic colonization, understood practically the theoretical models outlined above. Ironically, Wakefield worked out the answer while he was in debtors' prison, thinking about how it would be possible to re-create English society in new lands like Australia. English society rested on landownership by the gentry and hard work by the landless laborers they hired. The only way to assure that the right sort of people ended up possessing the land while their social inferiors ended up working for them was for the state to set the price of land so high as to preclude landownership by the many.

This sounds simple enough, but *de jure* state ownership of land did not necessarily convey *de facto* control (Duncan-Baretta and Markoff, 1978). Both would-be escapees from the labor market and would-be sheep graziers challenged state ownership and the state's monopoly of violence. The effort to institute state control and ownership over land sparked conflicts in all the Southern Hemisphere societies between states on the one hand, and both the intermarried and intermediary populations that had emerged from the first waves of migration and the remaining indigenous peoples on the other. Hone Heke's Maori in New Zealand, Ned Kelly in Australia, gauchos and Monteneros in Argentina and the Méti in prairie Canada all asserted local usages and qualified property rights against emerging states (Denoon, 1983). And these groups were all well armed, as weapons were an essential part of their 'means of production.'

In the Australian colonies and New Zealand the state proved strong enough to institute and maintain property rights, suppressing outlaws and more or less enforcing the principle of crown ownership of land by forcing squatters to pay rent. In Argentina the state was weak, almost nonexistent at periods, and so had a harder and more violent time instituting a monopoly of violence and property rights over land. Where the Australian colonies could suppress scattered bushrangers with police actions, and New Zealand's colonies could match borrowed British regulars against the ferocious Maori, the Argentine/Buenos Aires government had to mount its own sustained military campaigns against organized revolts. Argentina thus ended up with a private kind of Wakefieldism where ranchers asserted control over all available land and backed their claim with private armies. Uruguay demonstrates the state's failure to institute its claim to land: gauchos defeated the state's armies, and labor control crumbled in the resulting anarchy until the 1890s. The institution of effective property rights, public or private, succeeded in preventing an overly large leakage of labor across the frontier in the Southern Hemisphere production zones. In turn this permitted Buenos Aires to abolish slavery and the slave trade in 1853, and, beginning in 1851, the Australian colonies began banning transportation of convicts to Australia.

The shift from coerced to free labor in all the new temperate producers helped boost output of foods and NFAs. In turn, increased imports generated a steady stream of European migrants. Competition from the new temperate producers forced many European peasants off the land. Crowding into nearby cities, they depressed wages, and both they and existing urban workers then took off for higher wages and more opportunity in the Southern Hemisphere and the United States. As in Ireland, the largest flows occurred when former labor-intense grain production zones encountered increased competition from grain producers further out, particularly in the Americas. The peaks of migration from the United Kingdom, for example, occurred in the 1840s, 1880s, and 1910s, coinciding with the arrival of grain from the old US Northwest, from the US Midwest, and from Argentina and Canada. Nineteen million people migrated from the greater British Isles during the 1800s. This migration also included many skilled workers attracted to the industrial activity that occurred in conjunction with agricultural production in the US and Australia.

Overall, 40 percent of the natural increase in Europe's population in the nineteenth century migrated, with about 60 percent, or 33 million, of these going to the United States (Brinley, 1973). Put another way, two out of every five surviving babies left Europe permanently. Argentina absorbed 5.4 million immigrants, Canada 4.5 million, Australia 1 million, New Zealand 0.5 million, and South Africa 370 000. With their arrival, local land prices rose to the point where the violent maintenance of land property rights became unnecessary. People had to work for wages. In recognition of that fact, workers in all of these societies agitated for bans on non-European immigration, hoping to slow immigration and thus keep wages high. Why, aside from racism, were they afraid of being swamped by non-Europeans?

Tropical Asia: forcing voluntary migration

European settlers in temperate climates feared Asian immigrants because Asians were also on the move. Although in proportion to total population fewer Asians migrated than Europeans, absolutely the numbers are almost the same. India and China supplied nearly 50 million migrants, most of whom traveled as indentured or quasi-indentured labor, to new and old production zones during the nineteenth century. One million Japanese also migrated as a mixture of free and indentured labor. These indentured Asians replaced or supplemented former African slaves in sugar production in the West Indies and Africa's coastal islands, and supplied labor for emerging tea, rubber, palm oil, and sugar plantations in Asia and the Pacific. Chinese became famers in Thailand, miners in Malaya, cut sugarcane in Cuba, quarried guano in Peru, and in more limited numbers mined, built railroads, cooked, and did all manner of things in Australia and the Pacific coast of North America. Unlike Africans, indentured Asians did not travel as slaves, at least *de jure*, although their *de facto* work conditions and lack of personal freedom at times closely resembled chattel slavery. What explains the *de jure* difference and the motivation for seeking indenture?

Europeans in Asia encountered relatively durable states and societies that were able to resist outright colonization. They also found that they, not the locals, got sick. Most of Europe's diseases originally came from Asia, so the local population had one up on the Europeans. Europeans remained largely (self-)confined to urban enclaves like Hong Kong or Shanghai's Bund. European firms and colonial governments found it difficult to get enough European labor to do anything more than man the top layers of their administrative and military networks. As a result, in Asia European enterprises had to rely on Asian labor, and European armies had to depend on Asian soldiers.

While Asia obviously did not have the kind of open frontier that European diseases created in, for example, the Caribbean, neither did it have an 'Irish' type frontier with truly surplus labor. A few areas aside, precolonial Asia, despite occasional famines, was not overcrowded to the point where the marginal product of the last worker was zero. The initial emergence of new commercial and export-producing zones did attract an inward flow of labor in search of higher wages from neighboring subsistence economies. Twenty million Chinese migrated 'internally' to Manchuria between 1900 and 1930, and several million Javanese migrated to Sumatra and Borneo, all seeking to establish their own farms. But local subsistence peasantries in Asia by and large avoided working on plantations. In Ceylon, the local Sinhalese population had an easy subsistence existence in the lowlands, just as native Malays had in Malaya. Why should a peasant family perform year-round work on a tea or rubber plantation when it could supplement its income by planting a few coffee or rubber trees of its own?

With peasants averse to moving, European colonial governments resorted to nonmarket mechanisms to get Asians to work for planters. Imperial tax policies and laws that encouraged an expansion of commercial production in settled areas had the effect of crowding peasants into smaller and smaller subsistence areas, just as in Ireland (Furnivall, 1956). Commercial agriculture tended to be more capital-intense than the subsistence or older market production it replaced. Workers displaced from these more intensely commercialized agricultures then flooded into newly opened, distant, export production zones elsewhere in search of any possible livelihood. In other words, rather than commercial agriculture drawing in labor from subsistence areas, the emergence of commercial agriculture often crowded workers off the land into subsistence areas and then into other commercial agricultural zones. Colonial governments encouraged Asian entrepreneurs to broker this labor movement. And some Asians used indenture to successfully re-establish themselves elsewhere.

In India, for example, British tax and land policies caused a massive emigration of Tamils from southern India to a variety of new export agricultural areas. The British assigned landownership to individual farmers, or *ryots*, and introduced a fixed land tax. As in Japan, the tax forced peasants to reorient production towards the monetized, commercial economy. As in Japan, weak peasants lost their land to stronger peasants. Unlike Japan, but rather like Ireland, the state did not use tax revenues to industrialize the country. Instead, British colonial policy promoted increased market share for imported textile and household goods. So where landless peasants in Japan became a new urban labor force, in India they either crowded onto the land left over from commercial production or opted to emigrate. China saw similar processes after the British forced the Ch'ing to legalize emigration.

Thousands of newly landless Tamils thus indentured themselves to work in the new rubber plantations in Malaya, in new tea plantations in the relatively empty highlands of Ceylon and Assam (in northeastern India), in new rice plantations in Burma, and in sugar and mining in Natal. Once there, they provided an expanded market for Indian and Burmese rice exports, speeding the reorientation of rice production towards export markets and the process of emigration in an echo of the temperate zone-European agricultural interaction. For example, from 1887 to 1897, 31 200 Tamils per year went to Sri Lanka as tea production tripled. By 1911, 366 000 Tamils constituted 80 percent of all plantation workers, and about 9 percent of Sri Lanka's population (Craig, 1970; Wolf, 1986). On the other side, areas like Malaya saw immigrant inflows at five times the level of Argentina.

Africa was even further from being an 'Irish' frontier, with a low labor-to-land ratio capable of absorbing a rough doubling of population before 1900, and few natural barriers to migration. Thus, even more coercion was applied to motivate wage work. British and French imperial authorities went to extraordinary lengths to generate labor supplies in Africa, replicating the Asian pattern. Imperial authorities had to employ hut and head taxes paid in coin and mandatory production of cash crops to force the local peasantry into the market. Getting wage labor was even more difficult, as the British found in their southern African colony of Rhodesia (Arrighi, 1970). African peasants in the Rhodesia area assimilated European plants and cultivation techniques.

Their ability to assimilate European agricultural technologies enabled them to compete with European farmers as a source of food for mining operations in South Africa proper. It also enabled those peasants who desired to maintain a subsistence existence with limited contact with world markets to do so at relatively high levels of consumption for relatively little effort (in other words, they had a backward-leaning labor supply curve).

In either case, would-be British agricultural employers found themselves at a disadvantage: they could neither engage Africans as workers nor compete with African peasant producers. Settlers first used their state to impose taxes, first in kind and then in cash, on African peasants, hoping that this would drive them into the labor market in search of cash wages. Settlers then turned to a policy of land expropriation, forcing peasants into a serf-like situation in which they offered their new settler landlords labor rents. Land expropriation also diminished the area available for subsistence production, forcing subsistence peasants to shift from direct production and marketing to sale of their labor.

The Rhodesian case shows even more clearly than southern India the degree to which the low land-to-labor 'Irish' situation was as much a creation of politically deployed violence as of market forces. In Africa, European settlers deployed political power to generate a labor force for internal use; in India, the colonial state imposed taxes and intermediaries whose actions then generated and facilitated labor migration; in the Southern Hemisphere, artificially high land prices kept workers inside the frontier. Aside from the postrevolutionary United States, simple market mechanisms rarely motivated migration for participation in a wage labor market. However, once states violently established production, the market became increasingly capable of generating its own labor supplies. The British abolished indenture in India in 1910 and banned immigration of indentured Chinese in 1914, while indenture continued in the Dutch East Indies (Indonesia) through 1945.

The shifting legal status applied to laborers, which arose mostly from differing population levels at the time those laborers came to the places where they worked, shows this clearly. Sugar and tobacco, which were most closely associated with slavery, took root at a point in time when population in the Americas was at its nadir. Extant slave systems in turn were extended to cotton production once settlers cleared Native Americans out of the southeastern United States. Slavery everywhere mutated into a kind of serfdom, with rents paid in labor or in kind (for example, via sharecropping in post-Civil War America). Indenture flourished at a later date. In Asia, empty places tended to be surrounded by full places, blocking the escape route for indentured labor. Plantation owners could therefore use foreign indentured labor for tea, rubber, and vegetable oil production. These workers could not cross the frontier in the same way that manumitted slaves had on the larger Caribbean islands and the Caribbean coasts.

The industrial revolution thus created a demand for agricultural products that the market could not at first satisfy. States and settlers in the periphery had to deploy organized violence and start production with noncapitalist labor forms. But the production of agricultural exports and of a labor force for those agricultural exports grew synergistically. The more temperate agricultural exports that Europe absorbed, the more Europeans became available for work in new production zones; in the tropics, the more that traditional production was commercialized, exposed to market competition, and driven to expand output, the more some workers there were displaced and made available for work in new production zones elsewhere. Did this mean that states became irrelevant and markets became self-sustaining? Not at all. As the next chapter shows, states had to intervene in other ways to constitute, maintain, and transform production in Ricardian export zones. The differential success of those Ricardian exporters rested in large measure on the differential abilities of their states to weather the periodic crises of transformation caused by the continued emergence of new competitors resulting from the continued expansion of demand from industrial Europe and later the industrial United States.

Chapter 6

Agriculture-Led Growth and Crisis in the Periphery

Ricardian Success, Ricardian Failure

> It is quite as important to the happiness of mankind that our enjoyment should be increased by the better distribution of labour, by each country producing those commodities for which, by its situation, its climate, and its other natural or artificial advantages, it is adapted, and by thus exchanging them for the commodities of other countries, as that they should be augmented by a rise in the rate of profits.
>
> *David Ricardo*

Ricardo's two sources of happiness are synergistic. Britain's industrial revolution and successful Kaldorian late industrialization in parts of Europe, the United States, and Asia both relied on Ricardian development elsewhere and made it possible. The cyclic expansion of industrial country output engendered similarly sized expansion in peripheral agricultural production. States violently created new production zones in successive waves, inducing the massive waves of involuntary and voluntary migration seen in Chapter 5. But as we argued in Chapter 2, the opportunity to produce agricultural goods for an industrial core did not guarantee exports or development. Value produced per acre was necessarily low out in the periphery. Furthermore, while trade flows were complementary and fairly stable, the investment flows that accompanied them were not.

This chapter examines Ricardian development strategies at two levels. First, at the unit level, looking internally at the periphery, it asks how some peripheral areas used Ricardian strategies to develop in order to answer why some did relatively better. Different state policies created different outcomes in the periphery as peripheral states responded to their common Gerschenkronian and Kaldorian collective action problems, and needed to generate the same rapid increases in output necessary to get Verdoorn effects. Second, at the system level, it asks what consequences Ricardian development had for the global economy and how Ricardian developers interacted with each other. As in industrial Europe, relative success for some developers meant failure for others. Moreover, individually rational investment decisions in specific Ricardian developers proved collectively irrational, as rapid increases in any one region's exports collectively turned into overproduction and drove down prices. In turn this invalidated prior investment decisions based on the expectation of continued high prices. Because borrowed foreign capital financed most Ricardian development, this crowding out generated a series of global financial and/or debt crises. Even though Ricardian exporters could generate large volumes of exports, these did not generate revenues sufficient to service foreign debts. This dynamic also played out for manufactured Ricardian exports in the late twentieth century. While this chapter concentrates on the nineteenth-century debt crises, and Chapter 11 on the late twentieth-century ones, I will be calling out parallels as I go along.

Successful Ricardian development depended on state intervention to position an exporter advantageously in world markets and to reduce the peripheralizing effects of market pressures. In other words Ricardian developers faced the same Gerschenkronian and Kaldorian problems late industrializers faced. Ricardian states outdid late industrializers' states in their interventions, because states creating agricultural export systems not only had to direct investment into productive activity, but also create a labor force from scratch. In the European settlements in the Southern Hemisphere and in North America the state organized inward flows of labor and capital, while constructing both society and economy. These states controlled a fairly high proportion of investment, deploying as much as one-quarter to one-half of all investment at different times during the nineteenth century. These proportions equal or exceed those in the twentieth century's late industrializers.

This investment, primarily in rail systems and other social overhead capital, enabled private producers to generate massive exports of agricultural and other primary products. The greater the volume of exports flowing back through *imported* railroad systems, the lower the fiscal stress Ricardian states felt, and the less likely it was they would default on their overseas loans. Capital markets recognized this and rewarded successful states with lower interest rates (Flandreau and Zumer, 2004). At the same time, easily glutted product markets punished all Ricardian agricultural developers with falling prices for their exports, creating common periods of crisis in the 1850s, 1890s, 1920s and 1980s. These states then tried to reorient their economies around new Ricardian exports. The centrality of state policy shows why externally imposed colonial states could easily hamper development, but also why those same well-institutionalized colonial states often did better at organizing short-term economic booms compared to legally independent states.

Putting aside the question of relative state competence, all Ricardian developers faced an extra, significant limitation that was not present in Kaldorian strategies. Raw material exports can create a dynamic, growing industrial economy, contrary to arguments that they create insurmountable obstacles (Innis, 1930; Lewis, 1978; Berend and Ranki, 1982). However, both food and nonfood agricultural (NFA) exports were vulnerable to the phenomenon expressed by Ernst Engel's law: as income rises, the proportion of income spent directly on food and fibers declines. This phenomenon led to 'boom and bust' cycles in Ricardian developers. Booming demand for a particular export led many countries (and individual producers) to borrow money to initiate production; production volumes soared; the market saturated; prices fell; borrowers suddenly found themselves illiquid or insolvent. Paradoxically, falling prices did not stimulate increased consumption in industrial areas;

instead, consumers diverted their extra income into higher-quality foodstuffs and other new goods. This pushed production outward, creating new competitors in export markets.

Successful long-term development for Ricardian developers thus rested on their ability to shift from one commodity to another, higher-value-added commodity when the first commodity experienced price declines. Alternatively, they had to be able to use the local demand for industrial inputs created by temporarily booming agricultural exports to create local industry. Most Ricardian developers managed the first, but only the United States, Australia, Canada, Sweden and perhaps Denmark managed both of these in the nineteenth century. Most lived through a series of boom and bust cycles until the Depression of the 1930s, when a second set of Ricardian developers tried to shift to Kaldorian industrialization strategies (Reynolds, 1985).

Colonial governments imposed an additional barrier to Ricardian development. Colonial governments are blamed – correctly – for deliberately hindering industrialization during their tenure. However, industrialization did occur in Asia, because, as we saw in Chapter 4, market segmentation prevented European firms from penetrating local markets. Successful Japanese industrialization and competition hindered Indian industrialization as much as British imperial authorities' connivance with British exporters. Colonial governments hindered future development in a more significant way when they deliberately created low land-to-labor areas in order to create a supply of labor for the European agricultural enterprises that were absorbing open land. The oversupply of labor depressed wages and thus inhibited investment across the economy. Why substitute expensive capital for cheap labor?

Ricardian developers' profound reliance on foreign capital to fund investment compounded their inherent internal difficulties in generating development and growth. The majority of nineteenth-century overseas investment went to agricultural and mineral exporters. All investment is inherently risky, but this investment carried two additional risks. First, virtually all borrowing was done in hard currency, usually pounds sterling. But many borrowers did not have hard domestic currencies. Their ability to service their debt thus rested on their ability to generate an export surplus roughly equivalent to their interest payments, or on the ability to continue to attract foreign capital inflows. Second, borrowers typically contracted loans at rates which made sense given the high prices present at the beginning of a boom. Yet, as the Lewis raw materials cycle (Chapter 3) ran its course, raw materials markets saturated and high prices gave way to low prices, making loans difficult if not impossible to service.

This chapter concentrates on Ricardian development in temperate agriculture, comparing Australia, Argentina, and the US Midwest to show how a Ricardian strategy could lead to industrialization. It will stint tropical agriculture for two reasons. First, temperate agriculture was far more important for the world economy during the long nineteenth century. Second, even in the relatively favorable terrain of the temperate zones, where states were at least nominally independent, demand for exports rose rapidly, and wages were high, industrialization using a Ricardian strategy proved difficult. If few states succeeded under favorable conditions, it should not be surprising that areas with unfavorable conditions failed. As with late industrialization, failure was the norm and success unusual. Then the chapter turns to the global, financial side of Ricardian development, showing how Ricardian strategies tended to be fratricidal.

Temperate agriculture and Ricardian development

The most important agricultural exporters of the nineteenth century were the European settler colonies of North America, the Southern Hemisphere temperate zone, and Siberia, followed by Asia's three great rice export zones. Brevity and analytic clarity suggest calling these the new agricultural countries (NACs), a designation that runs parallel with the label newly industrializing countries (NICs). The problems of agricultural development run parallel to those of industrial development. Second, the World Bank uses the label NAC for poor countries that shifted from 'traditional' agro-exports to new kinds of agro-exports in the 1980s and 1990s (see Chapter 12). This shift is precisely analogous in causes and outcomes to the shifts occurring in the nineteenth-century NACs.

Four temperate zone NACs became self-governing British Dominions: three North American colonies (confederated as Canada in 1867 and incorporating all of British North America by 1949), six Australian colonies (federated in 1901), New Zealand, and four southern African colonies (federated as the Union of South Africa in 1910). The NACs also include the Latin American southern cone, which wars sorted into Uruguay, Argentina, Chile and Brazil's Rio Grande do Sul province. These were called informal dominions because their economic and social ties to Britain were as close as those of the formal Dominions but without, of course, the political tie (Denoon, 1983; Platt and Di Tella, 1985). The American Midwest constituted a dominion over which Britain and the US East Coast contested. Finally Siberia was a major source of Russia's wheat exports and of internal dairy 'exports' back to Russia's imperial center. (By this reasoning Manchuria, a frontier zone inside China, could also be considered a NAC, since it was a major source of food exports back to 'mainland' China and, like Siberia, a major recipient of internal migration.)

In tropical Asia, Burma (Myanmar), Thailand and the Mekong Delta (southernmost Vietnam) also resembled the temperate settler colonies. In Burma, for example, immigrant Indians and Chinese servicing the rice export zone around Yangoon composed half the urban population by 1900 and 7 percent of the total population. The rice zone's population, acreage and exports expanded four, seven and twelve times respectively in the last half of the nineteenth century (Mitchell, 2000). Thailand saw a fivefold increase in exports and massive Chinese immigration.

The United States aside, the NACs' economic significance in the nineteenth and, to a lesser extent, twentieth centuries is generally overlooked. The temperate NACs supplied Britain with roughly 40 percent of its imports after 1880, split roughly in half between the United States and the other NACs net of Siberia. This is well out of proportion to the other NAC's population, which all told amounted to only half of France's by 1900. The temperate NACs also disproportionately received British capital exports, accounting for 60 percent of British foreign investment, or 40 percent excluding the United States. Put differently, in 1913, Australia, with a population of just over 4 million, generated more British imports and exports than Imperial India, with a population in excess of 300 million, and owed Britain more money than India. On the import side the six Southern Hemisphere NACs imported 125 000 miles of British-produced rails, and the United States another 125 000. Together, this amounted to roughly Europe's total rail trackage by 1914.

The NAC's qualitative impact on the division of labor is even more important. By making food cheap, US and NAC exports enabled a rapid expansion of the British domestic market and its internal division of labor without a corresponding rise in nominal wages. In 1800 the average British worker family spent 75 percent of its budget on food, half of which went for bread. By 1900 only 33 percent of the budget went for food, and the average diet included considerable quantities of dairy and frozen meat from the NACs. Real wages in Britain rose about 60 percent from 1860 to 1900 because of cheaper imported food. In Asia, the rice NACs had a similar effect on food costs for the indentured labor in the new tin, rubber, and palm oil export zones. I will briefly touch on the most outstanding case of a successful Ricardian strategy, the United States, and then turn to the more typical cases in the NACs and the tropics.

Ricardian growth in the United States

The United States emerged as the most successful Ricardian developer, first, simply, because it was first, and thus commanded advantages similar to those Britain enjoyed from its industrial revolution, and second because the US federal and subnational states also resolved many of the Gerschenkronian and Kaldorian collective action problems producers faced. United States exports of staple foods to the Caribbean sugar islands started as early as the 1600s. In the 1800s, the United States emerged as the major overseas exporter of cotton and later foods to Europe. Because of its high productivity and falling oceanic transport costs, it easily competed with and displaced exports from peasant-based agricultures in Eastern Europe by the 1860s. The only limits to US cotton and food exports ultimately came from US own rising internal consumption and from tariffs imposed by importing states. In this respect, the United States and its apparently endless supply of cheap land played the same role in the nineteenth century that China and its apparently endless supply of cheap labor plays today with manufactured goods exports.

Meanwhile the state(s) intervened to provide many of the collective and private goods needed for export agriculture. The Revolution, the refounding of the United States as a stronger federal state in 1789, and the Civil War all constructed a powerful and durable state apparatus (Bensel, 1990). This state created capital and a labor force simultaneously. As Chapter 4 noted, individual states all intervened to capitalize rail and canal transport in the pre-Civil War period. After the Civil War, the land grant system helped capitalize transcontinental railways, linking the agricultural heartland to export markets. Land grants were a particularly efficacious form of subsidy, because the value of the land the railroads received in part depended on their ability to promote agricultural production in adjacent areas. Railroad firms thus had an interest in maximizing exports, and most US railroads made more money from land sales than from transportation in their formative years. The federal state meanwhile avoided the costs of borrowing abroad, and instead shifted those risks to the private owners of railroads. Land grant railroads proved a superior policy choice compared to the alternatives that appeared in other NACs, like foreign-financed direct state ownership or subsidy of railroad operating costs. These contributed to later debt crises.

The federal state also structured labor markets. It defended slavery in the South (until 1863) while allowing free migration to tip the demographic balance towards free labor markets. Despite the use of slave labor in the southern states, migrants found the United States irresistibly attractive. The Revolution made land somewhat freely available to a flow of European religious and political dissidents; the Civil War-inspired 1862 Homestead Act, which gave farmers 160 acres for free if they cultivated it for five years, magnified this. From 1870 to 1915 the number of farms and farm acreage tripled. US and other NAC food exports then drove European peasants off the land, providing a steady stream of immigrants to the United States and other NACs. Many migrants stayed in cities or peopled Midwestern towns, providing labor for new industries. Finally the US state also upgraded labor by mandating free public primary education.

The state also provided capital for the agricultural sector. In the pre-Civil War cotton South, the subnational states organized a flow of capital to private planters. The states set up quasi-public banks by giving them state bonds. Potential and existing planters could get capital by mortgaging their land to these banks; in return, the banks then gave the planters those bonds. Planters would sell those bonds in the global capital market, receiving British pounds, which they could then use to capitalize up production. When those planters sold cotton overseas, they received pounds and dollars that they could use to pay the bank; the banks used those dollars to repay the state; and the state used those dollars to repay the original British lender. At least, in principle; many planters and a few states defaulted! Default or no, cotton production exploded in the 1800s, rising from 3000 bales in 1790 to 180 000 bales in 1810, to 732 000 bales in 1830, and, finally, to 4.5 million bales in 1860.

Finally, the federal state, through the US Department of Agriculture (USDA) Extension Service, resolved farmers' characteristic Kaldorian collective action problems, which is their inability to generate and disseminate information about production rapidly, and their incentive to pass off inferior grades of grain and meat for better ones. (These problems hindered Argentine grain exporters up until 1914.) The USDA's grading services prevented farmers from cheating, improved the image of US exports in world markets, and motivated farmers to shift towards higher value crops. The 1862 Morrill Act created the great system of land grant colleges. These initially specialized in agricultural R&D, generating a vast amount of technical and scientific information, new seed varieties, new machinery, and marketing information the USDA then helped disseminate. When the growth of cotton output began to level off, corn (maize) and wheat output and exports picked up because of this extensive state support. Corn output doubled from 1870 to 1900; wheat output doubled from 1870 to 1880 and then rose another 20 percent by 1900.

Strong Ricardian success created the local incomes that induced industrialization. Rapidly rising agricultural exports generated incomes that were widely dispersed over many family farms. In turn this created strong demand for industrial inputs and for processing of agricultural outputs that fed into a wide range of industries attached to agriculture. On the output side, for example, from 1850 to 1880 flour milling was the single largest industry by value of product in the United States, the fourth largest by value-added, and generally the highest or second highest in terms of capital intensity, with productivity per unit labor twice that of the US manufacturing average. On the input side, by the 1870s agricultural machinery accounted for 25 percent of US machinery production. Equally important, farm families consumed many generic manufactured metal goods, including items like kettles, pots, plows, stoves, axes, nails, guns, and saws (Page and Walker, 1991). Much the same processes drove Hungarian industrialization before 1914 (Berend and Ranki, 1982).

Despite their small scale, these diverse industries accounted for roughly one-third of US manufacturing output by 1890. Most were made using the efficient 'American system' of standardized production that had developed to supply New England farmers. Transportation investment and agricultural output dynamized each other. The provision of thousands of small simple engines for the steamboats plying the 30 000 miles of navigable rivers and canals in the United States facilitated the adaptation of the American system by heavy industry. Finally the state also helped manufacturing, with tariff protection, quality assurance, export promotion and the violent opening of markets in Latin America and Asia (Becker, 1982). Tariffs shifted incomes from farmers and export markets to emerging US industry, speeding investment and growth. This enabled firms to generate their own solutions to the productivity problems they faced (and which we will discuss in the next chapter).

Ricardian exports in the other temperate NACs

The expanding European demand that pushed wheat production into the United States and Russia also pushed sheep-raising for wool out to the southern hemisphere, replacing the wide variety of idiosyncratic hunting economies based on intermediary populations that Chapter 5 mentioned. Until the 1840s, the NACs were largely economically irrelevant to Europe, which supplied its unmechanized woolens industry from its own hinterlands, like Scotland, Spain and Central Europe. Consequently, they remained relatively underpopulated. As late as 1825 the nonindigenous population of Australia was around 70 000. In contrast, Barbados, a small island, had a European population of 10 000 as early as 1700. As in the tropics, coerced labor (except for New Zealand) represented a last-resort choice for these uneconomic imperial outposts given their highly permeable frontiers and high land-to-labor ratios.

Two developments changed this. First, the reorientation of Europe's peripheral agriculture to the British town forced its own peripheral wool growers to shift to finer, higher-value wools. This change opened a space for the NACs to supply coarser wool. Second, wool textile production was mechanized in the 1830s. With rising demand, producers and potential producers in the NACs found themselves unable to expand production as much as they would have liked. Potential wool producers lacked labor for the reasons discussed in Chapter 5. They also lacked capital in two senses. On the one hand, they personally lacked the capital necessary to expand production by buying more sheep, setting up homesteads, and shearing sheds, and to carry them through the growing season until they could harvest their wool and get paid for it. On the other, their raw colonial societies lacked even the most rudimentary infrastructure, including the infrastructural *sine qua non*, transportation. Where European planters in Asia confronted an enormous but unusable pool of labor, would-be graziers in the NACs confronted an enormous but unusable landscape. Price signals alone could not induce capital and labor to migrate to the NACs. Instead, NAC states had to create themselves in order to resolve the Gerschenkronian problems hindering expanded wool and hide production.

In the ideal response, states abolished coerced labor but closed the frontier so as to herd migrants into the labor market. States used their own credit to borrow overseas capital for infrastructure investment. This infrastructure investment, primarily in rail systems, opened new land for productive exploitation and also provided employment for new migrants. Sale of this new land allowed states to amortize their debts and to sponsor more immigrants to work on newly opened land. Rising demand for land and the infusion of foreign capital also permitted existing or speculative landowners to capture large capital gains from selling their landholdings. These landholders and speculators constituted a powerful social group pressing for further integration with the British economy – they were the domestic face of British hegemony. Ideally, this process created a self-sustaining cycle in which foreign investment funded railroads, which opened new land, which attracted new migrants, whose imports of consumer and capital goods provided the state with customs revenue to service its debts, thus sustaining the state's creditworthiness and allowing speculators to pressure it to borrow more money for yet more railroads. First, however, there had to be states.

In each country the political struggles of the 1850s and 1860s revolved around efforts to create new states or expand existing state structures and activities that could provide Gerschenkronian collective goods. The core structures of these states mirrored those in Europe. In the 1850s and 1860s agricultural exporters tried to establish consistent and centralized fiscal apparatuses and to assure internal order by monopolizing the means of violence. NAC states' behavior is understandable. All of these states were instrumental states that strove to maximize the private good of the graziers who controlled them (Denoon, 1983). In these extremely small societies, government and economic elites almost completely overlapped, either in one person or through extended families. Rising land values conveyed huge capital gains on these landowners.

Britain's passage of the Australian Colonies Government Act in 1850 created a space for the emergence of local constitutions, legislative arrangements, and institutions. Each Australian colony took control over customs and land sale revenue. All began systematically to stamp out bushrangers (small-scale sheep-rustlers living off the land). And all forced sheep graziers to acknowledge crown ownership of land through payment of land rents.

In Argentina, creating a central fiscal and military apparatus took more time. Argentina's longer history of settlement left it with several competing and autonomous centers of power after the overthrow of Spanish rule. One, Uruguay, split off. After export-oriented graziers overthrew the dictator of Buenos Aires province in 1851, a decade-long civil war erupted between the inland provinces and Buenos Aires. The steady convergence of the economic interests of Buenos Aires and the other provinces with access to water transport provided a basis for compromise, because those other provinces also wanted to enter the wool trade. Despite its control over customs revenue, Buenos Aires was never able fully to centralize control over other revenues or fully to establish control over the provincial militias. This makes the significance of being first for the United States clear; it was busy exporting and growing while others were trying to create states.

In the 1850s both Argentine and Australian graziers sought more reliable labor supplies. Once the shift from coerced to free labor discussed in Chapter 5 was complete, both Australia and Argentina subsidized transport costs for British and European migrants. Each averaged over 20 000 immigrants per annum in the 1860s; by the 1880s nearly 100 000 people per annum migrated permanently to Argentina and nearly 40 000 to Australia. One in seven Britons migrated to Australasia; Argentina absorbed 10 percent of European migrants to the Americas. Even so, graziers still had to pay extremely high wages to attract European migrants. These high wages forced graziers and other employers in these societies to search for high-productivity production methods. Paradoxically, this helped attract capital rather than driving it away: high productivity meant higher profits. None the less, the NAC states had to organize a flow of capital just as they organized a flow of labor.

As with labor, the NACs initially faced an absolute shortage of capital.

Unlike late-industrializing Europe, where the creation of new forms of intermediation sufficed to pull existing capital out from under mattresses and into investment in railroads and factories, the NACs needed both new forms of intermediation and the capital itself. They adopted the US model, and imported capital by floating public bonds and private corporate enterprises in Britain; they also created legal structures that facilitated private borrowing. Domestically, an inherent contradiction between the way they raised public debt and facilitated the expansion of private debt brought most NACs into a debt crisis by the 1890s. Put simply, railroad development allowed speculators to cream off gains in land values the state needed to amortize railroad debt. (An external contradiction will be discussed later.)

Each state established a legal context for railroad development and began borrowing abroad for capital to develop railroads. In Australia each individual colony borrowed directly on the London bond market, and built and operated its own rail system. From 1861 to 1890 these rail systems expanded 2.5 times as fast as GDP in general (Butlin, 1972: 16). By 1890 southeastern Australia had 10 500 miles of railroads. Unlike grain, wool could be profitably transported over land about 80 miles.

Argentina opted for a mixed public and private system. As part of the deal cementing an end to the civil war of 1851–62, Buenos Aires agreed to use customs revenue and central government borrowing to subsidize the construction of more private railroads, guaranteeing their profit rates and buying some of their stock shares. The most important was the Central Railroad, connecting inland but sheep-grazing Cordoba with the river port Rosario. The central state also built rail lines in the less economically active interior provinces. By 1900 Argentina had about 10 350 miles of railroad. In both countries the extension of railroads inland opened up millions of acres of land for export-oriented production.

Each state also established a legal regime for private individuals to mortgage land, creating a basis for private credit. In both Australia and Argentina graziers contracted about half of each country's foreign debt. Until the 1850s mortgages on land were not legal in Australasia; the shift to Dominion status enabled local states to legalize mortgaging. Argentina did not really get a mortgage system until the Banco Hypotecario de Buenos Aires was established in 1872. Mortgage finance was not readily available in Uruguay until about 1896.

States loaned their creditworthiness to the private sector to enable overseas borrowing. Argentina imitated the US South. The state loaned its bonds to local banks, which then sold state bonds to overseas investors in order to raise specie that they could use to back their loans to agriculturalists. Landowners then mortgaged their land to those banks, assuming that their increased production and exports would generate enough specie to pay the bank. The bank then repaid the state for its bonds with this specie, and the state could use the specie to buy back its bonds from overseas investors. States went beyond simply creating a legal framework to help capitalize private enterprises in ways that ultimately conflicted with their ability to repay public borrowing.

The extension of railroads created enormous speculative opportunities, because railroad building created a fictitious capital in land. Generally, land has economic value only to the extent that production occurs on it. Access to railroads increased the value of land by increasing the potential value of the production that would be carried out on it. Landowners could then borrow against this increased value.

NAC states tried to capture the increase in land values created by the new transportation networks, and thus earn enough money to pay back the debt they contracted while building or subsidizing railroads in the first place. Generally, however, private actors captured these speculative profits through the contemporary version of insider trading. Either by advance knowledge (typical of Australasia) or simply by appropriation of the land in advance of the state's assertion of ownership (typical of Argentina), private speculators generally captured the increase in land prices. These insiders then sold land to outsiders, typically new migrants. Outsiders paid what they perceived to be a fair market price, based on the stream of income they expected from wool produced on the land they were buying. The states' failure to capture increased land values created a potential fiscal crisis that could and did undermine the entire process of state-led development. Despite this situation, states' success in organizing inflows of capital and labor created classic Gerschenkronian spurts for the NAC wool economies. Sheep flocks and wool exports in each country grew exponentially. In 1813, Australia had 50 000 sheep; by 1850, 16 million; by 1880, 60 million; and by 1895, almost 110 million. Wool exports paralleled this, rising from 28 000 tons in 1860 to 342 000 tons in 1910. Argentina lagged behind slightly, with 250 000 sheep in 1815; 5 million by 1850; and 61 million by 1880.

Leading-sector agribusinesses in the NACs were highly capitalized and highly concentrated enterprises, just like leading sectors in late-industrializing Europe. The NACs saw the first widespread application of the joint stock company to the production of agricultural goods. In both Argentina and Australasia, large landholders and large corporate bodies predominantly owned sheep stations. These enterprises relied on a fully proletarianized but itinerant workforce to shear sheep. This workforce presented a considerable political problem for the state. In Argentina graziers controlled shearers with private armies, vote rigging, and careful mixtures of shearers from different areas. In Australia, workers could vote and by 1890 were capable of mounting a general strike. Finally a few large commercial banks and financial agencies dominated lending to the pastoral sector. These firms were bi- and sometimes multinational in orientation, usually being chartered and capitalized in Britain. In effect, these commercial firms, which aggregated the savings of millions of Britons for use in large-scale overseas enterprises, replicated and anticipated the role played by industrial investment banks in Continental Europe. These fully capitalist enterprises retreated after the common debt crises in the NACs during the 1890s, giving way to less fully capitalist family farming. Were things different in the tropics?

Ricardian exports in the tropics

Ricardian development in the tropical NACs largely proceeded along lines similar to those in the temperate NACs, with one key exception: well-institutionalized states were generally colonial governments hostile to local industrialization; independent states (even if only *de jure*) generally lacked the institutional capacity to promote industrialization above and beyond what the market naturally generated. Colonial states systematically supplied Gerschenkronian collective goods for the agriculture exports they desired. Colonial administrations imposed export crops in several cases (bringing, for example, rubber from Brazil to Malaya and tea from China to India and Ceylon [modern Sri Lanka]). The independent states had difficulties supplying agriculture with Gerschenkronian collective goods. Aside from this, the state played basically the same role it did in the other NACs, establishing a legal regime for private property in land, borrowing overseas to build transportation infrastructure, and ensuring labor supplies. As in the temperate NACs, the better they did these, the greater their competitive advantage relative to other suppliers in the same markets.

As Chapter 5 noted, in much of the tropics labor had to be imported. Even though European diseases did not depopulate Asia as they had the Americas, the political costs of clearing thousands of settled peasants off the land meant that export production often took place in relatively empty areas. There, it was easier for would-be planters (often former colonial administrators or local government officials!) to steal land unhindered. But this in turn meant that planters had to import labor. Railroad construction also proceeded along lines similar to those in the temperate NACs. Colonial or local states floated bonds overseas to finance state-owned networks or to subsidize foreign-owned firms, and these networks directly served new export production zones. They often paid extremely high interest rates on these loans, reflecting creditors' reasonably accurate perceptions of their lack of tax capacity to service loans.

When local states successfully combined capital, labor, and crop, they experienced the same kind of explosive growth in output as the temperate NACs. Overall, tropical exports increased by 270 percent from 1883 to 1913. Brazil's pre-World War I coffee exports doubled five times to peak at 7.8 million tons annually in 1900–10; Colombia's soared from 4080 tons to 132 000 tons from 1878 to 1924; Ceylon's tea exports rose from 1 million pounds to 194 million pounds 1882 to 1914. In each country rising exports induced local industrialization to provide agricultural inputs and process outputs, just as in the temperate NACs. In Colombia, for example, a textiles industry emerged to provide clothing and bags to family farmers producing coffee. Overall manufacturing grew 5 percent per year from 1905 to 1925 and employed 15 percent of the labor force. In British-run Ceylon, where plantations dominated and workers' income was thus lower, manufacturing output only grew 2.8 percent a year and employed only 10 percent of the labor force by 1911 (Craig, 1970).

However, just as with the temperate NACs, tropical exporters also generated their own debt crises. Domestically, their weak fiscal apparatuses could not collect enough revenue to service their debts. Externally, they faced a harsher version of the rising competition and falling price problem all the NACs encountered, because in many cases colonial governments deliberately created intra-imperial sources of supply for tropical products. Brazil's success with coffee stimulated market entry by other producers and states in Latin America, colonial Africa, and colonial Asia. The coffee market became glutted, and prices began dropping around 1900. Brazil defaulted in 1898–1900, and then made only partial debt payments in the next decade. Its major competitor, Colombia, also defaulted for part of that decade. Colonial governments avoided default by simply passing lower world market prices on to their subordinated workforces as lower wages and higher taxes. This, however, impeded local industrialization by slowing domestic market growth.

The failure of Ricardian strategies: the crisis of the 1890s

The crisis of the 1890s was a debt crisis with simultaneously international and domestic causes and ramifications. First we will look at the international aspects, asking why and how money was loaned, and what were the systemic sources for financial crises. Then we will turn to the domestic side of the debt crisis in order to explain the shift from highly modern capitalist production forms to family farms, and the shift both within Ricardian strategies and from Ricardian to Kaldorian strategies. What caused these common crises, and why did they create family farming in all the temperate NACs except Uruguay and Chile? I will also set up the discussion of the emerging markets financial crisis of 1997–8 through some relevant comparisons in the text.

Ricardian debt crises: systemic factors and solutions

Understanding the evolution of the global debt crises of the nineteenth century requires understanding why and how the money was lent, and why it was borrowed. This investment in understanding pays dividends when later chapters look at later financial crises. Nineteenth-century offshore investment was enormous, even by today's standards. Relative to gross world product, those international investment flows dwarf post-World War II flows by a factor of about two to three. The temperate NACs, including the United States, owed about £3.5 billion to European creditors by 1914, or about $355 billion in 2007 dollars. Total European foreign investment by 1913 amounted to about £7.5 billion, or $760 billion. Because the entire world economy then was perhaps only one-tenth of its size today, adding a zero to each number gives a better sense of scale. Between 1873 and 1914 the British invested an average 5 percent of their GDP overseas, enabling Australia, Argentina, Canada, and other nations to finance between 30 and 50 percent of their gross capital

Table 6.1   *Distribution of British foreign investment by area, 1913 (£ million)*

	Value	%	of which Railroads (%)
Europe	219.0	5.8	2.0
US	754.6	20.0	16
Other temperate NACs	1718.0	45.7	12.0
Tropical Empire	478.5	12.7	9.0
Tropical Non-Empire	593.4	15.8	8.0
Other	103.4	2.7	n/a
Total	3763.3	100	47.0

Source: Based on data from Fishlow (1985: 394).

formation from overseas sources. By 1913 British investors' stake in overseas economies equaled half their stake in their own economy (Edelstein, 1982: 22, 27). The French and Germans averaged outflows of 2 percent to 2.5 percent of GDP. By contrast, during the 1920s the United States lent about 1 percent of GDP overseas annually. In the peak years of US direct investment overseas and during the 1970s recycling of petrodollars, outflows rarely breached 1 percent of US GDP. Even in the peak year for Japanese overseas investment, 1987, they lent less than 1 percent of GDP. Naturally this means that today's late-industrializing debtor countries rely much less on foreign capital for investment funds. Few countries used foreign capital for more than 25 percent of capital formation, and then only in peak years. Table 6.1 presents a geographic breakdown of nineteenth-century overseas investment.

Europe, and particularly Britain, lent so much money because *ex ante* returns looked large. As previous chapters noted, the division of labor could expand only as fast as the supply of food and raw materials for urban workers and manufacturing activity. Manufacturing output and its labor force expanded more rapidly than agricultural production through most of the 1800s, raising relative prices and profits for agricultural goods. Few lenders consciously attempted to keep agricultural production in sync with manufacturing growth. However, high agricultural prices made would-be agricultural exporters out in the NACs willing to pay relatively high interest rates to get capital, and lenders quite reasonably invested for the maximum return. These dynamics also created a perpetual tendency towards oversupply and thus a debt crisis (from the point of view of creditors) or a profitability crisis (from the point of view of borrowers) as prices cycled downwards. This same dynamic drove foreign investment in Southeast Asia and China in the 1990s, as firms shifted labor intense production to these low-wage areas.

Differences between the social structures of European agricultural production and NAC production made NAC agricultural production more profitable than European, even after transportation costs. Europe was cluttered with noble landlords and peasants, neither of whom necessarily had to accommodate market forces. Noble landlords inherited their land and thus avoided mortgages; moreover, without the whip of mortgage payments they thus could

Table 6.2 *Global agricultural productivity 1800–1910, unweighted averages[a]*

	1800	*1830*	*1860*	*1880*	*1900*	*1910*
High-productivity agricultural exporters[b]	12.3	13.6	22.1	30.1	38.3	48.4
Industrial Europe[c]	7.5	8.4	11.6	13.7	17.5	20.3
Low-productivity agricultural exporters[d]	4.6	5.1	6.0	6.4	7.5	8.5

Notes:
[a] Millions of direct calories produced per male agricultural worker. Note that these are best-guess estimates.
[b] Argentina, Australia, Canada, Denmark, New Zealand, United States
[c] Belgium, Britain, France, Germany, Netherlands, Sweden, Switzerland
[d] Austria-Hungary, Greece, Norway, Portugal, Romania, Russia, Spain
Source: Based on data from Bairoch (1991: 12).

cream off and consume rents, raising European production costs. Similarly, peasants could avoid market pressures by reverting to subsistence production or sending extra children off to the city or the Americas. With few exceptions, Central and Eastern Europe landlords and peasants ignored market pressures and so continued using archaic production methods on small plots. Thus, European agriculture continued to be a low-productivity agriculture supporting many rural mouths through rents and direct consumption (see Table 6.2). In contrast, the NACs could adopt modern large-scale production methods once coerced labor regimes ended.

Lagging European agricultural productivity produced a highly complementary investment and trade pattern in which European industry spun off some of its profits into high productivity agriculture largely outside Europe, thus lowering its raw materials and food costs, and enabling even higher industrial profits and more investment. Industrial demand for raw materials meanwhile validated the profitability of investment outside Europe. The major exceptions to this pattern are states whose strategic concerns caused them to direct private investors towards their allies. France put about 25 percent of its investment in Russia, its counterweight to Germany. Germany put about 25 percent in Austria-Hungary, Romania, and the Ottoman empire, its corridor of states running southeast to the Mediterranean and supplying it with food and fuels (Feis, 1930: 49–59, 73–80).

Investment occurred in sequential waves to the specific geographic area that seemed the most promising location at that time. Each investment wave swamped each area with capital, enabling the construction of an entire rail network, rather than piecemeal additions. Argentina and the US cotton South caught the first investment wave in the 1820s and 1830s. The United States and Canada caught the second wave, building their first intercontinental railroads in the 1860s and 1870s. Russia, the Ottoman empire, and Egypt also borrowed heavily during this period. Then New Zealand, Australia, Argentina, and southern Africa caught successive waves in the mid-1870s, early 1880s, late 1880s, and 1890s. In the immediate pre-1914 period, South Africa, Argentina, Russia and especially Canada caught the last big wave.

Almost half of all nineteenth-century British investment went directly to railroads, and a further 25 percent went indirectly, through government borrowing, to railroads and other social overhead capital. The remaining 25 percent went to directly productive enterprises. In effect, money never really left Britain – only rails and other physical goods did. Over 70 percent of this lending was in the form of *portfolio* investment, in which lenders do not control the enterprise. Instead, states, local entrepreneurs, and a bevy of bi-national corporations controlled the actual deployment of capital.

Infrastructure investment done as portfolio investment reinforced local actors' gains from collaborating with British global economic hegemony. While overseas investment yielded rates of return well in excess of British domestic investment opportunities, it yielded less than other investment opportunities in the NACs and the United States (Edelstein, 1982: 233–49). Local investors were better positioned to capture those opportunities because of transportation and information barriers facing investors. Thus nineteenth-century investors overwhelmingly chose portfolio investment over direct investment and most investment banks acted as intermediaries and not as principals in investment transactions. This had important consequences for the emergence and resolution of the 1890s debt crisis, so we need to examine why investors chose portfolio investment, even though it yielded lower gains than direct investment might have.

Investors favored portfolio investment because of the limits imposed by organizational techniques, political and prudential preferences for arm's-length transactions, and the structure of nineteenth-century banking. In foreign direct investment (FDI), lenders actually establish or buy a corporation overseas and run it. The modern transnational corporation is the pre-eminent example of FDI (Chapter 11). Successful FDI requires high levels of supervision to generate profits. In portfolio investment, lenders receive their payback as invariable interest on loans or as rents on land and buildings. Portfolio investment thus leaves the detailed, day-to-day management of firms to the borrower. Most British firms did not have the organizational sophistication necessary to supervise overseas ventures on a month-to-month basis, let alone day-to-day.

Britain's overt unwillingness to get militarily embroiled in foreign countries' domestic politics after the 1850s also inhibited direct investment. Direct investments had no guarantee of security from violent or legal forms of expropriation. Portfolio investment in public debt was somewhat safer, but by no means guaranteed. Out of 90 defaults by indebted states in the long nineteenth century, only two resulted in military action, seven in some kind of cession of sovereignty to foreign states, and seven others in a cession of sovereignty to foreign private investors themselves (Suter, 1992: 92–3). Debtors ceded sovereignty by allowing foreign experts to take control of, for example, their customs houses, thus assuring creditors that tax revenue went to service debt first (Flandreau and Zumer, 2004). British investors thus tended to avoid direct investment except in areas of exceptional political stability, such as the United States, or places where British law prevailed, such as the self-governing or directly governed colonies.

More subtly, however, the concentration of investment in government and infrastructure rarely made it necessary for the British to resort to overt or covert pressure on recipient governments. Colonies obviously were subject to imperial vetoes on default. But even in formally sovereign countries and in the partly sovereign, self-governing formal Dominions, formal supervision was largely unnecessary. The largely instrumental states in the NACs wanted to retain their creditworthiness because the landowning class dominating those states needed overseas capital to make money. Land speculation yielded fantastic fortunes and routine production more moderate ones, but both would evaporate if the flow of inward investment dried up. Equally so, Southeast Asians borrowed to speculate in real estate in the hope that continued FDI would generate enough exports to validate their speculation.

The banking structure also inhibited direct investment, particularly by British banks. British commercial banks specialized in short-term lending for trade purposes; they abhorred holding physical property or equities even in Britain. British merchant (that is, investment) banks preferred to act as inter-mediaries in transactions between savers and borrowers. They avoided being direct creditors. Neither commercial nor merchant banks, therefore, wanted direct investment, and when, through either accident or default, they found themselves in possession of real property they disposed of it as quickly as possible. Conversely, the legal infrastructure in many investment areas also deterred direct investment. Setting up limited liability corporations was diffi-cult or impossible. Therefore, even firms that were wholly owned and run in the NACs often incorporated in London and then drew on the London share or bond markets for their capital.

What went wrong?

In 1889 Baring Brothers, one of the largest London investment banks, failed to sell a large issue of Argentine bonds. Shortly afterward, in 1890, the Argentine government defaulted on some of its bonds, driving the value of Barings' holdings to zero, bankrupting Barings, and causing a decade of finan-cial turmoil. From its 1890 peak of about £100 million per year, total British overseas lending collapsed to about £23 million in 1898. Countries that could not or would not default fell into economic depression as net capital inflows shifted to net outflows during this decade. The effect was similar to the collapse of the Thai baht in 1997.

Put simply, individually rational investment and lending decisions created collectively destructive outcomes for borrowers and lenders. Borrowers borrowed and lenders loaned in the expectation that today's prices would continue into the future, permitting borrowers to earn enough money to service their debts and retain enough profits for investment. But because everyone invested in production of essentially similar goods, with fairly low barriers to entry, and because there was a lag between the time borrowed money was invested and the time production began, everyone underestimated the volume of output that would emerge on world markets and thus overestimated the price they could get for their production. For example, the creation of multiple new sources of wool production drove down wool prices. Most export commodities experienced price declines from 1871 to 1895. Textile fiber prices fell 40 percent; grains 34 percent; and sugar, tea and coffee prices 46 percent (Saul, 1985: 14). In the 1990s, Southeast Asian economies experienced a similar 20 percent erosion in unit prices (Kaplinsky, 1999).

Secondarily, because much borrowing was for railroads and other infrastructure, there was a long gestation period between the time the loan was contracted and the time that production actually began. Rail lines did not appear overnight, and building up a large enough pool of livestock also took several animal generations, even when new graziers had access to supplies from older areas. However, payments on new debt began immediately, requiring either continued borrowing or a decrease in discretionary imports. Countries typically borrowed more money to cover their current interest payments, just as many people (unwisely) make only the minimum payment on their credit card. Interest on the initial debt thus was rolled over into the principal of the debt.

In practical terms, countries quite reasonably ran balance-of-payments deficits in order to bring in rails and other equipment, but then shifted to imports of consumer goods when the initial infrastructure investment led to rapid employment growth. Because NAC and colonial states relied so heavily on customs revenues, they often had no choice but to allow continued imports; stopping consumer imports would have simply precipitated an earlier crisis as revenues fell. As we have already noted, governments had difficulty capturing all the gains their investment generated and thus had trouble servicing their debts. Instead, the NACs pushed crises off to the future, hoping that export revenues would catch up with debt service demands for foreign exchange. Southeast Asian and other emerging markets similarly relied on excessive short-term debt. They believed that they could easily refinance this debt, even when it exceeded local foreign exchange reserves.

Consequently virtually all the NACs were in a state of *illiquidity* – that is, they lacked enough cash on hand to meet today's debt payments, but they had every reason to believe that sometime in the near future their new production systems would generate enough cash flow, *would* make them liquid enough, to meet debt payments. Investors, however, were ill-equipped to distinguish between illiquid borrowers and *insolvent* borrowers. Insolvent borrowers would not be able to make their debt payments either today or in the future, because their new production systems were relatively less competitive and so unable to generate enough cash flow, ever. They were bankrupt. When lenders perceived that some borrowers were insolvent, they ceased lending to everyone, driving illiquid borrowers into insolvency when those illiquid borrowers could no longer rollover old debt. Thus what started as individually successful, debt-financed Ricardian development strategies became *collectively* unsuccessful. The investment gamble proved wrong for most borrowers, and thus also for lenders, though not for the banks organizing the flow of investment funds.

Speculators' appropriation of most of the rise in land values deprived NAC states of the revenues they needed to pay back their overseas debt. Without this revenue, NAC states found themselves unable to continue borrowing abroad and thus to continue building railways and other infrastructure. London bankers were aware of the NACs' revenue problems, and began to demand higher interest rates on NAC bonds and to shut some borrowers out of the market. Between the periods 1880–5 and 1890–5, Australian borrowing fell by almost half; by the second period, debt service exceeded new borrowing. Capital flows to Argentina ceased from 1890 to 1895 after Buenos Aires defaulted. Argentina's default simply revealed the underlying structural problem of agricultural oversupply, just as the Thai decision to break the baht's peg against the US dollar revealed overproduction in Asia.

The 1890s debt crisis was resolved fairly painlessly for these banks, because of the structure of intermediation, that is, the financial institutions linking lenders (savers) to borrowers. In the 1800s, investment banks generally facilitated a transfer of funds from savers to debtors but rarely directly held debt themselves. Because debt largely took the form of bonds, default threatened the bondholders and not the investment banks. Bankers made money by taking a cut out of every bond sale. Thus, debtor defaults rarely threatened banks with financial catastrophe, and banks were willing to arrange debt relief and reorganization, bridging loans and new bond flotations as long as debtors tried to get their house in order. Baring's collapse was the exception; it occurred only because Baring had been caught holding Argentine bonds it intended to sell. Generally it was the many widows and orphans, the actual small bondholders, who lost from these defaults. They organized the Corporation of Foreign Bondholders (CFB) to protect their interests, but this protection proved much weaker than that which the International Monetary Fund (IMF) provided for creditors in the 1980s and 1990s financial crises (Flandreau and Zumer, 2004). For their part, banks worked out new bridge loans, partly to save Baring, partly to generate new income from these transactions. British banks underwrote two restructurings for Argentina, allowing it to roll debt over until booming export volumes and prices made it liquid again.

The 1890s crisis was also resolved rather painlessly from a global macroeconomic point of view, because of the complementary nature of economic relationships between debtor and creditor countries that Lewis described (Chapter 3). Debtors exported primary products almost exclusively, while importing manufactured goods. The crisis of the 1890s scared British investors away from foreign investment, reducing lending in the 1890s to three-fifths of its 1880s level. By redirecting their investment into the domestic economy, they caused the British economy to expand. After derisory 8 percent nominal growth over the entire 1880s, British GDP roared ahead with 27 percent growth during the 1890s. Renewed growth restored demand for debtors' exports, driving up primary product prices and enabling debtors to service their debt.

Ricardian debt crises: internal factors and solutions

In the NACs, though, these debt crises were anything but painless. Falling export prices made it difficult for indebted (corporate) individuals and states to carry the fixed burden of the debts they had contracted to finance development. The obvious solution to a fixed-debt burden was to increase productivity and production, shifting to higher-value-added crops with rising demand in Britain. Then a new round of Ricardian development could start. But getting from A to B involved domestic political struggles and often new injections of foreign capital that debt-burdened states had difficulty obtaining. The continued expansion of Europe's industrial population pushed agricultural production zones further out, but did not guarantee that the entire first round of Ricardian exporters would make it into the second round.

The rising interest rates and the reversal of net capital inflows in the 1890s broke the virtuous cycle of NAC growth. Less lending meant fewer new railroads, fewer new railroads meant lower land sales, lower land sales fewer immigrants, fewer immigrants slower customs revenue growth, and slower or lower customs revenue made debt service more problematic. The debt crisis had a private side too. First, speculators had rushed to invest in land over the frontier, expecting continued expansion of the rail net. Their states' fiscal crises prevented railroad building, trapping millions of pounds of speculative investment in overvalued land. Second, declining wool prices meant that even real producers who had bought productive land when wool prices were high now found themselves unable to meet mortgage burdens that had been hypothecated on the basis of high and rising wool prices. Speculator and producer mortgage defaults made banks the owners of millions of acres of land. Banks could not recoup their initial investment by selling this land, because falling wool prices also drove down land prices. (The 2007–9 mortgage crisis had the same dynamic, but you must wait for Chapter 14.) This double debt crisis also triggered efforts by workers to organize economically and politically. Producers' efforts to squeeze out the maximum return from their properties in order to service increasingly burdensome mortgages caused confrontations with their workers. Australasia saw a general strike followed by several smaller but violent strikes in 1890, and Argentina experienced civil disorder in the early 1890s and a series of violent general strikes in the 1900s. Workers' parties emerged in both countries in this period.

How could states, speculators, and banks escape their economic dilemmas? How could states control the new unions and workers' parties? Partly by design, partly by accident, states tried to create a class of small landholders to resolve these difficulties. If extensively produced commodities like wool could not yield enough revenue per acre to support both mortgage payments and the grazier, then perhaps more intensively produced commodities like grains, meat, and dairy would. The very success of prior Ricardian development in flooding Europe with basic grains had pushed urban incomes up to the point where workers there could now afford these foods. However, precisely because these commodities were intensively produced, they were less suited for large corporate enterprises.

Family farms, in contrast, operated on the right scale to produce meat and dairy products, and with machinery could also handle grain production. Family farms were also more resilient than fully capitalist enterprises, which had to pay both wages to workers and profits to their owners (Friedmann, 1978). In contrast, family farms did not accumulate profit or pay wages to family members in the strict sense. They merely survived, at a level they found tolerable, after paying their fixed obligations to creditors and suppliers of inputs. Thus, family farms could ride out periods of economic turbulence and declining prices more easily than corporately organized farms.

NACs trod a variety of different paths to family farming, but in each case people with power made rational decisions that shifted their production profile closer towards that which a Thünen analysis would predict. In Argentina, graziers defaulted on their loans or devalued them through inflation. Free from debt, they upgraded their cattle and sheep populations, breeding for meat, not hides and wool. They hired immigrant Italian families to produce grain on their land, integrating meat and grains in a complex and highly productive rotation. This change is visible in the changing ratio of fatter crossbred animals, which could be used for high-value frozen and chilled beef, to scrawny native cattle, suitable only for low-value jerked and salted meat. In 1895, just after the crisis, the ratio was 1:1, but by 1908 it had risen to 10:1. Grains replaced wool as the major export. Wool composed 58.1 percent of exports in 1880–4, but by 1900–4 was down to 26.5 percent; grains were only 5.2 percent of exports in 1880–4, but by 1900–4, 48.3 percent (Schwartz, 1989).

Australia saw similar changes, but more slowly than in Argentina, because of Australia's inability to default. There, banks foreclosed on graziers and then sold land to family farmers. The state subsidized these sales by advancing low-interest mortgages to would-be farmers. In New Zealand graziers subdivided land among their children, breaking estates up into more manageable units. The state also subsidized the creation of new family farms. Because these new family farms generated greater revenue per acre than wool grazing had, banks could sell off former wool estates at prices high enough to recoup their initial investment. Exports increased 250 percent from 1896 to 1913, with wool falling from 47 percent of the total to only 35 percent, and dairy and meat products rising from 17 to 36 percent (Schwartz, 1989).

The temperate zone NAC's wheat, meat, and dairy products produced a second successful Ricardian boom. All the NAC states supported this shift with a new round of infrastructural investments, borrowing anew to build a second, denser network of railroads and to establish agricultural research centers; things the United States had already done 40 years before. These new farms generated increased exports that saved the state from its own debt crisis. Increased exports meant increased imports, and thus increased customs duties. This allowed the state to renew borrowing and railroad building. Family farming also constituted a circuit breaker between the state and the restive working class in the temperate NACs. These new small property owners evidenced a potential for upward mobility, and also created a solid mass of voters for conservative parties.

This second round of Ricardian success re-created the cycle experienced in the first round of Ricardian success. By the 1920s and 1930s, meat and dairy export markets were glutted, and the NACs as well as the tropical Latin American agricultural exporters experienced a second severe debt crisis (see Chapter 7). The recurrent crises related to Ricardian strategies forced a shift to manufacturing-based economies. The foundation for this shift to manufacturing had already occurred as a natural result of Ricardian-based growth.

From agriculture to industry in Ricardian development

The debt crisis induced a shift from extensive production of wool to relatively more intensive production of grains, dairy, and meat products. It also created an opportunity for the first stages of industrialization in some of the NACs. More farmers meant broader demand for daily necessities, as in the United States. Construction, food processing for local and export markets, and light industry emerged in all the NACs at this time. This agricultural export-led industrialization in light industry occurred across most agricultural exporters. The NACs experienced greater success than either tropical or Eastern European agricultural regions, but much less than the US Midwest. In Southeast Asia the issue has been whether these economies could shift to higher value-added manufacturing in the face of low-wage Chinese competition; most have not.

Grain and dairy exports generated the greatest impulses for industrialization (Berend and Ranki, 1982). First, these goods tended to be produced by family farmers, creating a relatively flat distribution of income that enlarged the local market for light consumer goods. Small industrialists could easily jump into the production of garments, furniture or food processing, especially milling and beer making. All of these had relatively low capital requirements. Second, family farmers relied heavily on machinery. Wheat farmers needed it to compensate for the fixed quantity of labor inside the family, while dairy producers needed cream separators and refrigeration equipment. The larger and more sophisticated the overall economy, the more likely that machinery production would start endogenously. In the smaller agricultural export economies, agricultural machinery production had strong Gerschenkronian aspects. Both Canada and, to a lesser degree, Australia became producers of harvesting and other grain production equipment by virtue of tariff protection for local producers. Australia used this in turn to promote a local steel industry. Argentina, lacking iron ore, coal, and any deliberate industrial promotion policy, achieved industrialization only in a few light consumer goods.

The same pattern can be seen in dairying equipment. Sweden became the world's largest producer and exporter of dairy equipment, partly by accident and partly because its tight links to the vibrant Danish dairy export sector enabled existing machinery producers to capture demand for equipment. Other dairy producers had to compete with first mover Sweden, so a dairy equipment industry emerged in the United States only behind tariff barriers. Outside the United States, industrialization in the Ricardian periphery depended crucially on local social pacts between manufacturers and labor that expanded the potential domestic market. Australia shows this most clearly, because Canadian industrialization was distorted by its proximity to the United States and by the US firms' early multinationalization into Canada. In Australia during the early 1900s, local manufacturers and labor exchanged high regulated wages for tariffs and other forms of protection from outside competition. High wages expanded the market for locally produced products, in turn spurring increased investment and thus increased employment in a primitive kind of Keynesianism. The agricultural sector and foreign consumers bore the cost of this protection and higher wages via a disguised export tax on the agricultural and minerals sector.

These mild Kaldorian industrialization strategies were extremely fragile. They depended on timing: were world markets for agricultural products expanding? They depended on agriculture's ability to invest, increase productivity, and remain competitive despite the imposition of additional costs. And they depended on a low minimum scale for entry to key industries. When Juan Peron tried the same strategy in Argentina in the 1940s and 1950s, none of these things was true. Stagnant agricultural markets reduced the utility of agriculture as an engine for the rest of the economy; draining investment resources from agriculture for industry provoked a drought in agricultural investment and declining production; and the minimum scale for entering key manufacturing sectors probably exceeded Argentina's domestic capacity both to consume output and to generate investment funds at that time.

As with the industrial late developers in Chapter 4, successful Ricardian developers in Europe's agricultural periphery had to provide Gerschenkronian and Kaldorian collective goods for producers. Using borrowed money to provide those goods exposed these states to insolvency when uncoordinated investment in agricultural production inevitably produced a crisis of overproduction. The macroeconomic complementarity between industrial Britain and its raw materials suppliers helped the best positioned Ricardian exporters to grow again. But it did not ameliorate all of the inevitable political tensions these crises produced. In colonial Asia, anti-imperial and nationalist sentiments emerged from the stagnation of real wages in the face of vastly expanded production (Bassino and van der Eng, 2006). In the temperate zones, the destruction of large-scale agricultural firms in some countries during the 1890s debt crisis created a class of family farmers who found it harder to oppose nascent industrialists. As in the United States these industrialists convinced states to use tariffs to subsidize industrial growth. Political tensions with Britain's Ricardian periphery combined with the very real conflicts in Britain's relations with Kaldorian late industrializers in Europe and the United States to erode both these macroeconomic complementarities and British hegemony. The next chapter examines this erosion.

Chapter 7

The Collapse of the Nineteenth-Century Economy

The Erosion of Hegemony?

> The superiority of Prussian enterprise over British lies in good organization; this outweighs many major advantages of the English.
>
> *Werner Siemens*

British decline?

By the end of the nineteenth century, all the institutions of British hegemony were slowly decaying. The major western European states had abandoned free trade during the 1870s and 1880s, insolating themselves from the peripheralizing effects of Britain's market. After 1890, even Britain itself began a slow retreat into its colonial markets as protection in Europe and the United States and declining industrial competitiveness eroded its global market share. Surpluses in imperial markets offset rising British deficits with third parties like Germany and the United States. The slow shift away from Ricardian to Kaldorian strategies in the new agricultural countries (NACs) presaged rising protectionism, to Britain's ultimate loss, in agricultural production zones as well. The international monetary system proved increasingly vulnerable to crisis with the decentering of trade from Britain. Industrialization by Germany and the United States created zones in which the mark and dollar, not the pound sterling, were used for exchange. Britain's share of world import markets also declined relatively in the run-up to 1914, decreasing incentives to cooperate with Britain. Britain's share of world trade fell from its mid-century peak of about 30 percent to 14.1 percent in 1913, while the US share rose from 8.8 to 11.1 percent and Germany's from 9.7 to 12.2 percent. By 1929 the British share had slipped further, to 13.3 percent, despite World War I's detrimental consequences for Germany (Lake, 1988: 31).

British hegemony declined at the bottom – dominance of production – and at the top – dominance of global finance. The British economy continued to enjoy absolute growth. But its productive base declined relative to those of the United States and Germany, compromising Britain's ability to export. Both challengers captured increasing shares of third-party, nonimperial markets, forcing Britain to rely on its empire. From above, Britain's ability to offer access to its own import markets declined, limiting the incentives it could offer for cooperation. Declining export share forced Britain to finance its trade imbalance out of its existing overseas investments. In the past, investment income had been plowed back into more overseas investment, enabling the British to extend their financial control over the major supply regions. Now it only kept the British from losing ground. Finally British control over global financial flows diminished with the rise of central banks or monetary authorities in the major economies. New central banks made it less necessary for countries to park funds in London, and less necessary to rely on the pound sterling for trade. This undercut Britain's ability to engage in a form of arbitrage where Britain borrowed money from debtor countries on a short-term, low-interest rate basis, and then loaned those countries their own money on a long-term, high-interest rate basis.

The erosion of British hegemony was to a degree endogenous to the success of the processes animating British hegemony. British success in creating agricultural supply zones also made cheaper foods and non-food agricultural (NFA) goods available to other countries. British rail exports similarly helped by enlarging late developers' domestic markets and those of neighbors. British competition motivated industrialists in Germany and the United States to create a range of institutional and technological innovations in order to survive. Starting from relatively low levels of output, both experienced substantial increases in output and thus Verdoorn effects, propelling them past British productivity levels. Both also used trade protection to shelter their domestic markets. Politically, Britain's success in creating highly competitive export-oriented agricultural producers overseas exacerbated political pressures for protection. As the extension of rail networks exposed more and more of Europe's microeconomies to world markets, it created a potential for protectionist alliances between European agriculturalists and industrialists.

This chapter first discusses the nature of British hegemony, then shifts to the erosion of British hegemony from below and above, and ends with the disintegration of the nineteenth-century world economy in the interwar period.

British hegemony

Britain's superiority in the manufacture of textiles and railroad-linked goods was the bedrock for its hegemony during the nineteenth century (see Chapter 4). These allowed it to dominate world export markets for manufactured goods and conversely to become a major market for other countries' NFA exports. British hegemony ultimately rested on an import market big enough to induce cooperation and to cause its suppliers to reorganize their production processes in ways that favored Britain (Hirschman, 1980). As British pre-eminence in production decayed, so, too, did the basis for cooperation with Britain's particular ways of organizing world trade.

But Europe's departure from free trade signified the erosion of British hegemony at the margins, not at its core. The core of British hegemony in and over world markets lay in the complementary, market-based relationship between Britain and its raw materials-producing zones, not in Britain's trade with the European continent. Protection on the continent (and in the United States) by itself did not undermine British hegemony or immediately reflect declining hegemony. Rather, successful late development subsequent to protection undermined British hegemony by creating alternative industrial centers whose market pressures created their own agricultural peripheries. These competing Thünen towns threatened, but never displaced, Britain's dominance over its agricultural periphery. Still, the threat was large enough to induce Britain to resort increasingly to political, not market, mechanisms to maintain its dominance. These efforts began with informal preferential tariffs in some colonies and culminated in the Ottawa Agreement of 1932, which set up a formal preferential imperial tariff.

Hegemony arises from the convergence of interests between the specific groups making state policy in the subordinated countries and those making policy in the hegemon, and is solidified in irreversible investment decisions and habits of the mind. Market pressures emanating from the hegemon's industrial zone start this convergence. In the nineteenth century, potential suppliers' desire to cash in on British demand for raw materials established a durable free trade system signaled by a continued reliance on Ricardian strategies. Free trade in this core area survived until most of Britain's suppliers opted for or were forced to choose Kaldorian strategies during and after the Great Depression.

The convergence of interests among Britain and European late developers and the United States was more tenuous. This convergence involved the late developers' desires to gain access to cheap capital goods imports and to finance those imports via exports to Britain and other areas. Britain gained access to markets this way, but never permanent access. Once these late developers could produce capital goods locally, they closed off their markets and began preying on third-party markets in Britain's periphery.

Free trade among complementary economies

Free trade among complementary economies did not pose problems, at least until agricultural exporters began using Kaldorian strategies to develop manufacturing sectors. Agricultural imports allowed Britain to expand its internal division of labor and to become an almost exclusively manufacturing-based economy, at least relative to its European and North American competitors. By 1914 only 8 percent of the labor force remained in agriculture, and after 1870 acreage under cultivation contracted by 30 percent. Agricultural exporters meanwhile used the British market to enrich themselves.

Because the NACs were empty places, they faced low political and economic costs from cooperating with Britain's free trade zone. Britain's access to cheap foods and raw materials leveraged its initial industrial supremacy; the NACs came into being as supply zones precisely because the British industrial behemoth and its import market existed. The NACs' Ricardian strategies, whether locally adopted or inherited from colonial administrations, provided the soil in which British hegemony flourished.

Initially 80 percent of exports from the formal Dominions went to Britain, and virtually all their foreign borrowing came from Britain. The informal dominions, though not legally bound to Britain, show a similar pattern; about half of US exports in the 1850s went to Britain, for example. Exports meant money, and capital inflows meant capital gains for existing property owners.

Britain consolidated its hegemony by offering local elites massive incentives to cooperate with British trade and financial arrangements. Competition among would-be exporters for British capital and for the profits accruing to those using best practice agriculture disciplined those elites, allowing Britain to avoid the costs of overt intervention. Put bluntly, better-behaved states – those that enforced property rights, paid interest, and docilely expanded production – got lower interest rates. Smaller economies, economies with political authorities that were not committed to gold, and economies with weak tax capacity all paid higher interest rates on their public and private debts, reflecting greater uncertainty about repayment. This spread could be enormous: Uruguay, lacking an effective state until the end of the century, highly indebted, and with a fiduciary internal currency, paid interest rates on its public debt almost two-and-a-half times as high as those paid by the British state in 1889. In contrast, the premiums demanded for the Australasian colonies' public debt averaged only one-third over that for British public debt (de Cecco, 1986: 396).

This competition gave Britain access to cheaper raw materials than its competitors. Finally, because the supply zones relied on British capital, Britain obtained a considerable portion of its imports as loan repayments; Britain ran a consistent and growing trade deficit during the nineteenth century. All in all, these relationships were the core of British hegemony and more important than Britain's relationships with European economies.

The emergence and persistence of free trade in the complementary British-dominion economic system needs little explanation. When the British opened their market to agricultural imports, all of the great agricultural exporters reduced their tariffs to revenue levels. Only the United States stands out with an early protectionist tariff, reflecting the political dominance of the late-industrializing areas in the Northeast and parts of the Midwest over agricultural exporters first in the South and then in the Midwest. Those elites created a market rivaling and then surpassing Britain's. Consequently, most US agricultural production went to domestic markets by 1900.

This complementary system eroded under the pressure of US and German export drives, and when agricultural exporters attempted industrialization. Latin America was the most important of the third-party markets not under direct colonial domination. There British exporters lost ground relative to German and US exporters after 1880. Although British exports roughly doubled from 1890 to 1913, German exports tripled, and US exports more than sextupled. By 1913 combined US and German exports to Latin America exceeded Britain's (Platt, 1973: 99–100). Meanwhile, the Germans carved out their own sphere of influence in Central Europe, and German exports largely went to European destinations. Consequently, Britain became less and less important as a market for peripheral agricultural exporters.

While third parties imported less from Britain, they remained disproportionately reliant on British finance. British lending, instead of helping British domestic industry, thus helped US and German industry to expand by lowering their raw material costs and expanding their export markets. This undermined British competitiveness more than did the British investment banks' traditional indifference to long-term lending to British industry. From the point of view of third-party countries, there was still no reason to abandon free trade. To the contrary, they could have their British financial cake while eating higher-quality US and German imports too. And since British exports continued to rise in absolute terms, producers there remained divided over trade protection. In the long run, however, Britain's declining share of exports and imports reduced the incentives for elites in the periphery to cooperate with Britain, while undermining British industrial supremacy.

Free trade among competitive economies

The more difficult question concerns free trade among competitive economies – for example, among Britain, Europe's late industrializers, and the United States. Bilateral treaties reducing tariffs gave way to protectionist tariffs by the 1880s. This suggests but does not prove that the sequencing of late-industrialization efforts determined receptivity to British efforts to promote free trade. The classic bilateral tariff treaty is the 1860 Cobden–Chevalier Treaty between Britain and France, but Louis Napoleon III's unilateral reduction in tariffs on imported iron rails in 1853 anticipated this treaty (Kindleberger, 1975; Nye, 1991). Initially, France could not produce enough iron to supply local demand for rails. Maintaining a tariff would have slowed the expansion of its rail net. Cobden–Chevalier extended the earlier tariff reduction, and gave French exporters access to the much larger British market. French exports of wine and high-quality wool textiles funded imports of capital goods.

Germany presents a similar, but more successful story. In the early 1800s it was a typical supply region. Prussia provided Britain with well over half its grain imports (see Figure 5.1) and other German states about 70 percent of British wool imports. But as Germany industrialized after 1860, it became increasingly like Britain in its raw material needs, and turned Eastern Europe into a major food supply zone despite its low productivity (Offer, 1989). Like France, Germany initially reduced tariffs on imported rails during its first great railroad spree. But it raised tariffs on rails, textiles and other manufactures during the 1870s to promote industrialization and maintain a fiscal base for its military (Weiss and Hobson, 1995). Once domestic output caught up with domestic demand, the need for imported capital goods also evaporated. Instead, pressure built for Germany to export ever larger quantities of goods, as Leo von Caprivi, Chancellor of Germany, 1890–4, noted: 'We must export. Either we export goods or we export men. The home market is no longer adequate' (quoted in Hobson, 1997: 56).

The great depression of the 1870s – so called because it was marked by falling prices and profits despite rising output – created additional pressure for protection. The British drive to export rails and create new agricultural protection zones succeeded in bringing millions of new acres into production. Meanwhile steamships lowered the cost of shipping grain from New York to Liverpool by 80 percent, 1868 to 1902; globally the steam engine cut oceanic freight costs by two-thirds from 1880 to 1900 (O'Rourke and Williamson, 1999: 41). The subsequent flood of cheap imported grain caused falling agricultural prices and rural distress everywhere in Europe. European producers pressured their states for relief, which they received through higher tariffs. French grain tariffs after the 1870s equaled 40 percent of world market prices by the 1880s, and German tariffs 30 percent.

Successful late industrialization also created pressures for protection as overcapacity emerged in basic producer goods like iron and steel. During the 1870s, steel production generally used the Bessemer process. However, its follow-on technologies – the open hearth furnace using electrically powered loading equipment – required a much larger scale of production than the Bessemer process to be profitable. Producers thus sought to assure themselves the greatest possible share of the domestic market. By the 1880s and 1890s, industrialists were able to find agricultural allies for protectionist policies (Gourevitch, 1985). Yet if the British had generated and dominated the new leading sectors, they could have sparked a new round of growth centered on superior manufacturing and restored the political bases for their hegemony. Why did the production bedrock for their hegemony erode?

The erosion of British hegemony from below: production

Ultimately British hegemony eroded because its productive base eroded relative to that of its two main competitors, Germany and the United States. The third Schumpeterian leading-sector cluster (sometimes called the 'second industrial revolution') emerging in the late nineteenth century centered on electricity, chemicals, better steels, and personal transportation in the form of bicycles. British manufacturers had access to and indeed invented some of the hard scientific technologies in this cluster. But they lacked four soft (managerial and organizational) innovations present in US and German industry: professionalization of management; cartelization of industry; electrification of production; and Taylorization of production processes.

The new hard technologies of the 1890s created enormous opportunities for firms to profit from economies of both scale and scope (defined below), if they could successfully create managerial structures and workplace processes to take advantage of those opportunities. German and US firms translated these innovations into higher rates and absolute levels of productivity growth and national income. US labor productivity grew by 2 percent per year from 1890 to 1907 compared to British growth of 0.1 percent; by 1909 US productivity was over two-and-a-half times as high as British productivity in 15 major industries (de Cecco, 1984: 27). From 1870 to 1913, US GDP grew 4.9 percent annually and German GDP 3.9 percent, while Britain's grew only 2.6 percent.

Why did the British miss out on the chemical/electrical cluster? For the most part British firms did try to adopt the new hard technologies and enter new product markets. The key difference is that British firms did so without fundamentally changing their managerial or production structures. Their failure to adopt the new organizational technologies decreased their ability to draw maximum benefit from the hard technologies they did adopt. Broadberry (1998) argues that this failure occurred as much outside manufacturing as it did inside, and that at an economy-wide level, the shift of labor from agriculture to manufacturing helped German and US gain relative to Britain.

Hard technologies and firm structures

Economies of scale come from using the same highly specialized (and expensive) machinery to produce enormous quantities of the same standard product. Spreading the fixed cost of this investment over many units of output lowers the final cost per unit produced. The new process technologies in activities such as food canning and processing, soap and chemical production, steel production, oil refining, and transportation required enormous investment in product-specific production and transportation equipment, such as large tilting furnaces and mechanized feeder systems in metal smelting (Chandler, 1990). These investments were profitable only if plants could run at high levels of capacity utilization and throughput, which allowed their large fixed costs to be spread out over many units of production. If they were run at low capacity utilization or throughput, then per-unit costs were high because each unit had to bear a proportionally greater share of the cost of amortizing a big investment in fixed capital. High-capacity utilization implied relatively continuous usage of the machinery, and thus created pressures for stable sources of inputs and stable ways to market output.

Simultaneously, systematic research and development created possibilities for economies of scope. Economies of scope come from using the same knowledge to produce similar, though not identical, products. Firms with dedicated research and development (R&D) facilities could apply the knowledge they produced to a wide range of goods using similar production processes, like organic chemicals. The first university-industry complexes, forerunners of areas like Silicon Valley, started in Germany's chemical industry and in US agriculture. The German chemical industry combined university brain power with waste products from coal mining to develop a wide range of organic dyes for the textile industry and an even wider range of organic pharmaceuticals, soaps, and fertilizers. By spreading research costs and production knowledge over many products, the Germans drove down costs. By 1913 a typical large chemical firm like Bayer spread its research knowledge over 2000 different marketed dyes. Similarly, the US Department of Agriculture's Extension Service systematically channeled knowledge generated in agricultural colleges to farmers.

The professionalism of management

Only a new kind of firm – the multidivisional firm – could adequately capture these economies of scale and scope. The new US and German multidivisional firms were bigger than, and handled management, marketing, and manufacturing differently from, Britain's family-run firms. Larger firms could more easily make the investment in dedicated production and research facilities needed to capture the new scale and scope economies. In turn, these firms also needed more professionally trained management in order to use these investments efficiently. They needed marketing professionals in order to develop stable consumer markets for high levels of output. They also needed to reorganize manufacturing processes to prevent workers from interfering with the flow of production and the introduction of new production technologies. Professional managers not only replaced the bevy of cousins with imprecise responsibilities found in British firms but also displaced their owner-manager CEOs.

These new firms first emerged in the United States because of the difficulties railroads encountered managing continental-scale operations. The railroads created complex pyramidal structures in which tasks like finance, personnel, purchasing, R&D, operations, and legal matters were centralized into specialized internal divisions, while daily supervision was decentralized to regional offices. Eventually, this format diffused to the entire manufacturing sector in the United States. Banks enforced a similar process in Germany, albeit with initially smaller firms. In the United States, modern corporations also characterized the service sector (Broadberry, 1998).

The cartelization of competition

The amalgamation of many small firms into a few larger firms permitted larger investments in these new technologies. It also increased the risk of over-investment and what the Japanese like to call 'excessive competition' and 'price destruction.' Too many firms flooding the market could drive down prices and eliminate any profit, so producers sought to discourage competitors from creating too much new capacity. They did so through implicit or explicit efforts to create cartels, or trusts. Through cartels (or trusts), firms coordinated their investments, selling prices, and production volumes in order to prevent overcapacity and dangerous levels of competition. The much smaller number of large firms in any given sector made it easier to do this than in older, more fragmented industries.

Cartelization took different legal and financial forms in the United States and Germany. In the United States the passage of the Sherman Anti-Trust Act (1890) made cartels and cartel agreements illegal. In Germany, however, not only were cartels legal, but also cartel agreements were enforceable contracts. Thus, German firms often retained their separate identities inside the cartel structure, while US firms had to merge their organizations into one company in order to avoid prosecution. In the long run, this approach enhanced the US competitive position in world markets in the new industries by forcing a more thorough reorganization of production.

This difference also enhanced German banks' power. In Germany banks typically were larger than firms and used their control over access to capital to persuade recalcitrant owners to participate in cartels. Although later these cartels often gave way to a formal amalgamation of firms, no legal or financial necessity impelled this change. US multidivisional firms developed out of smaller firms. To get around the Sherman Anti-Trust Act, they incorporated themselves as new firms, floating new issues of stock shares to capitalize themselves and make payouts to the owners of the old firms. Most banks were too small to finance these new enormous firms. As a result, banks had less power over these corporations than in Germany.

These cartels took advantage of state policies that protected industry through high tariffs and helped them to maximize scale economies through military purchasing. High tariffs enabled cartels to capture their local market and then use that as a platform for expanding into foreign markets. Cartels dumped production into overseas markets at low prices, accepting short-term losses in order to maximize output and thus spread their fixed costs over the longest possible production run. At the same time, state purchases of armaments helped absorb steel and engineering goods (Hilferding, ([1910] 1981; Kurth, 1979).

By World War I, most of the 200 largest firms in Germany and the United States were multidivisional firms. For example, in the United States firms representing 65 percent of steel production capacity amalgamated into US Steel in 1901. Similarly, in Germany the amalgamation of the electrical machinery industry under AEG and Siemens created firms that, in effect, combined the German equivalents of Western Electric, Westinghouse, General Electric, and the larger public utilities under one corporate roof. In contrast, before World War I, fewer than 10 percent of the 200 largest British firms were of the new multidivisional type (Chandler, 1984).

British firms made hesitant moves towards amalgamation. They organized federations of firms, or cooperatives, in the textile and consumer goods sector but not in producer goods or heavy industry. Cooperatives purchased raw materials and intermediate goods jointly, raised capital jointly through cooperatively owned banks, and sometimes marketed jointly. Yet individual families/firms retained control over production decisions. These families made no effort to coordinate production or to change the scale of production. In textiles, this represented a reasonably successful adaptation to competition from abroad (Lazonick, 1990). In producer goods industries like basic metals, in chemicals, and in machinery, however, this cooperative solution was inadequate. Globally, Britain's two-thirds' share (in 1880–4) of machinery exports from the four leading economies fell to only one-third by 1909–13. More telling, by 1912 General Electric, Westinghouse, and Siemens – US and German firms – controlled two-thirds of the electrical equipment production inside Britain (Ellsworth, 1950: 421–2; Chandler, 1984: 497).

British slowness to adopt new organizational forms led to glaring differences in the production of one of the key goods of the era, steel (Stone, 1974; Lazonick and Williamson, 1979). From 1850 to 1880 the British dominated world iron and steel production, accounting for about half of production and almost three-quarters of world exports. By the 1880s, however, the British had already begun to lose ground to the United States, where the average Bessemer furnace (used mostly for rail production) produced three times as much as the average British furnace. A bigger change came with the shift from Bessemer to open hearth furnaces. Although the British actually adopted the new hard technology somewhat earlier and more thoroughly than did US or German producers, they did so in the context of a relatively stagnant domestic market. Consequently, the British tended to build relatively smaller furnaces than either competitor, attaching them to existing steel mills without changing the organization of work. Total British steel output rose only 3.4 percent per annum from 1890 to 1913, compared with 9 percent growth in US output (Elbaum, 1986: 58).

Meanwhile the United States and Germany continued building railroads at high volumes. Between 1880 and 1914 the United States added over 150 000 miles of track (three times the total British and German trackage combined) to its system, and Germany about 16 000. These extensions permitted US steel firms to build furnaces that were much larger than those in Britain. US and German metals producers thus benefited much more from Verdoorn effects than did the British. Growing demand also permitted the construction of completely new mills, whose layout incorporated new strategies for organizing work processes and new auxiliary technologies for steel making. By 1913 the average US or German open hearth furnace was twice the size of the average British open hearth furnace, and US and German firms had captured around 15 percent of the British domestic market for steel (Chandler, 1990: 491).

The electrification of production

German and US metal smelting firms built larger-scale production facilities because this enabled them to use electrically driven machinery for loading ore into the furnace and unloading molten metal, and thus attain higher throughput. This passed Verdoorn effects on to the electrical goods industry, spurring its growth. Again, British electrical goods firms had to sell to a slow-growing metals industry whose scale of production did not justify such machinery. Electrification of production overcame many of the limitations inherent in steam-powered machinery, as well as being much more productive than hand methods for loading and unloading furnaces.

Bulky and immobile steam engines had to be placed in close proximity to production sites. These engines delivered motive power via multiple leather belts looped around a large rotating shaft in the ceiling of the factory. This made it difficult to deliver precise amounts of power to individual machines. It also made it difficult to rearrange machinery on the shop floor in order to change the flow of materials or introduce new production methods. Electrically driven machinery overcame these problems. Fractional amounts of metered power could be applied to specific machines, making it possible to machine metals more cheaply and to finer tolerances. This precision was critical for making interchangeable parts. Electrically powered cranes, tilting furnaces, and roller belts in the steel industry replaced human-powered charging and draining of the furnace, as well as the transport of hot raw steel, allowing bigger furnaces to run continuously.

Because British firms tended to be family owned, they could not afford to shut down what often was their only furnace to reorganize production around the new technologies, while their larger US and German competitors could selectively shut down works for reorganization. If their sales had been falling absolutely, British family firms might have risked shutting down to reorganize. Because the absolute level of sales continued to rise slowly, and continued to be fragmented over a large and diverse number of steel shapes, British firms had fewer incentives to make such costly and risky investments.

The Taylorization of work processes

Electrification only boosted productivity if work processes could also be changed to take maximum advantage of electrical machinery. Work processes had to be 'Taylorized': management needed to reduce or remove workers' ability to control the flow of materials and the pace of work in order to make electrification profitable. Existing work processes in the steel and related industries gave workers considerable control over output levels. Workers in mining and steel production were paid piece rates based on the volume of output and world market prices per ton. Skilled workers in the steel industry and shift bosses in mining acted as subcontractors, promising to produce a certain volume of output for the mine/mill owner, and then hiring enough unskilled workers to turn out the contracted amount. Until the advent of open hearth furnaces and electrification, owners accepted this system because it minimized their risks; workers shared in gains and losses when prices rose or fell because wages were linked to world market prices. This system blocked full utilization of electrical machinery and newer, larger furnaces. Skilled workers (master contractors) had no desire to increase their workload, and owners could not really use wages to induce more work since wages were linked to world market prices. Skilled workers' control introduced bottlenecks in what was potentially a high-volume production system.

Just as their fragmented and stagnant market deterred British metal firms from introducing electrical machinery, it also deterred an attack on the existing system of labor relations. As individual owners, British mill owners could not compensate for lost output at their mill by increasing production at someone else's mill. At the same time, long institutionalized arbitration boards kept the labor peace, but they also perpetuated the system of tonnage-based wages.

The reverse was true for US and German mill owners. They faced a rapidly growing and absolutely large market and so had huge incentives for trying to destroy impediments on the use of electrical machinery. Cartelization in the United States and Germany facilitated coordinated lockouts of workers. Owners also found allies in unskilled workers, whose wages and job security were limited by the subcontracting system. US and German owners attacked unions with abandon. Krupp led the way in Germany, combining an extensive welfare system (which Bismarck imitated nationally) with equally extensive police surveillance to pre-empt unionization. In 1892 Andrew Carnegie locked out the skilled steelworkers' union at his Homestead steel mill. Within two years, the skilled steelworkers' union was destroyed, and mill owners began introducing electrically driven trolleys, casters, cranes, and mixers, creating a form of continuous casting. The price of American steel dropped by two-thirds over the decade, and the elimination of many jobs made possible a 50 percent rise in wages as productivity rose by 300 percent. Unskilled workers benefited most from this hike in wages.

Although British mill owners adopted parts of the new technologies, they did not adopt the managerial and work practice changes associated with it. What occurred (or did not occur) in steel more or less occurred everywhere else in the British economy. The British did not quite miss the boat on the new cluster of leading sectors, but they sailed dinghies while the competition used cigarette boats.

Conclusion: decline from below

British firms' reluctance to innovate both reflected and reinforced their market situation. Experiencing and expecting slow growth, they resisted investment in new, high-productivity machinery, new ways of organizing work processes, and new approaches to organizing their firms. In contrast, US and German firms made self-validating investments in the new technologies. US steel production doubled every 10 years in the 1880s and 1890s, and then doubled every five years in the 1900s as electric machinery and Taylorism swept the industry. By that point, total US iron and steel production was four times British output. German iron output doubled roughly every 15 years from 1870 to 1914, and steel output every seven years. Rapid increases in output led to rapid increases in productivity; rising productivity meant lower prices; lower prices meant increasing demand; and increasing demand meant higher output. Table 7.1 shows the differences in new investment and output clearly.

Once US and German firms squeezed the British out of their respective domestic markets, they used profits from sales there to subsidize exports into the large and lucrative British market as well as third-party markets. Britain imported US-produced sewing machines, agricultural machinery, bootmaking machines, light machine tools, and processed foods, and German-produced steel products, electrical goods, specialized machine tools, and quality chemicals. By producing for both domestic and export markets, US and German firms were able to run at full capacity. Their size in turn dissuaded competitors from challenging their control of their market. Firms like Singer, for example,

Table 7.1 *Investment and growth in the three leading economies, 1870s–1914*

1. Net domestic capital formation as a percentage of net domestic product					
Britain		*Germany*		*United States*	
1875–1894	6.8	1871–1890	11.4	1869–1888	13.9
1895–1914	7.7	1891–1913	15.0	1889–1913	12.9

2. Annual percentage increase in manufacturing output per capita			
	Britain	*Germany*	*United States*
1881/85–1896/1900	0.9	3.9	2.1
1896/1900–1911/13	0.7	2.5	3.2

Source: Based on data from Saul (1960: 39–41).

controlled about 80 percent of world sewing machine production and, along with a host of other US firms, were able to transnationalize into the British market, pre-empting competitors.

The failure to innovate thus affected global market shares in manufacturing (Table 7.2). Britain provided 26.3 percent of US imports in 1899, compared to Germany's 18.7 percent. Although the British share rose slightly to 26.5 percent in 1913, Germany leaped ahead of Britain to supply 30.7 percent of US imports. Similarly, the US share of Germany's imports jumped from 12 to 21 percent in the same period, while the British share declined from 15 to 8.1 percent (de Cecco, 1984: 27). Meanwhile, the United States and Germany were Britain's two largest sources for imports, particularly for machinery, chemicals, processed foods, and some kinds of metals. Britain's ability to export goods from the new leading sectors waned as the United States and Germany muscled out its domestic producers. In turn, this reinforced Britain's dependence on relatively unsophisticated colonial markets to balance its trade accounts. Selling to unsophisticated customers does not force producers to upgrade production, and apparently this strategy helped erode British industry's competitive position (Lazonick, 1990).

Table 7.2 *Share of world exports of manufacturing by Britain, Germany, Japan, and the United States, various dates, %*

	1881	*1899*	*1913*	*1929*	*1973*	*1987*
Britain	43.0	34.5	31.8	23.9	9.1	7.3
Germany	16.0	16.6	19.9	15.5	22.3	19.3
Japan	0.0	1.6	2.5	4.1	13.1	16.3
United States	6.0	12.1	13.7	21.7	15.1	12.6

Source: Based on data from Broadberry (1994: 294).

The erosion of British hegemony from above: international trade and finance

The declining British trade presence

Britain's trade and finance relations with its periphery reflected the erosion of British hegemony from below. The United States and Germany began to force Britain out of third-party noncolonial markets and construct counterhegemonies in Latin America and Central Europe. Both used credit and investment to prise open markets and create zones in which the dollar and the reichsmark rivaled sterling, shifting trade towards themselves. By 1914, the mark was used more widely in Europe as a reserve currency than sterling. Consequently the British increasingly relied on their enormous and politically created trade surpluses with India and a few other colonies to offset their trade deficits with Germany and the United States; both of those countries ran deficits with India. In 1910, for example, Britain's £60 million surplus with India offset a £50 million deficit with the United States.

Having failed to launch its boat on the tide of new hard and soft innovations associated with the chemicals/electricity cluster, Britain lost way in global export markets. More and more, Britain had to use its investment income to cover its trade deficits; more and more, investment went overseas because of a relative lack of industrial demand for investment funds at home. In the long run, this situation diminished Britain's ability to consume other people's exports. British productive weaknesses eroded the foundations for cooperation.

This erosion of British hegemony was just that, however – an erosion. Although the United States and Germany had surpassed the British in specific sectors, neither as yet had the kind of overwhelming productivity advantage needed to displace Britain. The German economy still had lower overall productivity than Britain, reflecting the protection of an obsolete agricultural sector. Only Germany's larger population gave it a larger market overall. Although the United States had both higher overall productivity and a larger population, it was still a net debtor in the pre-World War I period. The British meanwhile retreated into their domination of global finance to maintain their hegemony (Arrighi, 1994). How did this work?

British hegemony and international finance

The international monetary system is usually considered in abstract terms, but this treatment has the effect of disconnecting the monetary tail from the investment and production dog. The monetary system is not just a means for making exchange easier. Today, as in the late 1800s, the monetary system reflects two variables: domestic political arrangements and the scale of international investment. Abstractly, international money exists to make nonbilateral, nonbarter transactions possible, particularly those that are discontinuous in time and thus impossible without some form of credit. Like the domestic monetary supply, an efficiently functioning international money should provide a source of liquidity that grows in tandem with the growth of transactions and the economy in general. If it does not, then either inflation or deflation can occur, both of which are destabilizing. The key attraction of monetary systems based on gold (and other precious metals) is also their key problem: the global supply of money cannot be increased through policy decisions. This makes metallic money, as well as systems of paper money tightly connected to a metallic base, immune to inflation. However, metallic money risks deflation for this same reason – it cannot be expanded to stabilize continuously falling prices.

From 1870 to 1914, the fact that the gold standard worked owed more to a large and growing supply of credit instruments, including stocks and bonds, than to any expansion in the supply of metallic money. Increased credit money accounted for 90 percent of the expansion of the global supply of bank reserves from 1816 to 1914 (Triffin, 1964: 2–20). In turn this expanding supply of credit money rested on London's privileged position in international trade and finance, and on Britain's exploitation of that position. The classic description of how the gold standard actually functioned better describes how international money functioned before 1850, while descriptions of the early post-World War II gold–dollar standard provide better explanations for the period 1850–1914. How was the gold standard supposed to work?

In the classic understanding of the gold standard system, precious metals served as the basis for both international and domestic money. Banks, including the primitive central or official banks of the time, bought and sold gold or silver at fixed rates, exchanging bank notes for metallic money, and creating new notes only when their gold reserves expanded. If a country imported more goods by value than it exported, a net outflow of specie occurred in one of two ways. First, domestic purchasers could remit specie directly to sellers to pay for imports. Second, as foreigners redeemed bills of exchange and bank notes taken as payment for their exports, banks would have to remit gold to foreigners. This drain of specie money would cause bank reserves to fall, making banks call in loans and their bank notes (paper money). In turn, this situation would cause deflation – a fall in the price of goods in local currency terms – making imports more expensive and exports cheaper. The flow of specie would then reverse itself as the change in relative prices made imports decline and exports grow. The converse was also true: successful exporters would experience rising prices as their metallic money supply grew, which in turn would price their exports out of other countries' markets but make imports cheaper, causing an outward flow of specie.

This system seemingly eliminates all the perplexing and political problems of international trade. As long as national currencies are not debased, their exchange relationship to gold gives them fixed exchange rates versus other gold-backed currencies. Similarly, the fungibility of domestic and international money means that balance-of-payments disequilibria automatically equilibrate through flows of gold. As long as all banks play by the rules and do not prevent gold flows, replace gold currency with paper money, or debase the currency, everything should work automatically (aside from time-lags).

This system is actually a better description of the period before 1850, which is to say before the Bank of England was given a monopoly of paper currency issue in 1844, and before the transatlantic telegraph cables linking New York and London in 1851 combined with the explosion of British overseas lending after 1860 to create a unified transatlantic asset market. By the late 1800s, verbal acknowledgment of the gold standard's rules accompanied constant disobedience of them (de Cecco, 1984: 1–20; Eichengreen, 1985). Central banks in England, France, and Prussia seem to have intervened freely to prevent gold outflows, as did monetary authorities in smaller countries after 1900. The system worked through exchanges of sterling balances and bills of exchange within Britain, among British and non-British banks, rather than through gold flows between countries. Intra-bank exchanges eliminated the need for physical flows of gold. Instead, net claims favoring Britain would usually be settled by new long- or short-term borrowing in Britain. If the claims were unfavorable to Britain, an increase in the Bank of England discount rate (the 'bank rate') would usually suffice to draw in an offsetting flow of short-term capital, thus obviating the need to export gold from Britain. The monetary system thus mirrored the complementary flow of investment and goods in the real economy.

This system worked for three reasons. First, world trade, though not identical to trade with Britain, closely approximated it until 1900. Sterling and sterling-denominated bills of exchange drawn on London banks could thus be used as a substitute for gold in international transactions. Outstanding international bills of exchange on London banks roughly approximated British trade at any given time. A whole group of London banks specialized in the buying and selling of bills of exchange at varying rates of discount. These banks helped the market for bills to clear. They bridged the time gap between otherwise offsetting flows of bills for export and import payments from any given area. Bills also avoided the problem of the gold supply not growing in tandem with trade. Gold output lagged behind trade during the great depression of 1873–96. Trade grew at an annual average rate of 3.3 percent from 1870 to 1913, but the supply of physical gold grew only 1.4 percent per year from 1873 to 1892, and then only 3.7 percent per year up to World War I (Triffin, 1964: 2–20). Therefore, the expansion of trade relied heavily on the creation of credit forms of money.

Second, the sterling-based gold standard relied on the enormous volume of paper assets created by British investment overseas. Investment flows meant that balance-of-payments deficits could be financed for extremely long periods of time without requiring any adjustment – any shipment of gold or constriction of the money supply – on the part of the deficit country. Theoretically, this was not possible under the gold standard. Practically, however, the United States and many other agricultural exporters consistently ran trade deficits from the 1860s until 1900. The stocks and bonds created by British investment were used to settle outstanding claims (Foreman-Peck and Michie, 1986).

Securities (stocks and bonds) substituted for money. So-called finance bills were created when holders of the same security simultaneously sold and bought that security on both sides of the Atlantic. For example, a Canadian importer of British machinery would need pounds sterling to settle his debt to the British machinery producer, but, of course, received Canadian dollars from his customers. Using Canadian dollars, this Canadian might buy Canadian railroad bonds or stocks in the amount he owed, and transfer ownership to his bank. The bank would then sell the bonds/stocks in London, receiving sterling to pay off the machinery producer. By 1913 transactions like this settled three-fifths of bills exchange. The value of simple bills of exchange roughly corresponded to the value of British trade. But the value of finance bills rested on an asset base which was a multiple of British trade. Thus, this asset base could be tapped whenever the rate of growth of the physical money supply or of bills of exchange fell short of the growth of trade. This asset base also grew procyclically: rising trade usually entailed higher profits for firms, which meant rising capital values for their shares and higher interest rates on bonds as the demand for credit grew. In turn, this expanded the potential money supply. The so-called gold standard system of the late 1800s was thus actually a sterling–credit money standard. Gold remained the ultimate backing for money, but a backing that was rarely if ever relied on.

Finally, the institutional structure of international banking also stabilized the system. The Bank of England maintained a relatively small gold reserve, approximately £28 million. It could afford to do this because Britain would experience a gold outflow only when it ran large trade deficits – but those deficits were usually with agricultural exporters in Britain's periphery. These exporters in turn typically parked their trade surpluses in Britain, in the many colonial and quasi-colonial banking systems anchored in London, to protect themselves against their own trade deficits. The London branches of these banks held sterling balances that effectively functioned as a country's 'gold reserves.' In 1892 foreign and colonial banks based in London had funds amounting to about £370 million; these rose to £952 million by 1908 – or roughly one-third to one-half of total bank funds in Britain (Foreman-Peck and Michie, 1986: 399–405). India's funds and monetary gold base, firmly under the control of colonial authorities, constituted a significant portion of this. These funds were often deposited in British commercial banks, who then used this capital to finance their discounting of international bills of exchange.

This institutional structure meant the gold standard was not economically neutral. In effect, Britain ran a system of financial arbitrage. Peripheral countries loaned British banks money at low interest rates, reflecting British banks' inherent creditworthiness and the short-term time period for the loan. Then, those same British banks turned round and reloaned the money back to peripheral countries at higher interest rates, reflecting the longer-term of the loan and the inherently lower creditworthiness of overseas borrowers. Debtors were loaning their creditors money to be loaned back to them at higher interest rates. This situation rested in the first place on superior British manufacturing and productivity, which created an available pool of profits waiting for reinvestment. In turn this pool drew in peripheral savings that enlarged this pool of capital. This practice worked to the disadvantage of the economically weak. It is not accidental that the Deutsche Bank was founded in 1870 to help take over the financing of Germany's foreign trade, ultimately shifting it from a sterling to a reichsmark basis. In the absence of such behavior, this structure reinforced the inferior position of agricultural exporters in the system, making it hard for them to pursue anything but a Ricardian strategy. Later we will see that the US ran a similar system in the 1990s and 2000s (Chapter 14).

The stability of the monetary system rested on the stability and value of the stocks and bonds making up Britain's foreign investments and on the stability of the periphery's deposits in Britain. The monetary system thus faced only two serious threats to its stability. First, a series of defaults by Britain's supply zones could undermine the credit money used in international exchange. Second, withdrawal of peripheral deposits in London could force either punishing increases in Britain's domestic interest rates, or force a devaluation of sterling. This had both short- and long-term aspects. In the short term, any financial panic might move peripheral depositors to redeem sterling balances for gold. This is what happened in 1914 and 1929–32 (de Cecco, 1984: 7). In the long term, the more trade the periphery did with non-British industrial economies, the less reason they had to deposit money in London. The rise of a US-dollar-based zone in Latin America, and of a reichsmark-based zone in Eastern Europe, thus fundamentally threatened Britain's ability to keep international payments activity in Britain, to defend the pound sterling, and to live off other people's money.

All this was disguised, because the gold standard was superficially politically neutral, in the sense that it could not be used as an instrument. Political authorities had at best blunt instruments for influencing the money supply. The Bank of England could raise and lower its discount rate, and thus affect the underlying flow of short-term bills of exchange, but it could not control the long-term evolution of the money supply. The money supply ultimately rested on the supply of securities created by the capitalization of economic growth on a world scale. The Bank of England could not use monetary policy to punish British enemies. While markets could be such an agent of punishment, they did not define enemies in a political sense, but only in the sense of 'a good credit risk is a friend, a bad credit risk an enemy.'

This political neutrality reinforced the structure of incentives that underpinned informal imperialism in the NACs. Countries could opt out of the gold system and pay only economic penalties, expressed as higher interest rates. Except in the formal Dominions, elites retained control over their money supply, as the Argentine case demonstrates. There, ranchers opted to go off gold in the late 1880s so as to devalue their debts in a time of falling world market prices for their exports. When world market prices began to rise, they opted to go back on gold in 1900. The relative absence of extraeconomic coercion reinforced the elites' perception that participation in the British system was discretionary and to their benefit.

World War I and the collapse of British hegemony

Without some catastrophe, British dominance probably would have continued for some time. As it was, a catastrophe came along. World War I and the Great Depression finished off an otherwise slow process. World War I destroyed the fundamental bases for British hegemony. The War accelerated US growth, fundamentally disordered exchange rates, and left the British with much larger overseas liabilities at a time when the holders of those liabilities had no reason to leave money parked in London. The gold standard rested on massive investment flows out of Britain, partly financed by equally large short-term flows into Britain. It also rested on a presumption that gold would be freely exchangeable for paper money at fixed parities. European economies' underlying ability to support the gold standard through investment flows disappeared after 1914. Wartime inflation destroyed convertibility. This discussion will look first at monetary and trade issues, and then at the link between trade and investment. Monetary problems alone could not have destroyed the institutions of the nineteenth-century economy, but investment and trade problems could and did.

Exchange rates

World War I aggravated the underlying weaknesses of the gold standard. First, differential rates of inflation destroyed the old pre-war exchange rate parities. Setting 1913 price levels at 100 for all countries, by 1920 price levels in the United States were 221; in Japan, 259; in Britain, 307: in France, 488; and in Germany, 1000. The sharp deflation in 1920–21 also occurred unevenly across the major industrial countries. Pre-war parities no longer reflected countries' underlying competitiveness in world markets. In turn this made it unlikely that a neutral balance of payments would emerge from trade flows priced using those parities. Efforts to get new parities that reflected real underlying levels of productivity failed. The relationship between parity levels, prestige, overall economic activity, and the value of creditors' assets created enormous political incentives to set exchange rates either too high or too low.

Britain (1925) and Italy (1922) set their exchange rates too high for political reasons. Britain's heavy reliance on food and raw material imports made an overvalued pound attractive, by making imports cheaper. Naturally the power of Britain's financial community also made this an easy decision. But this decision was self-defeating, as it priced British exports out of world markets. The French set their exchange rate relatively low (1926) in order to maximize exports, and they indeed gained world market share. For its part, the United States tended to sterilize its current account surpluses by hoarding gold, thus taking demand out of the world economy, and worsening things for everyone.

In the crisis of 1929–32, these unresolved exchange rate problems erupted into open competitive devaluations. The British tried to counter a series of bank failures in Austria and Germany by extending sterling credits to those countries. The smaller European countries feared this would weaken sterling, and they also needed to offset their losses on holdings locked up in Central European banks. They began to convert their holdings of sterling into gold to boost their reserves, producing a run on the pound and forcing Britain off the gold standard. At that point, many countries devalued their currency either to maintain parity with the falling pound or to maximize their export surplus. This action in turn set off successive rounds of devaluation.

In varying degrees, virtually every country then resorted to currency controls in order to manipulate the value of its currency and to control the level of imports. Currency controls forced exporters to turn foreign exchange earnings over to the central bank or some other authority, which then allocated foreign exchange to importers chosen for political or economic development reasons. Obviously, this ended the freely exchangeable currencies of the gold standard period.

Trade

World War I also disrupted the pre-war trade system. Protectionist tariffs were widespread, but trade otherwise was largely unregulated. During the War, however, states imposed direct trade controls to assure adequate wartime supplies of raw and finished goods. For example, during the War the British state bought as much wool and butter as Australia and New Zealand could produce, at guaranteed prices, through joint organizations like the British Australian Wool Realization Authority. Wartime trade organizations stayed in place postwar as voluntary organizations, financed by taxes on producers. These organizations attempted to regulate trade in primary commodities and built up enormous buffer stocks as prices fell during the 1920s.

Again, the Depression intensified this break with pre-war patterns. States began using explicit quotas to regulate the volume of imported goods. States worked out bilateral exchange agreements that replaced the old multilateral (often triangular) patterns of exchange. These bilateral deals segmented the world's markets into blocs. One bloc centered on Britain, including British colonies, dominions, and a few of Britain's more important trading partners like Argentina and Denmark; a second centered on Germany, including Eastern Europe; a third centered on the United States, including Canada and parts of Latin America; a fourth centered on Japan and its northeast Asian empire.

This segmentation into blocs hurt some countries more than others. Lacking a significant imperial market, and so competing on the basis of productivity rather than power, the United States suffered the greatest fall in exports. Countries unable to export were also unable to import, and so they began encouraging the production of commodities that in an open market would have been uncompetitive. During this period many European countries became self-sufficient in wheat production, for example; this was one reason why US grain exports fell (de Hevesy, 1940). The interaction of trade stresses with the enormous shift in global investment patterns caused by the war set the stage for the 1930s collapse. A stylized model of trade and debt conditions will help show why.

A stylized model of the interwar period

A stylized picture of the world economy in the 1920s clarifies the salient issues. Imagine an international economic system with three types of countries: a large developed country that is also a large net creditor; several other, and often smaller, developed countries that are only marginal net creditors or perhaps even marginal net debtors; and a large group of highly indebted developed and less developed countries (LDCs) that are mostly primary product exporters. To service their debts, the developed and LDC agricultural periphery must either run large trade surpluses with developed countries in general or attract new lending to cover cumulating deficits on the investment income side of their accounts.

All developed countries that are themselves net debtors must run trade surpluses with the creditor country in order to prevent their own net investment income deficit from cumulating into more debt. (These developed countries obviously cannot run surpluses as a group with developing countries as a group, because this would only expand the latter's deficit and thus debt.) Economic stability in this system depends on the large creditor country either running a current account deficit, and thus boosting exports from debtor countries, or directly financing debtors' ongoing current account deficits. When the large creditor either cannot or will not provide either type of finance, trade flows will tend to contract as countries try to maximize their merchandise surplus by restricting their own imports. This individually rational restriction is collectively and systemically pernicious, however. By reducing everyone's exports, restriction forces all countries to further close their markets and perhaps default on their debts. In this situation, the large creditor must act as a lender or market of last resort, in order to prevent a collapse of markets as individually rational decisions cumulate into collective disaster. If for some reason the major creditor country no longer can provide credit directly, all other countries will immediately be forced to reduce their imports. The more abrupt the contraction of lending, the more abrupt the efforts to constrict imports will be. How did the interwar period resemble this stylized picture?

The structure of international debt in the 1920s

The problem: round one

World War I undid the relatively complementary debt structure created by British nineteenth-century lending. The war created a massive overhang of European debt on top of the existing high levels of debt outside Europe, while eroding Britain's creditor position. Neither Europeans nor Britain could import as much from the agricultural periphery as they had before the war. At the same time, both the Europeans and Britain had to export more to cover their increased debt payments. This conflicted with the agricultural periphery's need to expand its exports.

As Chapter 6 observed, the agricultural periphery had contracted high levels of developmental debt before 1914. By 1914 many peripheral agricultural exporters had foreign debts amounting to their combined gross domestic product and fairly high debt-to-export ratios. But Britain in effect traded its interest earnings for food, enabling this periphery to service its debts. Similarly, the industrial European countries paid for imported foods and raw materials by exporting to Britain and the agricultural periphery. Britain's trade surplus with major colonial markets such as India paid for its imports from Europe. The war destroyed these complementary flows in two ways. First, by creating overcapacity in global agriculture, it caused serious price declines that made debt service more difficult for the periphery. Second, it reduced British and European ability to import from the periphery.

During the war the agricultural periphery massively expanded output of foodstuffs and raw materials to supply European combatants. Wheat acreage outside Europe expanded by 34 percent during the war (Malenbaum, 1953: 236–7). After the war, the Europeans resumed local food production. The ensuing oversupply of agricultural products drove primary product prices down an average of 30 percent from 1923 to 1929, well in advance of the Depression. Falling prices made it harder for Ricardian agricultural exporters to service their debts, because they now had to export a greater volume of merchandise in order to earn the same amount of currency for debt service. Worse, by exporting more, they drove prices down even further.

If the agricultural exporters had encountered open markets, falling prices might not have been as big a problem; after all, the agricultural periphery had survived falling prices in the 1880s. However, all of the European industrial countries began protecting their markets, again well before 1930. What was going on in the periphery's traditional European markets? Rising European protectionism reflected efforts by indebted European countries to maximize their own export surpluses. After all, the Europeans had their own debt problem. Continental Europe emerged from the war as net debtors, because of inter-Allied borrowing; Britain's net creditor position was severely eroded by war debts. Only the United States emerged from the war as a major net creditor. This shift in the status of most European industrial nations, including Britain, upset the balance between flows of capital and goods achieved in the nineteenth century.

In Continental Europe, this situation forced each country to try to maximize its dollar or pound sterling surplus in international trade in order to have foreign exchange to service its foreign debt. Ultimately, everyone needed dollars to pay off their debts to the United States. Meanwhile, German reparations aggravated existing debt-related trade imbalances. If the Germans ran current account surpluses large enough to pay their reparations, this would unbalance the accounts of both traditional debtors and other non-European countries. German nonpayment, however, put additional burdens on the new European debtors, particularly France.

Before the war, the larger European countries had generated surpluses by running merchandise surpluses with Britain or by skimming off surpluses that their tightly controlled colonial economies made with the external world, including the United States. Thus, Britain offset trade deficits with the United States and Europe through trade surpluses with and investment income from the NACs; they in turn ran trade surpluses with the United States and Europe. The postwar terms of trade decline and debt overhangs in the periphery forced those areas to restrict imports. Colonial empires thus generated less foreign exchange for the imperial countries at a time when those countries needed to rely even more heavily on their colonies. Nor could European countries run surpluses with one another to pay the United States; one country's surplus implied a deficit (and crisis) for another.

Britain's own declining competitiveness and weakened position as a creditor hampered its responses to this problem. Its heavy wartime borrowing from the United States transformed it from the international system's major creditor into a marginal net creditor overall and a net debtor *vis-à-vis* the United States. As a net debtor to the United States, the United Kingdom had to run either a bilateral trade surplus with the United States or a huge surplus with other countries that themselves ran surpluses with the United States. For example, in 1923 British exports to the United States amounted to a bit over £61 million. But the British government alone needed to find about £33 million annually to service war debts to the United States. Britain ran an annual average merchandise trade deficit of roughly £260 million during 1923–29. Overall, its current account surplus amounted to only about £100 million (Falkus, 1972b; McNeil, 1986; Pullen, 1987: 143).

As noted above, the 1925 British policy choice to set convertibility between the pound sterling and gold at pre-war parities aggravated the situation by lowering Britain's ability to export. Overvaluation increased imports and decreased the incentive to invest in the domestic economy. Capital formation as a percentage of British GDP during 1921–9 fell by about 25 percent compared with 1900–13 levels. Its economy weakened, Britain had difficulty maintaining the pre-war structure of debt and trade. Diminished exports ultimately meant diminished imports and lending. Unable to do both, Britain mostly bought and only grudgingly lent. In the 1920s Britain lent less than half as much overseas in real terms as it had lent in the pre-war decade. Britain did buy more, however. While this helped its debtors generate the revenues they needed to pay back their debts, it also increased the United Kingdom's merchandise trade deficit by 43 percent in real terms compared to the pre-war decade. Consequently, Britain ran down its overseas assets to pay for the increase in imports. As a result, Britain's invisible (interest) trade surplus fell by about 20 percent during the 1920s (Orde, 1990: 328–9).

Unable to support global lending and trade flows by themselves, the British tried to lead by example and to promote cooperative solutions to the problems of German reparations and overseas debt. US lenders, however, hesitated to commit capital outside of traditional areas like Canada and Central America, or the politically secure (Germany excepted) European countries (Moulton and Pasvolsky, 1932). Britain also helped sponsor four failed multilateral conferences on mutual tariff reduction.

Why couldn't debtors simply increase exports to the United States in order to earn dollars for debt service? European countries and the periphery alike found it very difficult to run surpluses via direct exports to the United States (Falkus, 1972b). Few European countries or agricultural exporters had goods marketable in the United States. The United States was self-sufficient in most natural resources and agricultural products; it drew much of its supply of tropical products from captive sources like Liberia (rubber) or Central America (fruit).

Exporting manufactured goods to the United States was also difficult. The United States had high tariffs. More important, World War I began the domination of highly productive, Taylorized, assembly-line methods of production in the United States. This productivity advantage made it impossible for Europeans to export all but a handful of products to the United States. The European countries' share of finished manufactured exports to the United States plummeted after World War I, reflecting a more general decline in the share of manufactured goods in US imports and a sharp increase in their share in US exports, from 35 to 45 percent (Falkus, 1972b: 607). The United States actually increased its trade surplus with Europe during the 1920s, because even countries, like France, that had vigorously assimilated US-style mass production, ran deficits with the United States. Figure 7.1 lays out these trade flows schematically, while also revealing the Devil's hand at work in starting the Depression.

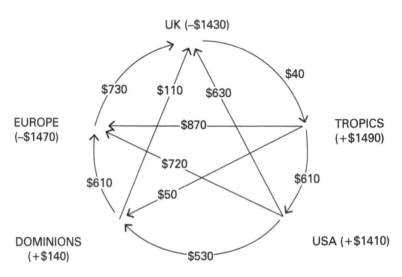

Source: Data from Hilgert (1943: 395).

Figure 7.1   Structure of net world trade surpluses, 1928, $ million (figures in parentheses are global trade balance for each area)

The solution?

If countries couldn't export more to the United States, only three things could make international transactions balance. First, Germany could be made to provide the reparations the European Allies demanded. The failed French occupation of the Ruhr proved this would not happen. Second, creditors could write down the debt overhang from World War I, freeing debtors' cash for commodity trade. The United States did write down small parts of inter-Allied debt after 1924 (Pullen, 1987).

Third, the United States could become a lender of last resort to the world, financing the debtors' dollar deficits. During the 1920s the United States lent about $10 billion overseas. By way of comparison, this $10 billion in real terms equaled about one-quarter of all nineteenth-century lending by all creditor countries; rivaled the post-World War II Marshall Plan (though over a longer time period); and represented in cumulative terms an export of about 12 percent of average US GDP in the 1920s. The United States more than recycled its current account surpluses during the 1920s, much as Japan and China recycled their current account surpluses in the 1980s, 1990s and 2000s. US lending helped delay an explosion in tariff levels from the 1920s to the 1930s.

US lending began in earnest with the 1924 Dawes Plan and its associated reductions in inter-Allied debt (McNeil, 1986; Schuker, 1988). The $100 million government-to-government Dawes loan to Germany sparked a flood of US lending overseas. From 1924 to 1929, the US financial community floated $6.4 billion in loans, roughly double the 1920–3 rate. About 75 percent of this went directly to foreign governments. European and peripheral debtors recycled this US lending as debt payments to and imports from Britain. This indirect US help for Britain and British exports in turn helped Britain to resume its lending, albeit at lower levels than before the war.

US lending inadequately solved the imbalance of primary flows among trading countries. Compared with simply having the United States import more, lending only put off the eventual day of reckoning. For if the flow of capital were shut off, the underlying problem not only would remain, but would also have been worsened by five years of additional debt accumulation. And this is precisely what happened. For example, debt service for the major British colonies and dominions increased from $725 million per annum in 1923 to $900 million by 1928, implying that a proportional increase in exports had to occur precisely as prices were falling (Kindleberger, 1973: 84).

The system could keep going only if the United States continued lending. However, economic events and policy in the United States brought an abrupt end to capital outflows. By the end of the 1920s, loose monetary and regulatory policies had encouraged speculative excesses, including a near doubling of the stock market from 1926 to 1929. Hundreds of firms rushed to issue equity to raise capital for assembly lines. The 1929 crash, in which the stock market slid to half its 1929 peak, precipitated a recession. This recession trapped the billions of dollars invested in additional capacity during the late 1920s, as well as wiping out speculative financial gains. Although the Federal

Reserve initially moved to increase liquidity in 1929, the money supply contracted by about 20 percent from 1931 to 1932. And the state did little to bridge the gap between the enormous increase in supply that assembly lines created, and stagnant industrial wages.

During the 1920s, a few US transnational manufacturing and financial firms had made large, long-maturing investments in Europe and consequently forged tight and complex ties with European financial and industrial circles (van der Pijl, 1984). By 1929, about one-fifth of all US portfolio investment was in foreign, albeit mostly short-term, bonds (Frieden, 1988: 64). But domestic economic and political realities defeated this group's desires to bind the United States to Europe's fate during the 1930s. Most US firms were still oriented to the domestic market, and US holders of liquid capital were not as tied to Europe as transnational manufacturers. Even the regional Federal Reserve banks, which had considerable autonomy before 1935, prioritized their local economy over the international economy (Eichengreen, 1992: 11). After the 1929 stock market crash, capital stopped flowing overseas. Without a last-resort lender or buyer, most countries tried to generate trade surpluses by resorting to tariffs to shut out imports. International trade collapsed by two-thirds from 1929 to 1932. In turn this crushed the agricultural periphery. From 1928 to 1933, export revenues for the 41 largest primary product exporters fell 50 percent (Eichengreen and Portes, 1986). All of them defaulted on their foreign debt, except Argentina and the formal Dominions. In turn the British government took direct control over foreign lending, while US private capital flows evaporated. The structures and institutions defining the world economy of the long nineteenth century were dead.

Consequences of British decline

British decline (and American ascent) before and after World War I was reflected in and reinforced four fundamental changes in the international political economy. Each change germinated in the interwar period but did not develop fully until after World War II. First, foreign direct investment (FDI) began to replace portfolio investment as the mode for overseas investment, and investment shifted from agricultural production to manufacturing. Since major agricultural producing areas lay inside the United States, US firms went abroad looking for markets for manufactured goods, not sources of foods and NFAs. Before World War I and even more so before World War II, the most successful and technologically advanced US firms – Ford, General Electric, National Cash Register, Otis Elevator, Dupont, Singer, and so on – set up production in Britain. German firms like Hoechst (chemicals) and Siemens (electrical equipment) also made FDI in Britain. Absolutely, this investment was small, supplementing more traditional investment flows into raw materials extraction – for example, US copper mining in Chile or German iron mining in Morocco. But it was both a harbinger of things to come and an indicator of Britain's decline. If British firms could not compete with foreigners producing in Britain, drawing on the same labor and raw materials pool as British firms, they could not compete with them elsewhere.

Second, US and German firms' intrusion into British home markets created a novel problem for Britain. Now it was Britain that had to adapt, adopt, or create new institutional innovations so as to be able to compete with best practice manufacturing elsewhere. Britain now faced the challenges of late development and deindustrialization through competitive processes. Britain's former industrial success and the huge market this had created might guard against an absolute decline in living standards, but it did not guarantee future increases or competitiveness. The United States would face the same challenge after the 1970s.

Third, the old complementary trade patterns between Britain and geographically peripheral agricultural economies began to give way to intra-industry trade of differentiated and branded goods among high-income, developed areas. The old trade patterns rested mostly on an exchange of commodities between Britain and the periphery: railroad systems in return for bulk foods such as wheat and frozen meats. In the new, emerging intra-industry trade pattern, Fords were exchanged for Mercedes. This signaled a shift from a purely Thünen world to a world much more like that captured in Krugman's model.

Finally, by 1914, fully articulated rail and steamship networks connected all parts of the world. Substantial parts of Europe still remained only diffusely connected to the world economy, but the beginnings of trucking would soon fill in the holes in the lacelike pattern of areas tied together by steam transport. As this happened, true domestic markets began coming into existence in countries besides the United States, Britain, and NACs. These domestic markets would begin to have greater importance than foreign markets; intra-national markets began to matter more than inter-national markets. The rise of direct investment from one developed country to another also signaled this shift, as manufacturing firms moved to secure access to their most important markets.

All of these changes foreshadowed shifts that would bloom in the interwar period and then mature fully after World War II. In the meantime, World War I swept away British hegemony while making German hegemony politically untenable in Europe. The world economy then experienced an extreme and probably unavoidable period of instability in the 1920s and 1930s, before the United States invented a new set of institutions to replace Britain's decaying ones.

The breakdown of British hegemony completely disrupted the international economy. With virtually all countries resorting to exclusionary tariffs, using currency devaluations to position their exports favorably in the few remaining open markets, and either defaulting on their overseas debts or refusing to lend more money, the value of world trade dropped by over two-thirds from 1929 to 1932. Because this collapse of trade seemed both cause and effect of the horrendous economic costs of the Great Depression, it imbued policymakers with a profound distaste for all the measures they saw as responsible for that collapse: bilateral trade treaties, managed currencies, exclusionary tariffs, and default. Aversion to these policy responses would color every institution of the international system America re-created after World War II. None the less, a newly hegemonic America could have constructed many possible international orders around these aversions. The substance of the international system the United States created grew out of the particular domestic compromises achieved in US politics during the 1930s and 1940s. The remainder of the book, and Chapters 8 and 9 in particular, deal with these compromises, the essential elements of US hegemony after 1945, and the degree to which that hegemony is now in decay.

Part II

The Fall and Rise and Fall Again of Globalization

The Depression, US Domestic Politics, and the Foundation of the Post-World War II System

British hegemony declined because British firms could not master the hard and soft technologies in the electricity, chemicals and continuous-flow production leading-sector cluster. American hegemony was built on the subsequent petroleum, car, and assembly-line cluster. This cluster allowed the US economy to continuously expand its productivity lead over the rest of the world from the late 1890s until roughly 1960. This new Schumpeterian cluster encompassed petroleum as an energy source, motor vehicles as a new mode of transportation and as a consumption good, and consumer durables as an additional consumption good. At the level of production processes, the common factor was the marriage of continuous-flow processes with high levels of component and product standardization; in short, the assembly line. This cluster diffused unevenly to Europe in the 1920s and 1930s and then more broadly in the 1960s; Japan's transformation of this cluster in the 1960s posed a new challenge to US manufacturing; by 1990 it had diffused to China, India, and Brazil. By then, the developed countries had moved on to the silicon, microelectronics and team-production cluster. The emergence of the car cluster and the shift to electronics revived the global challenges that Britain's industrial revolution posed: Could countries avoid being left behind? Whose rules would govern international trade? How would supply and demand balance?

The collapse of British hegemony in the 1920s and 1930s magnified these problems. Immigrant, capital and commodity flows bounced back to pre-war levels during the unstable 1920s. Given a proper global architecture, the 1920s might not have given way to the Great Depression and World War II. But there was no social support for a US global role. The United States could not generate a stable domestic institutional structure for balancing the vastly increased supply the assembly line permitted against adequate demand. Consequently the United States exported its surplus production, depressing most other industrial economies. America's inability to cope with the macroeconomic consequences of assembly-line production and to export that solution led in part to the Great Depression of the 1930s and in turn to World War II. Both events sharply reduced all global flows. The Great Depression had enormous political consequences because the combination of rail and road transport exposed microeconomies everywhere to market forces.

The Depression's deflation proved politically and socially unsustainable.

Like the deep recession of 2007–9, the Great Depression created a political opening for massive state intervention to balance supply and demand in ways that also provided society with protection from the market's volatility. Internationally, World War II created an opening for the export of the US domestic solution for balancing supply and demand that was consistent with restoring global economic flows to their nineteenth-century levels. This chapter first discusses the consequences of the new leading sector. Then it turns to the constellation of US domestic interests that emerged from the Depression in order to understand institutional solutions to the problems of stabilizing domestic and global demand after World War II.

Cars: or, the disruptiveness of a new leading sector

American firms produced about 4000 cars in 1900. But 900 of America's 1100 car producers never built more than two cars, considerably limiting Verdoorn effects and economies of scale. By 1910, production had risen to just under 200 000 cars per year, or less than the annual output of a US car factory today. By 1921, output was 1.5 million vehicles, and pre-war production peaked in 1929 at 4.6 million. The sudden jumps reflect the transition in the industry from low-volume stationary assembly to high-volume assembly-line production. Henry Ford made this transition first, by insisting on extremely high levels of standardization and interchangeability for parts going into the Model T in 1908, and developing sophisticated logistical practices to assure a steady supply of parts. Standardization and logistics permitted Ford to introduce the tightly scheduled, machine-paced assembly line in 1913–14. By 1929, Ford accounted for two-fifths of annual car sales, while seven other firms split the remainder.

Ford combined all the elements from the prior cluster of leading sectors – professional management, cartel control over competition, electrification of production, and Taylorization of work processes – with continuous-flow production and superior supply chain management. This combination yielded spectacular increases in productivity. Ford's first crude final assembly line cut production time by half. Applying this to the entire production process cut total production time from 13 to 1.5 hours in 1914. This gave Ford an unbeatable edge over his domestic and foreign competitors until they too adopted the assembly line.

During the 1920s Ford produced about 20.5 cars per worker per year; partly reorganized US firms produced 4.3 cars per worker; and Europeans largely using stationary assembly produced 2 cars per worker. None of Ford's hard technology was particularly novel at first. Ford's system was a managerial innovation. The United States actually lagged behind Europe, particularly Germany, in many technologies such as electrical engineering and chemicals. Yet the assembly line revolutionized production across virtually the whole range of US manufacturing industries, propelling them far ahead of foreign competitors.

Specific problems created by US industrialization

The new leading sector created four problems, which first surfaced during the interwar period and blossomed after World War II. The first problem had two aspects emanating from the links among economies of scale, productivity, and continuous-flow production. The diffusion of the assembly line out from the car industry and into allied industries like refrigerators, washers, dryers, and radios meant that major portions of the economy became vulnerable to sudden changes in aggregate demand. Continuous-flow production required large investments in machinery that could be used to produce only one type of product (Piore and Sabel, 1985). This investment guaranteed a high level of productivity, in the sense of a high volume of goods produced per unit of labor applied. But high productivity did not guarantee high profitability unless this machinery were used continually. Unstable demand discouraged investment by raising fears of cyclically high unit costs and low profits; inadequate demand could trap fixed investments by creating excess capacity.

So problem one boiled down to two questions: how could demand for products produced on continuous-flow principles be stabilized? And how could the increased supply of goods be balanced with increased demand? In the short run, the absence of any solution to this problem was an important domestic cause for the Great Depression in the United States. In the long run, domestic politics in the United States created the institutional basis for postwar Keynesianism, which matched supply with demand and stabilized that demand. The end of this chapter discusses how these institutions emerged in the United States, while Chapter 9 discusses their diffusion overseas.

The return of displacement competition

The second problem was the return of displacement competition. US innovation of the assembly line threatened to displace the uncompetitive production systems of other countries just as Britain's mechanized textile production had obliterated premodern textile producers. American firms' foreign direct investment (FDI) into Europe threatened European firms in their own home market. How could the Europeans compete? In the 1920s, European employers attempted to introduce the assembly line and other American managerial styles in the face of considerable labor resistance (Maier, 1975). A European version of American-style production did not emerge until after World War II had destroyed both employers' old capital stock and, through systematic deportation of leftists to concentration camps, most European unions. Chapter 10 deals with European fears and responses to this problem, as well as considering multinational firms in general. Eventually, European firms assimilated US production technologies, and the Marshall Plan recast unions along more cooperative lines. Europeans stabilized their domestic markets through generous welfare states, agricultural subsidies, and centralized collective bargaining systems. The Japanese response, which took a different form, will be considered in Chapter 13. Successful European and Japanese adaptation of the assembly line enabled them to challenge US producers, disrupting the economic basis for stability in the postwar global economy.

The end of Ricardian growth based on agricultural exports

The third problem: the Depression and memories of World War II food shortages closed the window for Ricardian strategies based on agricultural exports. Developed countries opted to stabilize local agricultural incomes and output with price and quantity controls as well as import controls. These policies stabilized farm income in the United States, Western Europe and Japan. But they posed an enormous obstacle to continued Ricardian development using agricultural exports. Initially, the intensive application of science and machinery boosted developed country agricultural productivity, reducing the need for imports. But even when falling transport costs and continued industrialization pushed Thünen rings further out, developed countries limited growth in food imports. As demand for peripheral agricultural goods began to fall as a proportion of total demand, peripheral economies found it hard to earn a living as a national economic unit totally oriented towards external trade. This occurred despite absolute increases in peripheral agricultural exports, for those exports and the income they generated increased much more slowly than local population.

What could replace agricultural Ricardian development strategies? In the 1930s, most peripheries avoided change by joining one or another imperial bloc and continuing a Ricardian strategy. Those that could not join, starting with Brazil and Mexico, switched to Kaldorian growth strategies based on domestic market-oriented industrialization. These inward-looking import substitution industrialization strategies rested on social pacts that stabilized urban real wages and offered considerable protection to nascent manufacturers at the expense of the agricultural sector. In short, the Australian model of shifting rents from raw materials exports to protected infant industry diffused to Latin America.

After World War II rapid expansion of global trade created an opportunity for export-oriented Ricardian strategies based on manufactured goods exports. In a few cases in Latin America and especially East Asia, these turned into full-fledged Kaldorian strategies for development. These strategies produced the so-called newly industrialized countries (NICs), which exhibit all the classic symptoms of late industrialization (Chapter 4). Chapter 11 deals with the shift from Ricardian to Kaldorian strategies in East Asia (including China), Eastern Europe and Latin America.

States and the re-emergence of the global market

The first two problems, and to a lesser extent the third, created the fourth problem: could global trade and monetary systems consistent with domestic political and economic stability be (re-)created and by whom? Britain's ability to use its import market and financial resources to organize trade and money collapsed during the 1930s. The United States was the only plausible replacement as a hegemonic economy, but lacked the solid domestic backing that British financiers and textile exporters provided for Britain's role. This chapter details the political maneuvering in the United States that created a domestic coalition willing to support a limited international role. Chapters 9 and 12 examine the evolution of those monetary and trade systems as US domestic political compromises unraveled and new economic interests emerged.

The new postwar order temporarily reversed the continual state orchestrated formation and penetration of markets that occurred before 1914. As Karl Polanyi argued, states responded to the dislocating effects of market pressures and the extreme 1930s deflation by sheltering both capital and labor from markets (Polanyi, 1957). States erected formidable barriers to international trade out of the bricks of quantitative restrictions on imports, foreign exchange controls and allocation, control over capital movements, selective exchange rate devaluations, and bilateral trade deals. They also stepped in to regulate directly output and investment in the entire economy, particularly in agriculture and services. These interventions were both a cause and effect of the subsequent collapse of world trade and investment flows.

In the 1930s, the foreign trade of most industrial countries fell to about two-thirds of the level prevailing before 1914 relative to GDP; international investment largely disappeared. These levels were akin to those in the early nineteenth century, when trade and capital flows connected only the littoral and riparian skins of nations whose interiors were largely composed of micro-economies. US policy immediately after World War II aimed at a careful reopening of specific international markets. Essentially, only manufactured goods entered freely into world trade, and free exchange of currencies was permitted to facilitate that trade (Ruggie, 1982). Consequently world trade and capital flows did not recover to pre-World War I levels until the 1970s and did not surpass them until the mid-1980s (McKeown, 1991). The entire period from 1929 until the 1970s constitutes a significant divergence from the trends unleashed by the industrial and transportation revolution of the nineteenth century. The post-1970s period returned the world to nineteenth-century trends and their associated financial turbulence, culminating in the 2007–9 systemic crisis.

The international institutions that US policy created reflected, sustained and ultimately undermined this divergence from historical patterns. First, these international institutions protected domestic economic growth and macroeconomic stability by largely limiting international capital flows to official transfers and direct investment, and by limiting trade liberalization to manufactured goods only. This helped maintain full employment while risking higher inflation. In Europe this compromise meant that states could use publicly owned service sectors and financial targeting to encourage quite rapid economic growth. State direction permitted large riskless investments and equally rapid increases in manufacturing output by reducing volatility. By the 1970s this increased output flowed into world markets, depressing prices and profits in what eventually became a rerun of the first great depression – that of 1873–96 (Brenner, 1998). While the car cluster had not fully run its course, it had saturated rich country markets.

In the postwar period the United States consciously gave European and Japanese firms access to its domestic market for manufactures, so that its allies could do their part to contain the Soviet Union. In effect, the United States reversed course on its 1920s policy of exporting its surpluses, and instead imported other countries' surpluses. Consequently, the United States felt the overcapacity and falling prices consequent to the maturing of the car cluster first. This undermined both the economic ability of the United States to sustain the role of the dollar as an international currency, and the political consensus sustaining the regulation of the service economy. Similarly, because the US domestic consensus never permitted stringent capital controls akin to those in Europe and Japan, capital began to leak overseas, undermining the stability of the US dollar as an international currency.

Expediency and domestic politics drove the United States to pursue the destruction of the postwar monetary order and begin a conscious reopening of global capital, agricultural and service markets as its dominance of manufac-tured goods markets waned. This shifted the global economy back towards patterns that more and more resembled those of the nineteenth-century global economy. By unleashing competition in agriculture and the service sector, and by encouraging the growth of a global capital market, the United States has forced other states to consciously introduce markets into sheltered areas of the economy, producing the old-new phenomenon people labeled as 'globaliza-tion' in the 1990s. The US state also fostered the emergence of new leading sectors built on electronics and biotechnology (Hurt, 2009). Ultimately, imprudent deregulation of the financial sector brought the second era of deregulation to an end.

The rest of the book thus discusses the temporary suppression of global markets and their re-emergence as US hegemony broke down from below and above. US efforts to resuscitate its hegemony led it to reintroduce markets to the financial and service sectors, thus extending the global market into areas that had been sheltered from market forces since the Depression; and with deleterious consequences. But we must first see why the US acquiesced in the suppression and regulation of those same global markets.

From British to US hegemony

American hegemony in the international economy after 1945 reflects two paradoxes. After World War II, the United States possessed an unparalleled level of economic, moral, and military superiority. These strengths were already visible in the 1920s. None the less, in contrast to Britain's unilateral style of hegemonic leadership in the mid-1800s, the United States pursued a more cooperative style of leadership. In a limited way before World War II, and much more so after, the United States constructed a series of multilateral international organizations in which US pre-eminence but not dominance was assured (Latham, 1997; Costigliola, 1984). What explains this paradox, and US unwillingness to act decisively before World War II?

Three intertwined political and economic factors militated against an effort at a unilateral US hegemony. Politically, no US domestic consensus for an international role existed. Many US political actors opposed any international role for the United States, particularly in the 1920s. Internationally oriented US actors needed European help to sway their domestic opponents towards a larger US role. This meant that those internationally minded actors could not put forward institutions that embodied unilateral US dominance. Instead, postwar structures and institutions had to reflect European interests too. Those European interests, meanwhile, inclined towards making international economic flows serve domestic growth and full employment, rather than allowing them relatively free rein (van der Pijl, 1984).

Economically, in the short run, the geopolitical necessities of postwar reconstruction precluded any immediate return to the kind of externally oriented, complementary international economy over which the British presided. Economically, in the long run, the strong preference for macroeconomic policies oriented towards full employment and economic stability precluded the kind of free movement of capital typical of the British period. Most states preferred to retain capital controls in order to deter capital flight to the United States or to direct investment in order to assure growth. Even in the relatively free market United States, the state directed capital into a variety of preferred channels, including housing, agriculture, education, and power generation, as well as defense-related industrial ventures.

In economist Charles Kindleberger's famous formulation, global economic leadership went missing in the 1920s because while the British wanted to continue playing hegemon, they could not afford to, while the United States, which could afford this role, did not want it. But Kindleberger's formulation obscures how America's particular form of economic integration into the global economy hindered its leadership role. The innovation and diffusion of the assembly line in the US economy made the United States the largest economy in the world. But for most of the 1920s the sheer physical size and internal dynamism of the US economy drew producers' attention inward.

State power and interests ultimately reflect the power and interests of the social groups supporting the state, and a powerful bloc of US business interests that sold little in global markets was indifferent to international problems. This nationalist or isolationist group, centered in the Midwest and in Midwestern heavy industries, successfully stalemated efforts to assert US leadership by a second, more internationalist group, centered in the eastern seaboard, East Coast industries that were already multinationalizing, and eastern elites centered in the major New York City banks.

But even the internationalist groups initially had tenuous ties to world markets. The United States found its global periphery internally, in its own southern and western regions. The increasingly important car industry did not export more than 10 percent of its output until 1926, and half of those exports went to temperate agricultural producers like Canada, Australia and Argentina (Dassbach, 1993: 364–5). Yet by 1929 US domestic demand could absorb only 80 percent of local car output, even though US wages were already considerably higher than European wages.

Even if US policymakers had understood the consequences of the US mis-match between supply and demand in the 1920s and 1930s, and thus the need for a new deal at home and abroad, the US state was too weak to pursue this deal. The state lacked the institutions needed to tap into the resource-rich domestic economy. Institutionally, it lacked an effective central bank (and thus any way of coordinating domestic and international monetary policy), deployed an army approximately the size of Portugal's, and relied on informal and personal contacts to coordinate macroeconomic policy with other countries. The income tax affected a thin slice of the population.

The Depression and World War II changed much of this. The war enhanced the US government's ability to control its domestic economy and the global economy, and to confront potential challengers with unchallengeable military might. The assembly line permitted the United States to build the world's largest navy and air force. US experience in managing multidivisional firms translated into the capacity to handle the complex logistical task of supplying military forces deployed worldwide, for only the United States actually fought a *global* war from 1941 to 1945.

The war also created a capacity for domestic economic management. The war transformed the Federal Reserve system into a true central bank, and the Office of Price Management bequeathed to the state and the Federal Reserve the personnel, experience, and machinery to control aggregate demand and prices. The war expanded the reach of income taxation to the bulk of the working class, giving the state an enormous and broad source of revenue. A self-consciously Keynesian and expanded Bureau of the Budget taught the executive branch how to spend that money in the pursuit of macroeconomic stability (Katznelson and Pietrykowski, 1991).

The war also changed *intentions,* partly by changing perceptions of self-interest on the part of the nationalists and partly by creating a third group: security internationalists (Schurmann, 1974; Frieden, 1988). This new group, centered in the emerging sun belt/gun belt aerospace industrial bloc, broke the deadlock between nationalists and internationalists. The third group saw its economic future tied to a US global military presence. The incomplete resolution of this three-sided struggle over US state policy inclined the United States towards a reliance on international agencies to handle global economic problems rather than the unilateral policies typical of the British model.

The political problem: coalition-building in the United States

Three contenders in US politics

During the 1920s and 1930s US passivity towards international economic problems reflected a political deadlock between two groups of firms and farmers. The first group, which, following convention, we can call *nationalists,* was made up of firms and farms oriented almost exclusively towards the domestic market. These were steel and iron firms, railroads, coal mines, machine tool manufacturers supplying those firms, the banks that financed them, and the thousands of Midwestern food-producing farmers whose production by the 1920s was mostly consumed at home. These firms were largely oriented towards domestic markets, and, because they produced undifferentiated goods like basic steel or coal, they did not have the technological advantages needed to transnationalize into Europe.

In fact, some were uncompetitive and supported higher tariffs during the 1920s and 1930s; farmers by extension supported state efforts to subsidize exports. They were suspicious of any initiatives by the US state to channel loans to Europe, fearing that this would make capital more expensive in the United States. This group had strong connections to the Commerce Department, which for many years had acted to support US exports but not overseas investment. Their strong ties to the Department of Agriculture became even stronger when the state began directly regulating agricultural output after 1933. The Republican Party largely represented this group.

The second group – the *internationalists* – included car firms, electrical equipment makers (including makers of consumer electronics), producers of electrically powered machinery, and the oil firms. Although these firms sold the majority of their production in domestic markets, their incorporation of continuous-flow production processes made them extremely competitive in world markets. Consequently, all of them sold an increasingly substantial portion of output overseas or had transnationalized into Europe, Latin America, or even the Pacific before World War II. Roughly 15 percent of car firms' investment and nearly a quarter of machinery firms' capital was in foreign countries, compared with an average level of 6.5 percent for all US manufacturing (Frieden, 1988: 65). This group also encompassed two other elements traditionally oriented towards world markets: the large New York banks that financed US international investment and trade, and the cotton and tobacco South. In the 1920s roughly half of cotton production – America's largest export, followed by oil and cars – and one-third of tobacco production were exported. This group had strong connections to the State Department and to a lesser extent the Treasury. The Democratic Party largely represented this group after 1932, adding the industrial group to its existing base in the southern states.

Put simply, the first group did not see how spending tax money and political capital on saving Europe or the international economy during the 1930s advanced their interests. The second did. The first group dominated the executive in the 1920s, and the second in the 1930s, but the balance between them was too fine during these periods to produce any decisive outcome. US policy in the 1920s and 1930s thus made only hesitant and erratic moves towards a larger international role.

For example, during the 1920s, the United States pursued limited and contradictory policies towards international economic stabilization. The US Treasury orchestrated the 1924 effort to stabilize the hyperinflating German economy and to settle the war reparations question by providing start-up capital for a new German central bank and a new (and hopefully stable) currency, the reichsmark. But the Treasury had to do this by inducing private lending institutions, such as J.P. Morgan and Company, to underwrite the $100 million Dawes Plan loan. Meanwhile, nationalists had successfully instituted a procedure that allowed the State Department to veto private flows of capital overseas. Nationalists and internationalists also fought twice over debts left over from World War I, with nationalists demanding full payment while internationalists favored a write-down of debts to the United States (Pullen, 1987). Finally, the New York Federal Reserve Bank also maintained close ties and tried to coordinate policy with the Bank of England, but largely because of the close friendship between the banks' heads.

Franklin Roosevelt's election in 1932 shifted policy in a slightly more internationalist direction, but only after an initial effort at unilateralism. FDR delinked the dollar from gold just before the 1933 London World Economic Conference to help restore US farm incomes. At that conference, the British proposed an international fund to help stabilize currencies and to remove controls over capital movements, a forerunner of the International Monetary Fund (IMF) created in 1944. The United States rejected this proposal; instead, in 1934, Roosevelt devalued the dollar by ending gold convertibility. Fears of further competitive devaluations and trade restrictions led Cordell Hull, then secretary of state but also a long-time representative of southern cotton interests, to press for a more multilateral approach in both money and trade policy. Roosevelt obtained legislation empowering the executive in international trade negotiations. The 1934 Reciprocal Trade Agreements Act (RTAA) shifted negotiating power over tariff levels from Congress to the president, bypassing the vested interests that had passed the highly restrictive Smoot–Hawley Tariff in 1930. It did so only for limited periods of time, requiring Congress to renew this delegated power. The 1936 Tripartite Monetary Accord created a basis for cooperation among the central banks of France, Britain, and the United States to control exchange rate fluctuations in their currencies. It paved the way for a return to a mixed gold–dollar standard. Finally, in 1938 the United States and Britain agreed to a trade pact, partly to counter Germany's rising power.

Breaking the foreign policy deadlock

These two domestic groups, the nationalists and internationalists, remained deadlocked until the war changed every one's positions, partly by changing the nationalist group's calculation of interests, partly because, as mentioned earlier, a third group emerged to tip the balance between nationalists and internationalists, and partly because it created within the state itself an enlarged set of bureaucracies that consciously defined US security interests in terms of an expanded global economic role.

The nationalists' position changed in response to the domestic and international consequences of World War II. The great state-sponsored expansion of aggregate demand during the war revealed the utility of a macroeconomically interventionist state to the nationalist group. Steel mills that had run at one-third capacity during the 1930s suddenly found demand forcing them to expand capacity. The nationalists conceded the need for Keynesian policy, as long as it was oriented towards the domestic market, but they wanted Keynesianism via massive tax cuts, not via a continuation of the enlarged and intrusive wartime state. They also wanted to try to roll back the power of the new and militant labor unions, like the Congress of Industrial Organizations (CIO), which had emerged during the late 1930s. The war also permanently removed their temptation towards a genuinely isolationist foreign policy, even though they continued to see domestic markets as the ultimate source of American prosperity. They grudgingly acquiesced in a larger international role for the United States through the Marshall Plan and the 1948 Vandenberg Resolution expressing US willingness to intervene militarily in Europe. Militarily, however, they favored a small, cheap army based on selective service, which would limit the size of overseas armies (Eden, 1984).

In contrast, the internationalists' intertwined domestic and international interests motivated them to push for a strong US presence overseas. Because labor peace was essential for continuous use of assembly-line factories, they favored an accommodation with the new labor unions as long as management controlled investment decisions (Rupert, 1995). They also favored Keynesianism, but they argued that full employment ultimately required the expansionary effects of further exports. In 1947, the peak year for immediate postwar exports, some 5 million jobs and 7 percent of GDP relied on exports. The internationalists also hoped to tempt Midwestern farmers out of the nationalist bloc with subsidized overseas grain sales. More exports were impossible without help for European reconstruction and without efforts to open world markets.

Internationalists thus wanted the United States to take up Britain's old pre-World War I role and restore an open trading order, free capital movements, and convertible currencies. While they preferred an accommodation with the Soviet Union, they ultimately settled on George Kennan's idea of containment to provide a measure of security for Europe. Kennan's vision called for control over at least three and preferably four of the five great industrial zones in the world: the United States, Britain, Continental Europe, Japan, and Russia. Thus internationalists favored permanently occupying Germany and Japan to assure US security interests, and revitalizing those economies to assure domestic stability. Internationalists also argued that American prosperity depended on access to the raw materials provided by Southeast Asia and Latin

America, the so-called Grand Area (Shoup and Minter, 1977). Thus, they favored universal military training and a large conscript army in Europe to deter any Soviet attack, aggressive decolonization of the European empires to attain political stability in and economic access to the Grand Area, and permanent international institutions to regulate trade and money. Overall, the internationalists favored a state that was much more intrusive internationally and domestically than that which the nationalists favored.

The war created a third, initially small, group – *security internationalists.* During the war, military procurement reversed the centralizing tendencies in Krugman's model and industrialized part of the US agricultural periphery. Shipbuilding, aircraft, and electronics production moved to the Pacific Coast and the South. The security internationalists' interests merged with those of existing West Coast groups oriented towards Asian markets. The military component of this group faced massive cutbacks in spending as the United States demobilized. The civilian component faced sagging export sales as the early phase of decolonization destabilized Asian markets. They coalesced around an expansion of military spending aimed at rolling back the Soviet Union, and even more so the People's Republic of China after 1949. They therefore had some interests in common with each of the older two groups. Like internationalists, they favored expanding the state: domestically, they wanted more government spending and thus taxation; internationally, they wanted a strong US presence overseas, especially in Asia. Like nationalists, they feared the power of labor unions, which they saw as communist-dominated and with whom they had had numerous conflicts during the war (Seidman, 1953). Finally this group was tightly connected to the new security bureaucracies in the US state, which magnified its political power.

This third group resolved the old pre-war deadlock, because two groups could line up along a common axis of interests against the remaining group. Mutual accommodation produced a series of compromises after 1944 on international economic and security issues. While significant conflicts over the conduct and content of foreign policy continued, convergent interests permitted some consistent policy. The internationalists and security internationalists combined to press for a major international role for the United States. As the nationalists wanted, this would not be an expensive, unilateral role. Instead, the United States would attempt to create multilateral institutions in which all countries would be expected not only to cooperate but also to contribute. Thus, the IMF would act as a lender of last resort, but not by forcing the United States to accept any increase in imports that might cut into domestic firms' sales. Similarly, the internationalists had to settle for the General Agreement on Tariffs and Trade (GATT), which was a watered-down version of the International Trade Organization (ITO) they had originally wanted, but which had also threatened Congress's prerogatives over trade and even more so agricultural policy.

Anticommunism supplied the common ground for nationalists and security internationalists, so US efforts to restructure the world economy were justified by an ideological crusade against communism at home and abroad, even if this took priority over the internationalists' economic interests (Krasner, 1978). Economic (and arguably strategic) interests might have inclined the United States towards accommodating the new People's Republic of China in 1949, as France and Britain both did. US security interests, defined by internationalists in terms of containment, tended to favor adding China to the collection of states containing the Soviet Union. However, security internationalists' ties to the old Kuomintang (KMT) regime, now displaced to Taiwan, prevented recognition of the new People's Republic. Finally, the security internationalists demanded a greater level of hostility to the Soviet Union than the internationalists might have preferred. In contrast, nationalists and security internationalists could agree that priority should be given to air and naval forces, and thus implicitly to nuclear weapons as well, rather than to the universal military training that internationalists favored.

Economics and politics: supply, demand and macroeconomic regulation

If compromises among these three groups dictated the *form* the US foreign policy took, the domestic political compromises over how to cope with the economic consequences of mass production dictated the *content* of foreign economic policy. The assembly line and other continuous-flow production processes yielded enormous economic gains from a combination of economies of scale and productivity increases. But the economic rationality of mass production rested on its profitability, and this was hostage to three different problems created by mass production's very productivity.

First, mass production was not profitable if demand was unstable. Mass production assembly lines were highly efficient because they used large systems of capital goods dedicated to the production of a single commodity. These systems were profitable only if they ran at something approximating full-capacity utilization. Unstable demand created unpredictable periods of low utilization. Low-capacity utilization concentrated the large fixed capital cost over a smaller number of units, raising prices and limiting turnover and profits. High-capacity use, however, could create a virtuous circle of low per-unit costs, high sales, high turnover, and high profit rates. These high profit rates would then encourage and fund even more investment in labor-saving machinery and higher productivity. This virtuous circle was vulnerable to unstable and inadequate levels of demand. Thus, while mass production might be more productive than other systems in terms of output per hour of labor, in economic terms its profitability rested on conditions that were largely outside the firms' control. Fear of surplus capacity related to the business cycle thus inhibited investment in mass production processes, despite their absolute productivity advantages over other types of production processes.

The economic rationality of mass production was therefore hostage to its supply rigidity. Because dedicated facilities had to be used continuously, supply could not be changed; instead, some way had to be found to both stabilize demand and raise it to a level adequate to absorb supply. The first efforts at monopolization and/or cartelization offset unstable demand by restricting output to a level well below average demand. As the proportion of mass production firms grew in the economy and as they became more dependent on one another, this unilateral solution could not work. If a few firms misjudged markets or acted out of narrow self-interest, all would suffer (Piore and Sabel, 1985).

Second, even when demand is stable, the absolute level of demand determines the extent to which mass production techniques can be used. Although mass production increased the average worker's productivity, wage increases and thus the ability to consume lagged behind productivity. While many mass production firms raised wages in the United States during the 1910s and 1920s, they did so with an eye not towards balancing supply and demand but towards stabilizing their own workforces. Ford's famous $5-a-day wage aimed at lowering labor turnover from a crippling 300 percent per year to more tolerable levels.

Finally, the assembly line was extremely vulnerable to strikes. Because of the high level of interdependence among all the different components and subassemblies flowing into or down the line, a strike by only a small fraction of workers could paralyze the entire line. During the 1930s, US workers took advantage of this through the sit-down strike. This tactic allowed them to shut down assembly-line production while limiting owners' ability to respond with violence.

Unionization and macroeconomic stabilization

In the United States, unionization and government efforts to stabilize prices and incomes helped resolve these problems. Franklin Roosevelt's victories in 1932 and 1936 created a climate favorable to unionization. When the economy began to climb out of depression in 1935, workers used sit-down strikes to pressure employers to recognize unions, give higher wages, and provide a measure of dignity at work. The automobile industry had experienced catastrophic levels of underutilized capacity after annual demand fell from over 4 million cars in 1929 to under 1.5 million in 1932. When demand recovered to nearly 3 million cars annually in the period 1935–7, firms were reluctant to risk prolonged strikes. In 1935 the United Autoworkers Union (UAW) conducted its first sit-down strike. In 1937, a record 28 million person-days of labor were lost to strikes.

The Congress moved to help workers. In 1935 it passed the National Labor Relations (Wagner) Act, which the Supreme Court affirmed in 1937. This Act confirmed the legality of unions and established conditions for collective bargaining. This law was reinforced in 1938 by the Fair Labor Standards Act, which set a minimum wage and created a uniform 40-hour workweek. The number of unionized workers rose from 4 million in 1934 to 15 million in 1945; by then, about 70 percent of industrial workers were unionized, and many employers offered nonunionized workers union-level wages to preempt unionization.

Workers and/or employers may or may not have understood the macroeconomic consequences of unionization. In hindsight, however, unionization resolved most of the problems of macroeconomic stabilization associated with the assembly line. Successive deals linked wage growth to economy-wide productivity growth, not only increasing aggregate demand but assuring a balance between supply and demand. Long-term contracts with generous health and unemployment benefits stabilized aggregate demand by removing the long-term risk of going into debt to buy cars and houses. Wage increases linked directly to productivity gains assured some balance between supply and demand. The United States promoted its style of unionization in Europe after the war, diffusing this particular solution to demand-side stability (Maier, 1976; Rupert, 1995).

The US-style exchange of wage and productivity gains comported well with the more systematic supply-side interventions occurring in Europe and Japan (Shonfield, 1964). These states actively coordinated investment from the 1950s to as late as the early 1980s. In France, for example, as late as 1980 the state provided about 40 percent of credit in the economy; in Japan the state provided roughly 20 percent of gross fixed capital formation. These targeted investment streams created macroeconomic stability, allowing private firms to continuously invest in new technologies and rapidly expand industrial output. Regulation (and nationalization) of broad swathes of the service sector enhanced macroeconomic stability and industrial expansion. State-owned enterprises in transport, energy generation, and telecommunications announced long-term investment plans, financed them with subsidized capital, and bought equipment from pet domestic suppliers. Health and education bureaucracies acted similarly. Economically this meant most of the economy grew at a predictable pace, fully sheltered from the international market. Politically, it created millions of stable jobs with predictably rising wages (and a predictably rising tax base).

All this conflicted with the free market norms and practices of the pre-World War I British-dominated international system. In that system, economic cycles were allowed to run their course, and production levels rose and fell in response to demand. If firms could not survive through a recession/depression, they went out of business. Internationally, supply and demand came into equilibrium through the pulsation of people and capital from Europe and to the agricultural periphery. These pulsations mirrored domestic waves of expansion and stagnation. Over the long run, nations' trade surpluses and deficits matched because the international production structure was complementary. In the new system, however, trade became more and more intra-industry trade, where countries exchanged differentiated manufactured goods.

Everyone thus tried to damp down the business cycle to make mass production profitable. Firms produced through recessions, gambling that demand would eventually catch up with supply; unions demanded rising real wages; states accommodated both by expanding the money supply during recessions. States could not allow trade surpluses or deficits to disrupt their management of aggregate demand. By the same token, they could not allow large international movements of capital that might disrupt their ability to manage their own macroeconomy in accordance with local political demands.

The multilateral organizations that US political compromises created thus acted to contain world market forces. These organizations rested on a broad consensus about the strategic subordination of international capital flows and the priority of domestic growth, even though conflicts over the implementation of that consensus were frequent. The United States and the European countries present at Bretton Woods all agreed on the continued utility of controls on the international movement of capital (Helleiner, 1994: 33–8). Controls permitted individual states to determine domestic market outcomes and assure full employment. Organizations like the IMF and ITO/GATT provided an arena for regularizing tactical conflicts over money and trade. States' control over capital flows and investment gave them control over strategic issues.

The rise of multilateral organizations

Domestic political compromises thus determined the form and content of US hegemony. Britain was largely content to act unilaterally and rely on markets to enforce its interests. The United States created and acted via a host of multilateral international institutions that reflected an underlying elite consensus on the need for stability. The IMF would act as a lender of last resort, supervising and supporting fixed exchange rates among currencies. The International Bank for Reconstruction and Development (IBRD, or World Bank) and the Organization for European Economic Cooperation (later, OECD) would help European economies recover from the war, shortening the period in which controls over trade and capital flows were necessary. GATT, the successor to the still-born ITO, would help maintain open markets by supervising an orderly reduction in tariff barriers.

The substantive missions of these multilateral organizations reflected the prevailing preference for macroeconomic stability (van der Pijl, 1984). While these new organizations were supposed to undo the deleterious consequences of states' suppression of world trade in the 1930s, this mission was subordinate to states' overriding desire for full employment and macroeconomic stability. But the Depression had offered up contradictory lessons about economic closure. While closure had precipitated the Depression, the Depression and war suggested that a closed economy was a prerequisite for full employment and stability, because no single country could bring global supply and demand into balance. By contrast, states with the proper tools could attain domestic macroeconomic stability. And because the political consequences of unemployment had been so horrific, no political party anywhere would risk letting markets rule unimpeded. These organizations thus embodied contradictory conclusions drawn from the domestic and international lessons of the Great Depression of the 1930s.

The domestic lesson of the Depression was that giving the international market and more particularly surplus producers an unlimited ability to influence domestic production and employment was a recipe for disaster. Before World War I, states could not really control the domestic money supply. However, the war gave them the tools and motivation for doing so. Most observers linked high unemployment in the 1930s to the attractiveness of fascism and communism. Thus, having spent the better part of a century systematically opening up their interior microeconomies to world market forces, states now had both political and economic reasons to limit the impact of international economic fluctuations on their domestic economies. Allowing the international market to affect the money supply and investment would mean that states had lost control over their internal economy.

This domestic lesson conflicted with the supposed international lessons of the 1920s and 1930s. Keynes summarized those lessons pithily, calling for 'the freest possible economic interchange without discriminations, without exchange controls, without economic preferences utilized for political purposes and without all of the manifold economic barriers which had in [his] judgment been so clearly responsible for the present world collapse' (Gardner, 1969: 42). Those lessons seemed to indicate that any deviation from liberal principles would throw the international economy into conflict and a downward spiral. Keynes, however, also argued that this free exchange was possible only when there were mechanisms to force trade surplus countries to come back into balance.

Therefore, each of the multilateral international organizations created by the United States and its European allies reflected states' determination to have their domestic cake while dining in international markets. These institutions would promote a liberal economic order similar to the pre-World War I order – up to the point where that order conflicted with the principle of domestic full employment and stable demand. John Ruggie (1982) has called this contradiction 'embedded liberalism,' arguing that a preference for a liberal international monetary and trading order was embedded in a set of institutions ostensibly oriented towards preserving domestic economic stability. Furthermore, the US position on these agencies' missions reflected the unsettled dispute among the three US political factions.

These twin constraints on international institutions can be seen clearly in fights over the establishment and mission of the IMF and in the failure to establish an ITO and the substitution of the more limited GATT. These fights began at the very first US and British meetings held in 1941 to map out the postwar world, and they continued through to the 1944 Bretton Woods Conference, which planned the postwar monetary order. Disputes over the ITO continued into the 1940s. In the long run, given this contradictory compromise, these institutions could work only so long as the United States was able to absorb surplus production from other countries and convince those same countries to use dollars as the international currency.

The International Monetary Fund

In principle, the IMF's mission reflected the liberal international lessons of the 1920s and the Depression: the world needed stable, fixed, and realistic exchange rates. Fixed exchange rates would prevent countries from using competitive devaluations to expand their exports (or minimize imports). As before 1914, freely exchangeable currencies would be backed *de jure* by gold and *de facto* by dollars (instead of pounds). The IMF would act as a lender to support those exchange rates when countries ran temporary balance-of-payments deficits. The United States and Britain, the major actors at the 1944 Bretton Woods Conference, disagreed on how to get balance, however. After all, given fixed exchange rates, balance could be achieved in one of three ways. Depression era-style direct import controls could be used, but the United States and Britain both agreed that this policy had been a disaster. Second, an imbalance of payments meant that a country consumed more than it produced, leading to more imports than exports. Imports (demand) and exports (supply) could be brought into balance by deflating the economy, inducing a recession, and thus lowering demand for imports. Third, balance could be created by increasing domestic supply, lending money to support ongoing economic activity, and thus increasing exports or import substitutes. The United States and Britain disagreed as to which of the last two methods should predominate. (Asian countries were largely unrepresented at Bretton Woods.)

John Maynard Keynes led Britain's delegation to the conference. Consistent with his *General Theory* (1936), he put the maintenance of a stable macroeconomy and full employment ahead of creditor interests and the maintenance of fixed exchange rates. Instead of local economies adjusting to global pressures, the global economy would adjust to local desires for full employment. Keynes, followed by the Europeans, proposed that the IMF act as a global central bank. The IMF would create a fiduciary or paper money – money without a gold backing to assure its value – called the bancor. Countries running balance-of-payments deficits could borrow this paper money and use it to buy exports from countries running balance-of-payments surpluses. Countries with balance-of-payments surpluses would have to accept this fiduciary money for their exports and then turn around and use it to import more from deficit countries. Debtor/trade-deficit countries would thus avoid having to deflate their domestic economy. Keynes also wanted the IMF to have the power to force surplus countries to revalue their currency, which would decrease their ability to export. Keynes' plan put the burden of adjustment on trade surplus, creditor countries. This contrasted starkly with the old gold standard, in which outflows of gold and foreign exchange from deficit countries automatically forced deflation.

The United States, on the other hand, favored a mix of policies that reflected the balance among its different political groups. Nationalists were skeptical about funding the IMF at all, let alone permitting it to create a fiduciary currency. They favored having deficit countries induce local deflation to return to balance. Internationalists favored a stronger IMF. However, because they realized that the United States would naturally be the world's largest (and perhaps only) creditor/surplus country for quite some time, they also favored limiting the ability of other countries to draw on US resources as Keynes desired. Instead, they were willing to allow trade deficit countries to use nonmonetary means – temporary discrimination against surplus countries' exports – to bring their international payment position back into balance while borrowing small amounts from the IMF.

The US position largely prevailed, because the British understood clearly that postwar US financial assistance was conditional on an outcome closer to US preferences. Both sides agreed on fixed exchange rates, but any re-/deval-uations by more than 1 percent, not Keynes's 5 percent, needed IMF permis-sion. Deficit countries, not surplus countries, were expected to bear the cost of restoring balance through deflation. The IMF was capitalized at $8.8 billion, more than the original $5 billion in the US proposal, but much less than Keynes's $26 billion. The IMF could not force surplus nations to change their exchange rates. And, rather than having an automatic right to borrow IMF funds, deficit countries had to seek IMF approval for borrowing in excess of half of their initial contribution to the Fund. Though this jumps ahead to the last chapters, it is worth noting that Keynes had his revenge: When the US became a debtor/deficit nation after the 1990s it had no way to induce credi-tor/surplus countries like Japan and China to expand their imports from the US.

The International Trade Organization

Where the IMF dealt with monetary issues, the ITO was supposed to deal with trade and investment issues. Like the IMF, the ITO grew out of the interna-tional lessons of the 1930s. On the one hand, the efforts of individual countries to boost their exports through devaluation, dumping, and state-controlled bilateral trade and to cut their imports through quantitative restrictions, higher tariffs, and currency controls had proven completely futile. On the other hand, US initiatives from the 1934 Reciprocal Trade Agreements Act onward had shown that mutual accommodation might engender rising exports for all. During the 1930s, Cordell Hull used this authority to negotiate more than 20 accords, covering about half of US trade and facilitating a rough doubling of exports from their 1932 low point (Kindleberger, 1973: 233–5).

As with the IMF, strategic agreement on the need for multilateral control of trade did not preclude tactical disagreement between the United States and Britain. Both sides agreed to prohibit quantitative restrictions except under extreme balance-of-payments difficulties or in relation to agriculture. Both also agreed to lower tariffs, since more trade probably meant more employ-ment. Beyond that, conflict. Pre- and postwar US policy sought to open up closed French and British imperial markets to US goods (Shoup and Minter, 1977; Thorne 1978). The United States wanted across-the-board tariff reduc-tions along most favored nation (MFN) principles. Hence, any nation that lowered tariffs for goods imported from one country would have to lower them for goods imported from all countries that had MFN status with the importing country. MFN-type tariff reductions would eliminate imperial preference systems, benefiting highly competitive US firms.

In contrast, the British wanted to lower tariffs while retaining the 1932 Ottawa Agreement system. This placed higher tariffs and occasionally quotas on goods imported from outside the empire, giving imperial producers a competitive advantage. From Britain's point of view, these minor preferences were much less an obstacle to trade than the absolutely high US tariff levels created by the 1930 Smoot–Hawley Tariff. In addition, because British firms could not compete with US firms in third-party markets, the British government feared a rapid erosion of the large sterling balances those countries still held in London.

Because employment and profits visibly lay at the heart of this disagreement, negotiations over the ITO were much more contentious than those over the IMF. Even if people and firms understood the arcane nature of the monetary policy governed by the IMF, its effects were more diffuse than specific barriers to physical exports and imports. Consequently, the ITO talks remained deadlocked. In a sense, the United States, Britain, and their allies could compromise over the IMF more easily because uncertainty about the postwar environment made precise calculations of losses and gains difficult. However, the failure to secure an ITO before the war ended and world trade began to revive inhibited the continued pursuit of a compromise. The war had aggravated the uncompetitiveness of British firms (Smith, 1986). It had also depleted Britain's overseas investments, making merchandise exports even more important for the British trade balance. In the United States, the 1946 elections gave the Republicans, and thus the nationalists, control over Congress. They forced the executive to agree that any tariff reductions that imperiled US industries would be subject to an escape clause permitting the United States to continue its tariff in full force.

A face-saving compromise made it possible to finish writing the ITO's charter in 1947, and 50 countries signed it in Havana in 1948. The ITO was unable to get congressional approval, however. In the absence of any comprehensive ITO agreement, tariff negotiations continued along the lines laid down by a protocol contained within the ITO charter, called the General Agreement on Tariffs and Trade. While Congress also refused to approve GATT, it proved a durable, if limited, venue for tariff negotiations. All the areas excluded from GATT – nontariff barriers, agriculture, services, and investment flows – would later become the focal point of the 1980s and 1990s trade negotiations that set up the World Trade Organization.

The international institutions set up under US auspices reflected the specific compromises made in US domestic politics to create an institutional structure to balance supply and demand in a mass production economy. Internationalists overcame nationalists' hesitance about foreign adventures by sharing international regulatory institutions with Europeans. Precisely because those organizations rested as much on European (and later Asian) cooperation as on US power, US power had to be exercised in positive sum ways. The United States could not unilaterally impose solutions without risking a flight from the organizations it had created. At the same time, those international organizations had contradictory missions. They were to prevent a recurrence of the Great Depression by enforcing a liberal economic order, but not at the expense of full employment and continued domestic expansion in the economies participating in those organizations.

Despite conflicts, these institutions succeeded in recreating an integrated global economy by the 1980s. Yet success was self-liquidating. The diffusion of the car leading sector to Europe and Asia undercut US manufacturing supremacy. As Michal Kalecki (1943) had predicted, the pursuit of full employment to assure macroeconomic (and political) stability led to inflation and renewed class conflict. Diffusion and conflict undercut the social bases of support for the Bretton Woods institutions. This prompted an unsuccessful search for new institutional forms and content to balance supply and demand in what had once more become a global and increasingly unstable economy. The subsequent chapters examine this process in specific issue areas.

Chapter 9

International Money, Capital Flows, and Domestic Politics

> ... above all, let finance be primarily national.
>
> *John Maynard Keynes*

In 1992 a hotel in the small New Hampshire resort community of Bretton Woods was sold as part of the Resolution Trust Company's fire sale of properties acquired from collapsed savings and loan banks. This event accurately symbolized the final passing of the post-World War II international economic system. For the 1944 multilateral conference that created the IMF and set exchange rates took place in that hotel, and its owner's bankruptcy emerged from the deregulation of the controlled financial systems characteristic of the Bretton Woods period. Regulated finance, minor crises and inflation gave way to deregulated finance, major crises and deflation as global supply began outstripping global demand. Yet there was constancy within that process of change: both Bretton Woods and the subsequent regime reflected the exercise of US power. The US state sought and benefited from international financial systems that permitted the United States to live outside the normal trade-offs across domestic consumption, domestic investment, and investment abroad. The United States abetted the emergence of the large pool of unregulated international mobile capital that undermined the Bretton Woods monetary order, to avoid constraint.

The Bretton Woods deal embodied two fundamental tensions. The first lay between the imperatives of domestic macroeconomic stability and growth, and adherence to a circumscribed but liberal international trading order, that is, between the domestic and international lessons of the Great Depression (Ruggie, 1982). Put simply, countries had to balance their international pledge to maintain a fixed exchange rate against a simultaneous promise to local firms and workers that governments would print as much money as was needed to maintain full employment. Ultimately these two *political* promises could be kept only if international trade and investment flows were fairly small relative to the size of the world's major economies. If trade and particularly capital flows returned to their pre-World War I proportions, however, either domestic monetary policy autonomy or the international monetary system of fixed exchange rates had to disappear.

This was true because, as the economists Robert Mundell and J. M. Fleming had shown, governments could simultaneously achieve only two out of the three policy objectives of fixed exchange rates, international capital mobility, and monetary policy autonomy (Caves, Frankel, and Jones, 1990;

Table 9.1   *The Mundell–Fleming trilemma: three possible monetary orders*

Policy Choices	Gold Standard	Bretton Woods	1971/75 on
Fixed Exchange Rates	**Yes** fixed against gold (but market premia)	**Yes** fixed vs $, $ fixed vs gold	**No** floating rates (many LDCs – pegs) (EU – an internal peg via ERM/ EMS)
Capital Mobility	**Yes** but few instruments	**No** capital controls in Europe, Japan	**Yes** many instruments
Monetary Policy	**No** few central banks; but Bank of England could move system	**Yes** central banks manipulate money supply; governments provide credit	**Yes** weak, operating indirectly through exchange rate

Frieden, 1991). This meant first, that three broad policy constellations existed, and second, that the choice among them was a political choice, because different policy constellations favored different social groups. Table 9.1 lays out the three Mundell–Fleming worlds, which correspond roughly to the gold standard period (in principle), the Bretton Woods period, and the contemporary era (but also the gold standard era in practice). Capital mobility under the gold standard era favored creditors and capital. Capital controls under Bretton Woods advantaged workers and debtors insofar as these controls permitted full employment and artificially low interest rates.

The second fundamental tension in Bretton Woods lay between its *de jure* cooperative structure and a *de facto* fundamental asymmetry between the United States and the rest of the world. The United States provided the international currency and served as the major source of export growth for most countries and thus for new global demand. This made it the only country that had the power to break the rules established at Bretton Woods. Any political decision about Bretton Woods' future ultimately rested on US perceptions of its national interests (Calleo, 1982; Gowa, 1983; Henning, 1994). US security interests, understood broadly, determined when and how the United States would act to restore, repair or reject the Bretton Woods system. US security interests 'understood broadly' means that the United States has consistently if not always successfully sought to prevent the emergence of peer military and economic rivals. The United States thus sought differential growth, that is, above-average growth as compared to its rich country economic rivals, in order to prevent those rivals from displacing the United States from the center of the global economy (Nitzan, 1998; Schwartz, 2009a). The ability to act without constraint with respect to consumption and investment has enabled the United States to attain differential growth.

During the classic Bretton Woods period, US security worries focused on the communist bloc. Thus the US ignored the domestic economic consequences of its support for Bretton Woods. In any case, these appeared to be minor, because international trade represented a small part of the US economy, and other countries' willingness to hold dollars meant that the United States could for a time run balance-of-payments deficits without fear of a forced devaluation.

But as foreign production recovered, so did foreign penetration of the US market. This compromised America's position relative to Europe. The international side of Bretton Woods had become inconsistent with domestic economic growth, and thus with firms' profitability, politicians' desires for re-election, and state power. The United States was on the wrong side of differential growth favoring its nominal allies. The United States then abandoned Bretton Woods, fully deregulating capital flows and shifting to floating exchange rates in the 1970s. This allowed the United States to generate new global demand and to position US manufactured exports more favorably in world markets. As long as the United States could generate new assets and foreigners were willing to buy them, the United States could monetize its trade deficits. Financial deregulation solved the first issue.

The Bretton Woods monetary system broke down because of two decisions by the United States. First, the United States never imposed comprehensive capital controls like those in most of the Euro-Japanese economies. Because US investors could gain higher returns overseas, capital tended to leak out of the United States. Moreover, chronic US current account deficits also fed this pool of liquid capital. As this pool grew, international capital movements gradually became large enough to swamp countries' efforts to establish independent monetary policy. International capital flows thus increasingly limited the room for European- and Japanese-style *industrial* policy. Creditors and the financial industry seized on this growing difficulty as evidence of the futility of capital controls, and pressed for liberalization. By the 1980s most countries had abandoned capital controls.

Second, the United States consciously decided to let exchange rates float in the belief that dollar depreciation would advantageously position US manufacturers in world markets. Until the 1970s, exports plus imports amounted to less than 10 percent of US gross domestic product (GDP), in contrast to 30 and 50 percent of GDP for the major European economies. This asymmetry diminished by the 1980s, when trade amounted to more than 20 percent of US GDP. Given an inability to directly redress US manufacturers' uncompetitiveness, the United States used its power to change the rules of the exchange rate game. A depreciating dollar in principle positioned US exporters more favorably in global markets, though it did not solve the problem of global oversupply. However, an appreciation for the systemic effects of decreased growth elsewhere tempered this predatory behavior. Too strong a dollar hurt US manufacturers, but too weak a dollar hurt growth in foreign economies that were debtors to the United States. Consequently US exchange rate policy oscillated between driving the dollar down to boost US exports and growth, and allowing the dollar to strengthen so that US consumers could import enough goods to drag other economies out of various financial predicaments. This 'yo-yoing' eroded the Bretton Woods commitments to full employment and social protection.

The United States also changed the rules of the game for trade. Under Bretton Woods only manufactured goods were tradable. The United States, however, possessed large and growing competitive advantages in services and agriculture. It pushed to replace the General Agreement on Tariffs and Trade (GATT) with the World Trade Organziation (WTO) to make services and agriculture tradable (Chapter 12). The nontradability of services and agriculture was an essential part of macroeconomic stability in Europe and Japan, so this also eroded the Bretton Woods employment commitments.

Domestic macroeconomic stabilization became more difficult as the Bretton Woods' capital controls and fixed exchange rates eroded. In this sense the international financial system has gone back to the nineteenth century, when volatile capital flows determined countries' ability to sustain payments deficits, asset sales lubricated international trade, crises were common, and Bank of England intervention occurred only during crises. Unlike the nineteenth century, though, global trade complementarity did not assure a long-term balance between supply and demand. How did we get from there to here?

Back to the future in money and capital mobility

The international monetary system passed through three distinct phases on its journey towards the past. In each phase the United States provided new liquidity and new demand for the global economy in amounts that reflected the continued role of the US dollar as the international reserve currency, US domestic political struggles, and US efforts to maintain its relative power position. From 1945 to 1960 the United States unilaterally ran the international monetary system, and funded other countries' continued balance-of-payments deficits with a mixture of publicly controlled capital and foreign direct investment (FDI). From 1960 to roughly 1975, as the other industrial countries began running trade surpluses, the United States continued to act as the source of global liquidity but faced increasing challenges from holders of internationally liquid assets culminating in the 1971 dollar devaluation. From 1975 to the mid-2000s the international monetary system came to resemble the nineteenth-century system with respect to balance-of-payments financing and capital flow patterns. Capital flows went from rich countries to poor countries, private actors dominated flows, and assets rather than cash or gold backed international lending and money. The dollar's value oscillated as the US state balanced pressure from manufacturers and the finance sector. As this period came to a close in the 2000s one condition reversed, signaling the degree to which supply and demand were out of alignment: capital began flowing from poor countries, particularly China, to rich countries, particularly the US. By the mid-2000s public lenders dominated these flows, a clear sign that politics was driving markets rather than the reverse. The unparalleled US ability to create new financial assets lubricated this process as the financial sector became politically dominant.

The United States acquiesced in the transformation of its trade deficits into rising foreign debt. Like Britain, the United States ran a global system of arbitrage, borrowing short-term at low cost from the rest of the world, while investing long-term at higher returns into the world. And like Britain, the United States used this arbitrage to help fund its increasingly large trade deficits, freeing the United States from the normal trade-offs. Unlike Britain, the United States was a large net international debtor by the end of the 2000s. This debt reflected the fact that only the United States was willing and perhaps able to create the demand needed to absorb global surplus production. The breakdown of the Bretton Woods compromises broke the link between wages and productivity in rich countries. Productivity continued to rise, but median incomes did not. US assets filled the gap, as Chapter 14 discusses in more detail.

Using the US dollar as reserve currency created a contradiction between liquidity and confidence. Only the United States could and would provide international liquidity, but in part its ability to provide liquidity was a function of countries' and private actors' willingness to hold dollars and dollar-denominated assets; this was 'Triffin's dilemma' (Triffin, 1960). For the dollar to function well as an international currency, it had to expand roughly in line with the expansion in world trade. Otherwise, the shortage of dollars would cause falling prices in world markets – deflation. Deflation would remove world trade as an engine of growth for many economies, and it raised the specter of the deflationary 1930s. World trade was expanding at a rate of 8.5 percent a year during 1961–73, well in excess of the rate of growth in the global gold supply (about 1 percent to 2 percent a year). Thus, gold alone could not provide international money in the late twentieth century any more than it had in the nineteenth century. Instead, the United States either had to print enough dollars to facilitate growing world trade, or generate assets to back new money, or both. If not, deflation would occur.

Yet, if the United States printed enough dollars to create international liquidity and put them into circulation by running an imbalance of payments, it would ultimately undermine confidence in the fixed exchange rate for the dollar. Since world trade was growing faster than the US economy (because US manufacturing could not expand output profitably), printing enough dollars to keep up with global trade meant that the US money supply was expanding faster than its own economy. This could lead to several problems. If the United States ran a balance-of-payments surplus, then US inflation would soon rise above European rates. Alternatively, if the Europeans ran a trade surplus and accepted and held dollars, then they would experience inflation. Finally, productivity and output in the United States was not rising rapidly enough for the United States to be able to validate its dollars by exporting goods. Quite the contrary – rising European and Japanese productivity and their undervalued exchange rates combined to allow them to penetrate the US and third-party markets in the 1960s through 1980s, just like Chinese production would do in the 1990s and 2000s. This undermined the value of dollar holdings. The United States could have confidence by choking back the supply of liquidity in world markets, but it could not easily have liquidity and confidence simultaneously. Each of the four phases reflects different assessments of the tension between liquidity and confidence, and the way that these related to US economic gains relative to US competitors.

Phase one: American unilateralism, 1947 to 1958–60

In phase one, the United States unilaterally ran the world's monetary system. Other countries set their currency's exchange rate by reference to dollars, and held dollars as their reserves. States controlled the conversion of local currency into foreign currency and vice versa, and thus also controlled inward and outward overseas capital investment. Contrary to the Bretton Woods plan, free currency convertibility and an easing of capital controls did not occur until the end of the 1950s.

The Bretton Woods architects' optimism derived from their misjudgment about what had destabilized world trade. They thought that open trade could resume once each country stabilized its currency. However, as in the 1920s, the vast productivity gap between the United States and Europe (about 2.5:1) and Japan (5:1) made it difficult to export to the United States. Europe and Japan needed time not just to rebuild what the war had destroyed but also to assimilate US assembly-line and continuous-flow technologies. The only way these countries could earn enough dollars to balance their international trade would be to drive wages and living standards back down to Depression levels. This was politically unfeasible. It was also strategically inconsistent with the US desire to control four of the globe's five key industrial areas.

Since its allies could not earn dollars, the United States simply supplied them with dollars and thus liquidity, allowing them to reconstruct their economies along US lines without further depressing living standards. One-time transfers, like emergency loans to Britain and France or the Marshall Plan, provided about $26 billion (about $240 billion in 2007 dollars) to Europe. US overseas military forces, a flood of US tourists, and investment by US firms establishing subsidiaries in Europe also provided Europeans with cash. All three flows turned a US merchandise trade surplus into an overall current account deficit. Unlike the recycling of the US merchandise surplus in the 1920s, these flows did not create new debts.

The United States easily reconciled liquidity and confidence concerns during this period. European reconstruction with US aid provided a boost to the US economy. Marshall Plan and other aid amounted to a global fiscal stimulus of about 4 percent of US GDP for three years (around 2 percent of global GDP). US military spending and aid were two of the largest net negative entries in the US balance of payments, running at a fairly consistent $5 billion to \$6 billion through the 1950s and 1960s. Meanwhile, Europeans and others unquestioningly held dollars because no alternative existed. Without dollars, they could not buy food, oil and machinery on global markets.

Even if necessity did not dictate that Euro-Japanese central banks hold dollars, the United States' productivity edge and massive reserves created plenty of confidence in the dollar. With gold reserves of roughly \$25 billion in 1948, the United States could more than back its pledge to convert any of the dollars held overseas into gold at \$35 per ounce. Moreover, US inflation rates were lower than the Euro-Japanese rates, providing a useful hedge against local devaluations. Finally, US manufacturing's absolute productivity edge meant that the United States could probably redeem overseas dollars through exports. As it was, only Euro-Japanese currency controls, tariffs, and the peculiarities of local markets held back a flood of US exports in the 1950s. So, during this period, a 'dollar' standard operated, with most countries' central banks using their holdings of dollars as their financial reserves. Exchange controls meant that few private individuals held dollars, but even they had incentives to hold them rather than trying to exchange them for gold. States controlled the bulk of global capital flows.

Phase two: Bretton Woods works, 1960 to 1971 (de facto) or 1975 (de jure)

By 1959, the European economies had recovered from the war, closing the economic gap with the US. They began to abandon currency controls, though many continued capital controls. US multinational firms had helped European producers bridge some of the productivity gap between Europe and the United States. The Japanese (at least formally) abandoned currency controls in 1964. During this period the Bretton Woods system operated much as it was intended to – and almost immediately the tension between liquidity and confidence emerged, much as Triffin (1960) had predicted. The United States' productivity advantage had declined relative to European and Japanese producers. In addition, Euro-American inflation rates steadily converged during the 1960s, thereby highlighting the fact that the dollar was just another paper currency. By 1960, too, dollars held overseas roughly equaled US gold reserves, opening the dollar to speculative attacks. If all foreign-held dollars were cashed in, the United States would have to balance its current account or devalue the dollar, because no gold would be left to redeem new dollars accumulating overseas.

The US government initially responded to the erosion of confidence in the dollar in two ways. Internally, it created a variety of soft capital controls to try to stem the movement of dollars overseas. It tried to raise short-term interest rates above long-term rates to attract capital back to the United States; it imposed the Interest Equalization Tax, which reduced yields on higher-paying loans to Europe relative to equivalent US securities; and it imposed the Voluntary Foreign Credit Restraint Program and Foreign Direct Investment Program to set ceilings on lending from US banks and parent companies.

None of these worked. Firms and banks quickly found ways around lax regulations, while more stringent regulations would have been politically impossible. The Kennedy administration also cut taxes to spur faster domestic growth and restore the US–European growth differential.

Second, externally, the United States used its political power to pursue central bank cooperation in defense of the dollar and other currencies (Zimmermann, 2002). The major central banks set up a 'gold pool,' agreeing to swap gold among themselves to support the dollar at $35 per ounce of gold, and agreeing to support one another if speculators attacked their currency. Until 1967, the Euro-Japanese central banks, France excluded, held and tried to sterilize dollars. 'Sterilize' means that, after they accepted dollars from their citizens and exchanged them for local currency, central banks then tried to raise local interest rates to mop up this new emission of local currency. Holding dollars thus forced them to choose more inflation or slower growth (Parboni, 1981). The United States also encouraged an upward revaluation of the German deutschemark as a controlled and disguised devaluation of the dollar.

These responses failed to prevent the long-term erosion of confidence in the dollar. After the gold pool failed to prevent a run on the British pound and dollar in 1967, the United States asked the Europeans to replace it with a new two-tiered gold market. In this new arrangement, central banks agreed to exchange their currencies at the old Bretton Woods par values only among themselves, while in a second private market, gold and currencies would exchange at market rates. Privately, Germany agreed not to exchange its growing pile of dollars for gold. *De facto*, the two-tier gold market and German promise amounted to a US default on its promise to back up dollars with gold.

The material basis for the erosion of the dollar lay in the growing pool of capital held as eurocurrencies and the relationship between this pool of capital and the emerging US trade deficit. The eurocurrency market began as communist countries' dollar deposits in London banks. US multinationals avoiding taxes and oil exporters parking funds swelled this pool of stateless deposits. Because these deposits fell outside normal domestic banking regulations, banks accepting eurodollar deposits could lend more cheaply, pay depositors higher interest rates, and still make higher profits.

Faith in the US dollar fell as the eurodollar pool – initially a collection of US IOUs – grew. By 1970, eurocurrency deposits amounted to five times US gold reserves. (By 2003 the eurocurrency market deployed over $16 trillion, substantially larger than US GDP that year.) Eurodollars (and later eurocurrencies) were the physical manifestation of the US inflation and balance-of-payments deficits. Had the United States been able to export more goods, eurodollars would perforce have come home as payment for those goods. So the growth of eurodollars in the days of European capital controls mirrored the increasing inability of the United States to export manufactured goods and earn back the dollars it spent buying other countries' exports.

The US's deteriorating export capacity in turn derived from rising inflation and slowing productivity growth (see Table 9.2). President Kennedy planted the seeds for inflation, expecting that his tax cuts would produce, first, growth,

Table 9.2 *Inflation rates and industrial productivity growth in the United States, EU countries, and Japan, 1950–76, selected years*

	Inflation Rate			Productivity Growth 1950–76 (annual increase, %)
	1960–65	*1966–70*	*1971–75*	
United States	0.3	4.3	6.8	2.8
Germany	2.6	2.6	6.3	5.4
France	3.7	4.2	8.8	5.0
Britain	3.1	4.6	13.1	2.6
Italy	4.5	2.9	11.5	4.3
Japan	5.9	5.4	11.6	8.3

Sources: Based on data from OECD (2008c) and Parboni (1981: 93).

second, new tax revenues, and thus, finally, a balanced budget. (This was more or less what Reagan expected in 1982 and George Bush in 2001–3.) If the United States had been a truly closed economy, or had been able to deploy effective capital controls, this fiscal stimulus would have caused increased investment in the domestic economy. Productivity might have continued to grow rapidly as businesses sought solutions to the tight labor markets of the 1960s. But businesses could take their money and invest anywhere they pleased, including overseas – and they did. By 1970 manufacturing firms were making about 25 percent of their new investment overseas, increasing productivity in America's competitors, not the United States. While US investment overseas increased US control over global production, it also worsened the US balance of payments, as US transnational firms substituted overseas production for US exports (Gilpin, 1975).

Phase three: dollar 'yo-yos,' 1971–5 until the mid-1990s

By 1970 US inflation rates had reached the average level in Europe, and the United States ran its first trade deficit in merchandise goods – a sign that its economy had weakened considerably. Import penetration in manufactured goods had doubled to 16 percent by 1971–3, reflecting especially a worsening deficit with Japan. These various bits of bad news drastically decreased confidence, causing a massive outflow of gold from US reserves. So in August 1971 Nixon unilaterally devalued the dollar by 10 percent, raised tariffs by 10 percent, and made the dollar inconvertible into gold. Nixon delinked the dollar from gold in order to stimulate the US domestic economy through increased exports, and so assure his re-election and close the relative gap with Europe. Bretton Woods was dead.

Bretton Woods, murdered by Nixon in 1971, was finally buried via the Second Amendment to the IMF's charter in 1975. This amendment 'legalized' floating exchange rates. But rates had been floating *de facto* since 1971. Floating exchange rates appeared to diminish the confidence-liquidity dilemma by diminishing the German and Japanese ability to export. The

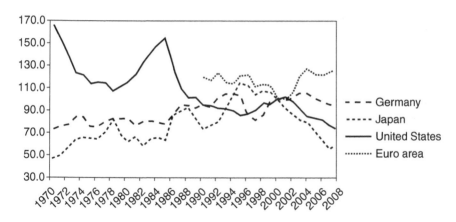

Source: Based on data from OECD (2008b).

Figure 9.1 *Relative unit labor costs, G3 countries and Euro area, 1970–2008, common currency basis, 2000 = 100*

deutschemark rose nearly 50 percent and the yen almost 30 percent against the dollar by 1973. The US state could now promote domestic growth rather than having to defend the dollar's exchange rate. Détente with Russia and China permitted the US state to focus on competition with Europe and Japan.

The burial of fixed exchange rates opened the door to US efforts to manipulate the dollar's exchange rate in pursuit of more manufactured goods exports. (Chapter 12 discusses trade negotiations to open the door to agricultural and service exports.) Carter, Reagan and Clinton all produced yo-yos in the value of the dollar in an effort to lower US manufacturers' relative unit labor costs (RULCs), and thus make them more competitive in world markets (in Figure 9.1 a falling trend indicates greater price competitiveness). But consistent trade deficits under Carter, Clinton, and especially Reagan, increasingly undermined the United States' ability to pursue unilateral policies by expanding US net foreign debt.

The Europeans tried to insulate their monetary policies and growth from the US dollar yo-yos by recreating Bretton Woods at a regional level. They tried to fix exchange rates among European currencies through the 1972 and 1975 currency 'Snakes,' the 1979 European Monetary System (EMS), and finally the 1999/2002 currency unification under the euro. The first Snake died quickly. A reconstituted Snake emerged in 1975, but collapsed in the face of substantial US dollar devaluations in the late 1970s. In an eerie replay of the Snake's second collapse, the falling dollar and the costs of German unification in the late 1980s undermined the EMS in a spectacular crisis in 1992–3. The euro so far has survived difficulties reconciling divergent inflation and growth rates in the European Union, but it remains to be seen if it will survive the strains created by the 2008 global financial crisis.

Both academic theorists and politicians thought that the shift to floating rates after 1973 would help countries avoid having to choose between competing international and domestic needs. Under Bretton Woods, an effort to slow inflation by raising interest rates acted directly on the economy. Rising interest rates induced actors to slow investment and lower debt-financed consumption. As Keynesian multipliers reduced everyone's consumption, demand for goods and services would fall, easing inflationary pressures. Because of capital controls, foreign capital could not crowd into the economy in response to high interest rates. Conversely governments could also artificially lower interest rates to induce extra investment without fear of capital flight.

But as capital controls proved harder to maintain in the face of a growing pool of eurodollars, attempts to inflate the domestic economy in order to have full employment put great pressure on the exchange rate and central bank foreign exchange reserves, for speculators would attempt to sell local currency against other stable currencies. In turn, falling reserves would cause deflation, undoing local policy. Theoretically, with floating rates central banks would not be obliged to use their reserves to buy their own currency. Floating the currency would decouple decisions about domestic policy from exchange rate pressures.

These theoretical hopes about floating rates proved illusory, because monetary policy no longer acted directly on the whole economy once capital controls were removed and exchange rates floated. In the contemporary period, monetary policy in most countries can be used to speed up or slow down the economy only through its effects on the exchange rate, and thus through its effects on the traded sector of the economy, rather than directly as under the Bretton Woods system (see Table 9.1 above). An effort to lower inflation by raising interest rates in the context of free capital mobility would draw in foreign capital seeking high returns. As investors exchanged foreign currency for local currency to make their investment, the local currency would appreciate relative to foreign currencies. A rising currency would then price local exporters out of world markets; as demand for exports fell, exporters would reduce investment and lay off workers. Similarly a rising currency would also make imports cheaper, leading import-competing firms to reduce levels of investment and hiring. These investment and wage reductions in the traded sectors of the economy would then lower inflationary pressures. But few countries, particularly in Europe and Japan, could tolerate the political costs of rising unemployment in the traded sector of the economy, because both firms and workers in that sector were highly organized. Nor could they tolerate the economic costs of decreased exports, because they both feared a long-term erosion of their position in overseas markets and because trade deficits led to an accumulation of costly foreign debt.

These political pressures exacerbated the growing imbalance between global supply and demand. The recovery and expansion of European and Japanese production flooded goods markets with excess supply (Strange and Tooze, 1981). But Europe's tight labor markets and its search for monetary insulation from the United States diminished growth in demand. Germany acted as the monetary anchor in Europe's variations on a regional Bretton Woods, but unlike the United States, Germany prioritized domestic monetary stability over 'international', i.e. European, liquidity. And the Japanese state similarly compressed domestic demand. Under Bretton Woods, the US unilaterally filled the gap between global supply and demand by absorbing excess exports. But Nixon's whole purpose in ending gold convertibility was to shift part of the responsibility for generating demand back onto the Europeans and Japanese.

Only international policy cooperation could resolve the supply–demand gap given capital mobility. If everyone reflated at the same time, then exchange rates and trade deficits would remain reasonably stable as demand caught up with supply. If states pursued discordant policies, however, most unilateral efforts to reflate would cause exchange rate gyrations and damage the initiator's economy. But governments in the United States, Germany/Europe, and Japan had diverging interests, and so pursued contrary policy goals, with choices by the United States producing oscillations in exchange rates – the dollar yo-yos – and thus the world economy.

Yo-yo number one: the dollar goes down

During the 1970s Nixon, Ford and Carter all allowed the dollar to decline roughly 20 percent relative to other currencies in order to increase US exports. The rapid fall in US RULCs led to a temporary trade surplus, but the 1973 oil shock led to a temporary strengthening of the dollar as oil exporters agreed to recycle their surpluses into US banks and treasury debt (Spiro, 1999). The fundamental policy divergence in this environment lay between the United States and Germany. The United States wished to pursue a rapid reflation policy, whereas the Germans wanted to keep down the inflation induced by the oil shock. This policy divergence continued in later decades, as more rigid European labor markets created continual central bank fears of inflation.

The Carter government tried to reflate the US economy after the 1973–5 recession induced by the oil shock. This started the first global yo-yo in the dollar's exchange rate by widening the US trade deficit and flooding the world with US dollars. Carter's policy raised the dollar back to 100 percent of its 1971 exchange rate level from the roughly 80 percent of 1973. Carter's policy caused GNP growth rates well in excess of the European average in the second half of the 1970s. On average, the major European economies grew about 3 percent per year in real terms after the 1973–75 recession, while the United States grew about 4.5 percent. However, the Carter administration's policy tools – mostly fiscal deficits but also lower interest rates – caused growing US inflation and a flight from the dollar. By 1980 US inflation had doubled to 13.5 percent, and the trade balance had gone from surpluses in 1975–6 to deficits averaging an unprecedented $30 billion per year, driving the dollar's value down to 72 percent of its 1971 value by 1980. This yo-yo in the dollar's value, more than twice the 10 percent devaluation Nixon had ordered in 1971 and in both directions, disrupted European and Japanese efforts to use exports to the United States to revive their own economies and their efforts at monetary stability.

Unilateral US reflation had led to differential growth in the United States as compared with Europe, and thus initially strengthened the US dollar. But as the dollar rose, making US exports weaker, Carter tried to drive the dollar's relative value down in order to use exports to sustain domestic economic expansion. Reagan would repeat this oscillation but more violently; Clinton more gently. Meanwhile, the Europeans tried to stabilize exchange rates inside Europe around the German deutschemark, in the second currency 'Snake' arrangement. The Snake collapsed as currencies appreciated at different rates against the dollar and as European countries pursued different domestic policies. The deutschemark experienced the most extreme appreciation, rising nearly 50 percent from 1976 to 1979. To maintain parity with the deutschemark, the weaker economies would have had to appreciate their currencies to levels that threatened their growth. Thus, one by one, countries put domestic concerns ahead of exchange rate stability and dropped out of the Snake.

From the Europeans' point of view, the problem continued to lie in the United States' efforts to escape constraint by dining out on its international credit card. The United States refused to accept the costs of the first oil shock by allowing the price of domestic oil and natural gas to rise to market levels. Ford's and Carter's attempts to pull the economy out of the 1973–5 recession relied on excessive credit creation in the US economy. As long as the United States gave artificial boosts to demand, it would run balance-of-payments deficits and have higher inflation.

From the United States' point of view, the problem lay in Euro-Japanese free riding: these governments refused to reflate their economies and thus absorb some of their excess manufactured goods production as well as US service and agricultural exports. By reflating alone, the United States risked higher inflation rates and trade deficits than did the other major economies, which was what put downward pressure on the dollar. Since a reflating US economy helped pull the other economies to export more and thus grow out of their recessions, the United States thought those economies should also bear part of the risk of increasing inflation. Conversely, the United States also accused the Japanese and Europeans of 'dirty floating' – of deliberately manipulating their currencies to keep the dollar's value from falling. Carter was willing to cooperate with the Europeans and, if necessary, to intervene in foreign exchange markets to bring currencies back to what his administration thought were equilibrium exchange rates.

At the 1978 Bonn G7 conference, the Americans, the Japanese, and the Europeans tried to work out a basic deal on coordinated reflation (Putnam and Bayne, 1987). The United States agreed to tighten monetary policy and to decontrol oil prices – that is, to accept the decline in national income that had been caused by the oil shock. Paul Volcker, an advocate of low(er) inflation, replaced Arthur Miller as chair of the Federal Reserve Board in 1979. The Germans and Japanese agreed that, like the United States, they would serve as the 'locomotives' to pull the world economy out of recession, lowering their domestic interest rates and using fiscal policy to reflate their economies.

But the Bonn agreement had perverse consequences that drove each country to go it alone in the next round. The 1979 oil shock delayed US decontrol of oil prices. Meanwhile, European and Japanese central bankers felt that their efforts at reflation only caused growing fiscal and trade deficits and higher inflation in their own countries. Japan's inflation doubled to 8 percent, its overall fiscal deficit hit 4.4 percent of GNP, and it had a current account deficit of 1 percent of GNP in 1979 and 1980. Germany's inflation rose to 6 percent, the fiscal deficit hit 5 percent of GNP, and it ran its first trade deficit since the 1950s. In each country, the government's net debt position roughly doubled as a percentage of GDP, causing net interest payments and thus fiscal deficits to rise. These domestic costs made the Germans and Japanese particularly insistent that the United States not abuse its asymmetrical power and that it sort out its domestic problems before they would act to coordinate macroeconomic policy again.

Yo-yo number two: Reagan's roundtrip
Under Reagan, the United States again resorted to unilateral action for domestic economic and political reasons. After 1979 Volcker raised real interest rates to unprecedented levels in an effort to choke off US inflation. This combined with the 1979 Iranian-revolution oil shock to plunge the world back into recession. High interest rates, however, started a second yo-yo as the dollar rose to 130 percent of its trade-weighted 1971 value in 1985. Domestic and security concerns motivated the Reagan administration's unilateral pursuit of a stronger dollar. Reagan pursued very tight monetary policies in order to stop inflation, which both the Japanese and Germans agreed with. The United States and the Euro-Japanese, however, diverged on fiscal policy as a tool for reflation. For domestic political reasons, the Reagan administration preferred to cut taxes immediately but to put off spending cuts until sometime in the future. The tax cuts of 1981, designed to cement the Republican Party's 1980 electoral coalition, caused enormous fiscal deficits as the Reagan administration simultaneously expanded the US military. Germany and Japan pursued precisely the opposite policy mix: they wanted first to bring down spending slowly, and then to loosen both monetary and fiscal policy to reflate their economies. The high levels of public debt and fiscal deficits inherited from the 1978 locomotive effort made them deeply suspicious of the Reagan approach.

Reagan's enormous and rising fiscal deficit successfully reflated the domestic economy, but domestic reflation combined with a rising dollar made it harder to export and much much easier to import. This unstable situation, with high interest rates keeping the value of the dollar higher than the evolving trade deficit would have permitted, suited the Europeans and Japanese. Their economies reflated precisely because import penetration of manufactured goods in the United States rose from 20 percent in the 1970s to 32 percent by 1985. From 1980 to 1985, external demand generated one-third of Japanese GDP growth and three-quarters of German GDP growth. This free ride on the expanding US trade deficit may have suited the fiscally and monetarily conservative finance ministries and central banks in these countries, but it placed them in a dangerous situation: they had no control over long-term macroeconomic policy as long as the United States pursued a 'go-it-alone' strategy, but the reverse was not as true. If they went it alone, they could not hope to influence US policy. The United States drove growth in the world economy, and because it did, it could potentially choose to slow growth as well. With the dollar at unsustainably high levels in 1985, both Japan and Germany had reason to fear the consequences of a free fall in the dollar and the US economy. So the United States still held the cards. If the United States could negotiate a deal with one or the other of the major economies, then it could distribute the benefits of US reflation differentially.

By 1985 and 1986 the domestic and security concerns motivating Reagan administration policy had changed. On the security side, the Soviet Union was visibly weakening. The domestic sources of the Reagan policy shift lay in the erosion of the manufacturing sector because of the high dollar. The high dollar had cost the US manufacturing sector about 1 million jobs, and even in the highly efficient agricultural sector it had led to import penetration in markets like wheat. The trade deficit jumped from $12.5 billion to $178.7 billion, from 1980 to 1986 (both in 1982 dollars). Capacity utilization in US manufacturing fell from 1984 to 1986, despite economic recovery (Henning, 1994: 276–7). Reagan's manufacturing constituencies began pressing for relief, so Reagan began looking for ways to lower interest rates and the dollar's value against other currencies. Reagan thus combined efforts to divide and conquer the other rich economies with efforts to get monetary cooperation. In its divide-and-conquer efforts, the Reagan administration tried to play the Japanese card against the Europeans and the French card against the Germans (and especially the Bundesbank) in hopes of getting a pact with everyone.

But Reagan also pursued cooperation with the other major central banks to prevent a precipitous fall in the dollar. The Japanese and the Germans were inclined to cooperate because a precipitous fall in the dollar's exchange rate would hurt their externally driven economies. At the Plaza Hotel in New York in September 1985, after the dollar had already fallen about 10 percent from its early 1985 peak, these countries agreed to lower the dollar another 10 percent, and to lower interest rates if the United States cut its fiscal deficit. The Euro-Japanese price for this deal was the subsequent Gramm–Rudman–Hollings Deficit Reduction Act of December 1995. As it turned out, the dollar slid by about 40 percent against the yen and the deutschemark during 1985–7, as speculators magnified central bank actions. Japan and Germany ran larger fiscal deficits, and after 1985 domestic growth picked up in both countries.

The United States tried to divide and conquer its competitors by playing the French against the Germans and the Japanese against the Europeans. The French disliked the very high interest rates imposed by the German Bundesbank on the rest of Europe via the EMS. To weaken the Bundesbank, the French preferred relatively firm exchange rate signals as triggers for intervention by central banks in the five largest economies. These automatic signals would constrain the Bundesbank's ability to exert deflationary pressure in the

EMS. The price the United States asked, however, proved too high for the French: a serious effort to liberalize trade in agriculture at the upcoming Uruguay Round of the GATT talks (see Chapter 12).

Unable to move the Europeans, the United States pursued a separate deal with the Japanese, most prominently in the 1986 Baker–Miyazawa accord to lower the US and Japanese discount rates simultaneously. The Baker-Miyazawa deal of 1986 foreshadowed a series of bilateral alliances against Europe during the 1980s. Slow European growth, the falling dollar, and US–Japanese cooperation then forced the Germans to try to expand domestic demand. As at Bonn in 1978, the Japanese insisted on a quid pro quo. In return for a promised 6-trillion-yen increase in spending and further liberalization of financial markets, the Japanese insisted that the United States stick to its Gramm–Rudman–Hollings budget reduction targets.

This minimal degree of cooperation proved difficult to sustain. Just as at Bretton Woods, the divergent interests of creditor/surplus and debtor/deficit countries were unbridgeable. Just as at Bretton Woods, it was impossible to force trade surplus countries to increase consumption. Unlike at Bretton Woods, the United States was no longer a surplus country. The United States and France, united as net foreign-debtor and trade-deficit countries after 1988, tried to get the others to agree to specific exchange rate levels that would trigger automatic intervention to reduce surpluses for trade surplus countries. They also tried to get everyone to agree to a common set of macroeconomic indicators that would signal a need for reflation or deflation (Henning, 1994: 284–90). The two creditor countries, Germany and Japan, steadfastly refused to be bound by automatic triggers and a definite set of indicators. They wanted to put the burden of adjustment on deficit countries. Consequently, the G5 central banks and states could not agree on anything more than vague target ranges for intervention.

Like the 1971 Nixon shock, the dollar's exchange rate yo-yo under Reagan disrupted established patterns of growth in Europe and Japan, and shifted support for the dollar away from private capital towards public capital. As the yen rose after 1985, small and medium-sized Japanese businesses found it impossible to export. As providers of a big chunk of campaign financing for the ruling Liberal Democratic party, they screamed for relief from *endaka* (high yen). Instead the central bank lowered its discount rate by nearly half, in the period 1986–8, provoking explosive and eventually unsustainable increases in stock market and property values. In Europe, declining exports forced two EMS realignments, which in effect devalued the French franc. These pressures forced non-US central banks to support the dollar in 1987; about 75 percent of the capital inflow into the United States that year came from central bank interventions buying dollars. This, however, was not an ideal situation for the United States, as it rendered the dollar's international centrality hostage to political decisions. The dollar's shrinking share of foreign exchange reserves through 1990 reflected this weakening. While the dollar comprised nearly 75 percent of official reserves in 1978, by 1990 it had fallen below 50 percent as central banks diversified into various eurocurrencies (40 percent) and yen (10 percent) (Wooldridge, 2006).

Yo-yo number three: Clinton's yo-yo against the yen

The long 1990s (1991–2005) also saw US efforts to manipulate the dollar in its own interests. Chief among these interests was the revival of the dollar's central role, and of US domestic growth. Yet the decade started off unpropitiously with respect to US power and the dollar. Many feared that the rapidly strengthening Japanese yen would replace the dollar, and Japanese growth rates were well in excess of US growth rates. The early Clinton administration thus initially prioritized domestic manufacturing over finance and tried to balance the budget in order to lower domestic interest rates. It held the trade-weighted dollar constant at approximately 90 percent of its 1973 value until 1996, even as the yen rose by almost 40 percent against the dollar. But the Clinton administration had to reverse course when it realized that the rising yen threatened to cause a full-blown financial crisis in Japan.

Briefly, the recession created by the popping of the Japanese stock market and property bubbles in 1990 generated a falling yen and thus a huge increase in exports, particularly to the United States. In 1992 and 1993 the Japanese current account surplus hit 3 percent of GDP, similar to its mid-1980s level. In response, the Clinton administration talked the dollar down against the yen, eventually driving the dollar from 130 yen down to 80 yen. (Figure 9.2 shows the trade-weighted value of the dollar against the US current account deficit.) This made virtually all Japanese exports to the United States unprofitable, as Japanese firms chose to maintain their dollar prices and accept fewer yen. Clinton pressured the Japanese government to expand market shares for US goods like integrated circuits, cars, and food. Clinton's policy was targeted narrowly at Japan, for the dollar actually rose against European currencies in this period. But as the magnitude and depth of the Japanese recession of the 1990s became apparent, Clinton reversed course and allowed the dollar to rise

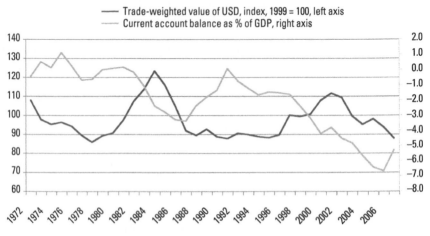

Source: Based on data from OECD (2008b).

Figure 9.2   *Trade-weighted US dollar exchange rate (1999 = 100) and US current account deficit (% of GDP), 1972–2007*

against the yen to boost Japanese exports and growth. Clinton's advisers feared Japan's recession would drag Asia and perhaps the entire world economy into a recession, or worse. By 1996 the yen was back to its early 1990s levels.

The rising dollar prioritized American finance over American manufacturing. This orientation intensified after the 1997–8 Asian financial crises (see also Chapter 14). Just as in the 1980s Latin American debt crisis, the United States accepted a rising trade deficit as the price for avoiding a melt-down of indebted Asian economies. Loose monetary policy in the United States encouraged consumers to borrow against their rising – but illusionary – home equity wealth. Mortgage equity withdrawal – borrowing against the difference between a home's market value and the mortgage debt already contracted on that home – generated $300 billion annually, in 1991–2000, and accounted for an increasing portion of US GDP growth after 1996 (Greenspan and Kennedy, 2007: 9, 17).

Because US growth began running well ahead of Japanese and Continental European growth, the dollar's international centrality waxed. Investors absorbed dollar-denominated assets, reinforcing the US growth advantage. Put too simply, Americans borrowed against their houses to buy cheap foreign goods and renovate their houses, driving unemployment down and tax revenues up. Reassured by US growth and fiscal prudence, foreigners recycled their trade surpluses as purchases of US securities, including bonds backed by US mortgages. These purchases lowered interest rates in the United States, encouraging yet more borrowing. And they also strengthened the dollar, making foreign goods even cheaper.

The George W. Bush administration reinforced all of these tendencies, by adding loose fiscal policy to loose monetary policy. Home prices were already appreciating at a rapid clip under Clinton, but the rate of appreciation doubled under the Bush administration. So too did foreign financing of mortgages for these homes. Foreign lending provided 10 percent of total lending in US credit markets in 1994; by 2005 it accounted for 25 percent (D'Arista and Griffith-Jones, 2006: 64). This made it possible to extract approximately $1 trillion in home equity each year in the 2000s. But this growth was unsustainable, as the 2007–9 financial crisis showed. Even before the crisis, the dollar's exchange rate versus the euro was in free fall. Though this crisis called the dollar's centrality into question, it also simultaneously troubled the euro, the only plausible replacement currency. While the future of the dollar is unclear, renewed US growth at rates above those of its peer OECD rivals would surely stabilize the dollar's position (Schwartz, 2009b).

Winners and losers

US policy produced winners and losers in the international economy. First and foremost, the United States served its own interests, periodically devaluing the dollar to increase the international competitiveness of firms exporting from the United States. Figure 9.1 (p. 207) shows how the three great devaluations of the dollar led to lower unit labor costs in the United States relative to the other two major OECD economies. The US share of world exports, from 1986 to 1998, steadily improved from 11.3 to 14 percent, while the German and Japanese share deteriorated from 20.9 to 15.3 percent. Relative to growth in their respective export markets (thus controlling for economic cycles), from 1986 through 1997, US, German, and Japanese export volumes respectively grew 2.4 percent, fell 2.3 percent, and fell 5.9 percent. The United States' use of the dollar was tempered only by its fear of global financial crisis. The massive Asian financial crises provoked a flight to the dollar, which made it possible for debtors to increase exports to the United States. From 1998 on, US export share steadily fell, precisely because US growth ran at levels well above the OECD average.

Second, in monetary policy coordination (and as we will see in trade policy, too), a tacit US–Japanese and then US–Chinese alliance against the Europeans eventually emerged. The basis for these alliances lay again in an asymmetry in the world economy. Both Japan and China had a disproportionate stake in the US economy. During the 1990s roughly one-third of Japanese exports went to the United States, and disguised exports from Japanese subsidiaries in East Asia increase this share. Absent those exports, Japanese growth would have been more miserable than it already was. Similarly, China's tripling of GDP, in 1990 to 2005, was partly due to its access to the US market, which allowed export volumes to rise sevenfold. In contrast, only about 10 percent of German exports went to the United States and about 3 percent to Japan. The Chinese and Japanese thus abetted US policy by buying increasing volumes of US securities, particularly Treasury Bonds.

US–Asian cooperation diverted the bulk of growth and the benefits of growth in the OECD area largely to the United States. To a limited extent this resulted from the systematic depreciation of the dollar against the yen and deutschemark in the 1980s and 1990s. From 1991 to 2005, the relatively mature US economy grew faster on a population-adjusted basis than nearly the entire OECD, and for a while it outgrew a few of the emerging Asian economies (Schwartz, 2009a). This allowed the United States to keep its share of global output constant at 20 percent, while Japan and Germany each lost ground. Differences in job creation tell a similar story. Overall, the United States added about 35 million jobs (though often low-quality jobs) and unemployment fell below 5 percent; Japan moved from extreme labor shortages to rising open unemployment, and, by some estimates, disguised unemployment of around 6 percent; and Europe lost about 2 million jobs, while unemployment rose to over 11 percent.

The Continental European response has been consistent: set up a zone of currency stability centered on Germany. With intra-European Community trade accounting for more than half of any given country's exports and imports, currency volatility inside Europe would have been costly and economically unbearable. The European Monetary System, which came into effect in March 1979, revived and strengthened the old currency Snake of the

1970s. EMS was a smaller version of Bretton Woods: fixed exchange rates relative to a weighted pool of EU currencies (instead of gold); a 2.25 percent band for stronger currencies and a 6 percent band for weaker ones; and mandatory intervention by central banks. Like Bretton Woods, it was vulnerable to conflicts between external monetary stability and internal growth. And indeed, the EMS unraveled 1992–3 as unemployment rates began rising. This did not prevent the launch of the euro in 1999. This irrevocable monetary unification is also subject to the tensions that severed the Snakes and wrecked the EMS. The 2007–9 financial crisis thus tests whether 'irrevocable' can withstand widening growth disparities across, and widening unemployment within, Europe.

The present structure: back to the future

By 2008 the international monetary system had come to resemble the asset-based exchange system of the nineteenth century. Although the current system is not a formal gold standard system, it functions much like the asset-based international money of the late nineteenth century. In the nineteenth century, capital flows overwhelmed the rudimentary or nonexistent central banks of the peripheral agricultural exporters, including the United States. Slightly stronger central banks in industrial Europe, particularly the Bank of England, were able to manipulate interest rates and gold stocks to maintain stability in their own domestic markets. As in the nineteenth century, international capital movements in the late twentieth century have become so large as to make isolated domestic monetary policy difficult even for the big three economies.

International stocks and flows of assets have become enormous when compared with those in the period 1929–70; they have returned to levels typical of the late 1800s. In 1980 the stock of international bank lending totaled about 4 percent of the combined GDP of the OECD countries, and the stock of internationally issued bonds totaled about 3 percent. By 1991 these had respectively risen to 44 percent and 10 percent of aggregate OECD GDP, roughly approximating the outstanding stock of overseas investment in 1914 in relation to developed countries. By 2008 outstanding international bonds alone amounted to $23 trillion, or about 60 percent of OECD GDP. As in the late 1890s, money can be moved internationally simply by selling assets in one place and buying them in another. Short of reimposing capital controls, central banks are powerless to halt this process. However, the recent *de facto* and sometimes *de jure* nationalization of banks will surely give central banks considerable informal influence over capital movements.

For the large economies, the removal of capital controls (in combination with the privatization of the publicly owned service sector) essentially killed the orchestrated growth of the Bretton Woods era. States could no longer use monetary policy and directed investment to generate rapid growth. As in the nineteenth century, growth now rests on the bottom-up emergence of new growth clusters. Outside of the United States, state efforts to create new regional economies around cutting-edge technologies largely failed. However, as in the nineteenth century, the international monetary system remains asymmetrical. The United States can still manipulate exchange rates in order to position its exporters favorably, just as the Bank of England could manipulate its discount rate to protect the pound sterling. And just as in the nineteenth century, rival powers disliked this and tried to generate their own financial power; this is the significance of European monetary union (EMU) and of recurrent Japanese and current Chinese proposals for something like an Asian Monetary Fund.

In the nineteenth century, the emergence of an asset-based monetary system had positive and negative consequences. Positively, it meant that large imbalances of payments could be sustained for extremely long periods of time, if both capital and confidence were available. Negatively, however, if both capital and confidence evaporated, a country could be drastically and immediately deflated. The Argentine or Australian experience of the 1890s was repeated in Mexico in 1994, and globally in the crises spawned by the 1997 financial crisis that started in Asia. These small economies face precisely the situation the agricultural periphery faced in the 1890s. Volatile capital flows can cause uncontrollable expansions and contractions in the domestic monetary supply. As in the nineteenth century, this can help developing economies grow. The US trade deficit was sustained well past the point anyone would have predicted, precisely because this large pool of international capital was available. Indeed, in 2004 the United States absorbed nearly 70 percent of global capital exports. But, as in the nineteenth century, a sharp reduction in this capital inflow could have catastrophic consequences. Chapter 14 will elaborate this in the context of the 1997–8 Emerging Markets financial crisis and the 2007–9 subprime crises.

Chapter 10

Transnational Firms

A War of All against All

> Trade in Asia must be maintained under the protection of our own weapons; and they have to be paid for from the profits of trade. We can't trade without war, nor make war without trade.
>
> *Jan Coen, Director-General Dutch East India Company, 1614*

The widespread emergence of professionally managed, multidivisional firms in the nineteenth century and advances in telecommunications made it possible for large numbers of firms to implant themselves permanently in the different national economies emerging before and especially after World War I. Before World War I, foreign entrepreneurs had been a pervasive feature in all developing economies, but whenever these immigrant entrepreneurs lacked a corporate structure based in their original home economy they rapidly became indistinguishable from locally rooted firms.

Structural features of the post-World War II global economy accelerated the diffusion of multinational enterprises. The priority given to local employment meant countries only slowly reopened their markets to global trade after World War II. This conflicted with the enormous competitive advantages US firms enjoyed from their ability to manage the assembly line and market on a continental scale. Many US manufacturing firms thus chose to shift a part of their production overseas into those relatively closed markets, becoming transnational corporations (TNCs). This was the only way they could expand their global market share. As European and Japanese firms recovered and expanded, they too ventured into foreign markets to protect or expand their market share.

In contrast to most nineteenth-century manufacturing firms, which manufactured within one national economy and exported finished products to other countries, TNCs dispersed a substantial portion of their production, service, and sales operations into their major overseas markets. They replaced exports with production in former export markets. Although most of these firms operated 'multinationally' – that is, operated relatively autonomous branch plants in the closed economies typical of the Bretton Woods period – eventually many began to integrate their operations into fairly intricate continental and often global divisions of labor. By 2006 the stock of inward foreign direct investment (FDI) was over $12 trillion, direct *overseas* production by TNCs was roughly $5 trillion (about the size of France and Germany combined), and direct TNC production accounted for perhaps one-tenth of world output and half of global turnover (UNCTAD, 2008: 10, 207).

The proliferation of US-based TNCs before and after World War II presented a magnified version of the displacement competition threat that the British industrial revolution posed to European industry. Mira Wilkins (1974) sketched out the basis for displacement:

> What impressed Europeans about American plants in Europe and the United States [in the 1920s and 1930s] was mass production, standardization, and scientific management; in the 1960s Europeans were remarking that American superiority was based on technological and managerial advantage [and] that this expertise was being exported via direct investment.
>
> (1974: 436)

Host countries feared that TNCs would take control of commodity or supply chains in leading-sector industries, and use this to dominate the local economy. TNCs' intrusions into the domestic markets of other countries thus called forth responses like those in the nineteenth century as states sought to create competitive local firms. Host states' responses and local firms' learning and imitation helped competitive laggards catch up with firms using best practice technologies in manufacturing and, to a lesser extent, services. Once these firms caught up with transnational US firms, they, too, began to transnationalize their operations in order to maximize the return on their particular managerial or technological advantages. By the 2000s TNCs from developing countries began taking over older leading sectors like steel and cement.

By the end of the 1980s, direct foreign investment had created three rough regional blocs, characterized by high levels of bilateral trade and investment flows, and centered on the United States, Japan, and the European Union (EU) (UNCTAD, 1991: 31–66). The dominant economy in each bloc also received substantial investment flows from the dominant economies in the other blocs, although Japan remained relatively impervious. In 2007, for example, intra-OECD FDI flows reached $1.2 trillion, and accounted for about 70 percent of all FDI. And about 70 percent of flows to developing economies went to the eleven largest recipients, with China and Hong Kong getting nearly one-third (UNCTAD, 2008: 72–3, 253–6).

This regionalization in turn caused a profound change in the nature of international trade. As world markets gradually reopened during the 1960s and 1970s, TNCs were able to integrate their production flows on a global scale. By the end of the 1990s, roughly half of the trade of developed countries occurred *within* firms as part of their administration of globally oriented production plans, and local production displaced inter-regional exports. For example, the value added by US firms *located* in Europe exceeded all US firms' exports to Europe by 70 percent.

Politically imposed trade barriers provided the initial impulse for transnationalization. But by the 1990s most cross-border investment conformed to the Krugman model in Chapter 2, with rising intra-firm trade merely signaling that the process of dispersion occurred inside firms rather than through arm's length exchanges. Dispersion followed a clear wage and skill gradient.

Politics mattered in a different way. As with nineteenth-century rings, state activity concentrated production in a few favored locations. States intervened because the new TNCs accelerated the diffusion of hard and soft best practice manufacturing technologies. In the worst case, being ignored by TNCs condemned an economy to stagnation. TNC investment alone might contribute to a manufacturing-based Ricardian strategy. And where states evolved an effective industrial policy in response to the displacement threat TNCs posed, they could generate a Kaldorian strategy that propelled them near the ranks of the developed economies. This chapter looks primarily at TNCs themselves and developed states' efforts to control TNCs and shape a Kaldorian strategy. This discussion largely concerns efforts to control the lucrative parts of different value chains. Chapter 11 discusses developing countries' strategies in light of this struggle, while Chapter 12 discusses dispersion in the context of international trade institutions.

The old transnationals

Transnational firms have always existed; recall the Dutch East India Company. These transnationals were simply one way of moving capital internationally in order to capture resources, usually raw materials and climate-specific agricultural products, absent from the home economy. These earlier transnationals were not really transnational (or multinational in the sense of operating in a range of different countries) in either political or economic terms. Most of them connected European economies with colonial or quasi-colonial economies. When they dealt with local or host states, they were often simply dealing with extensions of their metropolitan state. For example, firms like Royal Dutch Shell or Unilever operated primarily in Dutch and British colonies. These transnationals thus often operated within a single legal space, even though their operations were far-flung and global. Even outside formal colonies, the gradual extension of European state power secured various forms of extraterritoriality for transnationals, allowing them the right to operate under their domestic law rather than local law. Nor were the early transnationals particularly transnational economically. Most of them simply extracted raw materials for processing back in the metropolitan economy. The maritime-based connection between urban metropolis and the raw materials periphery was closer and more organic than the low level of integration between the maritime-oriented economy in the metropolis and its own interior microeconomies. The competitive advantage these firms possessed essentially boiled down to the use of political and military power. As we saw in Chapter 1, violence was part of the means of production for these firms.

Consequently, considerable conflict arose between host countries and transnationals extracting raw materials. Put plainly, the basic conflict between hosts and extraction TNCs was about who would capture the rent inherent in production of relatively scarce raw materials. Rents inhere to all nonrenewable raw materials and often to many renewable ones. By definition their replacement cost is higher than the cost of extraction; otherwise, substitutes would be used immediately. In addition, the last unit of supply coming onto the market generally has higher production costs, generating rents for producers with lower costs. These rents can be captured by either the host or the TNC, or they can be shared between them. During the period of direct colonization, TNCs captured the entire rent because the 'host' government existed to support TNC operations. Even with nominally independent states, corrupt governments and the absence of any bargaining skills meant that hosts appropriated little, if any, of this rent and that what they captured in turn was personally appropriated by politicians.

After decolonization, a bargaining situation emerged. TNCs controlled technology and investment capital that were otherwise unavailable to potential hosts. Hosts, on the other hand, controlled access to their raw materials. The distribution of rents between host and TNC depended on the relative scarcity of the raw material in question, the relative scarcity of investment capital, and the relative scarcity of extraction technologies (that is, the difficulty hosts faced in trying to learn or buy extraction technologies). In general, the scarcer the raw material was relative to demand, the more plentiful capital and the easier technological transfer, the greater were the opportunities for hosts to maximize their share of rents, and, if the reverse, the greater was the TNCs' ability to maximize their share of the rents. Whatever the initial bargain struck between TNCs and hosts, bargaining power inevitably shifted towards the host. This became known as the obsolescing 'bargain' because, over time, bargaining power usually shifted towards the host, and thus the terms of the agreement became less acceptable to it, that is, obsolete (Vernon, 1971: 46–59).

Bargaining power shifted towards the host for three reasons. First, once a TNC commits itself to investing and actually builds production facilities, it must operate the facility to recoup its investment. So TNC bargaining power based on threats to relocate evaporate after the TNC invests. Second, over time hosts become familiar with extraction technologies. Finally, accrued rent itself can be used as capital, lessening reliance on external sources of capital. Thus, analysts of the obsolescing bargain typically speak of cycles in which TNCs bargain for a large share of the rent, commit to local production, and then find that hosts demand revision of the bargain in the host's favor. As the bargain obsolesces, hosts extract more of the rent through export taxes, social security contributions, bribes, and so on.

Constant interaction between hosts and TNCs has increased the sophistication of state strategies for capturing rents. Consider the oil industry. TNCs initially captured the entire rent, as the paltry royalties the major oil firms paid the Arabian Peninsula sheikhs show. Once the sheikhdoms became independent, and could rely on a generation of children schooled abroad, they realized the scale of exploitation occurring and began nationalizing oil fields to capture control over the rent. Oil TNCs then retreated back into their refining and distribution networks and used control over these downstream activities to continue extracting rents. They also began developing technology for tapping into offshore oil fields. Oil-producing countries responded by trying to form a cartel so as to present oil TNCs with a united front. The Organization of Petroleum Exporting Countries (OPEC) was virtually the only successful example of a raw materials cartel.

Most of the cartels foundered because, among other reasons, many raw material deposits occurred in *developed* countries in which the issue of rent was less salient. With more diverse economic structures, these developed countries had little reason to make common cause with LDCs. TNCs reinforced this division after 1973, shifting investment to politically safe, raw materials-rich countries like Australia, Canada, and the United States. Once more, oil exporters responded by using revenue captured in price booms to develop or buy refining and processing capacity or to develop new technology. Saudi Arabia, for example, built the world's largest basic petrochemicals complex. Even so, OPEC's power over the market has been erratic. It is strongest when rich country economies are running full blast. But driving prices up inevitably precipitates recessions in those economies, driving oil prices back down. This dynamic has driven much of the oscillation in oil prices since 1979.

The new transnationals

After World War I, this older pattern of TNC investment and its resulting conflicts was displaced by the rapid global expansion of US manufacturing firms. Again, firms sought to capture rents that would otherwise be unavailable to them, although these rents differed from those generated by absolute scarcities of raw materials. Firms wanted access to politically closed markets, or to pre-empt potential rivals. Second, just as the Krugman model in Chapter 2 predicts, wherever labor costs were greater than transport costs, labor-intense manufacturing could move out to regions with cheaper wages. As transportation and communication costs fell through the twentieth century, the incentive for manufacturing firms to disperse their production rationally along a gradient based on skill levels at different wages rose. Service sector firms supplying them followed in their wake.

Post-World War I FDI thus diverged from prior patterns. First, most investment went to developed countries – about 75 percent of FDI since 1945 – because that was where the money was. Second, related to this geographical shift, investment shifted from extraction to manufacturing. By 2006 less than one-tenth of FDI was for raw materials extraction, while manufacturing accounted for three-tenths and services for six (UNCTAD, 2008: 7). Third, TNCs at first seemed to reproduce their entire production complex in host countries, creating what some analysts have called 'multi-domestic' firms. This pattern was an artefact of the Depression and Bretton Woods era segmentation of national markets. As markets reopened, TNCs soon rationalized production along regional or global lines, becoming truly *transnational*.

How can firms transnationalize?

The conflicts these changes created can best be seen by first asking how firms can transnationalize. After all, in a world of perfect markets, FDI should not happen and TNCs should not exist (Kindleberger, 1966). According to international trade theory based on factor costs and comparative advantage, if a foreign company is capable of producing a product locally, using local labor and resources, then a local company should be able to outcompete that firm and drive it from the market. Local companies, after all, don't have to bear the costs of being foreign – of not being integrated into local supplier and marketing networks, of not being politically connected, of losing economies of scale, of bearing the cost of communications and transportation between dispersed operations. In economists' language, transaction costs are higher for foreigners. With lower transaction costs, local companies should be more profitable, and thus able to displace foreign interlopers from their own domestic market. Alternatively, the costs of being foreign should motivate would-be investors to choose portfolio investment rather than direct investment, or should induce firms to license their technology out to local firms and so still capture rents from that technology. What does international trade theory miss here?

Local firms' inability to compete and TNCs' existence indicates that TNCs must have some enormous competitive advantage and/or motivation for investment. Three complementary theories suffice to explain the TNCs' competitive advantages and motivations. These argue that oligopolistic firms transnationalize to attain market dominance and a continued flow of technological rents; that the natural evolution of production processes and markets along a typical product cycle motivated transnationalization based on a transient competitive advantage; and that the asymmetrical nature of markets for information (including technology) makes it more rational for some firms to transnationalize production than to sell or license technology. The oligopolistic rent-seeking model arguments are associated with Stephen Hymer (1972), Theodore Moran (1973) and Charles Kindleberger (1966); the product-cycle model with Raymond Vernon (1971); and the transaction cost approach with Oliver Williamson (1985) and D.J. Teece (1977, 1980).

Hymer and Moran argue that firms desire to pre-empt competitors and expand the ambit of institutional control. Firms compete in oligopolistic markets, using tightly held technology with potentially large economies of scale and in an environment in which the costs of gathering information about the future are high. Because firms compete in oligopolistic markets, they seek to pre-empt competitors in their existing product lines. Their technological advantage declines over time, as products run through a natural cycle, the so-called product life cycle. As this advantage erodes, production technology becomes more standardized, making it possible for firms in export markets to begin competing with the original, innovating firm. At this point, the innovator invests overseas to pre-empt competition.

How do technological advantages erode over the product cycle? Vernon's product-cycle model argues that products and production processes move through four distinct stages (see Figure 10.1). The market for a newly innovated product is unsure and small, and the optimal production technologies are unknown. Consequently, it is a luxury good, produced in small lots by skilled labor using general-purpose machines and at a fairly high cost. Competitive advantage rests on novelty and scarcity and proprietary technologies, which make high production costs less important. By the second stage, production technologies and the market are fairly certain, allowing the introduction of some dedicated machinery. This reduces production costs and allows the market to expand into the middle class domestically. It also makes possible exports to markets with similar income and consumption structures. These exports alert firms in the importing country that a market for these goods exists, but they cannot as yet acquire the technology to produce similar goods *competitively*. Much knowledge about production is embodied in workers' experience as tacit or firm-specific knowledge.

Cycle phase:

Characteristics	Innovation	Growth	Maturity	Stagnation
Location of production	home market, close to final sale	home market	home market, some overseas	mostly overseas
Capital intensity	low, general purpose machines	rises as mass production and special purpose machinery introduced	all mass production, stable demand, long runs	all mass production, stable demand, long runs
Labor quality	high, skilled labor, big 'engineering' inputs	Semi-skilled, big managerial inputs	largely unskilled, management codified	unskilled labor, low wages determine location of production
Barriers to entry	low barriers if have know-how, technology	more mergers, fewer entrants	low entry, oligopolistic competition	entry by foreign competitors (?)
Demand structure	luxury good, sellers' market, small number produced, extent of market unknown	more price competition, more middle-class buyers, market expanding	buyers' market, standard good, price sensitive large volumes	global mass market, differentiation to survive
Exports	no	to foreign luxury markets	FDI replaces exports to foreign markets, no imports	FDI displaces all exports, imports back to home
FDI	no	no		
Imports	no	no		market displace local production
Verdoorn effects	small, local effects	large, local effects	small local, large foreign	small, overseas effects

Figure 10.1   *Product cycle model*

By the third stage, continued expansion of the market combined with more experience has allowed for extensive standardization of production. The good is mass produced using dedicated special-purpose machinery and mostly unskilled labor. This special-purpose machinery replaces much of the workers' tacit knowledge, and so allows importing countries to use tariff and other barriers to encourage their firms to begin production, since the technical challenge is much smaller – simply buying the machinery transfers a significant amount of technology. Tariff barriers also stimulate the original producer to enter the market (if legally possible). The original producer hopes to pre-empt foreign competitors, or to limit their ability to use Verdoorn effects to catch up with (or surpass) it. Thus, the search for continued oligopoly rents and the threat of market closure motivate the original producer to invest overseas, shifting the locus of production. This part of the argument is fully compatible with Krugman's simpler model for dispersion.

The original producer continues to have a competitive advantage relative to upstart firms, but this advantage erodes as those firms acquire greater tacit knowledge through contact with the original producer (which by virtue of having begun local production is now much closer and can be observed) and through Verdoorn effects. By the fourth stage, the product is fully mature, and, because market growth in the home country has leveled off, more and more production is shifted to overseas production sites. Wage costs become a crucial source of competitive advantage since the production process is well understood. Both the original producer and its imitators search for cheap labor, dispersing production to politically stable LDC sites.

Tacit knowledge plays a central role in the product cycle, because it explains why firms with technological advantages prefer to invest overseas, rather than simply licensing technology and taking a minority stake in a local producer. Williamson and Teece, for example, maintain that the transaction costs involved in selling knowledge, particularly tacit knowledge, are extremely high. Buyers cannot evaluate the value of such knowledge until they receive it, but once sellers show a potential buyer the information, why should that buyer pay for it? Potential buyers therefore offer sellers a much lower price than sellers will accept. Rather than selling knowledge cheaply, innovators accept the costs of investing overseas. Any profit is better than no profit.

TNCs' explicit and tacit technological advantages and their motivation to pre-empt competition show not only why TNCs can go overseas and compete, but also why host states often fear this kind of investment. Because TNC investment took place largely in developed countries, the kind of struggle that took place around those investments differed from that in LDCs. Host states feared that at best TNCs would deny potential Verdoorn effects to local producers by taking away part of their market and thus potential increases in output. In turn, this would cause economic or technological stagnation in their domestic economy. At worst, TNCs might establish a controlling position in a given commodity chain and use that position to capture the lion's share of value created in that chain (Nitzan, 1998). Most TNCs were in high-tech industries in the sense that they possessed some hard technology (such as US electronics and computer firms) or soft technology (for example, US car firms) that local producers did not have. By dominating growth sectors, TNCs would crowd out local firms, reduce local economic growth, and depress the pool of profits available for local investment.

During the Bretton Woods period, TNCs posed an additional macroeconomic problem for host states. Because TNCs often disposed of revenues that were not only greater than those of virtually all domestic firms, but sometimes also the entire host country, they weakened states' ability to control the growth and composition of local economic activity. (In 2008 Walmart, the world's largest firm, employed roughly the working population of Norway and had turnover slightly larger than Norway's or Indonesia's GDP.) TNCs might choose to increase or decrease investment for reasons totally unrelated to local macroeconomic policy, while their ability to draw on offshore capital markets made them indifferent to the changes in local interest rates states used to regulate the macroeconomy. Moreover, TNCs' economic activity could create new sectors, expand old ones, or displace existing producers. Shifts in the sectoral composition of the economy also change the kinds of social and political groups in that economy, destroying old or creating new political actors. Thus, TNCs could change the political and economic environment in which a given state operated.

TNCs often occupied a strategic position in the local economy, because they produced goods that were related to the new leading sectors. These goods combined a multitude of manufactured components, whose value existed only to the extent that they could be combined into a commodity package. Consider cars, which contain radios, glass, textiles, plastics, electronics, tires, and a variety of machined, stamped, and forged metal products. In the motor vehicle-petroleum industrial complex, upstream commodity flows from tens of thousands of small firms tended to converge on roughly 20 global assembly firms that constituted a bottleneck in the commodity chain. The new TNCs tended to control the key bottleneck processing step. Thus, they threatened to dominate all the subsidiary and supporting industries that clustered around the leading sector, because they could exert monopsony (single-buyer) pressures on upstream sellers and monopoly on downstream buyers.

The electronics industry has a slightly different architecture in which fewer components supplied by more nearly equal firms are combined into various end products. But even there, a few firms, like Microsoft and Intel, exert considerable power. Host states feared that these TNCs would exploit local component firms and consumers. Finally, the new-style TNCs changed the nature of trade from open market exchanges between firms and consumers located in different countries to a flow of goods and services inside a single company, albeit internationally. This change also undermined macroeconomic stability. Market signals alone no longer sufficed to stimulate/restrict exports and imports when a country ran trade deficits. Corporate planning – administration – structured trade flows.

Host states, however, could deploy various weapons against TNCs.

Because these new manufacturing TNCs largely invested in other developed countries, they confronted legal regimes backed by reasonably competent states. These states could manifest their hostility to TNCs through policies favoring local producers. At the same time, protection created a dilemma for host states. If states allowed foreign firms to directly invest in their economies, this would increase the possibility that foreign firms might monopolize the stimuli for income and productivity growth. On the other hand, if states banned foreign investment, their local firms might never encounter and assimilate the hard and soft technologies that gave TNCs their competitive advantage.

Post-World War I intracore transnational investment underwent two distinct waves. In the first, US firms invaded the world, but primarily Europe. In the second wave, first European and then Japanese firms invaded the United States, particularly during the Reagan administration's great fire sale of US assets in the mid-1980s. Finally the 1990s saw huge movements in both directions, as well as a massive shift of labor-intense manufacturing to a few developing countries. How did these conflicts play out first between US TNCs and European firms and states, and then between Japanese TNCs and US and European firms and states?

America versus Europe

In 1967 Jean-Jacques Servan-Schreiber, a French journalist, wrote a call to economic arms for France and Europe. *Le Défi américain* (*The American Challenge*) called for a wide range of state initiatives to remedy the competitive edge US firms held over European firms. Without these initiatives, Servan-Schreiber (1969: 15) claimed, 'fifteen years from now the world's third largest industrial power, just after the United States and [the Soviet Union], may not be Europe, but *American industry in Europe*.' Servan-Schreiber was wrong about two things: 15 years later, Japan was the second largest industrial power in the world, and the Soviet Union disintegrated soon after. Why couldn't European firms initially compete with US firms on their own home court? Why didn't US firms later swamp the Europeans?

Servan-Schreiber correctly identifies the source of the American challenge to European industry: US firms managed mass production much better than did their European competitors. Until European firms assimilated the soft technologies associated with the American art of management, they risked being displaced from their own home markets by US TNCs. In the long term, by occupying the dynamic and high-profit sectors of the economy, TNCs threatened to choke off locally controlled growth and to denationalize part of the local pool of investment capital. In the 1960s, US firms in Europe produced 80 percent of Western Europe's computers, 24 percent of its motor vehicles, 15 percent of its synthetic rubber, and 10 percent of its petrochemicals. Local firms shut out of dynamic sectors faced stagnant profits. Meanwhile, more than half of the capital invested by US TNCs in Europe came from local sources, including the eurodollar market, as local investors rationally sought the highest returns (Servan-Schreiber, 1969: 14).

Thus, from the point of view of the European states, allowing US FDI to occur meant opening the gates of the national economic fortress to a well-constructed Trojan horse. Those sectors directly competing with or linked to the TNC risked losing growth and market share to the invader. Letting TNCs in, however, created an opportunity to observe the carpentry secrets that allowed the horse to be constructed in the first place. If those tricks and secrets could be learned and mastered, then local firms could counter-attack and regain both domestic and international market share. European responses to the invasion of US car firms from the 1920s through the 1960s reflect these different dangers and opportunities.

US firms in Europe

US car firms transnationalized early in their industrial history, more or less along the lines predicted by stage two of the product cycle theory. Ford set up assembly plants in Canada, Argentina, Brazil, and Britain before 1918 to assemble completely-knocked-down car kits (CKDs). These were cheaper to transport than fully assembled vehicles. Continental Europe was the next logical site for these assembly plants. Assembly plants were the bridgehead for a shift of the complete production process to Europe and Britain (Vernon's stage three) during the 1930s. Local efforts to protect domestic industry triggered this shift. During the 1920s, European states restricted US firms' market share by imposing high and sometimes prohibitive tariffs. They also imposed high taxes based on engine displacement, which favored local producers of small cars rather than the large cars US firms assembled. Meanwhile, a few European firms adopted some of Ford's assembly-line techniques, further eroding the US firms' price advantages even in the large-car segment. US firms thus transnationalized into the European market at the end of the 1920s to protect their market and profit shares from the combination of state intervention and European catchup.

GM led the way, strategically buying up the most up-to-date competitor in each country: Vauxhall (UK) in 1925 and Opel (Germany) in 1929. Opel, for example, had gone farthest in introducing a basic assembly line (Laux, 1982). The French and Italian states prohibited GM from buying local firms. In contrast, Ford set up greenfield plants – new plants in open fields – in Britain and Germany in 1931 and France in 1934, transferring its production processes intact rather than having to deal with existing practices at a (relatively) backward European firm. As with GM, the Italian state rejected Ford's efforts to begin full-scale production.

The European response

Britain, France, and Germany responded to the evolution of the threat from imports to transnational production in distinctly different ways, depending on whether their states focused more on the opportunities or on the dangers inherent in FDI (Reich, 1989). Britain focused mostly on opportunities and disregarded the dangers, and France mostly on the dangers and not the opportunities, while Germany kept a wary eye on both. The outcome was distinctly bad for British industry, less so for French, and least so for German.

The British state permitted unrestricted FDI by US car firms, hoping that US managerial practices would diffuse to Britain's backward industrial sector. Diffusion did indeed occur, but slowly. Disregarding minor niche marketers of luxury cars, US firms simply displaced inefficient British rivals. By the 1970s, US firms accounted for over 50 percent of British car production. Because these firms had global planning horizons and investment options, they began systematically disinvesting from Britain in the 1970s in the face of persistent labor unrest and foreign exchange crises. Britain then found it could not regenerate a car sector without more foreign investment inasmuch as local managerial talent and organizations did not exist. Instead, Britain simply imported more cars as demand grew, straining its balance of payments. Consequently, the state invited in a second wave of TNCs, this time Japanese firms like Honda, Nissan, and Toyota. All three sought access to the highly protected European Union market. This wave of Japanese firms simply replayed Britain's experience with the US TNCs. However, by the end of the 1980s, British firms began slowly absorbing superior Japanese production practices.

In France the danger of displacement preoccupied the state to the exclusion of learning from TNCs. As late as 1927, the average French car absorbed 300 person-days of labor from raw materials to finished product, compared to 70 person-days in the United States (Laux, 1982: 102). Prohibitive tariffs, import quotas, and denying permission for FDI to anyone but Ford (and then quite late), preserved about three-quarters of the market for French producers. After the war, France nationalized Renault and supported Peugeot as it absorbed smaller and failing rivals. Pressured by their state, French producers assimilated US manufacturing practices. French firms had barely assimilated US production methods when even better Japanese car-assembly practices nullified the gain, obliging the state to continue to use tariffs and import quotas to contain the Japanese threat. By the 1980s France was a net exporter of cars, largely confined to the European market. The absence of competition within the French market weakened the ability of French firms to compete with stronger firms in the overall world market; Renault had to buy one-third of ailing, debt-encumbered, unprofitable Nissan in 1999 to get a piece of the Asian market. The French continue to resist the full force of market pressures from Japanese car firms, including those that have transnationalized into Britain.

Germany chose a middle path. During the 1930s the Nazi government had tolerated but disliked Ford's and GM/Opel's share of over half the mass market, creating state-owned Volkswagen (VW) to challenge the US pair. Occupied Germany could hardly refuse re-entry by the US producers like France did, but it could try to restructure its industry to gain maximum benefits from their presence. The state encouraged each local firm to concentrate on different parts of the market. German firms competed with the US firms and, to a lesser extent, each other, forcing them to attain world-market levels of competition and productivity. The quasi-luxury firms had an easier time doing this. VW had the harder task, but with overt and covert state aid it prospered. It added US levels of assembly-line productivity to German-style attention to details, remaining one of the few European firms, aside from luxury producers, that could export in large volumes to the United States. VW eventually built production facilities in the United States.

The Europeans attempt to catch up

How did the Europeans catch up? Practically, they didn't. By the 1980s, European cars still cost about 30 percent more than similar US-built cars, reflecting an equivalent productivity disadvantage (Altschuler *et al.*, 1984; Womack, Jones, and Roos, 1992). Only German firms and a few luxury producers absorbed by the US giants in the late 1990s could penetrate the US and Japanese markets. But European firms' survival mimicked earlier catchup patterns. As in the nineteenth century, state intervention basically bought time for local entrepreneurs, preserving space in the local market so that they could experience Verdoorn effects. Then it was up to local producers to become competitive. In the process of catching up, local producers generated novel innovations that ultimately brought them up to or past the competitive position of their rivals. In the nineteenth century, German and US iron and steel producers had used scale economies to catch up with Britain's smaller plants and then taken advantage of their more plastic labor forces to introduce high-productivity electrical machinery and surpass the British.

In the automobile industry in Europe, local firms benefited from the proximity of US TNCs. US firms trained local workers and managers who later cycled through locally owned firms. Similarly, the demands of US firms on local component producers forced them to introduce high-volume, US-style assembly-line techniques in order to win contracts for parts. To this, the Europeans added a hard technological edge and better design skills (Williams *et al.*, 1994). Their fragmented market forced them to make their cars distinctive. They used advances in design (frontwheel drive, econo-boxes, styling, lifetime service contracts) and in hard technologies (antilock brakes, electronic fuel injection) to set their cars apart from those of other local competitors. This fragmentation of the market placed the transplanted US firms at a disadvantage. While they had vast experience in high-volume assembly-line production, US firms had less experience producing and selling into highly differentiated markets. Thus, they gave up part of their advantage to come into the European market, while transferring part of their advantage to local competitors via imitation.

Finally, because protection forced US TNCs to produce locally, both the local components producers and the national (but partly TNC) car industry experienced far higher levels of growth than did the US industry. From 1950 to 1973, US car production grew from just under 7 million units to just under

11 million units, a 60 percent increase. But average production in that period hovered around 9 million units. European car production, including US TNCs, jumped from 1.1 million units in 1950 to just over 11.4 million units by 1973, with fairly rapid and steady growth, and then edged up to about 13 million units through the 1980s. Consequently, from 1950 to 1970 the European industry experienced extremely rapid increases in output and extremely rapid productivity growth. Both industries stabilized at around 16 million units per continent by the 2000s. Figure 10.2 shows the differences in the geographic location of production (see Table 13.3 for world market shares by producer), and reveals the extraordinary expansion of non-US, non-European production as Asia industrialized in the 1990s and 2000s.

Japan versus America (and Europe)

Servan-Schreiber had the satisfaction of being flattered by a hundred imitators about 20 years later, when a veritable deluge of books appeared in the United States on the theme of *le défi japonais*. (Ten years after that, the Japanese produced their own literature about the 'barbarians at the gate,' as US firms took advantage of Japan's financial crisis to buy firms and market share on the cheap, and the current decade will no doubt feature equivalent claims about Chinese firms.) These works eventually identified the source of Japanese competitive advantage in firms' superior management of mass production. US firms faced competitive displacement – the 20 percent of the US market GM lost from 1980 to 1999 essentially went to Japanese firms. The inrush of Japanese and European investment as the dollar fell raised fears that the United States was losing control of domestic economic management and the

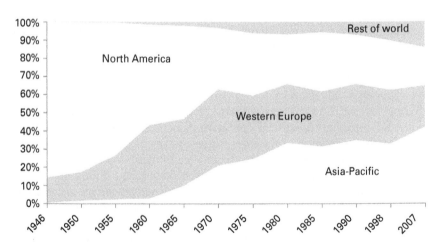

Source: International Organization of Motor Vehicle Manufacturers, http://www.oica.net/category/production-statistics/.

Figure 10.2   *Location of vehicle production, selected years*

economic high ground. Indeed, Japanese electronics and car producers did possess an overwhelming managerial advantage (see Chapter 13). Technologically, neither their products nor their production machinery were particularly advanced until the late 1980s. Their managerial advantage allowed them to export into the US and European markets, sweeping aside other small-car producers. By 1980 Japan had about 20 percent of the US market and just over 10 percent of the entire European car market; by 2007 all Japanese brands (local production plus imports) accounted for 38 percent of the US market and about 15 percent of the European market.

Just as in the past, the United States and European states tried to protect their domestic producers from the wave of Japanese car exports that started in the 1970s. Because the strictures of GATT prevented them from raising tariffs to any great extent, they resorted to the great and by then time-honored method of subverting GATT: the voluntary export restraint (VER) agreement (see Chapter 11). Like high tariffs and quotas in the 1920s and 1930s, VERs forced the Japanese to transnationalize their operations into their major developed country markets. Honda was first in the United States, Nissan in England, but the rest came soon after. Politically, transplants in the US soon became major players. They employed local workers, bought from local suppliers, and deliberately spread assembly plants across multiple states to influence as many politicians as possible.

Just as European firms learned from transplanted US firms, US firms eventually assimilated Japanese management techniques. Strategic alliances (Ford–Mazda and Chrysler–Mitsubishi) confronted the US partner with undeniable evidence of problems in their design, assembly, and component buying practices. Those firms began shifting to Japanese-style practices. By the late 2000s, US producers had cut the gap in the number of build hours per car from roughly eight hours to two hours. GM and Ford cut their supplier networks by 25 percent to create strategic alliances with the best suppliers and to shift part of the design work onto them, mimicking Japanese *keiretsu* structures (see Chapter 13). All three major firms enforced Japanese-style annual price reductions on component suppliers.

Just as with US firms in Europe, the Japanese invaders lost some of their original sources of superiority when they entered the US market. Toyota's ability to do just-in-time production, for example, derives in large part from the proximity of its supplier firms. Many are located literally next door to its main assembly plant in Japan. By shifting production to the United States, Toyota has been forced to ship components halfway around the world. To recreate its just-in-time inventory systems, Japanese TNCs had to develop a local (that is, US) components industry that was up to their quality and delivery standards. This forced those components firms to attain Japanese levels of productivity and quality, which helped the US assemblers create their own just-in-time systems. As in Europe, locals learned how to improve from proximity to a TNC competitor, while those TNC competitors lost part of their edge by transplanting themselves. The trend towards more managed trade (see Chapter 12) has accelerated the speed at which this assimilation occurs. The reality or threat that states might restrict market access through quotas or subsidies to local firms has prompted existing and would-be TNCs to enter into an enormous range of strategic alliances (OECD, 1999). These alliances facilitate a more rapid transfer of managerial and technical knowledge than that discussed above.

Meanwhile, back at the ranch ...

TNCs fought for market shares outside the developed economies as well. Two forces propelled manufacturing and service TNCs 'south' to LDCs. The first was a search for cheaper labor. The capital controls of the Bretton Woods system generated full employment at uniformly high wages in many developed countries, and while this helped profits by ensuring high rates of capacity utilization, differences in national wage rates put US and later European firms at a disadvantage compared with Japanese firms. As capital controls unraveled, firms began to shift labor-intense production steps to low-wage zones. Because this movement is intimately tied up with the dynamics of the Bretton Woods trade system it will be considered in Chapter 12. Second, activist states in Latin America and Asia began their own efforts to industrialize and to shift from agricultural exports to manufactured exports (not always the same thing). So the demand for low-wage labor found its supply. This will be the subject of Chapter 11. But in the meantime, you may as well know what happened.

Firms dispersed their production globally to avoid being locked out of major markets, and, when possible, to take advantage of variations in wages. While transnationalization was initially an overwhelmingly US phenomenon, the rest of the big economies raced to catch up. By 1997 the share of overseas production relative to total manufacturing output by firms headquartered in the United States was around 30 percent, while for Japan it was only 6 percent (OECD, 1999: 109). By 2004, foreign firms' turnover accounted for 21.5 percent of US GDP, and 5.2 percent of gross value added (OECD, 2008a). It might seem that the US was overrun by foreign firms, but US firms abroad generated 60 percent more value-added than foreign firms in the United States. Only Japan stands out with respect to low levels of foreign penetration: foreign firms' turnover amounted to only 5.4 percent of Japanese GDP, and only 1 percent of value-added. Table 10.1 provides data on the average stock of FDI that each major industrial economy had in the other two (treating the EU as a unit) from 1998 to 2006 (OECD, 2008b). The tightest connections existed between the US and European economies, with a strong Japanese presence in both of those economies but a much weaker presence of them in Japan. Undoubtedly, this reflects a variety of barriers to inward investment in Japan as well as two decades of economic stagnation. Simultaneously, Japan was relatively more invested in both the United States and Europe than in the rest of the world.

Despite this dispersion of production activities and sales globally, most TNCs remained firmly rooted in their home economies, whose particular institutional structures, including finance and labor markets, had constituted the initial competitive advantages that allowed the firm to become a transnational

Table 10.1 *Transnationalization in the Triad economies, 1998–2006*

		Average share of stock of direct investment from each country, %	
To:	From: US	Japan	Europe[a]
United States	–	41.5	48.6
Japan	3.8	–	2.5
Europe	52.4	23.9	–
Rest of World	42.8	34.6	48.9
Total, percent	100	100	100
Total, $ billions	1669.3	327.1	1541.6

Notes: [a] excludes intra-EU investment.

Source: Calculated from data at OECD, http://www.SourceOECD.org, date accessed 5 September 2008.

in the first place (Doremus *et al.*, 1998). Transnationalization of production thus tended to create continental/hemispheric production complexes rather than truly global production systems. On an aggregate basis, manufacturing firms transnationalizing into LDCs mostly went into nearby areas with low wages and stable, acquiescent governments. The biggest exception was investment by US manufacturing firms into the four Asian NICs and then China. But containerization and cheap fuel oil cheapened trans-Pacific transport considerably after World War II, facilitating this shift. However, the oil shock of 2006–7 – which saw prices roughly one-third higher in real terms than the 1979–81 Iranian Revolution oil shock – called into question production chains that reached 12 000 miles to China. One estimate put the increased cost of shipping a standard container as the equivalent of an 8 percentage point tariff increase (Shenfeld and Grauman, 2008).

This transnationalization also affected trade flows considerably. By the end of the 1980s, the majority of world trade was being conducted by TNCs shipping goods from one subsidiary to another. These flows reflected three patterns: the shipment of intermediate goods back and forth between high-wage, high-skill zones and low-wage, low-skill zones; the shipment of finished goods between different markets where TNCs had concentrated production of different goods; and traditional exports of finished goods from a manufacturing base to final markets. By 1996, TNCs accounted for about 33 percent of world exports. In the US economy itself, the world's largest open economy, TNCs controlled a fairly consistent 54 percent of US exports and imports during the 1980s, with US-based firms accounting for about three-fifths of that. TNC intrafirm transfers accounted for about 80 percent of TNC-controlled imports into the United States (Bureau of Economic Analysis, 2008). How did push-and-pull forces bring about this dispersion of production globally?

Chapter 11

Industrialization in the Old Agricultural Periphery

The Rise of the Newly Industrialized Countries

> The loss occasioned by protective duties consists, after all, only in values [i.e., money]; whilst the country thus acquires a power, by which it is enabled to produce a great mass of values. This loss in values must be considered as the price of the 'industrial training' of the country.
>
> *Friedrich List*

The dispersion of agriculture from the European Thünen town to the European settler colonies in the nineteenth century created modern, advanced agricultural production in those temperate zone colonies. The dispersion of manufacturing from the United States, Northwest Europe and Japan to select areas in Latin America, Eastern Europe and Asia is creating modern manufacturing in those areas, particularly China. Indeed, China, or China and India, is on a trajectory to regain its pre-industrial revolution share of world GDP. It is fashionable to cast this industrialization as a return to some natural distribution of global economic activity. But this is true only in the aggregate, and conceals both the actual process of (re-)industrialization and the nature of that manufacturing. We can pose the question this way: to what degree does the industrialization of China (or other peripheral areas) create a new Thünen town or a new, independent core manufacturing region, rather than a twenty-first-century manufacturing version of the nineteenth-century tropical agricultural periphery?

As with nineteenth-century late industrializers and Ricardian developers, we can view the current crop of industrializing economies collectively through the lens of the Thünen and Krugman models, and individually in terms of the degree to which local states overcame Gerschenkronian and Kaldorian collective dilemmas. This then allows us to consider how individual country outcomes created new adjustment problems in the global economy. Alice Amsden (1989: 143–4) summarizes the strategies thus way: 'The First Industrial Revolution was built on laissez-faire, the Second on infant industry protection. In Late Industrialization, the foundation is the subsidy [from the state] – which includes both protection and financial incentives.'

All peripheral states responded to the industrialized countries' massive intervention in domestic agriculture after World War II. European governments and later the European Union's Common Agricultural Policy made Europe self-sufficient in many foodstuffs and then an exporter of subsidized foods, displacing traditional agro-exporters from their markets. Simultaneously, rising income levels in Europe and America meant that the proportion of income spent on food and thus food imports declined steadily (Engel's Law). Because total population in the industrial countries continued to grow, so did peripheral agro-exports, but very slowly. The Argentinean Raul Prebisch argued that the slower growth of demand for agricultural goods relative to manufactured goods caused declining terms of trade, balance-of-payments crises, and thus economic stagnation in the periphery as stagnant export income had to be spread over a growing population (Prebisch, 1950).

Theorists like Prebisch thus called for a strategic shift from agriculture to manufacturing, that is, a shift from Ricardian to Kaldorian strategies trying to take advantage of Verdoorn's law. Viewed in the aggregate, this shift was successful. After 1960 peripheral countries in the aggregate typically grew twice as fast as the rich economies as a whole. This higher growth rate reflected a shift out of agriculture and into manufacturing in general, a shift that can be seen in the LDCs' changing export mix. The proportion of manufactured goods in total LDC non-oil exports rose from roughly 10 percent in 1955 to 65 percent in 1986 and in 92 percent in 2007. Meanwhile, foods and nonfood agriculturals (NFAs) fell from 77 percent to 8 percent. LDCs' share in global manufacturing exports rose dramatically, from 2 percent in 1965 to 33 percent in 2007 (WTO, 2008). But this aggregate success conceals quite divergent individual performances. Most gains accrued to nine countries – or, more precisely, five countries, one island, and eleven Chinese provinces, one of which has disputed ownership and one of which – Hong Kong – had a special deal. By the end of the 1990s, coastal China, Taiwan, South Korea, Hong Kong, and Singapore already accounted for nearly half of all LDC manufactured goods exports. Brazil, Mexico, Argentina, and Colombia accounted for another quarter. A few more Asian countries claimed another seventh, leaving the last seventh for the other hundred or so LDCs. The vast majority of LDCs remained agricultural exporters, or at best exporters of clothing. Consequently, even as late as 2003, the three largest LDC exports were still fuels (36 percent), clothing (20 percent), and agricultural products (17 percent), amounting to three-quarters of all LDC exports (WTO, 2008).

Late development in the agricultural periphery

Ricardian developers' varying success at shifting to industrial exports reflected their varying ability to master the problems Chapter 4 identified as inherent in late industrialization. The essential precondition for success was a relatively strong and autonomous state: could it control or influence society enough to extract capital, and invest it according to a consistent development strategy? As in the nineteenth century, states that were able to squeeze local agriculture avoided a reliance on borrowed foreign capital and crippling interest payments; similarly, states that could create or inherited local entrepreneurs avoided a reliance on TNCs. As in the nineteenth century, states that could repress local labor unions did so to maximize profitability and (re-)investment. As in the nineteenth century, most economies started out with Ricardian exports of labor-intense, low-value-added manufactured goods, and tried to shift towards more valuable exports. The usual distinction between import substitution industrialization (ISI) and export-oriented industrialization (EOI) is thus artificial. As we will see, most countries that adopted a pure ISI policy did so initially because global markets were closed, and in any case they continued exporting raw materials to fund ISI; most countries opting for EOI simultaneously did ISI too.

A mix of historical and geographic circumstances sharply circumscribed these options. A country's geographical location and colonial history largely determined its natural markets. In the nineteenth century, when only Britain plausibly provided an external motor for growth, this condition did not matter. In the twentieth century, however, the three biggest economic powers – the United States, Japan, and the European Community – grew at different rates and provided markets for different sorts of goods. Relatively slow European growth combined with protection of local markets to slow growth in Europe's neighboring LDCs. By contrast, Japan's relatively rapid growth and the interaction of Japanese export surges and US trade protection helped dynamize growth in East Asia, as we will see in Chapter 12. Internally, many states faced powerful local social groups that almost always constrained that state's ability to pick among various policy options. Just as in the nineteenth century, winners from earlier Ricardian development strategies often strongly resisted shifting their profits towards new industry.

As we will see below, only Taiwan and South Korea really succeeded in using their agricultural sector as an initial source of capital, and in allocating capital free of constraints. The other states typically borrowed abroad and allocated loan funds to favored local entrepreneurs, or tried to woo TNCs and direct their investment into promising sectors. This combination of constraints created four basic industrialization trajectories, listed in decreasing order of their success: an export-oriented, East Asian model linked to both Japan and the United States, in which early industrializers used foreign debt while followers relied on TNCs; a debt- and TNC-financed, ISI-oriented Latin American model linked to the United States alone; an export-oriented, TNC-financed southern European model linked to Western Europe; and an ISI-oriented, debt-financed Eastern European model linked to Western Europe, that shifted over to the southern European and Maghrebian model after communist regimes collapsed. India abandoned its self-reliant, low-debt strategy in the mid-1980s to pursue export-led growth, albeit in fits and starts. And China's enormous domestic market meant it could rely less on TNCs than the usual East Asian developer.

The following discussion omits Africa, because after 1955, sub-Saharan Africa was preoccupied with efforts to satisfy the *precondition* for late development: create a state (Bates, 1981; Callaghy, 1984; Fatton, 1992). The old externally imposed Ricardian strategies continued, leading for the most part to declining incomes. Meanwhile, a whole host of countries simply fell by the wayside because their economies were too small either to create manufacturing exports or to use them to generate backlinks to more sophisticated industry. There are 30 countries with populations under 1 million and a further 29 countries with under 5 million. Although manufactured exports are not impossible under those conditions, full-scale *late industrialization* probably is. The absence of a large domestic market makes it difficult for exports to induce significant backward linkages. The obvious exceptions – Singapore with a population of 3 million and Hong Kong with about 6 million – benefited from their location and prior capital accumulation, when they relinked with their traditional hinterlands.

The discussion in the next section contrasts a generic Latin American model, looking at Brazil, Mexico, and Argentina, a generic Eastern European model, and a generic East Asian model, looking at Taiwan, South Korea and China. While detailed, it will help clarify the importance of moving beyond simple Gerschenkronian strategies that create growth by mobilizing more factor inputs, to the kind of productivity growth that comes from resolving Kaldorian collective dilemmas. The end of the chapter deals with the systemic causes and consequences of the debt and financial crises of the industrialization process. One caveat is in order here: these countries are mostly the success stories. Therefore, while the discussion may at times seem to imply failure or wrongheaded choices, the reader should keep in mind the vast array of countries that would like to have the problems of these countries.

The Latin American path

Latin American industrialization occurred in three distinct waves. In each wave the state mobilized an increasing share of investment capital and channeled it to a new entrepreneurial actor. The first wave involved ISI in light industry (consumer nondurables) largely through private efforts, as well as the creation of a rudimentary capital goods industry under the aegis of the state. In the second wave, transnationals developed a consumer durables industry that again was oriented towards the domestic market, while the state continued to expand the capital goods sector. In the third wave, the state borrowed abroad to finance capital goods deepening and consolidation of an export-oriented consumer durables industry in an effort to displace the TNCs. The discussion will concentrate on Mexico and Brazil, as they were successful in all three waves.

Wave one: consumer nondurables

The first wave of industrialization in Latin America, around the turn of the century, was a natural consequence of these countries' original Ricardian strategies and resembled similar contemporary industrial spurts in Eastern

Europe, Australasia, India, and Japan. Local industrial entrepreneurs bene-fited from a kind of natural protection from external competition. Many basic goods were nontradables at this point because of high transportation costs: beer and basic food processing, construction materials, and, because of local tastes, some textiles. Producing and processing local agricultural output also spurred milling, machinery repairs, and sometimes machinery building. The low capital requirements for market entry facilitated this wave of industrial-ization. By 1914, local Brazilian and Argentinean firms had captured about 50 percent of their textile and garment markets. Production centered on the most dynamic agricultural export or mining area: São Paulo in Brazil, Santa Fe province in Argentina, and Monterrey in Mexico.

States consolidated this wave of industrialization during the Great Depression by adding overt protection and a conscious development strategy to the passive industrialization promoted by the old Ricardian strategy. The Depression caused Latin American exports to fall roughly 60 percent in three years. Declining export revenues drove Mexico and Brazil to default on their foreign debts. Soon after, their states intervened to create state-owned metals and petroleum industries, expropriating foreign producers in the process. They used foreign exchange controls to concentrate capital for investment, while also creating a basic administrative capacity to structure the market for industrial goods. Both states created labor unions that controlled an otherwise volatile labor force. Because of US concern to assure security in its own hemi-sphere while fighting a two-front war, both Brazil and Mexico managed to extract relatively high levels of resource and technical transfers from the United States during World War II, as well as considerable assistance in build-ing professional military and civil bureaucracies. In conjunction with this aid, Brazil's foreign debt was substantially written down and Mexico received a favorable rescheduling agreement. After the war, this aid prepared these two states to vault ahead of much richer and more industrial Argentina.

In Mexico the great state builder Lázaro Cárdenas nationalized the oil indus-try and railroads and established a state steel industry. He expanded the powers of the central bank, and he created the basis for substantial state control over finance through the state-owned Nacional Financiera (Nafinsa) bank and other banks specializing in rural and export lending. Nafinsa helped to expand indigenous heavy industry, using its control over US wartime aid in the 1940s to strengthen its hold on industrial capital formation. Like nineteenth-century German banks, Nafinsa took equity positions in many of the companies it funded, and by the 1950s the state would control between one-third and one-half of all investment. By the end of the 1940s Mexico produced most of its consumer nondurable consumption. Politically, Cárdenas forged durable alliances between the state and small business and between workers and peasants, incorporating those unions into the political party that ruled Mexico continuously until 2000, the Partido Revolucionario Institucional (PRI). PRI controlled and channeled demands to the state upward and state action downward.

In Brazil, Getúlio Vargas also rebuilt the Brazilian state, trying to centralize and professionalize power. Like Cárdenas, he nationalized railroads and oil, and he established state-run steel mills and coal/iron ore mines. By 1949 virtually all consumer nondurables and about half of capital goods consumption were locally produced. Like Cárdenas, Vargas established a strong state bank, the National Bank for Economic Development (BNDES in Portuguese), to control industrial finance. By the 1950s the state controlled 25 percent of investment, and by 1960 half of investment. Vargas repressed peasant revolts and unionized urban workers from above but failed to institutionalize his rule in a dominant political party such as PRI. GDP growth averaged 4.5 percent per year in the 1930s, led by a 6.1 percent expansion in industrial output (Maddison, 1985: 25).

Wave two: consumer durables and capital goods

After World War II, a second wave of industrialization occurred in consumer durables, particularly cars, but with TNCs as the major actor. Each state tried to use TNCs as an engine of growth for the local economy and as a transmission belt to carry new technologies to local firms (Jenkins, 1984; Kronish and Mericle, 1984; Bennett and Sharpe, 1985). Just like European states in the 1920s, these states hoped to create a local parts and components industry that later could move upstream into final assembly. Domestic content laws forced TNCs to locate manufacturing production, and not just final assembly of parts manufactured elsewhere, inside the local economy. The TNCs had various motives for cooperation. US TNCs saw local manufacturing as a way to stem the postwar erosion of their dominant market share; Europeans saw FDI as a way to gain global economies of scale.

In 1955 and 1956, Brazil set 80 percent and 95 percent content requirements for trucks and cars, respectively, while limiting the number of TNCs that could enter the country. Foreign exchange controls, devaluations, and high tariffs supplemented this policy, encouraging the new local parts producers to turn to the local capital goods industry for tooling and metals. The car industry expanded on the basis of local demand, particularly after the 1964 military coup encouraged a redistribution of income towards the top 20 percent of the population. Brazilian car production soared from fewer than 50 000 units in the 1950s to over 1 million units by 1978. This expansion pulled the rest of the economy along with it; by the late 1990s car production constituted roughly twice as much of GDP in Brazil as in the United States! Productivity in the car industry roughly doubled in the ten years after the 1964 coup, as the industry benefited from Verdoorn effects. However, TNCs' suppliers unexpectedly followed their assemblers into the Brazilian market, suppressing locally owned production. By the end of the 1970s, locally owned firms accounted for only half of component production, and by the 2000s domestic producers existed only in niche markets.

Mexico adopted local content legislation in 1962. Like Brazil, it limited the number of permitted models to maximize economies of scale, but it pursued a different strategy to preserve locally owned assembly. The state fostered a dual structure, allowing foreign assemblers but requiring component producers to have majority local ownership and requiring that engines be locally produced. This forced would-be TNC component firms to enter joint ventures with Mexican firms. Production rose to over 400 000 units by 1980. Like Brazil, it also experienced rapidly rising growth and productivity rates, especially during the late 1980s, when TNC producers anticipated the North American Free Trade Agreement (NAFTA) and invested heavily in parts and assembly plants. At the same time the Mexican state pioneered the use of export processing zones (EPZ or FTZ, Free Trade Zone) in North America by creating the '*maquildora*' program, which allowed tariff-free assembly of goods destined for re-export back to the United States.

Both countries ran into difficulties with their TNC-led strategies that echoed the fears generated by US transnational investment in Europe. Although each had tried to induce TNC investment with a mix of carrots and sticks (subsidies and domestic content laws), each state found that TNCs were content to live behind tariff walls without making any effort to bring local production to world market standards. Even though Brazil and Mexico were the most efficient LDC car producers in the 1970s, production costs were one-third to one-half above costs in TNCs' home factories. The TNCs also had no desire to export, and they had a high propensity to import the machinery they used. This induced the state to shift gears in the 1970s, when rising oil prices increased the need to export.

TNCs also dominated the strategic points in the production chain. Latin American countries feared denationalization of their economies more than the Europeans had. The Europeans, after all, already had some dynamic, export-capable industrial firms while Latin American countries did not. By 1970 foreign firms dominated the automotive, chemical, and machinery industries. TNCs controlled 40 percent of Mexican manufacturing production and 36 percent of the 400 largest Mexican firms, as well as 20 percent of the 400 largest Brazilian firms, accounting for nearly half of capital invested in manufacturing (Jenkins, 1984: 32–4; UNCTAD, 1991: 99–102). TNC control was magnified because TNCs tended to buy out the most dynamic existing local firms rather than starting up a new subsidiary. Finally, TNCs' pursuit of global economies of scale made them big importers of capital goods and sometimes parts, without generating any offsetting exports. All three Latin states therefore decided to ditch the TNC-led strategy. Instead, they would borrow directly in international capital markets to create locally controlled state and/or private industry.

Wave three: debt-financed industrial deepening

The basic problem with the TNC-led strategy was TNCs' disinclination to continue investing once the domestic market was saturated. By the early 1960s, for example, Brazil produced 99 percent of its consumer goods, 91 percent of intermediate goods, and 87 percent of capital goods (Baer *et al.*, 1987). ISI had exhausted itself as a growth strategy. Because the market served by ISI was small, Verdoorn effects could not pull local industry up to a world market standard of competitiveness, and continued protection for local producers sheltered them from the need to get there. Local firms generally were too small, too risk-averse, and too unprofessionally managed to undertake either exports or the assimilation of new technologies. The inability to export manufactured goods hampered further industrialization and vice versa.

The Latin states turned to export promotion and overseas borrowing to overcome these limitations. Foreign capital inflows would supplement subsidized exports until a new range of export-competitive industries was developed; inflows would help further expand the domestic market, generating additional Verdoorn effects; and foreign capital acquired as loan capital seemed free of the deleterious consequences of capital controlled by foreign TNCs. Retrospective analyses of this debt-led strategy have been critical because of the debt crises of the 1980s, but these strategies were both reasonable and reasonably successful, particularly with regard to Mexico and Brazil. They accounted for 40 percent of all LDC foreign commercial debt in the 1980s and had relatively well-disciplined states that executed reasonable debt-led development plans. Moreover, given real interest rates averaging about *negative* 6 percent on LDC debt in the late 1970s, and rising terms of trade, borrowing was a reasonably rational strategy. As in the nineteenth century, however, these conditions did not last for ever.

Brazil had the largest, most ambitious, and most successful of the Latin debt-led strategies. The state's strategy revolved around the creation and/or expansion of a wide range of state-owned firms in heavy industry. These would consciously contract with local suppliers for their inputs, and so their growth would spur the development of a wider industrial economy. By 1978 the state had both enveloped the local private sector and displaced TNCs as the engine of growth (Evans, 1979). The state supplied nearly all of the private sector's capital investment via BNDES, while state firms absorbed half of the private sector's output. At the same time, between 65 percent and 75 percent of capital goods consumption came from state firms making capital goods. As a result, TNCs' share of local Brazilian assets and markets shrank relatively. From 1969 to 1984 TNCs' share of local assets fell from 27 percent to 9 percent, while state firms' share rose from 28 percent to 50 percent and local firms' share stayed about the same. At the same time, exports of manufactures boomed, rising 15.4 percent per year from 1965 to 1970, and 26.7 percent per year from 1970 to 1975 (Fritsch and Franco, 1991). All of this growth rested on borrowed money: from 1970 to 1980 public foreign debt increased from under $5 billion to over $50 billion.

This strategy proved reasonably successful. From 1965 to 1980 Brazilian GDP tripled in real terms, led by industrial production, which quadrupled. After Mexico defaulted in 1982, the flow of capital to Brazil also ceased, paralyzing new investment. The entire economy went into a deep recession, from which it recovered only in the 1990s. None the less, the investment wave of the 1970s positioned Brazil as a successful exporter of manufactured goods such as small aircraft, cars and car components, armaments, and, of course, textiles and shoes. By 1989, 75 percent of exports were manufactures. By

2005 Brazil was making 2.5 million cars annually and was the tenth largest exporter of automotive products.

Table 11.1 below details export profiles for some countries discussed above and below, showing the outward shift of textiles and garment export production, and the substitution of electronics and automotive exports for those lower-value goods.

In Mexico the state also began systematically reducing the influence of TNCs after 1970. A 1973 law limited TNC investment. Instead, the state channeled an enormous amount of borrowed foreign money through Nafinsa, expanding foreign public debt from $6.8 billion in 1972 to $58.1 billion in 1982, and doubling its investments absolutely during the 1970s. Most of this investment went to state-owned or -controlled firms, particularly the state oil monopoly PEMEX, which absorbed 40 percent of government borrowing by 1979. The number of state firms increased ninefold during the 1970s, increasing the public share of GDP to 45 percent by 1979. The fiscal deficit also expanded to 15 percent of GDP, causing the current account deficit to grow to $12.5 billion in 1982.

Unfortunately, despite the *maquiladora* program, Mexico's export capacity was tied too closely to its oil giant, PEMEX, which by the end of the 1970s was generating about half of Mexican exports. Declining oil prices and rising interest rates after the 1980 recession destroyed Mexico's ability to continue servicing its enormous debt. Like Brazil's, Mexico's public foreign debt had gone from less than $5 billion to nearly $75 billion in 10 years. Mexico had to go to Washington for a bailout, triggering a general shutdown of lending to LDCs during the 1980s, just as Argentina's default cut off lending in the 1890s. Mexico weathered the 1980s better than Brazil in the sense that it experienced a smaller drop in per capita GDP. Its stable government controlled inflation and its proximity to the United States encouraged a wave of investment in *maquiladoras,* particularly for electronics and car parts (see Chapter 12). Thus, by the end of the 1980s Mexico was exporting more cars than Brazil, despite lower production levels (700 000 units in 1995 and 1.7 million in 2005). Automotive-related exports exceeded oil exports in 2007, and Mexico's automotive exports were three times Brazil's and nearly equaled Korea's.

The Latin debt-led strategies had the same key weaknesses described in Chapter 6 in relation to Ricardian strategies. First, the long gestation period between the contracting of foreign debt and the creation of export competence in manufactures delayed the onset of revenues from those exports. As late as the middle of the 1970s, over two-thirds of Brazilian, Mexican, and Argentine exports were still primary products; by the mid-1990s only one-third of Argentina's exports, half of Brazil's and three-quarters of Mexico's were manufactures. Manufactured exports didn't really take off until the 2000s, when TNCs integrated local producers into global commodity chains. So foreign debt accumulated all through the 1980s and 1990s; by 1997 Brazil's commercial debt has risen to $166 billion, Mexico's to $120 billion, and Argentina's to $101 billion.

Table 11.1 *Shares of exports of specific products in total merchandise exports of selected NICs, 1980–2007, percent*

		1980	1990	2000	2007
Brazil	Agricultural products	50.9	31.7	28.9	30.9
	Fuels and mining products	11.3	16.1	12.1	20.6
	Iron and steel	4.4	11.5	6.8	6.5
	Office and telecom equipment	2.4	2.2	4.3	1.9
	Telecommunications equipment	0.0	1.4	3.0	1.6
	Automotive products	7.2	6.6	8.7	8.7
	Textiles	3.3	2.5	1.7	0.9
	Clothing	0.7	0.8	0.5	0.2
Mexico	Agricultural products	12.7	8.6	5.5	5.8
	Fuels and mining products	62.9	28.3	11.0	18.5
	Office and telecom equipment	0.3	11.3	20.5	20.0
	Electronic data processing equipment	0.0	0.0	7.1	4.6
	Telecommunications equipment	0.0	0.0	11.6	14.7
	Automotive products	2.2	10.9	18.5	16.8
	Textiles	0.5	1.8	1.5	0.8
	Clothing	0.0	1.5	5.2	1.9
China	Agricultural products	24.3	16.5	6.6	3.2
	Machinery and transport equipment	4.7	17.8	33.2	47.5
	Office and telecom equipment	0.4	5.1	17.5	28.6
	Electronic data processing equipment	0.0	0.6	7.5	13.6
	Telecommunications equipment	0.0	4.3	7.8	12.0
	Automotive products	0.3	0.4	0.6	1.9
	Textiles	14.1	11.8	6.5	4.6
	Clothing	9.0	15.9	14.5	9.5
Korea	Agricultural products	8.8	4.6	2.5	1.7
	Office and telecom equipment	9.7	22.1	34.4	25.0
	Electronic data processing equipment	0.0	4.2	11.5	5.3
	Telecommunications equipment	0.0	9.7	8.4	10.9
	Electronic circuits and components	0.0	8.3	14.5	8.8
	Automotive products	0.7	3.5	8.9	13.4
	Textiles	12.7	9.4	7.4	2.8
	Clothing	16.9	12.2	2.9	0.5
Taiwan	Agricultural products	10.2	5.6	2.4	1.9
	Chemicals	2.5	4.2	6.2	12.0
	Office and telecom equipment	13.6	21.1	39.1	28.0
	Electronic data processing equipment	0.0	10.0	19.8	5.1
	Telecommunications equipment	0.0	7.5	4.6	5.0
	Electronic circuits and components	0.0	3.6	14.7	18.0
	Textiles	8.9	9.2	8.0	4.2
	Clothing	12.3	6.0	2.0	0.5
Hungary	Agricultural products	25.5	26.4	8.8	7.3
	Chemicals	0.0	12.8	6.6	8.2
	Office and telecom equipment	5.1	5.2	25.7	22.8
	Electronic data processing equipment	0.0	0.0	14.0	5.6
	Telecommunications equipment	0.0	0.0	10.9	16.4
	Automotive products	9.6	6.7	17.1	18.2
	Textiles	2.9	2.6	1.3	0.6
	Clothing	4.0	3.9	4.4	1.1

Source: Based on data from WTO on-line statistical database, http://www.wto.org, date accessed 15 December 2008.

Second, as in the nineteenth century, the Latin countries (and the rest of the countries described below as well!) all crowded into the same markets. Prices for textiles, garments, shoes, and even small cheap cars plummeted accordingly. At least ten LDCs tried to export small cars in the 1980s and 1990s, but only three had any significant success: Mexico, Spain, and above all Korea. The rest ended up with debt and car plants with overcapacity. The 1980s debt crisis, which this overcapacity partly caused (see below), dealt a fatal blow to continued state intervention in all three Latin industrializers. It triggered sharp falls in state investment, and led to privatization of state financial and industrial firms. By the end of the 1990s, none of these states had the directive capacity they possessed at the beginning of the 1970s. (The same dynamic played out in Southeast Asia in the 1990s.)

If China's explosive growth had not occurred, indebted Latin American economies would probably have stagnated in the late 1990s and 2000s. Instead, China's voracious demand for raw materials allowed Brazil and other economies to retire substantial portions of the foreign debt, albeit at the cost of a return to raw materials exports. By 2007 China's imports of iron and other ores were three times Brazil's total exports, and its imports of oilseeds were one-third higher than Brazil's oilseed exports.

Eastern Europe

Eastern Europe was roughly equivalent to Latin America with commissars until 1989. That is, Eastern Europe was a Ricardian agro-exporter like the Latin American countries, except that its natural market was split between industrial Germany and Britain. Consequently, Eastern Europe faced the same kinds of problems in shifting to Kaldorian strategies and industrializing that Latin American countries did after World War II. Socialist planning allowed the Eastern European states to resolve handily their Gerschenkronian problem of resource mobilization. But it completely prevented any resolution of the Kaldorian productivity problem. Like Latin America, Eastern European countries had to rely on TNCs' largesse to overcome their Kaldorian dilemmas.

Industrialization in Eastern Europe proceeded in three waves, as in Latin America, but only the first wave was identical to that in Latin America. In the second and third waves, the Eastern European states over-played their role in industrialization. During the Depression and the War, Germany was a more difficult and exploitative partner than was the United States in its relations to Brazil and Mexico. After the war, Eastern European countries tried to exclude TNC investment and buy TNC technology directly. Their disastrous experience with this confirms the importance of tacit knowledge in TNCs' competitive advantage, for they ended up buying machines they could not use efficiently or effectively; they neither acquired external tacit knowledge nor generated it internally.

Wave one: consumer nondurables

Eastern Europe's first wave of industrialization occurred exactly as in Latin America. Agricultural exports created rising local incomes, which in turn spurred local light industry during the pre-World War I period. In Hungary, for example, agricultural exports rose 300 percent from 1874 to 1914, spurring investment in milling and in food processing, in local textile production, and in construction (Berend and Ranki, 1982). As in Latin America, not all areas benefited equally from this wave of industrialization. Bohemia and eastern Poland did best. Bohemia (now the Czech Republic) developed into the Austro-Hungarian empire's major source of railroad equipment and textiles. The eastern part of modern Poland (at that time the westernmost part of the Russian empire) produced textiles and machinery for agricultural exporters in the Ukraine and other parts of the Russian empire.

As in Latin America, the Depression consolidated this early wave of light industrialization. Eastern Europe's agricultural exports fell 40 percent in volume terms from 1929 to 1932. This confronted these countries with the same choice Latin America faced: retain bankrupt Ricardian strategies or shift to Kaldorian strategies. But German policies and the weakness of these mostly new states precluded as complete a shift as Brazil or Mexico made in the 1930s. Czechoslovakia's and Poland's more coherent national elites and prior industrialization allowed them to move into rudimentary capital goods and heavy industry. Czechoslovakia expanded its native car industry. Poland used state control over trade to channel investment to state industries. By the start of World War II, the Polish state owned 100 percent of munitions and armaments production, 80 percent of chemicals, 50 percent of metals, and over 90 percent of air and rail transportation. By contrast, Yugoslavia and Hungary were too busy creating states and social stability to foster much new industry.

However, Eastern Europe suffered from Germany's deliberate efforts to assure itself a flow of raw materials during the 1930s and 1940s. Bulgaria and Romania were seduced by German willingness to pay above-market prices for their agricultural exports and so developed little more than their textile industries. By 1934 Germany had constructed a set of bilateral treaties with each Eastern European economy (except Czechoslovakia) exchanging German manufactures for their raw materials, and by 1938 80 percent of trade was clearing via bilateral barter (Berend and Ranki, 1982). This arrangement enforced a Ricardian orientation. Nominally the Germans paid very good prices for their raw materials imports, but practically all this meant was that Eastern Europeans accumulated credit balances, which they would never collect, in Germany. In any case, the war leveled most of Eastern Europe.

Wave two: Stalinist heavy industrialization

The second wave of industrialization in Eastern Europe took place under Soviet-style socialism. During this phase the Eastern European economies (re-)created heavy industry. Heavy industry is ideally suited to a command economy, since economies of scale predominate over economies of scope and since capacity utilization is important for macroeconomic efficiency. As in Latin America, the state sponsored this investment, literally mobilizing labor and capital to add heavy industry to the privately created pre-war light industry. Unlike Latin America, the state then socialized light industry and in some places agriculture as well. It financed capital goods imports with agricultural exports and exports of low-value manufactured goods like garments.

About ten years later than Latin America, these states also tried to encourage TNCs to help develop a local automotive industry. But the socialist Eastern European states could not countenance TNC ownership of assembly plants for ideological reasons. Consequently, they tried to get the benefits of TNC technology transfer without the hazards of admitting TNCs to the local economy. In order to wrest technology away from TNCs without actually letting TNCs operate inside their economies, the Eastern European states emulated the strategy LDC host states used when confronting raw materials TNCs: picking on the weakest firms with the least amount of vertical integration and thus the least market power so as to get the best financial deal.

This strategy failed miserably, for when Eastern European states picked on the weakest of the European car firms, they also got the weakest technology. Weak TNCs had an incentive to transfer technology, for this allowed them to amortize the development and sometimes production costs for older technologies and designs. As a result, the Eastern Europeans bought uncompetitive and obsolete technology and models. Poland, Yugoslavia, and the Soviet Union all obtained licenses and machinery to produce Fiat's 124 and 127 models; Romania licensed a Citroen model. The Eastern Europeans planned to sell these cars back into Western Europe as 'new used cars,' that is, as unused versions of an older car. The Eastern Europeans essentially bartered with the TNCs, buying machinery and factories by promising to pay the car firms back with finished goods. In contrast, Czechoslovakia rehabilitated its pre-war car industry and ended up with the best car industry of any of the Eastern European economies at that time. Strategically, the Eastern European states thus hoped to escape the trap of being raw materials suppliers to and garment assemblers for Western European economies.

But despite being good Marxists all, the Eastern Europeans did not realize that hard technologies alone do not constitute the means of production. The means of production also include the relations of production, or soft technologies that enable physical machinery to be used productively. The Eastern Europeans bought machinery from the TNCs without also getting the practical knowledge they needed in order to make the machines and factories run well, and their own relations of production prevented any innovative Kaldorian productivity growth. The melding of Italian and French car technology with Eastern European production practices produced cars that could barely compete against used cars in the Western European or US market. The Romanian-built Citroen, for example, never achieved the minimum quality standards that PSA (Citroen's parent) demanded for sales in Western Europe. Moreover, the Eastern Europeans were never able to operate their factories at maximum capacity, which limited potential exports. From 1973 to 1979, all five Eastern European car producers (including the Czech manufacturer Skoda) saw sales in Western Europe increase from about 50 000 units to about 90 000 units (Altschuler *et al.*, 1984: 178–9). By contrast, South Korean car producer Hyundai was selling 200 000 units in the US market three years after its market entry. And it did so by selling cars with quality and styling levels found in new, albeit basic, cars.

Wave three: borrowed money and collapse

Like Latin America in the 1970s, the Eastern Europeans also embarked on a borrowing spree. Much of the borrowing went to subsidize living standards rather than for productive investment. However, even productively invested funds were not used efficiently, because, as noted above, machinery alone does not constitute the means of production. The persistent inability to increase production and maintain quality standards created an Eastern European version of the Latin American debt crisis. Indeed, the crisis started earlier in Eastern Europe, with Poland's quasi-default in 1980 and with Yugoslavian and Romanian debt reschedulings in 1981.

The collapse of state socialism created an opening for Eastern European states, the European Union (EU), and TNCs to re-negotiate Eastern Europe's role as a periphery to Western Europe and particularly Germany. The EU helped Eastern European states avoid the chaos of the 1920s by reconstructing their state apparatuses faster and with more resources. Like Latin America in the 1990s, the Eastern European states inviting in TNCs in an effort to rehabilitate both their consumer durables and nondurables sectors. For their part, European TNCs opted to create a Mexico – a zone of low-wage labor for labor-intensive components or for labor-intense consumer durables. Initially, this investment targeted sectors and areas which were already most developed before World War II. Thus investment initially flowed into textiles and garments in Poland, electrical machinery and metal parts in Hungary, and cars and heavy machinery in the Czech Republic (see Table 11.1 above). But by the 2000s, TNC transfer of tacit knowledge had created new competencies, as with car production in Slovakia and Romania, or non-electric machinery in Poland, while reinforcing older ones, like consumer electronics in Hungary (Intracen, 2008). Hungary's consumer electronics exports rivaled Ireland's, while tiny Slovakia leaped into the top 20 car exporters.

East Asia – Taiwan and South Korea

The Taiwanese and South Korean states played the same Gerschenkronian role that Latin American and Eastern European states did: the state started many basic industries, and state or state-controlled banks channeled investment funds into the private manufacturing sector. The state also controlled access to the domestic market, using tariffs and quotas to exclude imports and capital controls to limit TNC access. The state systematically repressed labor. At the same time, divergent colonial legacies and better luck in the timing of industrialization allowed these states to also overcome Kaldorian dilemmas. Crucially, the absence of a strong landowning class allowed both states to systematically squeeze agriculture to fund industry (like nineteenth-century Japan), decreasing their reliance on foreign loans.

In the absence of any domestic political challengers, these states were able to make state aid to industry conditional on high levels of export performance and productivity growth (Amsden, 2001). Like Japan, these states sequenced export flows, using raw materials (and foreign loans) to capitalize a consumer nondurables sector, whose exports then capitalized and provided a market for a protected capital goods sector. Moreover, the dynamics of trade conflicts between Japan and the United States (see Chapter 12) provided both with a constant stream of new opportunities for increasingly sophisticated consumer goods exports. Both developed country producers wanted or had to shift production to East Asia. This assured that Taiwan, Korea and China benefited enormously from constant Verdoorn effects.

The two East Asian states also balanced the costs and benefits of association with TNCs differently than the Latin or European states did. They allowed TNCs to produce for export in enclaves within their economies or to subcontract to local producers. This shielded domestic producers from direct competition with TNCs while allowing domestic producers to observe how TNCs produced world market competitive goods and to learn or absorb tacit knowledge. The East Asian states also subsidized manufactured exports in order to boost production volumes and thus capture Verdoorn effects.

These states could do all this because they differed considerably from the Latin American and Eastern European states. State-building was much less problematic than in Latin America or Eastern Europe. The US military created disciplined militaries for Taiwan and Korea, as they were front-line allies confronting communist regimes on the Asian mainland. Thus, these two states were highly autonomous, built first and foremost around highly independent militaries. Furthermore, these states did not face a well-organized and politically entrenched landlord class, because the US-run decolonization removed Japanese landlords after World War II. Finally, Taiwan and South Korea received massive amounts of US aid, which, at least initially, rendered their states less dependent on local social groups.

Wave one: agriculture, capital investment, and consumer nondurables

Japanese colonization reoriented the Taiwanese and South Korean economies towards agricultural exports for the Japanese market. As in Latin America, industrialization began as a consequence of rising rural income. The Japanese state encouraged productivity increases via flat land taxes, just as it had done back home. Taiwan's per capita income in agriculture doubled as productivity rose, 1895–1945. This also allowed extremely high rents, which captured about half the crop for landlords and the state. World War II and US occupation opened the door to thorough land reform in each society. These land reforms eliminated landlords as a class by 1953 in Taiwan and 1958 in Korea.

Land reform positioned both states to capture rents that landlords had previously consumed or invested in more land. *The state's ability to divert agricultural rents directly to industrial investment constitutes East Asia's first big divergence from Latin America, and one which parallels the differences between Japan and Russia in the nineteenth century.* The two states diverted rents through taxes, control over the extension of credit to peasants, and some judicious price fixing. Both states created state monopolies for the purchase and export of rice and the domestic sale of fertilizer. They lowered rice purchase prices and raised fertilizer sale prices. This allowed the state to capture about 35 percent of total agricultural production. The Kuomintang (KMT) state in Taiwan performed this transfer process best, tripling the outflow of capital from agriculture as compared to the outflow under the earlier Japanese colonial administration, and providing about one-third of gross domestic investment during the 1950s. The KMT state used agricultural exports to fund capital goods imports for a range of state-owned heavy industries such as cement, steel, fertilizer, electricity, and chemicals. Because of South Korea's later land reform and postwar reconstruction, it was more dependent on US aid for capital formation during the 1950s. US aid funded roughly 80 percent of Korean investment in the 1950s, with the state squeezing Korea's peasants in the 1960s.

Other than the successful squeezing of agriculture, this first wave of industrialization (from 1945 to, say, 1965) closely resembled that in Latin America. Private entrepreneurs using family savings capitalized light industry while the state created heavy industry. Agricultural exports (rice, sugar, and the ubiquitous bamboo shoots and mandarin oranges) paid for capital goods imports. In Latin America the problem at this point had been to move past light industry into consumer durables, while still trying to finance capital goods imports with limited agricultural exports. Latin American states invited TNCs in to resolve this problem. Taiwan and South Korea again diverged critically from Latin America at this point. They used the TNCs more cautiously, and they used *manufactured,* not agricultural, exports to finance further imports of capital goods. This shift to manufactured goods exports is the second decisive difference between the Latin American and East Asian development trajectories. The decisive difference between Eastern Europe, which also used manufactured exports, and East Asia is that the state allowed the normal competitive pressures of the capitalist market to discipline privately owned exporters and force them to upgrade their productivity.

Wave two: simultaneous import substitution and export expansion

These differences permitted Taiwan and South Korea to use TNCs to generate more exports, and teach local consumer nondurables firms how to manufacture efficiently to world market standards and then use rising exports of consumer nondurables to accelerate the expansion of a highly protected capital goods industry. As these capital goods and heavy industrial suppliers to the expanding nondurables sector themselves grew, Verdoorn effects would make them more competitive. In turn, they too would be freed from protection and forced or induced to export. Eventually, the entire economy would be freed from protection and would be export competitive. Creative use of the export processing zone (EPZ) lay at the heart of this strategy. The EPZs concentrated on producing the three 'T's: textiles, toys, and trash (such as cheap clothing and shoes, plastic Star Wars figures, hibachis (barbeques), inflatable swimming pools), and so on.

The Taiwanese and Korean EPZs imitated Hong Kong, which, by virtue of its geography (an island), demography (too many people), and resource base (none), had become a completely open economy surviving by manufacturing low-end consumer nondurables, including and especially garments and junky trinkets. In 1965 Singapore went over to this model, and Taiwan created its own EPZ. Korea created its first EPZ in 1970. Any TNC could come to an EPZ and find cheap and willing labor (mostly peasant women earning extra income for their hard-pressed farm families), could bring in goods to be worked up without any tariffs, and could take worked-up goods out without any taxes. The predominance of female labor in EPZs, and the high segmentation of local labor markets, meant that male wages in the domestic market could rise without pricing EPZ exports out of world markets (Seguino, 2000).

Three environmental conditions helped make the EPZ-led strategy successful. First, the TNCs had an interest in finding low-wage but productive labor to do the labor-intensive processing steps in their production chain (see Chapter 12). This was particularly true for Japanese firms (Ozawa, 1979). Provisions in the United States and other developed countries' tax and tariff code which levied tax only on the value-added overseas for reimported goods encouraged this global dispersion. Second, the progressive lowering of tariffs following the Kennedy Round (1964–7) of GATT negotiations facilitated a rapid rise in global trade. Finally, during the war in Vietnam the United States bought significant volumes of exports from both Taiwan and Korea, helping to ease the balance-of-payments constraint during the beginning of the EPZ-led strategy.

Taiwan (and later Korea) benefited from the EPZ in many ways. Even the small wage earned by the EPZ's labor force represented a net addition to Taiwan's ability to import capital goods. Moreover, many TNCs subcontracted work to local firms, enabling them to gain access to world markets, to learn about the outside world's quality standards, and to produce at large volumes and thus improve productivity. Finally, when these local firms and many TNCs bought locally produced capital goods, such as machine tools, this expanded demand created in the EPZ to the domestic market, producing Verdoorn effects in the capital goods and local-use consumer nondurables sectors. Asian EPZs tended to have more local firms than in, for example, Mexico's *maquiladora* border regions, giving the two Asian states greater leverage over the economic use of EPZs and the evolution of local industry.

Both states used additional measures to spur exports and thus production volumes and Verdoorn effects. Both states used control over the banking system to allocate capital only to firms that met export targets. Firms willingly exported at a loss to get access to capital; once they succeeded in exporting, they naturally tried to lower their losses and eventually found themselves profiting from exports. Therefore, state policy subverted market pressures that might have kept production volumes, and thus long-term productivity growth, low. Once firms were competitive, the state exposed them to world market competition and moved protection further upstream to producers of more sophisticated goods or of capital goods and inputs. Exactly this process occurred in Japan before World War II; consumer nondurable exports drove heavy industrialization. Note that the magnitude or presence of protection did not differ much between Latin America and East Asia. In South Korea, for example, as late as 1990, protection redistributed as much as 13 percent of GDP, with most of this going to manufacturing (Lee, 1997: 1272). What differed was the *conditionality* of protection; in East Asia states made subsidies and protection contingent on export performance.

Wave three: between Japan and China

During the 1970s Korea and Taiwan began to diverge. For political reasons the KMT government in Taiwan wanted to keep the Taiwanese-owned firms that did most of the subcontracting and exporting small. It avoided borrowing and stayed out of the production of consumer durables for export. Instead Taiwan successfully shifted to the export of low-end, simple consumer goods to other would-be Asian industrializers, especially China, while supplying capital goods to those new exporters and moving its own production towards increasingly sophisticated light electronics and contract semiconductor production. By the end of the 1990s, Taiwan was supplying about half of the world's laptop computers and a substantial portion of high-end computer monitors, while doing most of the labor-intensive assembly in China. This strategy was moderately successful. Taiwan accumulated the world's largest hoard of foreign reserves by 1990, enabling it to weather both the 1980s and 1990s financial crises handily, and its per capita income rose to about half the level of US per capita income. Yet at the same time, Taiwanese growth slowed significantly and it found itself having to compete with low-wage China on the one side, and high-technology Japan and America on the other. China wanted faster technology transfer, which would enable it to compete directly with Taiwan. Japan and America offered more fertile fields for research and development. The continued upgrading of sophisticated light industry in the face of TNC efforts to closely guard the technologies that assure them technological rents is not assured.

In contrast, Korea opted to borrow heavily overseas to capitalize a range of heavy industries that could only be run by gigantic corporations. Like the Latin American borrowers, this strategy gambled that new export industries would mature in time to service debt, and as in Latin America this proved false. However, South Korea's existing expertise in light consumer goods gave it enough exports to weather the early 1980s more easily than the Latin Americans did. By the mid-1980s the consumer durables investments had matured, and Korea was exporting cars to the United States. Rapid expansion of these exports – Korean car exports zoomed from nil to nearly $1 billion by 1985, $6 billion by 1997 and $50 billion by 2007; exports of integrated circuits (mostly dynamic random access memories – DRAMs) hit $5 billion by 1990 and $33 billion by 2007 – then created Verdoorn effects that made Korean car producers about half as efficient as the average US car manufacturer, and DRAM manufacturers about two-thirds as efficient.

Korea's reliance on foreign capital and its choice of more commodity-like products created considerably more vulnerability than Taiwan's choices, though. Korean firms' extraordinarily high debt-to-equity ratios brought them to their knees in the Asian financial crisis. This allowed the United States to force the Korean states to disperse ownership of these firms allowing foreigners to accrue ownership of 42 percent of publicly listed firms (*Economist*, 13 October 2005). New Western owners of Korean banks, electronics firms and car manufacturers are not likely to pursue growth at all costs, as Korean firms did in the past. Korean-owned banks and firms continue to find their high levels of debt a weakness in any cyclic downturn. Moreover, past Korean growth relied heavily on keeping wage growth well below productivity growth, which has proven impossible in an era of democratic politics. Manufacturing wages doubled in the 2000s. Like Taiwan, Korea finds itself between a rapidly up-grading, low-wage China on the one side, and an established Japan and America on the other.

East Asia – China as the final frontier

China's scale and diversity encompasses a wide variety of regional outcomes that makes sweeping generalization risky, and I cannot pretend to be able to settle an ongoing historiographic debate about China's astounding industrialization in the past half century. China undoubtedly includes not just pieces of but the whole of the Korean, Taiwanese, Japanese and Brazilian experiences in different provinces. Nevertheless, there are substantial correspondences with our general pattern. These help explain how China began to recover its eighteenth-century one-third share of global manufacturing output after two centuries of relative decline.

Wave one: nineteenth-century agricultural export-led industrialization

Like our other nineteenth-century industrializers, China experienced a substantial export boom based on commodity exports, primarily oils, silk and cotton. The value of Chinese exports more than doubled, in 1880–1913. But other tropical exporters had even faster rates of growth, causing China's share of global exports to fall, and per capita exports were a fraction of other countries' levels (Lewis, 1970; Maddison, 2007: 54, 88, 173). This relative decline is somewhat deceptive. Exports were concentrated on a few regional economies, and half of all exports flowed through Shanghai (Maddison, 2007: 57). Those regional economies thus experienced the same kind of growth impulse that, for example, nineteenth-century Brazil or Mexico did, with somewhat the same consequences for industrialization in consumer nondurables. The Chinese imperial state started the first modern textile mill. By the 1920s, Shanghai had become a center of textiles and garment manufacturing, with in excess of 3 million spindles. Some of this was foreign, particularly Japanese-owned, but the majority were local firms, particularly in the silk textiles industry. These firms were export capable (Pomeranz, 2000).

Unlike the most successful nineteenth-century exporter-industrializers, however, China lacked a strong and effective state. Civil war raged from most of the late nineteenth century through 1949. This hindered industrialization and exposed China to considerable external predation, including Japanese occupation of Manchuria. China did not attain India's 1913 level of railroadization until 1995. As in Korea and Taiwan, however, Japanese colonization had some beneficial consequences. The Japanese reoriented Manchuria towards the Japanese economy as a supplier of coal and iron products, and built an extensive rail network and the rudiments of steel and vehicle production. Meanwhile, Japanese and local textile firms successfully substituted locally spun yarns for imports after World War I.

Wave two: heavy industry under state socialism

After 1949, the victorious communist party was able to construct a more capable state, and thus use both the usual tools for accelerating late industrialization, and, via collectivization of the economy, some of the ones used in Eastern Europe. Violent land reform and the expulsion of the KMT to Taiwan permitted the state to build industry on peasants' backs. Compulsory sales, taxes and the same price manipulation the Korean and Taiwanese states used allowed the Chinese state to divert most of peasants' surplus over subsistence into industrial investment (Ka and Selden, 1986). By 1959 gross fixed capital formation, largely in heavy industry, had nearly doubled to 44 percent of GDP. But peasants lacked the means to reinvest in agriculture, and collective agriculture lacked any incentives to increase productivity, causing an estimated 20–30 million peasants to starve.

While famine induced the state to relax pressure on the peasantry somewhat, the state was still able to sustain non-residential fixed capital formation at levels comparable to Taiwan and Korea from 1958 to 1977 (Maddison, 2007: 64, 68). This decisively shifted the Chinese economy away from agriculture and towards industry, more than tripling manufacturing's share of the economy. But productivity performance was much, much worse than in Korea or especially Japan. China's growth in this period was largely extensive, not intensive (see the discussion on perspiration versus inspiration in the final major section). The lack of productivity growth, which the disruptions of the Cultural Revolution aggravated, brought this period of growth to a close in the same kind of crisis that pushed Brazil and Mexico into a search for foreign capital and export markets in the late 1960s.

While the state's communist ideology removed the normal market incentives to increase productivity, it did compensate for this through massive investment in basic education. The number of students in primary education tripled and the number in secondary increased by a factor of ten, 1952–78, raising the average worker's level of education from 1.6 years to 8.5 years, in 1950–92 (Maddison, 2007: 66). Health care also became universal. Both contrast favorably with health and education deficits that have slowed growth in the Latin American economies. When the state finally reopened China to global markets in the 1980s, the relatively high education levels of low-wage Chinese industrial workers proved an irresistible draw for firms looking to shift labor-intense production offshore.

Wave three: workshop for the world

The heterogeneity of China's late development is most apparent after Party leaders gradually reintroduced markets after 1979. In essence, three different growth constellations emerged. Each constellation has a group of analysts who see it as the dominant impulse. Our concern here is not to adjudicate this debate, but rather show how each fits into the broader patterns observed in earlier chapters.

The first impulse was domestic market-oriented, labor-intense, and generally small-scale. Yasheng Huang (2008) argues forcefully that rural China supplied this impulse, first in agriculture and then in small and medium industry (as well as some larger firms). This impulse flourished in the 1980s. Huang argues convincingly that this impulse led to major gains for rural areas, particularly with respect to food supply. It also created huge savings that financed new investment. But manufacturing productivity during 1980–92 appears to have grown slightly slower than in the United States (which was itself in the midst of a prolonged productivity slowdown) (Ruoen, 1997: 144). Huang (2007: 42) also argues convincingly that from 1990 onwards, political elites systematically transferred resources from rural to urban areas and just as often to themselves. Rural incomes then grew at half the rate of national GDP, causing the labor share of GDP to fall. If true, this sits uneasily with Huang's broader argument about the vitality of Chinese capitalism, for China continued to have rapid economic growth through the 1990s and even more so into the 2000s.

Perhaps the combination of lagging productivity and resource transfers confirms the salience of the second great growth impulse, which is the transformation of moribund state-owned enterprises (SOEs) into more dynamic, profit-oriented firms. The state recapitalized these SOEs with funds Huang's rural billion generated, pushing domestic investment up to 40–50 percent of GDP. China's state also forced foreign investors seeking access to the Chinese market to create joint ventures with Chinese SOEs. This policy particularly targeted the strategic car, semiconductor and civil aviation sectors. Thus VW found itself married to Shanghai Automotive, Motorola to nine distinct joint ventures as the price for its one wholly owned subsidiary, and Airbus built a wholly unnecessary assembly line for its A320 aircraft family with two SOEs in Tianjin. Chinese productivity growth ran at levels well above those in the revitalized US economy, and 40 percent faster than in the 1980s. This would comport with Amsden's (1989) argument about the necessity for permanent, professional management to accrue, absorb, and deploy production knowledge, and might reflect a successful state industrial policy aimed at creating something akin to Korea's successful multinational, multisectoral *chaebol*. Because of China's huge potential and real market size, it has much more leverage than did Latin American or Eastern European economies with respect to separating technology from multinational firms. By 2005, for example, China's market for semiconductors was larger than either the US or Europe markets, although 64 percent of apparent consumption was exported in some finished product (PriceWaterhouseCoopers, 2005: 15).

The third great impulse came from foreign invested firms (FIEs), which started out largely doing EPZ-style assembly in the 1990s but increasingly shifted to complete manufacturing after 2005. FIEs accounted for about 60 percent of Chinese exports in 2005 (Naughton, 2007: 386). Many FIEs are apparently Chinese-owned firms whose investment capital was round-tripped via Hong Kong in a search for legal security. Nevertheless, FIEs' ability to produce at developed-country levels of quality via subcontracting or their own imported technology has allowed China to export in volumes that dwarf most other large developing economies. Exports accounted for between 30 percent and 40 percent of Chinese GDP over the past decade, compared to about 10 percent for Brazil. Initially much of this output was concentrated in a few sectors, like garments, toys and luggage, but by the 2000s FIEs were exporting a wide range of electronics, car parts and simple machinery (Athukorala, 2005, 2007). Like other late developers, surging exports both had considerable multiplier effects in the economy and eased the trade deficit caused by machinery imports. Politically, the growth of labor-intense manufacturing also helped absorb the millions of migrant workers streaming out of slower-growing rural areas (Huang, 2007: 113, 124).

China thus repeated and combined features of all the late developers we have discussed. The state created a disciplined and skilled labor force out of a peasantry dispossessed of its land. The state created and concentrated capital by exploiting peasant agriculture, and used that capital to fund a wide range of industrial activities. The state encouraged and used EPZs to generate foreign exchange and validate firms' ability to compete in international markets. And the state used access to its domestic market to wrest critical proprietary technology away from multinational firms. All this accounts for at least some of China's success in doubling its share of global GDP in 1980–2004 and increasing its share of global exports from 3.7 to 12.4 percent, in 1992–2005 (Athukorala, 2007: 8).

Yet China also combined many of the problems of those late developers. The consistent repression of domestic consumption to capitalize industry created the macroeconomic imbalances that are the meat of Chapter 14. It also began to undercut the supply of cheap but educated labor that powered both domestic and FIE production. Finally the reliance on subcontracting and FIEs for exports has prevented the majority of Chinese firms from capturing any brand recognition in rich country markets. Market power remains with the original contractor or retail firms, which explains why Chinese firms typically capture only 5 percent of the final value of goods sold offshore (Linden, Kramer, and Dedrick, 2007). It also means that these retailers – like Walmart, which accounts for 10 percent of China's exports to the United States) – retain the ability to shift production somewhere else. As well, the quality of exported Chinese-made goods from subcontractors is at best erratic and often disappointing, suggesting long-term problems retaining market share in a world where expensive oil adds to the cost of trans-Pacific shipping.

LDC industrialization in perspective, and its systemic consequences

The sources for successful LDC industrialization strongly parallel earlier efforts at late industrialization (Chapter 4), just as the systemic effects of successful industrialization parallel the effects of successful Ricardian development by agro-exporters in the nineteenth century (Chapter 5). States in successful industrializers overcame Gerschenkronian collective problems, generating capital for investment, channeling those investment funds through state-owned banks to favored entrepreneurs (including its own firms), and bestowing lavish subsidies for export and growth. States overcame local entrepreneurs' natural risk-aversion to pioneering exports. Military conscription transformed peasants into an industrial army, just as it did in Western Europe. Finally states organized collective R&D to speed technology diffusion. Simply mobilizing labor and capital – Gerschenkronian success – bestowed substantial long-term growth amounting to 5–6 percent annually on Brazil, Mexico, Taiwan Korea and lately China.

But what about overcoming Kaldorian problems? Paul Krugman (1994) famously argued that East Asian industrialization was more about perspiration (Gerschenkron) than inspiration (Kaldor). Krugman is right that the bulk of LDC industrialization – which includes many cases not considered here – involves extensive growth, rather than the intensive growth that is characteristic of successful development. In other words, while many LDCs managed to solve their Gerschenkronian problems and mobilize both investment and an increased labor supply, they did not overcome their Kaldorian dilemmas and produce the industrial deepening that defines development. LDC states' social bases affected their ability to industrialize. The Brazilian state's inability to override the immediate interests of local agrarian elites created one of the world's most skewed distributions of income, with the bottom 20 percent of the population receiving only 3 percent of GNP, and also made it very difficult to control its own fiscal deficit. Although Brazil has the world's eighth largest economy, its local industry has consistently faced a constricted domestic market.

In contrast, the South Korean state's suppression of landlords allowed it to generate capital investments that gave every worker in manufacturing about 80 percent of the capital stock of the typical US manufacturing worker and to dramatically improve productivity (Amsden, 1989; Baily *et al.*, 1998). Still, even in South Korea, it is notable that capital productivity is roughly half that in the United States, and that Korean output per worker has stalled out at about half that in the United States. South Korea's high rates of growth and income come from working 40 percent more hours than the typical US worker. Moreover, some of the very practices that permitted Gerschenkronian success – the systematic concentration of capital into manufacturing and the concomitant starvation of agriculture and services – now impedes more rapid productivity growth in the entire economy, as it might in China. While Korea's manufacturing workers enjoy a capital stock approximating a US worker's, the equivalent worker in South Korea's highly protected service sector has less than a third.

Much as the Krugman model in Chapter 2 suggested, a new set of Thünen-like manufacturing zones is emerging, arranged on the basis of relative productivity and knowledge intensity in manufacturing. High-relative-productivity, knowledge-intensive manufacturing still takes place in core areas, while low-relative-productivity, non-knowledge-intensive manufacturing out in the old agricultural periphery feeds the town with basic industrial commodities. The fact that some LDCs now export manufactured goods does not *per se* constitute development. As scores of potential and existing exporters of garments know, low wages are an evanescent competitive advantage. Wages are always lower somewhere else – even China's coastal areas face low-wage competition from Vietnam and Bangladesh. This process mirrors the inexorable outward shift of wool and other primary product exporters in the nineteenth century, complete with falling prices and debt crises in the earlier producers.

Finally, luck – timing, strategic location, and externally induced destruction of local social groups – was very important. Brazil, Mexico, Taiwan and Korea all extracted substantial financial and technical resources from the United States. US efforts to create professional militaries in these countries substantially aided the efficiency of their states' later industrialization drives. Finally, the US-inspired elimination of landlords in Taiwan and South Korea helped remove potential obstacles to industrialization drives initially financed out of agriculture. In terms of timing, the two East Asian states began industrializing just as world trade was experiencing rapid growth and TNCs stood ready to facilitate exports. These conditions made the apparent rewards of an outward-looking export orientation very high. In contrast, the Latin American and Eastern European states' industrialization occurred in a period when the potential rewards for export-oriented policies were quite low.

Table 11.1 above shows how different policy choices and environments affected the level of technology embodied in exports and the kinds of exports countries generated, adding a few comparison cases to the ones surveyed in this chapter. Clearly in each major regional economy, one country emerged as the winner in a specific sector or two, and equally so, the outward dispersion of labor-intense production continues. In automotive products, for example, Mexico is North America's winner, Spain is Europe's, South Korea is Asia's. Among the NICs themselves, the Asian countries show a clear technological advantage. And China is clearly the 800-pound gorilla of garments and a wide range of other labor-intense goods, even without adding in Hong Kong's re-exports of Chinese production.

Systemic consequences

The emergence of the NICs also had two large systemic consequences, partially signaled above. First, the emergence of a host of new exporters of low-value-added manufactures triggered the successive debt crises of the 1980s, largely centered on Latin America, and then of the 1990s originating in Asia but quickly spreading to the entire manufacturing periphery. Both parallel the 1890s crisis examined in Chapter 6. The third wave of industrial deepening in the NICs was largely financed with external money, namely bank loans during the 1970s and a mixture of TNC investment, bonds, and bank loans during the 1990s. In both cases, states took advantage of temporarily low global interest rates to promote local export production, and in both cases the lack of coordination among investors led to saturation of the market, falling export prices, and a financial crisis. In turn, these crises compressed consumer demand in developing areas, exacerbating global oversupply relative to effective demand.

Like the nineteenth-century dominions, the would-be NICs of the 1970s all gambled on a relatively narrow range of seemingly promising industrial sectors: textiles and garments, shoes, toys, basic steel production, and cheap cars. By the early 1980s their production was booming just as the Reagan–Volcker recession in the United States led to declining demand for those goods, and as protectionist policies in the United States and Europe set severe quantitative restrictions on the volume of sales. Falling demand collided with Volcker's 8 percent increase in the real interest rate, making it quite difficult for debtors to generate enough foreign exchange to service their debt. From 1974 to 1986, terms of trade for most LDCs fell about 60 percent rendering most NIC debtors illiquid, and a few insolvent. When Mexico threatened default in 1982, banks rushed to stop lending lest they increase their own risk of collapse.

Much the same pattern occurred in the 1990s, but in Southeast Asia. Southeast Asian economies had linked their currencies to the US dollar. As the dollar's value fell relative to the Japanese yen, both Japanese and US TNCs had an incentive to shift production there. Southeast Asian economies boomed, encouraging foreign banks and investors to lend more money for domestic investment. The US state supported this lending, because it financed exports of infrastructural goods to economies that needed more power generation equipment, new airports, new harbors and new urban infrastructure (Garten, 1997).

These individually rational actions by banks created a collective disaster, for they meant the cessation of lending to solvent but potentially illiquid debtors like Brazil, and even to solvent and liquid debtors like South Korea. In this respect, both situations resembled that of 1890. As in 1890, when the Bank of England coordinated a bailout, the US state had to step in to organize new lending in the 1980s and 1990s. But unlike the 1890s crisis, the 1980s crisis directly affected creditor states because the structure of intermediation differed. In the nineteenth century the British financial system facilitated a sale of developing country debt as bonds, but rarely directly held debt. In the 1970s US and other banks directly committed depositors' funds to developing debtors as bank loans. Default thus threatened banks with the loss of depositors' funds and bankruptcy; the major US banks' loans to LDCs exceeded their capital base. Rather than risk bank collapses, the fiscal core of the US government, the Treasury and the Federal Reserve, used the IMF to force banks to commit new loans to debtors. Similarly, US investment banks' exposure to the hedge fund Long Term Capital Management, which collapsed subsequent to the 1998 Russian bond default also motivated the US Federal Reserve to orchestrate a collective bailout of imperiled banks.

In all these bailouts, investors tended to retain the bulk of the debt at face value. The bailouts typically added the interest in arrears onto the existing debt, helping it to roughly double over the 1980s. *In effect, the banks forced debtors to continue borrowing, creating a bigger long-term problem.* Because 1980s debtors cut investment back by an average of 20 percent in order to service their debt, they reduced their ability to grow out of debt. This crippled the Latin debtors relative to the East Asian debtors, who continued to grow through the 1980s, while the Latin debtors piled up more debt. Investment levels similarly fell in Southeast Asia after the 1997 crisis. From 1996 to 2007, relative to GDP, Malaysia's fixed investment fell by about 47 percent, Korea's by 24 percent, Thailand's by 36 percent, Indonesia's by 19 percent, and even in Taiwan investment fell by 8 percent.

The refusal to write-down debt also disrupted the complementarity of economic flows between debtor and creditor countries. In order to make their debt service payments, and pressured by the IMF to maximize their noninterest current account surplus, 1980s debtors depressed their imports through massive devaluations and the proliferation of import controls. Debt or import cuts decreased economic activity in creditor countries, in turn decreasing demand for debtor exports. In the 1980s, the United States, for example, lost about $25 billion annually in exports to Latin America owing to Latin American debtors' efforts to maximize their noninterest current account surpluses. Creditors' exports to Latin America did not return to the absolute level of 1981, in *current* dollars, until 1988. In the aftermath of the 1990s crisis, Southeast Asian countries also maximized exports and restrained imports. They re-pegged their currencies to the dollar in order to remain competitive with China, and like China they recycled their trade surpluses with the United States as purchases of US government debt. In effect, they shifted purchasing power away from Asia and to the United States.

The second systemic consequence of NIC industrialization was an end to the process of global deindustrialization through displacement competition that had started with the British industrial revolution. The industrial revolution in northwestern Europe and North America decreased the share of global manufacturing outside those areas from about two-thirds of world manufacturing in 1800 to about 7 percent during 1900–50. By 2000 the LDCs had doubled their share of global manufacturing to about 30 percent, and global GDP to about half. In all likelihood this share will continue to rise as India and China grow. Thus, as in the nineteenth century, the emergence of new industrial centers poses a considerable challenge to older producers. All three major established centers of industrial activity, the United States, Europe and Japan, faced sharply increased competition in all their major markets from new industrializers, particularly those in Asia (OECD, 1998b: 208). By 1995, other East Asian producers had become the major source of competition for Japanese producers and a significant source of competition for European and US producers. LDC-based firms like Hyundai (cars), Mittal (steel), and Cemex (cement) were able to multinationalize into core markets, albeit in older industries.

Core producers often successfully shifted into higher-value versions of these products or entirely new markets. But this competition helped lead to rising income inequality and a considerable fall in manufacturing employment (Wood, 1994). Both trends helped undermine the political consensus underlying the full employment orientation of Bretton Woods period macroeconomic policy. Both trends also increasingly disrupted the global balance between supply and demand, creating conditions that caused the great financial crisis of 2007–9. The next chapter looks at how Bretton Woods trade policy inadvertently helped both undermine itself and speed NIC industrialization. Chapter 14 deals with the 2007–9 financial crisis.

Chapter 12

Trade, Protection, and Renewed Globalization

> Not only the prejudices of the public, but, what is much more unconquerable, the
> private interests of many individuals, irresistibly oppose [free trade].
>
> *Adam Smith*

Like the postwar international monetary system, world trade patterns moved back to nineteenth-century market-driven patterns between 1945 and 2007, reflecting two different processes. First, although the dynamics differed, new production zones emerged in both agriculture and manufacturing as Thünen and Krugman dynamics played out. In agriculture, rising urban-industrial populations continued to push cultivation outward much along the lines the Thünen model would predict. A new set of new agricultural countries (NACs) emerged, with old locations exporting what were for them novel agricultural goods, and new locations suddenly blossoming.

Falling transport and communications costs abetted firms' efforts to disperse labor-intense manufacturing along a wage–productivity gradient. Increased trade created increased competition in TNCs' domestic markets, which motivated them to search for ways to match wage levels to skill levels. But they found this difficult to do within any single industrial economy, because postwar labor legislation had homogenized wage levels within individual economies. TNCs' search for cheaper labor found willing suppliers in the would-be newly industrializing countries (NICs) discussed in the previous chapter. Where nineteenth-century agriculture went searching for cheap land, twentieth-century industry went searching for cheap(-er) labor. Nineteenth-century agriculture dispersed to find land without peasants and landlords; twentieth-century manufacturing dispersed to find labor without unions, job protection, and entrenched work practices. In both cases the reverse flow of goods helped undermine the social and production relations that had created the initial impetus to move, eventually weakening that impetus. Globalization is thus the re-emergence of 'normal' market-driven gradients linking wages and skill levels as the postwar consensus on containing markets broke down.

However, second, markets alone did not push this dispersal of industrial activity. As with global finance, and as in the nineteenth-century, market forces could not have (re-)emerged without state intervention. Obviously, states drove multilateral negotiations to remove Depression-era trade barriers. The failure to create an International Trade Organization (ITO) left only the ad hoc, 'temporary' General Agreement on Tariffs and Trade (GATT) accord. Like the legal framework surrounding the international monetary system, the

GATT framework regulating international trade balanced domestic employ-ment and political and macroeconomic stability concerns against the gains to be had from trade and political pressure from competitive producers. The GATT thus dealt only with manufactures, sheltering agriculture and the service sector from international markets.

Although GATT facilitated a gradual reduction in tariff barriers and a rapid expansion of world trade, it also contained numerous qualifications, exemp-tions, and escape hatches. States creatively used GATT loopholes to protect domestic producers. While tariffs were down to insignificant levels by the end of the 1980s, about half of industrial country imports were subject to VERs, quantitative restrictions, countertrade (bilateral exchanges) and negotiated offsets, a level of protection approximating that in the 1930s (Grieco, 1990). However, far from impeding market forces, this creative protection often ended up actually magnifying market pressures on those producers, by accelerating industrial dispersal and thus helping to give rise to the new manufactured goods exporters that the previous chapter dealt with at the unit level. The GATT's successor, the World Trade Organization (WTO), embodies a fundamentally different ethos, reflecting US desires to open up markets which the postwar consensus had left closed in the name of employment and macroeconomic stability. Declining US competitiveness in consumer goods manufacturing through the 1980s created political pressures in the United States to open up markets elsewhere for highly competitive US agricultural and services exports. This pressure culminated in the GATT's last round of trade talks, the Uruguay Round, which produced the WTO and in effect resurrected the old ITO. Trade talks continued under the WTO, albeit less effectively. The first WTO round collapsed in the face of the 1999 riots in Seattle. Resurrected as the Doha Round in 2001, these talks collapsed in the 2008 global financial crisis.

This chapter looks first at the legal regime governing trade. Then it addresses the dynamics described above, showing how trade liberalization and protection interacted to induce more dispersion, and how protectionist policies have had paradoxical effects, often worsening the competitive global market pressures on the very producers states were trying to protect.

States and the postwar trade regime

The effort to create an International Trade Organization

Like the legal structure enveloping international monetary relations, the legal structure governing trade reflected a tension between the international and domestic lessons of the Depression. Individual states' efforts to create trade surpluses and employment by closing local markets to imports had led to collective disaster in the 1930s, as world trade declined by over two-thirds during 1929–32. The 1930s protectionist surge hurt many major US indus-tries, and they pushed for freer trade after the war, along with European coun-terparts (van der Pijl, 1984).

Fear of renewed trade wars motivated efforts to construct a trade regime paralleling the money regime constructed at Bretton Woods. In 1948 over 50 countries signed a charter for an ITO which would provide comprehensive supervision of all aspects of world trade, including foreign investment flows, agriculture, and other commodities like oil (Gardner, 1969). Like Keynes's proposed International Clearing Union (ICU), the ITO had strong disciplinary powers, which it could use against countries setting up barriers to trade. But whereas Keynes's ICU was aborted, the ITO was stillborn.

The domestic economic and political importance of stabilizing incomes and employment killed the ITO. The Depression shifted control over agriculture into the hands of virtually every state in the world (de Hevesy, 1940). The Depression and the war also put states in control of imports and infrastructure services like telecommunications, power, rail and air transport. In recovering Europe, states naturally gave priority to imports of food, fuels, and essential capital goods over other goods. Thus, while competitive industries in many countries were willing to support efforts to get the ITO, they faced stubborn opposition from larger groups benefiting from protection. Britain wanted to retain its preferential imperial tariff. Agricultural countries poised to industrialize, like Australia, Argentina, and India, thought the ITO would strangle their infant industry in its cradle. Even the smaller European countries, for whom trade was essential, worried about a powerful ITO because of the centrality of the service sector and agriculture for political and economic stability (Gardner, 1969).

Free traders in the United States wanted even more free trade than the ITO aimed for, while protectionists feared they would lose control over US trade policymaking. Constitutionally, Congress has control over trade. In 1934, seeking to undo some of the damage of Smoot–Hawley and hoping to expand exports, Congress had passed the Reciprocal Trade Agreements Act (RTAA). But Congress certainly did not intend to delegate authority to anonymous international bureaucrats at the ITO rather than a president subject to political pressures and horse-trading (Destler, 1992). Congress refused to ratify the ITO in 1948. Instead, one component of the original ITO proposal, GATT, emerged as an ad hoc regulatory institution for international trade in manufactured goods. GATT's weakness was reflected in its small staffing, uncertain legal status, and the absence of street protests and nasty books about it until the WTO replaced it.

The General Agreement on Tariffs and Trade

The GATT quite literally embodied a set of compromises between the domestic and international lessons of the Depression. Nominally, parties to the agreement consented to enforce three principles in settling trade disputes and in regulating trade practices:

1. Transparency and trade barrier reduction: all nontariff barriers should be replaced with tariffs, and all tariffs should be lowered. Quotas, dumping, and subsidies were prohibited.

2. Nondiscrimination: all signatories agreed to give most-favored-nation status to other signatories. Any favorable trade conditions granted to one party had to be generalized to all signatories so that everyone would have exactly the same treatment. Customs unions or free trade areas with lower trade barriers were permitted, however.
3. Reciprocity: multilateral talks arranged mutual tariff reductions.

These principles informed seven rounds of tariff reduction negotiations lowering the average tariff on manufactured goods from 40 percent in 1947 to about 5 percent today. These tariff reductions seemed to spark an unprecedented expansion in world trade. From 1950 to 2005 the volume of trade has grown 40 percent faster than gross world product. By 2007 total world trade amounted to about $14 trillion, roughly equivalent to US GDP or 28 percent of gross world product. As early as 1997 global trade had roughly surpassed the proportion it held in the early 1900s.

Unlike the very broad ITO, GATT basically covered only manufactured goods. Yet the areas GATT neglected grew in importance after the war. At US insistence, the GATT excluded agriculture from 1955. By 1997 agricultural trade had shrunk from its pre-World War I predominance to about 10 percent of world trade, reflecting rapidly growing trade in services and manufactured goods. Trade in services, which was fairly small in the 1940s, was also omitted from GATT. By 1997, however, trade in services amounted to about 23 percent of world trade. Both agriculture and services were major US exports, and represented two areas where the United States had a trade surplus ($72.1 billion in 1998 and $120.5 billion in 2007) and Japan and Germany large deficits ($48.7 billion/$21.6 billion and $46.1 billion/$44.7 billion, respectively) (WTO, 1998, 2008). Meanwhile, GATT also contained several escape hatches that allowed states to depart *temporarily* from its principles even with regard to manufactured goods, if the rate of growth of imports threatened to create large-scale unemployment in a particular sector. These limitations to GATT produced increases in protection over time, and in turn protection spurred more dispersion. How? Let us look at agriculture first.

Agriculture under GATT

The rapid postwar expansion of urban population in northwestern Europe, in the US industrial heartland, and, as we have just seen, in late industrializers increased demand for foods and nonfood agriculturals (NFAs) while raising the implied rent on agricultural land near cities. Consequently, the old Thünen logic re-emerged as trade revived after 1945. Better, cheaper transportation and refrigeration should have pushed much global agriculture outward to the Southern Hemisphere New Agricultural Countries (NACs) and into other new lands, while reducing production somewhat in the United States. Europe, and Japan. Indeed, new semitropical suppliers emerged for some traditional temperate goods. But high levels of subsidy and protection for established producers slowed this outward shift of the Thünen rings.

Thus increased demand for beef and cotton in the United States and the industrialization of the US South pushed production of low-quality beef (for fast food chains) and cotton southward. Cotton acreage quadrupled in Central America, and low-quality beef production doubled, in turn displacing traditional subsistence agriculture (and many peasants). By 1970 43 percent of Central America agricultural land was grazing areas, and by 1980 about two-thirds (Dunkerley, 1988: 193). As in nineteenth-century Ireland, this displacement provoked violent peasant resistance and massive migration.

Meanwhile, just as refrigeration/freezing had permitted Southern Hemisphere producers to export meat in the nineteenth century, the declining cost and increasing reliability of refrigerated transport opened up tropical and Southern Hemisphere areas for products that until then had been grown only in proximity to cities. Traditional agricultural TNCs (like the banana TNCs) and former nontransnationalized food processors diversified into these new crops. They supplied cloned and thus standardized varieties of foods/seeds, and they used their control over refrigerated transportation to dominate the flow of goods from new supply areas to industrial country markets (Friedland, 1994).

These changes reconfigured the old nineteenth-century Thünen rings. While suburbs ate industrial country farmland, health-conscious yuppies ate more fresh foods, expanding demand for nontraditional fresh fruits and vegetables and flowers in the Southern Hemisphere and tropical locations. After 1980 tropical areas added Northern Hemisphere fruits and vegetables to their traditional repertoire of bananas and pineapples. Southern Hemisphere growers of oranges (Brazil and Australia), apples (South Africa, Australia, and New Zealand), and grapes (Chile) became off-season suppliers to Northern Hemisphere consumers. Similarly, producers of vegetables and fruits in Northern Hemisphere tropical climates – for example, Mexican (or Israeli or Moroccan) tomato, strawberry, and cucumber growers – extended the growing season's 'shoulders.' As in the nineteenth century, all the competitive producers had reasonably stable governments promoting export production with the usual tools; and as in the nineteenth century, these NACs competed with existing, local producers.

These new agricultural zones grew up around and in response to growing industrial centers. Not unexpectedly, each of the three major industrial nations drew foods primarily from nearby regions, with Mexico and Central America supplying the United States and Canada, and Mediterranean countries supplying northern Europe (Islam, 1990). However, preferential tariffs and quotas for former colonies, like the European Community's African–Caribbean–Pacific (ACP) system, created some odd trade patterns as well as significant trade conflicts.

Despite this continued dispersion of agricultural production, import quotas and production subsidies in all the industrial countries encouraged local overproduction of uncompetitive, high-cost, traditional agricultural goods.

Developed country farmers used their political muscle to maintain Depression-era protection. Agricultural protection cost OECD states and consumers a fairly consistent $260 billion (€225 billion) in the 2000s, amounting to about 30 percent of total OECD agricultural output and 1 percent of OECD GDP (OECD, 2006: 19–21). The EU, through its Common Agricultural Policy, was the most egregious offender in terms of the volume of food produced and the total amount spent on protection. CAP consumed around half of the EU's budget – €125 billion in the 2000s – versus €35 billion in the United States in the 2000s. European quotas for expensive bananas from its former colonies provided those colonies with $150 million at a cost to consumers of $2 billion, with most of the difference going to large EU agro-TNCs. Japan spent about $48 billion, despite importing more than half its calories and being the world's largest food importer.

Unlike the other two major industrial areas, the United States was directly hurt by developed country agricultural protection; in turn, its own policies largely harmed LDC producers. For example, Japanese and Korean quotas limited US exports of citrus and beef; quotas protecting US sugar producers limited cheaper LDC sugar exports. From the United States' point of view, however, at least the Japanese did not export subsidized food into the world market, like the EU.

The vested interests created by protection sometimes extend outward from agriculture into other sectors. For example, continued protection of Japanese agriculture has contributed to Japan's relatively high land prices. High land prices became built into the price of stock shares (since companies own land); into the structure of lending (land provides at least 30 percent of the collateral backing bank loans); and into people's expectations about retirement (via their ability to reverse amortize their landholdings). Removing protection and all the various tax breaks that make it rational to hold land in agricultural use in Japan now would put further pressure on land prices, which have never recovered from the bursting of Japan's 1980s bubble.

The continued significance of agricultural exports for the United States sparked trade conflicts with Europe as early as 1962, and the US Congress passed increasingly stronger laws demanding executive action to open foreign food markets (Nivola, 1993). Global conflicts over agriculture emerged because production subsidies naturally encouraged farmers to overproduce. By the early 1980s, the EU had achieved self-sufficiency in major food commodities and had begun to build up enormous stockpiles of uncompetitive wheat, butter, and meat. From 1980 to 1991 it spent nearly $100 billion to dump these stockpiles into world markets (EEC, 1991). This dumping hurt existing, competitive producers in the United States and Australasia. The United States then decided to ally with other competitive agricultural exporters (collectively known as the Cairns Group), and pursue agricultural trade liberalization through the Uruguay Round of GATT talks (Hathaway, 1987; Higgott and Cooper, 1990). The Cairns Group's market power – they accounted for 9 percent and 12 percent of EC12 and Japanese exports respectively in the late 1980s – and US willingness to help LDC agro-exporters in exchange for their acquiescence in stronger intellectual property rights rules also created strong motives for reform.

The United States generated a two-pronged strategy designed to divide competitive from uncompetitive EU farmers and net losers from net winners in Europe's agricultural subsidy game. The stick in the strategy was subsidized US sales of wheat to third-party markets in the late 1980s, which forced the EU to provide even larger export subsidies. In 1988 Britain (a net loser from agricultural subsidies) forced the EU to put production caps in place, and thus limit subsidies, for the first time. The carrot was the Reagan administration's 1985 proposed 'zero option' for agricultural subsidies: by AD 2000 everyone would remove all subsidies. The EC completely rejected this proposal (as did uncompetitive sections of the US agricultural community).

The United States then gravitated towards the Cairns Group's proposal to convert all forms of subsidy into tariffs and then gradually lower those tariffs. At this point, the Europeans wavered over accepting the principle that rural income support should be disconnected from production subsidies, which would help end overproduction. Finally, in 1992 the Europeans proposed 29 percent cuts in subsidies but no real shift away from production subsidies as a concept. The United States felt this would simply prolong the problem of overproduction and trade fights. With negotiations deadlocked at the end of 1992, the United States used a dispute over US soybean exports to impose selective punitive tariff increases in order to create a free trade community among the EU's competitive farmers. It slapped 200 percent tariffs on French and German white wines and British wheat gluten – all competitive products – to get the EU to cut subsidies for uncompetitive oilseeds, which it eventually, grudgingly, did. This pattern repeated itself for the next decade.

By the end of the 1990s, agriculture had passed under the WTO's ambit. The Uruguay Round Agreement on Agriculture nominally made agricultural trade conform with the GATT regime: all forms of protection were to be converted to tariffs and tariffs were to be reduced by 36 percent from 1995 to 2000; new export subsidies were prohibited and the volume of subsidized exports was to fall 21 percent; and aggregate farm support (including non-protection-related supports) was to fall 20 percent. Some of this trade liberalization has occurred, but at an excruciatingly slow pace. Domestic farm lobbies, particularly in the EU and Japan, still have €100–200 billion compelling motivations to lobby vigorously against liberalization. Indeed, agricultural issues ultimately killed the 2000s Doha trade negotiations. Doha re-ran the 1980s policy initiatives: the United States proposed zero-ing out export subsidies, which would disproportionately hurt EU producers; the French refused to cut any subsidies. The US Congress responded with increased subsidies. And poor countries insisted on safeguards against surging food imports.

The global consequences of agricultural protection are large, negative, and ultimately unsustainable given a growing population. Econometric analysis suggested that competitive food exporters stood to gain about $100 billion if all restraints on agricultural trade disappeared, while, of course, the uncompetitive states would save themselves the even larger cost of subsidies. Agro-exporting LDCs, most of which are heavily in debt, would gain about $30 billion of this additional export income. Although aggregate accounting about the LDCs makes less sense than ever, these numbers do indicate that the weakest economies suffer the most from protection. Thus, agricultural protection is not just a matter of expensive butter in France. *Subsidies for rich (and uncompetitive) farmers in the industrialized countries mean more poverty in LDCs.*

GATT, protection, and the global dispersion of industry

Manufacturing production also dispersed along a Thünen-like gradient of wage/productivity costs, much as the Krugman analysis in Chapter 2 would predict. What kinds of production dispersed and why? In general, falling transportation and communication costs enabled dispersion. From 1950 to 2000 average transport costs fell 10 percent, though this was only half the size of the nineteenth-century decline (Hummels, 2007; Jacks, Meissner and Novy, 2008). The container revolution accounts for most of this, given that 95 percent of international freight by volume moves on ships. By 2006 global container shipping capacity amounted to roughly 10 million standard units. Ever larger jet aircraft – which carry about 35 percent of goods by *value* – also lowered transport costs. Falling transport costs should have enabled more agglomeration in industries with high economies of scale, while causing labor-intense industry with low economies of scale to move in search of cheaper labor. Three different patterns of dispersion emerged from these two dynamics.

First, just as established agricultural regions faced competition from the nineteenth-century NACs, established labor-intense, low-value-added twentieth-century industries with low economies of scale came under increasing competitive pressure first from Japan and then from the NICs (Chapter 11). Like nineteenth-century stay-behinds, they pressured their states for trade protection. However, protection induced more rapid technical advancement in the new production areas, ratcheting up the competitive threat to established industry in the protected sector or economy. The NICs' own efforts to industrialize in sectors at the end of the product cycle, where technologies were very well understood and thus more easily transferred than in sectors in which tacit knowledge or extremely highly skilled labor was needed, accelerated this process. So dispersion and protection interacted, each driving increases in the other.

Second, even in more capital-intense industries the increase in global competition caused by the rise of Japanese and European exports of consumer durables and electronics put pressure on US firms to seek cost savings to remain competitive. They largely chose to do this by relocating new production to areas with cheaper, more tractable labor, rather than reorganizing production processes at home to increase productivity. This induced first a flight to their own (US) South, and then to the LDC 'south.' As this flight created rising incomes in the NICs, agglomeration occurred in order to get economies of scale in these new locations. This created another self-reinforcing cycle of dispersion.

Finally, newly emerging leading-sector industries with no pre-existing geographical structure dispersed almost immediately, locating production near major sources of demand and dispersing component production along a wage/productivity gradient. Thus emerging semiconductor firms shifted labor-intense assembly steps to Singapore and Mexico in the early 1960s. The rest of the electronics industry followed this pattern, both in Europe and Asia. In short, some industries were born dispersed, some achieved dispersion, and some had dispersion thrust upon them.

We can paint a more detailed picture of dispersion by looking first at wage levels and then at the nature of the production process. In general, the least skill-intensive sectors, producing undifferentiated commodities, have fled more skill-intensive areas not because of rents on land but because of rents on labor. But they have only done so when the production process is not tightly coupled in time or space, thus permitting unskilled tasks to be done at some distance from skilled tasks, or when scale economies are weak. Both aspects reflect insights generated by Charles Babbage, an English mathematician of the nineteenth century. He suggested that firms break up production processes into skilled and unskilled tasks (Froebel, Heinrichs, and Kreye, 1980). Rather than paying a skilled worker (who could command a relatively high wage) to perform a mix of these tasks, skilled workers could be detailed to do tasks requiring skills, and unskilled workers tasks not requiring skills. Workers could then be paid wages that matched their marginal productivity.

However, postwar efforts to maintain macroeconomic stability tended to homogenize wages inside the industrial countries. Unions succeeded in raising the share of wages in the total value produced and in compressing the wage structure, raising wages for the unskilled and semiskilled workers who constituted the bulk of union membership. This indirectly raised wages across the entire economy, especially the public sector, because many sectors bargained for wage increases comparable to those made by industrial unions. Unionization and tight labor markets defeated firms' efforts to 'babbage-ize' production and wage levels, and thus to maximize their profits. To 'babbage-ize' production, firms had to go outside their national economies to find nonunion labor.

If a search for lower wages explains why firms might *want* to disperse production, it does not explain why this search might take precedence over other pressures or, equally important, whether they *can* do so. Not all production processes are amenable to geographic dispersion. It is pointless to have a skilled worker install antilock brake systems in a car and then ship that car somewhere else to have an unskilled worker install windows. In contrast, cloth can be woven and cut using expensive machines requiring skilled operators, and then shipped elsewhere for assembly into garments by (relatively) unskilled sewing machine operators. In general, the more tightly coupled production processes are, the nearer in time and space each step in the process has to be for things to get put together right, and the less likely it is that a process will be dispersed. Conversely, the less tightly coupled production processes are, the easier it is to disperse production. Similarly, garment assembly has very low economies of scale, which enables dispersion to multiple locations. Car production has high economies of scale – 250 000 units for vehicle assembly and 400 000 units for engines – which inhibits dispersion to small markets.

Dispersion began with the low-value-added, labor-intensive steps of loosely coupled production processes in the rich countries. They faced the greatest wage pressures, for they no longer could compete with the wages higher-value-added, assembly-line-based industries offered local workers. The textiles and garment industry (at $583 billion about 4.3 percent of total world merchandise trade in 2007) was the largest of the migratory industries characterized by high labor intensity and low levels of coupling in the production process. Because of the low level of capitalization needed to enter this industry, many local firms in LDCs could start production. Yet because they often lacked the design, merchandising skills, and market access of developed country firms or retailers, LDC producers typically acted as subcontractors for those firms and surrendered much of the final value to the prime contractors.

In higher-value-added mass production industries (such as cars – at $1183 billion about 8.7 percent of world trade, with total turnover twice that), rising wages for unskilled workers motivated a search for places to assemble low-value-added components using cheaper labor. At first, only component production was dispersed, with components shipped back to assembly sites in high-wage areas. Eventually, however, even cheaper cars, once their entire production process had been routinized and debugged, could be shipped to low-wage areas as well, because virtually all skills had been incorporated into special-purpose machinery (recall the product cycle model in Chapter 10). This investment occurred in lumpy packages reflecting the higher threshold for economies of scale.

Finally industries born global, like electronics (at $1514 billion about 11.1 percent of world trade) immediately demonstrated a perfect 'babbage-ization' of production, supplemented by the same kinds of trade dynamics that characterized textiles and garments. This industry had scale economies similar to the vehicle industry, but in reverse: scale was greatest in components and lowest in assembly. Component production of, for example, DRAMs required a $2 billion factory. But assembly could be done at individual work stations, much as in garment assembly.

Textiles and garments

In the United States, Germany, and Japan, textiles and especially garment producers went south both literally and figuratively in search of cheaper labor as wages rose in each economy. The industry split into its somewhat higher-value-added, mechanized, tightly coupled textile branch (the spinning of fibers and weaving of fabrics) and its low-value-added, uncoupled assembly of garments from fabrics. For Germany and Japan, which lacked low-wage areas within their own borders, this required the transnationalization of production. Garment producers went first to southern Germany and then to low-wage Mediterranean countries like Yugoslavia and Tunisia. Japanese producers went to rural Japan and then to the Asian NICs. US firms at first had the good fortune to find the south inside their own country in nonunion, low-wage states like the Carolinas, Arkansas, and Georgia. US producers migrated south soon after World War II, because US wages were then the highest in the world. Producers in the other two countries did not begin to move until the 1960s, when economic recovery from World War II and the 'baby busts' caused by war casualties created local labor shortages.

Firms found transnationalization to be costly. In Germany and Japan, joint state–industry organizations facilitated the orderly relocation of the industry, finding sites, providing subsidized capital, and negotiating with host governments. In the southern United States, host 'state' governments subsidized an orderly relocation. Despite this aid, the US industry felt itself to be under extreme competitive pressure. The industry was also shifting out of cotton fabrics into synthetics, a higher-value-added good for the industry, but this shift required new capital investment too. Hence, the US textiles and garment industry began to demand protection. The US government's response set the pattern for virtually all US and European protectionist responses in manufacturing sectors thereafter. It also unwittingly intensified the long-run competitive threat the industry faced.

In 1955, the US industry began demanding protection in response to rising imports of Japanese cotton textiles and garments, even though imports amounted to only 2 percent of consumption (Friman, 1990). In 1957 the United States asked the Japanese to voluntarily restrain their exports, which they did. This first voluntary export restraint (VER) set the new pattern for protection. Nominally, VERs abided by GATT's rules. The Japanese, after all, could not be condemned if of their own free will they set a quantitative limit on their exports, while, since the United States ostensibly had done nothing, it could not be condemned for violating the principles of transparency and nondiscrimination. Practically, however, VERs violated the spirit of GATT as the United States was for all intents imposing a bilateral import quota on Japan.

Japanese producers responded to the VER rationally. The VER limited *Japanese* exports of *cotton* textiles. So Japanese firms, aided by their state, began shifting cotton textile production to the Asian NICs, while moving up the value-added ladder into synthetics at home. Then they could export *synthetics* from Japan and *cottons* from the NICs, evading the VER. Threatened US producers appealed to Congress for more protection, and Congress extracted a new, expanded VER, the 1962 Long-Term Agreement (LTA), as the quid pro quo for approval of the new round of GATT tariff reductions President Kennedy sought. The new VER expanded voluntary restraint to the four Asian NICs. Producers again responded rationally, shifting lower-value cotton production offshore and upgrading their own output. (Table 12.1

Table 12.1   *Fiber content of textile production, world and East Asia, 1959–83, selected years (percent)[a]*

	1959–61		1969–71		1981–3	
	S	C	S	C	S	C
World	22	68	38	55	51	45
Japan	19	58	41	37	54	35
South Korea	2	92	42	54	70	26
Taiwan	6	90	27	70	78	21

Note: [a]S = synthetics; C = cotton. Percentages may not total 100 because of the presence of wool and other natural fibers.

Source: Based on data from Anderson (1990: 151).

shows the shift in fiber content.) Between 1960 and 1970 imports of cotton textiles doubled in the United States, but imports of synthetics grew 10 times. The NICs and Japan also began diverting exports to Europe. The Europeans then rushed to sign their own bilateral deals with the major exporters.

Both despite and because of this proliferation of protection, textile and garment exports from the NICs exploded during the 1960s. Rather than let the United States divert the Asian steamroller into their market, the Europeans pushed for the 'catch-all' Multi-Fiber Arrangement (MFA), signed in 1973 and subsequently renewed every few years until 2005. The MFA allowed the industrial countries to negotiate detailed bilateral quotas for exports from developing countries. This agreement slowed but did not stop the flood of exports, particularly in garments and footwear. All that happened was that the NICs and OECD importers relocated production to ever newer (and cheaper) production sites. Consequently, OECD producers of textiles and garments shed about 75 percent of their workforce between 1952 and 2002 in the face of persistently rising imports (Audet and Safadi, 2004: 38).

By the 2000s the industry had seemingly stabilized along lines that might have been predictable in the 1950s. The higher-value-added textile segment of the industry had increased its capital intensity and productivity, and was largely located in the rich industrial countries and the richest NICs. In the United States, for example, the textiles industry (spinning and weaving) tripled its capital intensity after 1950, enabling it to maintain position as the world's third largest fabric exporter, with about 17 percent of global exports. Unsurprisingly, value-added was almost four times the average for LDCs. Meanwhile, the labor-intensive garment industry had gone even further south into Latin America, searching for cheaper labor. Consequently, US 'imports' of garments (often made from exported US textiles) amounted to $67 billion in 2002 (Audet and Safadi, 2004: 76–9). The same pattern is visible in trade between Western and Eastern Europe.

But by enforcing quantitative restrictions on imports from specific countries, the industry forced a more rapid movement into higher-value-added products and a more rapid geographical diffusion of textiles and garment production technologies than might otherwise have occurred. The Asian exporters would probably be making more garments and fewer textiles if they had been permitted to export garments more freely. Moreover, the development of a local textiles industry provided an enormous boost to local production of light machinery. Protection in textiles and garments created completely irrational outcomes from the point of view of firms wishing to stem competitive pressures.

Unlike agriculture, the WTO was successful in phasing out the system of quotas for textile and garment trade under the Agreement on Textiles and Clothing. Quotas largely disappeared after 2005. Because China is the world's largest exporter of garments ($81 billion including Hong Kong, or 30 percent of total world garment trade), all protectionist pressures now bear on it. Systemically, the rapid geographical dispersion of textile and garment production and exports was mirrored with footwear, toys, cheap stamped metal products, lighting products, cheap TVs, low-end electronics and simple machinery. As each new flood of manufactured exports collided with its relevant VER, production shifted outward in Asia (and elsewhere) to countries with lower and lower relative wages. Production shifted from Japan (a low-wage economy until the 1970s) to the first four NICs, and from there to Malaysia and Thailand, and from there to Indonesia, China and Vietnam.

Automobiles

A similar process of dispersion and protection occurred in car production, with three differences. First, unlike the textiles and garment production chain, where the intermediate good (fabric) was amenable to capital-intensive, high-value production, and assembly of the final good was labor-intensive, in cars generally intermediate components were labor-intensive, low-value-added goods and final assembly was capital-intensive with large economies of scale. Second, as Chapter 9 noted, the car industry was the paradigmatic sector for the postwar period: highly unionized and well paid workers provided a substantial portion of the stable demand that enabled full capacity utilization and thus high profits. Third, the capital intensity of car manufacturing and the importance of soft management technologies created very high barriers to entry. This meant that unlike textiles and garments, where LDC producers could jump into the market as subcontractors and then rapidly mature into independent firms, TNCs largely dominated the dispersion of production.

An invisible form of protection had shielded the US market from major car imports until the oil shocks of the 1970s. The US car market was oriented towards large cars. Over 90 percent of the cars sold in the United States had engine displacements of over 2 liters in 1970, compared with only 30 percent in Europe and less than 1 percent in Japan (Dunn, 1987). When the oil shocks of the 1970s suddenly caused consumers to downsize, US firms faced serious competition from high-quality Japanese and European cars. In particular,

Japanese firms using just-in-time production strategies posed a considerable challenge (see Chapter 13).

By the end of the 1970s the Japanese share of the US market had risen to over 20 percent, Chrysler faced bankruptcy, and all three domestic manufacturers were suffering enormous financial losses. In response, President Reagan negotiated a VER with Japan in 1981, capping car imports at 1.7 million units. Just as with textiles and garments, Japanese producers responded quite rationally to quantitative limits. They shifted from the small, cheap cars to larger and more expensive cars, loading their cars with nonnegotiable options. As Honda matured into Acura, Toyota into Lexus, and Nissan into Infiniti, Japanese producers' total sales value continued to grow despite constant unit volumes.

The VERs also forced Japanese firms to transnationalize their production, but this time into the US market, not to a third-party, offshore low-wage zone. Honda led the way, building a complete production complex capable of producing more than 600 000 vehicles, including some Acuras. The other Japanese firms rapidly followed. By 2005 Japanese firms' productive capacity accounted for 40 percent of US domestic production, displacing a considerable part of their own exports and US firms' production.

As with textiles and garments, the Japanese competitive threat also forced US car firms to disperse the labor-intensive, low-value-added parts of their production process. Because car *assembly* is tightly coupled in the US production paradigm (the production of most components *and* final assembly is tightly coupled in just-in-time production), car firms dispersed component production first. As with textiles and garments, US firms first went to their own local south. Employment in transportation equipment manufacturing industries grew rapidly in the Sunbelt states after 1950. This shift was less about high wages than about escaping union work rules that firms felt inhibited productivity. Thus, the even lower wages to be found across the border in Mexico were not attractive enough to motivate a wholesale shift in production locale until the 1970s.

During the late 1960s and early 1970s, car firms in the United States and Europe experienced extremely high levels of labor militancy. A new generation of workers, undisciplined by the Depression and wartime training, entered the factories, demanding better wages and more stimulating work in good working conditions. At the same time, US carmakers faced a new competitive threat as Japanese cars began entering the US market. The US companies thought Japan's competitive edge lay in lower wages. Although they were wrong about that (see Chapter 13), they began looking for low-wage sites to which they could shift work. Korea, with wages then at around $4 per hour, compared to the $20 US carworkers got, suddenly looked much more attractive. GM and Ford took equity positions in and began sourcing cars from Korean firms. Mexico, where hourly wages were $2 to $3, looked even better, was closer, and did not involve deals with other firms.

For its part Mexico made itself attractive by expanding its *maquila* program in 1983. The *maquila* program, started in the 1960s, was a Mexican version of the Taiwanese export-processing zone, but one that encompassed the entire border area, not just a specific city. In 1983 Mexico liberalized the rules governing *maquiladoras*. The number of *maquiladoras* and their employees quadrupled by 1996 to 2800 factories with over 650 000 employees, or 25 percent of total Mexican manufacturing employment. Roughly one-quarter of value-added in the *maquiladoras* at that time was car related, making it the second largest sector after the entire electrical/electronics goods group (garments were third); car-related *maquiladoras* employed about one-sixth of total *maquiladora* labor. The combination of the liberalized *maquila* law and US carmakers' desire to escape US unions helped drive this explosion of production in Mexico and exports to the United States. By 2007, cars and car parts provided one-sixth of Mexico's total exports, exceeding oil (WTO, 2008). Most of these exports were small cars; larger, more expensive cars continued to be produced in the major industrial centers. Ford's Mexican factory shows why.

Ford relocated production of the Mercury Tracer (the Escort's twin, now the Focus) to a plant in Mexico. Because the Escort/Tracer line was essentially a re-skinned Mazda Protégé, this plant could be built off the shelf as a duplicate of Mazda's own plant (Shaiken, 1991). The Mazda Protégé had been in production for over a decade and all the bugs in its design and production process had been worked out. Consequently, while Mexican workers were relatively unskilled compared to Japanese and US workers, Ford could use them. This Mexican labor did not need to know how to figure out the ad hoc solutions to the production problems that always crop up with new models; those problems had already been eliminated. Working with an established model, this Mexican labor produced cars with labor inputs and defect levels that rivaled those of Japanese producers.

In contrast, Ford retained production of more expensive, more sophisticated models like minivans and SUVs (sport utility vehicles) in US plants. These had more complicated components and trim features whose assembly could not be automated; US workers retained the 'tricks' that had been built into the machines operated by Mexicans. And Ford continues to launch new models in the United States, where more experienced production teams can figure out solutions to the myriad of things that go wrong in the first few years of production. Nevertheless, as Mexican skill levels improved, more complicated models were also produced in those factories.

Producers in Europe mimicked the US pattern, by creating a 'Mexico' in Spain and Portugal before 1989 and then cautiously creating a 'Mexico' in Eastern Europe. Ford, GM, and Volkswagen went to Spain, which now makes more cars than Britain (itself a low-wage host to Nissan, Honda, Toyota, and Peugeot). Volkswagen produces in both the Czech Republic and Slovakia, GM in Poland, Peugeot in Slovakia, and Renault in Romania. As with Mexico, Eastern European production sites have matured from cheap cars to more sophisticated models, such as VW-owned Skoda's Octavia, a version of the Audi A3. By 2000, nearly every major car producer had located half its output outside its domestic market (UNCTAD, 2002: 133).

Electronics

The dispersion of electronics across the entire Asian-Pacific Rim economy presents an almost perfect picture of dispersion along a wage/productivity gradient. Bernard and Ravenhill (1995) present a lovely analysis of the 'babbage-ization' of the manufacture of calculators. Production is organized by a Taiwanese firm acting as an original equipment manufacturer for a major Japanese electronics firm. The Taiwanese firm buys sophisticated machinery, solar cells, and liquid crystal displays from Japanese firms. These are made with high-skill, high-capital production processes. It sources a mid-grade microprocessor from a local Taiwanese firm (which uses Japanese equipment to make the chip). It ships these parts to Thailand along with plastic injection molding machinery (a mid-range technology). Low-waged Thai workers put all the pieces together.

A similar pattern can be observed in the organization of production of hard disk drives (HDD) by the firm Seagate (Ernst, 1997). Manufacture of the magnetic read head, a high-precision, high-automation task requiring large inputs of skilled labor, is done in the United States; so is manufacture of the basic media for the HDD, because this requires considerable scientific knowledge about materials. Software is written in California. Product design, testing, and quality assurance are done in Singapore, which now has a highly educated white-collar labor force. The actual assembly of HDDs is dispersed to low-wage Thailand, which does labor-intense assembly of basic HDDs for commodity PCs, slightly-higher-wage Malaysia, which has a more automated plant for more complex HDDs, and the high-wage United States, which makes specialized HDDs for laptops, video units and mainframe computers. The cheapest metal components come from Indonesia, where wages are the lowest, with the rest from Thailand and Malaysia.

Trade in services and the erosion of social protection

The manufacturing cases described above all represent declining or contested industries for the United States, even if, as we will see with cars in the next chapter, they have managed to improve their productivity. But as the US merchandise trade balance deteriorated in the 1970s and especially 1980s, it sought to completely overturn the essential purpose of the GATT. The GATT fit comfortably within the ensemble of postwar compromises that sought to subordinate international market forces in order to maximize domestic employment. In the immediate postwar period, the exclusion of agriculture contributed most towards this goal, until the liquidation of Western Europe's peasant agriculture reduced farmers' share of the economy and population below 10 percent in most countries. As agriculture declined in significance (if not in political power), GATT's exclusion of services and public procurement loomed larger. By the 1980s services accounted for two-thirds of economic activity and employment in most OECD countries. While these services were normally thought of as being 'nontradable,' their nontradability was politically created rather than natural. This was particularly true for four major services that constitute 25 percent of economic activity and also constitute a large share of manufacturing businesses' indirect costs: electricity, air and ground transportation, retail distribution, and telecommunications. The largest barrier to international trade in these areas was public ownership and/or regulation.

As with agriculture, the United States found itself possessing an enormous competitive advantage in these areas by the 1980s, but no way to enter markets for them. On average, by 1990, US firms in these sectors were roughly one-third more efficient than firms in the rest of the rich OECD (Pilat, 1996). Domestic deregulation of these sectors in the 1970s and early 1980s had forced US firms to become more competitive to survive in their home market.

The United States also possessed a large competitive advantage in manufacturing industries that supplied capital goods to public sector or state-owned enterprises (SOEs), like aircraft, telecommunications switching systems, airport equipment, power generation equipment, and prime movers. I will call these public sector capital goods. While theoretically as manufactures they were covered by the GATT, practically the close ties between government officials running SOEs, the firms making public sector capital goods, and the (often public) banks financing those firms meant that foreign bidders rarely had a chance to displace local competitors. Indeed, some states, Japan, France and Brazil particularly, used SOEs' purchases to develop producers of public sector capital goods where none previously existed.

So as with agriculture, the United States sought to open up markets in areas that the postwar compromise had closed to international and often domestic market pressures. As with agriculture, the United States used the Uruguay GATT Round to open up markets that had been left closed in the initial GATT compromise, precisely because they were central to the insulation of large parts of the population from market forces. And by doing so it undermined the essential nature of the GATT, even as it enlarged the scope for the use of GATT's procedural norms by including these areas under the WTO and WTO organized fora.

Thus, for example, one WTO protocol opened up public procurement to outside bidders. In civil airframe manufacturing, the United States and Europe signed a 'cease-fire,' capping and reducing public subsidies for the launch of new models. And a whole range of services like telecommunications, advertising, construction, and entertainment are being opened up through sector-specific negotiations organized under the General Agreement on Trade in Services (Cowhey and Aronson, 1993). Together with the WTO's protocol on Trade Related Investment Measures (TRIMs), this has permitted an enormous increase in cross-border sales of services and FDI in services. American airlines, telecommunications firms, electricity firms, and financial services firms, for example, have not been shy about buying up privatized or deregulated equivalents in other countries. The penetration of US firms like GE Capital into Japan's financial system, of American Airlines into Canada and

New Zealand, and of Enron (power generation and distribution) into Germany broke up cozy old alliances between public sectors and their suppliers, and created new networks of global trade. Aggressive expansion of US service producers helped increase the ratio of US MNCs' overseas sales to sales by foreign MNCs in the US from 1.3 to 1.5 during 1995–2004, indicating increased control over global production by US firms. And as noted above, services exports netted in excess of $100 billion for the United States.

Trade-related increases in markets

The brief cases described in this chapter show how the dynamic interaction of liberalization, protection and dispersion eroded the production side of the postwar system of protection from markets embodied in the GATT. GATT permitted more free trade in manufactures, but as it did so it generated powerful protectionist pressures as producers threatened by competitive imports used political, rather than economic, talent to protect their market share. With GATT blocking the use of tariffs, states responded to those political pressures by using quantitative limits, like VERs, to slow the flow of imports. This then triggered dispersion. VERs drove former exporters to transnationalize into their major markets or into third-party markets in search of export platforms; transnationalization forced local producers to disperse in search of cheap labor or back into the exporters' economy. Dispersion and transnationalization fractured not only the old protectionist coalition, but also the basis for the old postwar consensus on social protection and full employment.

Uncompetitive producers remained protectionist, but as some formerly protectionist firms became competitive, dispersed their own production, and did joint ventures with the 'invaders,' their motivations for supporting protection declined. Instead, they began to support free trade – meaning the ability to arrange global flows of goods as they wished. Often, however, this free trade meant a new free trade area that incorporated the places to which they had dispersed production but excluded the sources of invader-controlled imports. Thus, US auto firms were major supporters of the North American Free Trade Agreement (NAFTA) because it allowed the free flow of goods within North America. US firms have significantly dispersed their operations across the United States, Canada, and Mexico. In contrast, the flow of goods by US car firms between their US and European operations are fairly small. Similarly, big European TNCs appear to have been a driving force behind the Single European Act 1986, which created something close to a barrierless EC-wide internal market (Sandholtz and Zysman, 1989). Those Euro-TNCs largely operate within Europe.

The politics of the Depression and war produced a set of global trade rules in which trade flows were subordinated to full employment and social protection. Ironically, the real-world use of those rules created new material interests and trade flows that undermined both goals. Politically, states like the United States swung fully round and tried to re-create markets for goods and services in which they were competitive, but whose markets had been suppressed under the old postwar compromises. Politically, firms which dispersed their operations into new transnational production networks pressed for stable political regulation of flows among the various countries in which they now produced goods. Both pressures produced new rules regulating trade at the global and regional level which removed guarantees of full employment and removed social protection. And just as in the nineteenth century, the loss of social protection aroused the kind of mass popular resistance evidenced at the 1999 Seattle WTO meeting. Thus, trade and production, like money, showed a distinct movement back to nineteenth-century patterns. Are these patterns stable? The last two chapters look at the production and financial basis for US hegemony. They examine whether a stable set of international institutions is possible and why a series of global financial crises culminated in the great 2007–9 financial crisis.

Chapter 13

US Hegemony

Declining from Below?

It is not necessary to change. Survival is not mandatory.

W. Edwards Deming

At the beginning of the 1970s and again at the end of the 1980s, there were vigorous debates about the end of US global dominance, with pointed comparisons to Britain's nineteenth-century decline. US vulnerability to energy imports animated the 1970s discussion, while the apparent decline of US manufacturing relative to Japan and Germany animated the 1980s debates. Unsurprisingly, the great financial crisis of 2007–9 and the outsized trade deficits that preceded that crisis have animated a new debate about US decline. Is the United States in decline? The previous 12 chapters suggest that any answer requires answers to two prior questions: given that the old package of leading sectors has diffused to lower wage economies, can the United States generate and control a new package of leading sectors? What is the nature of the macroeconomic imbalances behind the US trade deficit, and what does this tell us about the sources of growth in the world economy? This chapter answers the former question by looking at the shift from the car/assembly-line package to the microelectronics package. Chapter 14 addresses the second question.

Just as hard and soft innovations in the United States and Germany undercut the basis for British hegemony in the 1890s (Chapter 7), innovations in Germany and particularly Japan undercut US dominance in manufacturing and thus eroded US hegemony in the 1970s and 1980s. Yet from the mid-1990s on, the US economy expanded more rapidly than that of its two peer rivals, and US productivity growth not only recovered but exceeded that in most rich countries. The financial crisis of 2007–9 revealed some of these US gains to be illusory. But the crisis also revealed that German and Japanese (and much Chinese) growth relied on US growth, suggesting that some of their gains were equally illusory and that they would have had trouble growing without the US stimulus. Both illusory growth and the subsequent crisis stemmed from inadequate income at the bottom of the population, across and within nations. As Chapter 14 shows, this meant that demand lagged supply except to the extent that new demand could be created via new (housing-related) debt.

By 1913 the US and German economies were outcompeting the British economy by professionalizing management, cartelizing competition, electrifying production, and Taylorizing work. These hard and soft innovations emerged out of the circumstances in which US and German industry found themselves as they tried to compete with the British in the new leading-sector package of steel, chemicals, and electricity. They successfully took advantage of their rapidly growing domestic markets and their weakly unionized and thus fairly plastic labor forces to create new production processes.

In the 1950s Japanese firms – particularly car firms – confronted an environment which forced them to create a similar range of innovations: at the level of firm organization, the *keiretsu;* at the level of production processes, *kanban* (just-in-time inventory); and at the level of the worker, responsible multiskilled workers via *kaizen* (continuous improvement) and total quality management. By the 1960s and 1970s these innovations – the three 'Ks' – diffused to a few sectors of the Japanese economy, making them highly competitive exporters. Those sectors encompassed most of the assembly-line-based, automotive and consumer electronics sectors that constituted the existing package of leading sectors in the mid-twentieth century, as well as the standardized parts of the new electronics leading-sector package.

In short, Japanese firms displaced US firms from substantial parts of the old package of leading sector industries. Japanese production innovations eliminated defects found in US versions of the assembly line, just as nineteenth-century US innovations eliminated defects in British metals production. But unlike the United States after World War I, the Japanese did not generate an entirely new production system, nor did their innovations spread to their entire economy and generate new ranges of economic activity. Unlike nineteenth-century British firms, the US state and firms managed to generate a new leading-sector package that revived manufacturing, stabilized the US share of the global economy, and expanded US firms' control over the global economy. Consequently, the United States was able to contain challenges by its rich-country peer rivals, either maintaining or expanding its share of global GDP, and expanding its share of rich-country GDP by an astounding 4.1 percentage points. (See Table 13.1, in which purchasing power parity (PPP)-adjusted GDP tends to diminish US GDP and expand China's, while exchange rate-based shares tend to do the reverse).

Table 13.1 *Shares of global GDP, percent*

	PPP Adjusted		Exchange Rate Basis	
	1991	*2004*	*1991*	*2005*
Germany	4.9	3.8	8.0	6.5
Japan	8.8	6.6	13.9	10.9
China and Hong Kong	8.7	15.2	2.3	5.6
US	21.3	20.8	25.6	26.8
US share of OECD-18	38.8	42.9		

Sources: Groningen Growth and Development Centre Total Economy Database and United Nations on-line database at http://data.un.org, date accessed 18 December 2008.

Renewed productivity growth underpinned the US revival. This productivity reversal, and indeed the reversal of below average GDP growth for the United States, was all the more remarkable given the continental scale of the US economy. A small economy, like Finland, can easily experience above-average growth based on success in one sector, such as mobile telephony. A multisector economy that has substantial weight in the group being averaged has to have across-the-board increases to rise above that average. US firms and the US economy achieved these broad gains through an information technology-driven transformation of substantial parts of the service sector. While manufacturing continues to be important in the same way that agriculture remained important in an industrializing world, the bulk of employment and economic activity have shifted to the service sector. Just as manufacturing growth structured global demand for agricultural products, service sector growth is now structuring global demand for manufactures.

In the service sectors that matter most to business – telecommunications, transport, power generation, and retail distribution – US productivity advantages over Japan and Germany were even larger than those in manufacturing (see Table 13.2). These services collectively account for about 20 percent to 25 percent of GDP in most countries. These were also the fastest growing parts of the economy in the 1990s and 2000s, as the microelectronics revolution affected the dissemination of goods and information, and as productivity and thus profit gains increasingly came from linking all parts of the supply chain on a real-time basis to facilitate the reduction of waste and reduce inventory costs. These are services the United States government assiduously tried to open to competition via the WTO (Chapter 11). This chapter will first consider the challenge to US manufacturing and then the US services sector response.

Table 13.2   *Relative productivity, G3 economies, 1990[a]*

	US	Japan	Germany
Manufacturing	100	66.5	78.5
Telecommunications	100	80.6	63.1
Electricity generation[b]	100	76.8	26.8
Air transport	100	52.4	62.1
Retail distribution	100	60.3	78.5

Notes:
[a] Index, US = 100, defined as output per employee (manufacturing); revenue per employee (telecommunications); gigawatt hours produced per employee; operating expense per ton/mile, inverted; distribution GDP per employee.
[b] Adjusted for differences in fuel sources.
Source: Calculated from data in Pilat (1996: 139–40).

Defects in the US-style assembly line

Inventory as production process

The assembly line constituted the central production technology of the car-entered leading-sector package that dominated the twentieth century. The Japanese 'fine tuned' the assembly line, and by doing so were able to run demand-driven assembly lines rather than supply-driven assembly lines. By the early 1990s, the major Japanese car firms had surpassed the US firms in raw productivity; adjusted for quality they probably surpassed US firms in the mid-1980s. How had the productivity advantages of the US version of the assembly line decayed? Struggles between management and labor impeded productivity gains in the US version. Before the 1970s these problems were irrelevant, because the assembly line and the integrated, multidivisional firm gave US firms an enormous competitive edge over non-assembly-line-based small firms outside the United States. But assembly-line technologies diffused, exposing not only the car but other industries to international competition in the1970s and 1980s. This revealed the vulnerability of US assembly-line production to the Japanese version.

Assembly lines are industrially and economically efficient because they use machines designed for a single purpose to make extremely long runs of the same product. Maximizing economic return on these machines meant maximizing the number of units produced, spreading the cost of the machines over the largest possible number of units of output. Anything that interrupted production created inefficiencies and lost profits. The limited range of operations for these special-purpose machines made them vulnerable not just to macroeconomic shocks (see Chapter 9) but also to disruptions in the flow of parts being produced or assembled.

US firms made three problematic choices with respect to 'balancing the line,' that is, making sure that parts flowed and workers worked in precisely the right rhythms to prevent disruptive bottlenecks. US firms opted to run their lines without regard to minor changes in demand; opted to accept high rates of defects rather than stop the line to fix work in progress; and opted for management practices that alienated workers. Each problem reflected managements' fear of interruptions, particularly by workers. US management in general opted to accept the costs of fixing defects *after* cars were assembled rather than accepting what they perceived as the larger costs of interrupting production to fix defects *during* production, while allowing workers greater autonomy.

In the US car industry, firms typically produced cars ahead of demand, in large factories dedicated to producing a single car model. Changing from one model to another meant shutting down a factory and losing production time. Management tried to avoid interruptions arising from the absence of the right number and kind of parts or workers at any given step in the assembly process forced a shutdown. For example, if workers ran out of engine valves obviously it was pointless to continue producing engines. Similarly, if too many workers were absent, the assembly steps they performed could not simply be skipped. US management reduced these risks by holding large amounts of parts and labor as 'buffer' inventory. These buffers provided management with insurance against defective or missing parts, including absent workers.

But buffers were expensive. Excess inventory and labor tied up money which could be invested elsewhere (or on which firms were paying interest). In the 1980s the typical US car firm held between two weeks' and two months' worth of inventory depending on the part. By contrast Toyota typically held two hours of inventory. Holding inventory also encouraged sloppiness. Firms could tolerate defective parts coming from their own subsidiaries or from subcontractors because excessive inventory assured that enough good parts always could be found. Firms also ignored defects created by the improper assembly of defect-free parts. If workers botched an assembly operation they simply let the car or subassembly continue moving down the line. Other workers would rectify the error later, in the repair bays at the end of the line. This was a disguised way of holding extra inventory. Defective cars could not be sold until they were reworked.

The organization of workers

Management's fear of production interruptions prevented them from giving line workers any discretion. Instead they 'Taylorized' work, assigning each worker one specific task typically involving a series of repetitive motions done over and over as each car came down the line. Management basically wanted workers to behave like robots, programmed by a separate white-collar engineering staff and supervised by foremen who 'fixed' broken robots by yelling at them. This hostile environment generated an equally hostile response from workers and their unions (Edwards, 1979; Lazonick, 1990). Workers' unions responded to job fragmentation by insisting on very rigid job categories and descriptions – as many as 200 per plant. All this increased managements' need to buffer labor, since workers couldn't be shifted from job to job. Distrust of workers also prevented management from asking workers for better ways to assemble products. This blocked firms' access to all of the tacit knowledge workers gained every day. Indeed, workers actively resisted transferring that knowledge to management, fearing that it would lead to speeding up of the assembly line and job losses.

Workers treated like robots, behaved like robots, and lost interest in trying to produce high-quality products. Doing so didn't affect how they were treated by management, didn't change their wage (which was linked to their job description), and didn't change the pace at which parts came down the line. This problem also affected white-collar workers. Because blue-collar workers were not allowed to think, US firms had to hire someone to think for them, leading to a proliferation of white-collar workers doing minor engineering tasks, quality-control, and various coordination activities, as well as an increase in skilled workers who did routine maintenance. In the 1980s' US car firms typically employed 12 percent to 30 percent more supervisory white-collar workers than

Japanese car firms, spread out over twice as many levels of management. Japanese firms used their supervisory labor savings to hire more engineering staff, and this combined with their flatter hierarchies to enable them to generate new models more rapidly (Pucik, 1984; Womack, Jones and Roos, 1992).

The car industry's great pre-war productivity leaps slowed to incremental gains in the face of conflict between workers and management. Management confronted an environment like that facing British metals producers in the 1890s: slow growth in total US sales and no way to export from the United States to Europe removed incentives to fight workers and risk major strikes. Instead, they fixed things at the margins until the crisis of the late 1980s.

The organization of firms

US firms also adopted two very different ways of organizing the flow of components among different companies to prevent interruptions. Component suppliers were either wholly owned subsidiaries of these multidivisional firms, coordinated via bureaucratic mechanisms, or they were completely outside the firm and coordinated via arm's length, market-based contracts. Each solution generated new problems.

Making suppliers into wholly owned subsidiaries did assure constant and consistent flows of inputs and maximized economies of scale. But this vertical integration insulated subsidiaries from competitive pressures and distorted investment choices. Internally produced goods had administered prices whose final price and 'profitability' could not really be known. Subsidiaries had enormous incentives for over-investment and were protected from the costs of their inefficiency. GM presented the extreme version of this, producing over 70 percent of its parts in-house.

Buying parts from outside subcontractors helped lower costs. Car assemblers could deliberately pit subcontractors against each other in order to drive parts prices down. While this subjected subcontractors to market pressures, it also assured that subcontractors had no incentives to invest in long-term quality control or in design staff. Because they could lose their contract at any moment they could not be sure of amortizing this investment, nor did they receive enough information from the big car firms to redesign parts in advance of model changes.

The uncompetitive structure of the US car market removed any incentives to cure these built-in inefficiencies. The 'Big 3' – GM, Ford and Chrysler – operated a cozy, high-profit oligopoly. From 1946 to 1973 GM had an after tax net profit of 20 percent on its assets, compared with the 9 percent average in all US manufacturing. It achieved this by simply setting the retail price of its cars at a level which assured this high rate of return. The other two followed GM's price leadership (White, 1982: 153–5, 168). Foreign firms did not appear to present a competitive threat, because US consumer demand appeared overwhelmingly oriented towards large cars. Only Volkswagen's 1.3 liter engine 'Bug' found substantial traction in the US market. But the US 'Big 3' used their enormous profits to subsidize sales of their small cars whenever foreign market share increased. US firms' ability to cross-subsidize small cars eased competitive pressures, discouraging any search for more efficient ways to meet the import threat. When the two 1970s oil shocks shifted US demand towards small cars, the US firms were caught off guard, particularly by the Japanese. But if the Japanese were lucky – the oil shocks – they also were smart. What did the Japanese do differently, and why?

Remedies in the Japanese assembly line

Kanban and balancing the line

US firms balanced their assembly lines by producing ahead of demand, by buffering inventory and labor and by trying to impose minute top-down control over workers' actions. Three things constrained Japanese firms from adopting US production techniques simply out of admiration. First, the 1950s and 1960s Japanese market was absolutely too small to make supply-driven, economy-of-scale-oriented production possible. Second, capital was extremely scarce in postwar Japan, making inventory extremely expensive to hold. Third, Japanese workers made different demands on management as compared to US workers, leading to different kinds of wage and supervisory arrangements.

With direct imitation impossible, Japanese firms innovated new managerial techniques to overcome the balancing problem. These techniques are summed up in the Japanese words *kanban* and *kaizen*. *Kanban* refers in English to the three zeros: zero buffering of inventory (sometimes called 'just-in-time inventory'); zero buffering of labor; and zero defects. *Kaizen* refers to continuous improvement of the three 'P's: production, products, and producers. While the Japanese borrowed liberally from Edward Deming's work on total quality management, the incentive to adopt and adapt came out of their competitive environment (Cusumano, 1985; Womack, Jones and Roos, 1992).

The entire Japanese car market amounted to perhaps 50 000 units in 1950 (about two days' production in the United States) and had risen to only 250 000 units by 1959. This was the output of the average US car factory, a factory moreover often devoted to the production of *one* model. Even worse for Japanese car producers, rural and urban transportation/hauling needs diverged more than in the United States, forcing greater diversity in models. In a market this small, Japanese firms could neither afford to invest in product-specific machinery nor maximize throughput by producing in advance of demand. Instead they tried to produce in response to demand, scheduling production only when they had enough orders to make it rational to temporarily reorganize their assembly lines around the new product. This forced them to learn how to make such reorganizations in record time.

Capital was extremely scarce in postwar Japan, and because the state tended to allocate capital to particular sectors, it often was impossible to get at any price. Firms could not tie up precious capital in inventory simply to buffer against defective parts. Instead, they looked for ways to produce only what was needed. The deceptively simple *kanban* (zero buffering) inventory system emerged from this situation. *Kanban* literally refers to parts cards located at each assembly-line station. When the parts supply at a given station fell to about a two-hour inventory, the worker there simply attached this card to a moving clothesline. The card went to a worker who would call the relevant parts producer, who often was located a few hundred yards away, to the main assembly plant. The supplier would make just enough parts to restore inventories to about a four-hour supply. Ideally, the new parts would arrive just as the assembler put the last part into the car moving down the line. Practically, this proved impossible to achieve, but it did keep inventory down to a fraction of a day.

A similarly simple system kept labor buffers at zero. Above each work station were a set of traffic lights, or *andon* (Dohse, 1985). Workers controlled the lights, setting the light to green if everything was OK; to yellow to indicate that they needed help or that something might go wrong; and, finally, to red to shut down the line in order to prevent defective subassemblies or cars from being produced. A red light would draw assistance from foremen and other workers. The *andon* light system was a beautiful way of showing management precisely where production flows were unbalanced, where subassemblies had to be redesigned for easier and defect-free assembly, or where excess labor existed. Counterintuitively, management loved to see yellow lights on everywhere at all times, not green ones. Green lights showed management places where they had too much labor and thus where a labor buffer should be pared down. Red lights located serious problems for management, which could then allocate engineering talent to solving that problem. Yellow lights told management that everything was flowing as efficiently as possible. The US United Auto Workers Union estimated that where its workers typically worked about 45 seconds out of any given minute, Japanese workers were working 55 seconds (Hamper, 1992).

Zero buffering could only work in conjunction with a zero-defects policy. Having very few parts on hand implied a risk of shutting down the line if parts were defective and could not be replaced immediately. Thus, zero buffering of parts implies zero defects in the components being assembled; parts had to be made right the first time. By putting pressure on components producers to produce and deliver defect-free parts, it also put pressure on them to introduce *kanban* and *kaizen* principles into their own production. Production process innovation at the main assemblers thus flowed into the entire automobile sector and other sectors.

Kaizen and multiskilled workers

The three *kanban* zeros highlighted waste and problems in the assembly process, and thus permitted and forced *kaizen*, or continuous improvement, on producers. Unlike the US system, in which management distrusted workers and tried to impose a rigid top-down control, the Japanese system gave basic responsibility for production to work teams, even to the extent of allowing workers to shut down the line by switching the *andon* light to red. This was once unthinkable in the United States. Why could Japanese firms allow workers this authority?

As in the United States, relations between management and labor in Japan historically were quite conflictual (Cole, 1971; Gordon, 1985). In the late 1940s and early 1950s workers and unions launched a campaign to seize control of the production process and of factories. Like similar struggles in the 1930s in the United States, this campaign generated a set of institutionalized compromises. Led by good Marxists, Japanese workers demanded job security. They forced employers to adopt the system of lifetime employment that the state created for its own skilled workers (Weiss, 1993). Japanese workers also wanted wages to be linked to need, not to specific jobs. The largest component in wages was based on seniority (the *nenko* wage), since older male workers were more likely to have families to support. Lest the reader get the impression that workers got everything they desired, management and the state broke the US-style industry-wide unions, leaving only unions inside each firm – so-called 'enterprise' unions. Until the 2000s, Japan's lifetime blue-collar employees had a relationship to their firm that most closely resembled that of 1960s US white-collar employees.

Lifetime employees confronted management with a fixed cost and thus incentives to increase employees' productivity by constantly training them and upgrading their skills. That way, workers could be shifted around the assembly line in response to yellow and red lights, could adapt to assembly lines that themselves were constantly changing as production volumes grew and new models were introduced, and could produce higher-quality cars. Multiskilling helped to zero buffer labor and parts, because workers had enough of an all-round view of the system to spot and remedy waste and other problems. Workers' suggestions provided most of the information needed to eliminate defects by re-engineering parts to make them easier to assemble.

For their part, workers had an incentive to cooperate with management because enterprise unions and lifetime employment tied each individual worker's fate/income to the fate/income of his firm. Since they typically worked in teams and received part of their wage as a bonus tied to individual and team productivity, they also faced intense social pressure to cooperate. This white-collar-like relationship allowed Japanese firms to get by with only half as many administrative layers as a comparable US car firm, because many of the tasks assigned to white-collar workers in the United States were carried out by blue-collar workers in Japan.

Keiretsu and the organization of entrepreneurship

US-style multidivisional firms sourced parts from either completely integrated subsidiaries or disintegrated subcontractors. In contrast, the Japanese developed a new entrepreneurial system of partially disintegrated firms, the *keiretsu*. Like *kanban* and *kaizen, keiretsu* emerged from the circumstances of the 1940s and 1950s. Pre-war Japanese firms were linked together in *zaibatsu*, a more centralized version of Germany's nineteenth-century bank-based business empires. Like their German counterparts, Japanese banks extended *zaibatsu* control by fostering new firms as new economic sectors emerged.

After the war, the US occupation authorities tried to break up the *zaibatsu* by prohibiting banks from holding more than 5 percent of any company's equity. The *zaibatsu* responded by having all their former subsidiaries purchase small amounts of stock in one another, decentralizing into the more horizontal *keiretsu*. If the former *zaibatsu* looked like a cone, with the controlling bank at its apex, the new *keiretsu* looked like spider webs, with an enormous number of small connections linking together the fates of a large number of nominally independent firms. As the automobile firms grew, they created similar kinds of vertical *keiretsu* based on their supplier networks. While *keiretsu*-like arrangements are not unique to Japan, until recently they were more pervasive there.

The *keiretsu* structure extended all the way out to the smallest firms. Toyota, for example, sourced parts from about 220 primary subcontractors, who in turn dealt with about 5000 secondary subcontractors, who dealt with over 30 000 tertiary subcontractors. (The typical car has about 10 000 discrete parts.) Eighty percent of these producers were located near Toyota's main assembly plants, facilitating just-in-time parts delivery (Florida and Kenney, 1988). In many cases Toyota had a substantial equity stake in those firms.

Keiretsu provided the advantages of independent subcontractors and vertically integrated subsidiaries without their disadvantages. Component suppliers that are not directly owned and controlled by the car assembly firms have an incentive to search for other markets, which keeps them competitive and helps them to innovate. However, because the assembler firms typically have a large equity stake in the component firms, component firms can be sure that they have a long-term relationship with their major customer. Thus, they have incentives to cooperate in parts design, to make long-term investments in better production machinery, and to integrate their production with the assembler's production to facilitate *kanban* practices. In conjunction with *kaizen*, *keiretsu* also helped speed up the design process for cars, allowing Japanese producers to generate and produce a new model an average of one to two years faster than US and European makers. Subcontractors could begin their own design and engineering work before assembler's plans were finalized.

Keiretsu also help minimize risk. During the period in which the state allocated scarce capital, *keiretsu* could pool capital from their firms to finance ventures in new sectors of the economy (such as computers in the late 1970s) or to finance risky and expensive development projects like new car models. Vertical *keiretsu* permit coordination across an even larger number of firms than even the largest US car firm can manage. The larger Japanese firms acquired about 80 percent of their parts from inside their *keiretsu*, but without having directly to manage component producers as a part of their own hierarchies. By the 2000s, even GM was sourcing more than half its parts externally.

Although *keiretsu* structures muted competition among a given set of firms, they did not mute competition among producers in specific industrial sectors. Because each *keiretsu* attempted to enter each major industrial sector, competition was quite fierce. During the 1960s and 1970s, when Japanese car firms made their greatest productivity and output increases, between seven and nine firms competed over domestic market share, compared with three in the US market. The three largest Japanese firms combined never achieved the dominance that GM had with its consistent 45 percent share of the US market in the 1950s and 1960s.

Kaizen and *kanban* essentially improved on ideas first generated in the United States. Similarly, *keiretsu* improved on the multidivisional firm. The multidivisional firm allowed a company to reduce risk and to allocate capital into new areas related to its original business, thus gaining economies of scope. *Keiretsu* permitted the same thing, but over a wider range of activity and without losing efficiency from bureaucratization created by mandatory internal purchases and sales from/to subsidiaries. The Japanese innovations thus perfected processes in the old automotive sector, rather than creating a new leading sector package. Nevertheless their innovations substantially changed production practices everywhere.

'All together now'

Kanban, kaizen, and *keiretsu* rapidly increased Japanese car firms' productivity. In the 1960s Japanese car firms were one-third less efficient than US firms. Continual improvement of the production process reduced the number of hours to produce a small car to US levels by 1976. By 1980 the Japanese had created a roughly 30 percent advantage in labor input (Abernathy, Cole and Kantrow, 1983: 58–9, 61). Not surprisingly, with this kind of advantage, Japanese exports had taken 25 percent of the US market by the mid-1980s; this figure rose to 45 percent by the 2000s. The inherent efficiencies of the Japanese version of the assembly line combined with Verdoorn effects as Japan's own car production doubled to over 11 million units between 1970 and 1980, making it the world's largest car producer and exporter. This rapid growth also made it impossible for Japanese producers ever to codify their production systems; they had to continually search for new and more efficient ways to do things.

In contrast, US firms' domestic production floated around 8 million units, and thus US firms' share of world production fell from 57 percent in 1960 to 25 percent in 2007 (see Table 13.3). As with late-nineteenth-century British metals producers, stagnation in the absolute number of units they produced hindered US efforts to figure out how to react to the Japanese threat. US producers had already codified their production systems. But unlike British firms, the US firms did assimilate a considerable portion of the Japanese practices, mainly deploying them in plants in their growing overseas markets but also in some domestic plants. US firms were able to assimilate variations on the innovations that gave Japanese firms their competitive edge. By 2008 US

Table 13.3 *Relative share of world car market by ownership of company, 1970–2008, selected years, percent[a]*

Country	1970	1975	1980	1985	1990	1998	2007
Japan	22.4	26.0	33.7	32.1	37.3	26.6	31.4
Big Three[b]	14.6	19.0	21.7	19.2	24.2	17.3	22.0
Rest	7.8	7.0	12.0	12.9	15.1	9.3	8.4
US Big Three	47.0	44.2	33.3	41.3	36.0	28.0	25.1
West European	30.7	29.9	33.1	26.7	24.8	23.5	26.4

Notes:
[a] Totals may not add to 100 because of rounding and excluded producers.
[b] Toyota, Nissan, Honda.

Source: Based on data from DRI International, *World Automotive Forecast*, various issues.

firms had essentially closed the gap in terms of labor hours per car. However, a substantial quality difference remained, and the US firms were of course saddled with legacy pension and health care costs that Japanese and European producers had passed on to their states.

Much like the European firms that learned from propinquity to US firms operating in Europe, US firms learned from joint ventures with Japanese partners, or from propinquity to Japanese firms' US factories. Ford's strategic alliance with Mazda gave it an open window on Japanese production advantages. Chrysler built new Japanese-style plants, with loading bays located near assembly points to facilitate *kanban* inventory control, and a determination to hold no more than eight hours of inventory and to use teamwork principles. All three firms changed relationships with their suppliers, building American versions of the *keiretsu*. Thus Ford, for example, reduced the number of firms in its supplier base by two-thirds, spun out much of its internal component production as the new firm Visteon, and took equity positions in critical suppliers, like Cummins Diesel. All three assemblers also stripped out superfluous white-collar workers, reducing them from 16 percent of the labor force to 12.7 percent by 1995.

By the 2000s, Japanese firms faced two new difficulties. First, their home market was stagnant, with sales breaching the 1991 level only in 2004–6. Second their ability to draw the best blue-collar workers out of the labor force and assure their loyalty through lifetime employment and rapidly rising wages also waned. These problems forced the minor players into bankruptcy or the hands of the bigger players. By 1999, a highly indebted Nissan had to seek outside financial help from Renault, Mazda came under Ford's direct control, and GM extended its holdings in Isuzu and Suzuki. Meanwhile the US firms made huge profits on SUVs. Nonetheless, US dominance of this declining sector is clearly gone, as can be seen in the persistent trade imbalance in cars and car parts with non-NAFTA producers, mostly Japan and Germany, and the ever-growing Asian share of the US market. The 2007–9 crisis forced GM and Chrysler into bankruptcy and partial government ownership. None the less, US domestic production replaces imports, even if that production is foreign owned.

Out with the old, in with the new: high-tech industries and services

Just like US and German producers in the 1890s relative to British ones, Japanese producers outclassed US producers in the mass production industries that made up the core of the old growth cluster. What about the new set of leading sectors, however? Japanese producers posed a similar threat to US producers in the high-technology – that is, leading-sector – industries of the 1980s and 1990s, but the Japanese challenge fell short of that generated by US and German producers in the nineteenth century. Ultimately, US firms, with help from their state, generated a new package of leading-sector industries and technologies.

The latest growth cluster is made up of information processing industries and their associated transportation and communications revolution, as well as the incorporation of high levels of information content in products. All of these have reduced the transaction costs associated with organizing production, delivering goods, customizing products for purchasers, and organizing purchases. Though no new source of energy has yet emerged, the new package is highly energy saving by reducing the need to move goods, and because many of its 'goods' are digital content. The ideal-typical product is an internet MP3 download.

The key technology in this cluster is the integrated circuit (IC) in its various forms, like memory chips (DRAMs), application-specific chips (ASICs), and microprocessor units (MPUs). The storage capacity of ICs has doubled every three years, from roughly 1 kilobit DRAMs in 1972 to 16 gigabit DRAMs in 2008. This advance has permitted a 30 percent per year decline in the cost of processing information since the 1960s, roughly *seven* times the rate of decline in the cost of cotton textiles during 1780–1815.

Much like the internal combustion engine, ICs supply the motor that drives a wide range of goods, turning mobile telephones into computers with more processing power than a typical large industrial firm owned in the 1970s. This hard innovation has facilitated a change in soft technologies of the production process, away from mass production using dedicated machine tools and towards a more flexible production process using more general-purpose tools and towards more teamwork. The totemic worker in this new production process is a 'white-collarized' worker – think software coder – who is paid for acting responsibly and applying his or her skills to the generation of newer products, organized in teams, and with an equity stake in the firm as the ultimate performance motivator. Bio- and nanotechnologies are parallel 'information processing' and transformation industries based on small team production of new content that is then commercialized and marketed by larger firms.

US firms made the major innovations in this cluster, but with considerable state help. Defense and space contracts funded much of the research effort prior to innovation, and government contracts helped push IC production far enough down the learning curve during the 1960s to make ICs commercially viable for civilian computing uses. With the largest collection of innovating and end-use firms, as well as the world's largest final market for computing, the United States naturally dominated this cluster well into the 1970s. At the end of the 1970s US firms had 70 percent of the $15 billion world market for ICs, the Japanese had only 15 percent, and European and other producers shared the rest. By the mid-1980s, however, Japanese firms had displaced US producers as the dominant makers of DRAMs and had taken a roughly equal share of the total world market. In 1972 the ten largest producers of ICs were US firms; by 1987 seven of the top ten were Japanese firms; but by 2008 seven of the top ten were again American. Why wasn't electronics a re-run of the motor car story?

The Japanese combined the strengths of *kaizen, kanban,* and *keiretsu* with judicious amounts of state-run industrial policy. This allowed them to catch up to and temporarily displace US producers on the basis of production expertise. The Japanese already had a large and growing end-market for ICs: their consumer electronics industry. Consumer electronics accounted for about 50 percent of IC consumption in Japan, compared with only 15 percent to 20 percent in the United States. This industry combined many elements of mass production with strong consumer desires for differentiated goods. The three Ks permitted the six big Japanese electronics producers to continually vary their models while still gaining economies of scale. All these electronics producers wanted to have in-house capacity to produce ICs, which were becoming an integral part of consumer electronics.

The Japanese state also wanted IC production. The Ministry for International Trade and Industry (MITI) had targeted information industries as early as the 1960s using the standard late industrialization playbook. They sheltered the domestic market, forced US producers to license their patents, delayed US FDI into the Japanese market, and used government purchases to stimulate local production. MITI also sponsored a huge joint R&D program in ICs in 1975, the so-called Very Large Scale Integrated Circuit (VLSIC) program. Roughly one-third of this program's funds were spent reverse-engineering the most advanced US IC manufacturing and quality-testing equipment. With their own equipment, the Japanese could make export quality ICs, and they entered the market for 16k DRAMs in the late 1970s, surprising US producers and capturing about two-fifths of the market, and by 1981 they had captured 70 percent of the market for 64k DRAMs. Japanese attention to quality – *kaizen* – proved their major advantage.

Japanese strengths in manufacturing turned into Japanese weaknesses during the late 1980s and 1990s though, as information technology end-markets became more about information (i.e. content) and not just processing. Moreover, the US state sponsored its own R&D projects and deregulated the service sector, which became a ferocious consumer of information technologies.

Japanese weaknesses stemmed in part from some of the very factors that gave them their competitive edge when they engaged in catchup activities (Kitschelt, 1991). While *kaizen* permitted, indeed encouraged, the constant incremental improvements needed for catching up, it hindered the kind of radical breakthroughs on which technological leadership ultimately rested. Japanese firms' common interest in catching up gave the state a common goal around which to organize their research (Okimoto, 1989). In new areas, however, firms had fewer common interests, and their *keiretsu*-driven struggle for market share made them wary of disclosing their strengths in those new areas. Nor did Japan have an adequate public research infrastructure for providing a stream of new technologies for firms to exploit. In contrast, US research universities, their associated research parks, and co-located software and industrial firms constituted a form of '*keiretsu*' involved in a '*kaizen*'-ing of basic technologies. Finally much of the Japanese system of social protection rested on comprehensive regulation of the service sector.

Two different US government policies also synergistically bolstered US competitiveness. First, the Defense Department (DoD) ran its own successful version of the MITI VLSIC program from 1979 to 1987. The Very High Speed Integrated Circuit (VHSIC) program generated and refined several generations of Digital Signal Processing (DSP) chips along with manufacturing technologies for progressively denser ICs. While DoD wanted DSPs for 'Star Wars' and other military uses, they also turned out to be the critical technology for wireless communication, like the now ubiquitous cellphone.

Second, the government completely changed the competitive environment in which these hard technologies were deployed by deregulating the service sector (see the next section). Until the late 1970s, telecommunications was a stable, predictable market, with stable, predictable, regulated prices, in which new technologies could be deployed in stable, incremental ways on the basis of long-term plans. By deregulating telecommunications (and aviation, finance, trucking, rail freight, power generation, etc.) the US government created an unpredictable market characterized by rapid changes in price and product. This enabled rapid penetration of new entrants offering ever better, ever more personalized service. In turn, this created demand for customized chips.

Finally the United States aggressively created Asian competitors for Japanese firms in low-value-added areas of the market. US firms helped Korean firms to begin production of DRAMs, and US firms allied with a whole range of firms in Taiwan and Singapore. These low-cost Asian allies helped US firms squeeze Japanese producers, reducing profits in low-end markets while US firms continued to dominate high-end markets and design-intensive sectors.

As a result, wherever manufacturing *qua* manufacturing was important and technology reasonably standard, Japanese firms tended to prevail; wherever technology was in flux and innovation, and design and market-responsiveness were important, US firms tended to prevail. Japanese firms tended to dominate the production of ICs going into industrial machinery, like micro-controllers, of highly standardized ICs, like DRAMs, and of the standardized components that went into, for example, personal computers, but they did not dominate production of design-intensive ASICs or the design and assembly of the various sorts of PCs. Japanese DRAM and component producers faced severe price competition from Korean and Taiwanese producers, whose governments subsidized the same kind of unprofitable market entry by large integrated firms that the Japanese had pioneered in their efforts to displace US firms in the 1970s and 1980s. By the end of the 1990s DRAMs had become a commodity business with low margins, with two Korean firms holding half the market. In contrast, US firms excelled in the design and roll-out of ASICs, customized chips designed for particular end-uses. Japanese producers progressively lost market share as ASICs were incorporated into more and more products, including the consumer electronics at the heart of Japanese industry. Firms like Apple, whose products absorbed 25 percent of global flash memory output in 2007, sourced ASICs and DRAMs from US and Korean firms respectively. US firms thus displaced Japanese firms, producing more than half of world IC output by *value* by the end of the 1990s and into the 2000s. ICs constitute about 5 percent of US exports.

Similar processes occurred in civil airframe manufacturing, which also typically constitute 5 percent of US goods exports. Boeing lost market share to Airbus during the 1980s and 1990s because of Airbus's earlier shift to new technologies like fly-by-wire, innovative wing and cockpit designs, generous government launch subsidies, and a shift towards smaller planes subsequent to airlines' adoption of a hub and spoke model for moving passengers. At the end of the 1990s Boeing responded to the Airbus threat with a comprehensive set of product, process and organizational innovations (Aboulafia, 2007; Newhouse, 2007).

US Defense Department contracts helped Boeing learn to use new carbon fiber composites to radically change aircraft production technologies. After experimenting with composite materials (and computer aided design – CAD) in the B777, Boeing made the leap to an integral composite body for the B787 airframe. This means that the fuselage tube is built up completely from composite fibers without any internal spars. This permits a more rigid, yet lighter and more fuel-efficient, aircraft. It also permits a huge reduction in the number of parts, and thus time and labor, required to build the plane. Airbus remained wedded to a panel-on-rib design for its fuselages, employing this technology even when using composite fiber panels.

Boeing also made a successful organizational shift towards a *keiretsu*-like structure. Unlike Airbus, which was essentially a creature of four EU states before being folded into the bi-national EADS, Boeing was a publicly held firm subject to share market pressures for immediate profitability. This limited Boeing's ability to fund R&D and to launch new aircraft. For the B787 program, Boeing adopted a new organizational format made possible by the successful use of CAD for the B777 program. Boeing brought its subcontractors in as risk-sharing partners, integrating their production processes using CAD systems. Boeing's risk-sharing partners invested their own capital into

Table 13.4   *Change in manufacturing productivity and GDP, 1991–2006, indices*

	US	Canada	Japan	Germany[a]	France	Italy	UK	OECD Average[b]
Real output per hour in manufacturing (productivity)								
1991	100	100	100	100	100	100	100	100
2006	206	146	164	168	182	116	161	171
Total manufacturing output (output volume)								
1991	100	100	100	100	100	100	100	100
2006	174	158	115	116	132	105	110	152
Change in real GDP per employed person, converted to 2002\$, PPP adjusted, 1991–2006, %								
	31.9%	23.8%	21.8%	22.7%	20.5%	13.1%	35.3%	27.5%

Notes:
[a] Data are for post-Unification Germany – the index level is not affected by unification.
[b] Includes Korea and Taiwan.

Source: Based on data from Bureau of Labor Statistics at ftp://ftp.bls.gov/pub/special.requests/ForeignLabor/prodsuppt01.txt.

Boeing's R&D and the B787 launch. Doing so removed share market pressures on Boeing, although it also generated some of the same sorts of difficulties integrating subcontractors that hurt Airbus. It also had the subtle effect of lessening subcontractors' willingness to share technology with Airbus, for fear of reducing their own profits from the Boeing venture.

Boeing's success at incorporating CAD and new materials into its production processes is not an isolated phenomenon. US firms have been better at incorporating information technology into their production across the board. The most compelling evidence comes from a series of fine-grained analyses about the adoption of new IT-based production and management practices in Europe and the United States, which show that US MNCs use more information technology and use it more productively than do other MNCs (Bloom, Sadun, and van Reenen, 2007). Table 13.4 displays the changes in productivity and output levels for the major OECD economies.

Are you being served?

These phenomena were repeated in the service sector. Because the service sector now comprises more than 70 percent of most developed economies, service sector productivity growth is essential for long-run economic growth. Deregulation of the US service sector put enormous competitive pressures on other countries' service sectors. Competition also forced US service firms to rapidly assimilate information technology into their production processes. US airlines thus pioneered the use of load management; retail firms like Walmart pioneered the use of point-of-sale information to manage their inventory and maximize sales per square foot; US railroads pioneered multimodal transport and conformed to the logistical demands of manufacturers using just-in-time inventory systems. Naturally these firms were not alone, for European firms like Ahold (food retailing) and Benetton (clothing) also used point-of-sale information. Overall, though, US firms outstripped European and Asian competitors.

American productivity growth after 1991 disproportionately occurred in the service sectors. From 1994 to 2004, total factor productivity in the US service sector rose 1.3 percent annually, while productivity declined by 0.6 percent annually in Germany and Italy, and barely rose in France (Amiti and Stiroh, 2007; Inklaar, Timmer and van Ark, 2007; van Ark, O'Mahoney and Timmer, 2008). Total non-farm US productivity grew about 2.5 percent per year during 1995–2005, a level that could not have been possible had service-sector productivity gains significantly lagged behind manufacturing gains (Bosworth and Trippett, 2007). The service sector accounted for 75 percent of total productivity growth, and within that, multifactor productivity growth (organizational changes rather than additional capital or labor inputs) accounts for the lion's share. The disparate levels of GDP change in Table 13.4 could not have occurred without changes in service-sector output and productivity.

This productivity advantage permitted US service firms, as well as a handful of foreign service firms, to go multinational in newly privatized service sectors. These firms generated an enormous trade surplus that roughly offset the total trade deficit on cars. The US trade offensive in services also helped reconstitute a new form of US dominance that dovetailed with the effects of liberalized capital markets. The trade offensive reduced the capacity of the European and Japanese states to manipulate their economies by using national champions as engines of growth. Local firms that consumed services, and built them into the price of their exports, became increasingly conscious of the need to buy services at world market prices so that they could compete with other firms that enjoyed those same low prices. This disrupted firms' adherence to collective local productivity and growth alliances. For example, Siemens supported deregulation and privatization of Deutsche Telekom once it realized it could not compete in world markets as a supplier of telecommunications equipment tied to a stagnant public utility.

If there is an analog to nineteenth-century Britain, it is more likely to be found in the EU than the United States. Although the EU produces substantially more science workers than the United States, it produces substantially less in terms of patents and cited output (National Science Foundation, 2007). EU-25 R&D spending was one-fifth lower than in the US as a share of PPP-adjusted GDP, and absolutely one-third lower, 1991 to 2003. EU output of high-technology manufactured value-added also has substantially lagged behind US and Asian output since the mid-1990s. The EU's share of global high-tech value-added fell from 28 percent in 1990 to 18.4 percent in 2003. The IT revolution can also be seen in the fact that US firms received a greater share of royalties and licensing income than foreign firms investing in the United States. In 1989 royalties and licenses accounted for only 2.1 percent of US exports of goods and services, but by 2005 they were 3.3 percent (Bureau of Economic Analysis, 2008).

From the bottom up, from the top down

The renovation of US manufacturing, the US services offensive, and the inherent limitations of the Japanese model allowed the US economy to expand more rapidly than its peer OECD competitors. On the one hand, the destruction of the US labor movement and the assimilation of Japan's three Ks – *kanban, kaizen,* and *keiretsu* – enabled US firms to generate enormous profits and enjoy profit rates well in excess of their OECD competitors. By running plant and equipment on multiple shifts, and by engineering waste out, US firms managed to increase output significantly without having to increase investment, and this in turn increased their profitability dramatically relative to their OECD competitors (see Table 13.5). At the same time, as noted above, core European economies and Japan were experiencing a decade or more of stagnation. The growth disparity caused aggregate EU-15 output per hour to decline 10 percentage points relative to the US after 1995.

Relative decline thus plagued America's peer OECD rivals, rather than the United States itself. While it is tempting to regard the 1990s and 2000s as purely a consumption bubble, the US economy experienced real gains in employment, fixed investment and output. Table 13.6 presents comparative data on these items, adjusted for differences in population growth, which would otherwise favor the United States. Even after this adjustment, the US economy created more jobs than did the German or Japanese economies. And more jobs meant more growth, which in turn created more investment in everything from housing to machinery.

Table 13.5 *Rate of return on private sector capital in the OECD area[a]*

	1970s	1980s	1990s
United States	19.5	20.8	25.3
Germany	11.8	11.2	12.9
Japan	17.2	13.7	13.8
Average, G6[b]	13.0	12.6	13.6
Average, 12 Small OECD[c]	10.9	11.0	12.1

Notes:
[a] *Relative* changes are more important than *absolute* levels in this table, given difficulties in measurement.
[b] Canada, France, Germany, Italy, Japan, United Kingdom.
[c] Australia, Austria, Belgium, Denmark, Finland, Ireland, Netherlands, New Zealand, Norway, Spain, Sweden, Switzerland.
Source: Based on data from OECD (1998c: 100).

Table 13.6 *Population adjusted percentage change in main economic indicators from 1991 to 2005*

	USA	OECD Average	Germany	Japan
GDP (real, local currency)	33.5	28.1	17.3	13.3
Absolute number of Employed	1.8	3.0	–2.9	–2.7
Absolute number of Unemployed	–24.8	6.8	91.5	109.7
Gross fixed capital formation	79.9	48.2	2.7	–13.5
GFCF in Metals/Machinery	159.8	100.1	19.0	22.8

Source: Calculated from OECD National Accounts data at http://www.sourcewOECD.org, date accessed 1 June 2007.

From 1991 to 2005, real US per capita GDP increased 60 percent faster than in the Euro-land economies, enabling a slightly faster increase of 64 percent in personal consumption. Despite housing finance systems' importance in creating more aggregate demand – discussed further in Chapter 14 – US *non-residential* private fixed capital formation also increased at three times the rate in anemic Euro-land and more than ten times the rate in ailing Japan – and, surprisingly, at more than double the rate of US consumption. Consistent with Verdoorn's law, US manufacturing productivity and value-added increased at roughly double the pace in Continental Europe and Japan during 1991–2005, indicating that the American expansion was deep as well as broad. Finally, the United States also generated nearly half the OECD's net new jobs.

US firms also grew faster overseas than foreign firms grew in the US market during 1995–2004. Despite a 10 percent increase in the dollar's exchange rate over that time period, which diminishes measures of overseas activity, their overseas value-added increased by 40 percent, while turnover nearly doubled to 7.8 percent of gross world product, and about 13 percent of OECD GDP (UNCTAD, 2006: 332–3; Bureau of Economic Analysis, 2007: 46; OECD, 2008a: 378, 382). Moreover, despite slower growth in other rich countries, the ratio of US MNCs' overseas sales to sales in the United States by firms doing FDI into the United States also rose from 1.3 to 1.5 in 1995–2004. So US firms' productivity advantages translated into relatively greater control over production at home and abroad.

But was this revival of US hegemony from below matched by a revival at the level of global finance? After all, the United States ran a cumulative $6 trillion trade deficit from 1991 to 2007, although almost half of that occurred during 2003–7, at the height of the housing bubble and the Bush administration's fiscal irresponsibility. This trade deficit translated into a rising level of absolute and net foreign debt. By 2007 the United States owed $16 trillion absolutely and about $2.5 trillion net to foreign creditors. Could a hegemonic power also be an indebted power? Moreover, as we will see, net US debt was intimately tied to the housing finance debacle that sparked the 2007–9 global financial crisis. This is the topic of the next chapter.

Chapter 14

US Hegemony and Global Stability

Reviving or Declining from the Top Down?

> Under the placid surface, at least the way I see it, there are really disturbing trends: huge imbalances, disequilibria, risks – call them what you will. Altogether the circumstances seem to me as dangerous and intractable as any I can remember, and I can remember quite a lot.
>
> *Paul Volcker, 16 February 2005, Stanford University*

The American state used its position of dominance to try to construct something close to hegemony via the cluster of policies we label globalization: liberalization of international trade and capital flows, and liberalization and marketization of domestic finance and the public sector elsewhere. America's postwar dominance rested on its productive capacity, its enormous market, its control over global oil supplies, its ability to act as a lender of last resort in crisis, and its military power. Chapter 13 covered the first issue, but we cannot hope to cover the rest of these in this chapter. Instead this chapter will concentrate on the interaction between international financial liberalization and global growth. While this picks up the oil story, it necessarily stints military issues, which I leave to others.

US efforts at liberalization destroyed the institutional foundations for balancing global supply and demand constructed at Bretton Woods. The removal of controls on international capital flows and the expansion of the General Agreement on Tariffs and Trade (GATT) into the World Trade Organization (WTO) helped break the link between productivity growth and wage growth in the rich economies. Pre-1970s, rising wages validated rising productivity, because wage bargains linked wage growth to productivity, demand to supply. From the 1970s onward, the global economy has experienced oscillation and financial crises as production has expanded faster than demand (Brenner, 1998). By the 2000s, a huge imbalance had emerged between US overconsumption and Chinese overproduction. The corresponding financial manifestation of this imbalance was China's enormous accumulation of foreign assets, and American homebuyers' enormous accumulation of mortgage debt.

Naturally, each financial crisis differed in its specifics. One central thread, however, is that each effort to bring supply and demand back in line created the conditions for the next crisis by patching over the lack of demand with new debt, just as in the 1920s. The United States has used these crises to further the extension of market forces into other societies, particularly into the service sector, further weakening the connection between production and wage growth. Instead, as in the 1920s, the United States has generally served as the final source of demand by creating new debt. Unlike the 1920s, it has done so by using the dollar's reserve currency status to simply monetize part of its consumption, offering ever larger volumes of US assets to global financial markets. China and Japan, for their part, play roles similar to that of the United States in the 1920s. Where the United States hoarded gold, avoided imports and offered new lending to the world, China and Japan also hoard dollars, avoid imports, and lend to the United States by way of creating additional demand for their goods.

The United States has used its central position, its ability to create demand by offering new dollar-denominated assets to the world, to systematically reshape political economies elsewhere. In each financial crisis in the newly industrializing and new agricultural countries (NICs and NACs), US policy has tried to dismantle state-run industrialization programs and open up service-sector markets, particularly in finance, not only so that US firms can export to these economies but also so they can 'get a piece of the action' as owners rather than simply lenders. In Europe and Japan, US policy has tried to create markets in what were publicly owned or publicly coordinated service-sector markets, weakening the utility of this sector for social protection and government-sponsored growth. The US commitment to global economic stability thus presented the rest of the world with a Faustian bargain: the price of stabilization and new growth was often a reorientation of domestic political structures that made older growth and welfare models untenable (Gowan, 1999). At the same time US policy was internally contradictory: the intensification of market pressures and the increasing gap between supply and demand made financial crises more likely.

This cycle has played out four times since 1971, culminating in the massive financial crisis of 2007–9. The 1970s oil shocks sucked billions of dollars of demand out of rich economies. Resolution of this crisis involved the recycling of petro-dollars as new debt to would-be LDC developers, primarily in Latin America (see Chapter 11). The 1980s debt crisis demolished LDC demand. Increased US government debt, funded via the recycling of US trade deficits with Japan as 'Toyota-dollars,' then bridged the demand gap. The invisible (to Americans) US debt crisis of the late 1980s and early 1990s, when the falling dollar devalued billions of Japanese-held Toyota-dollars, led rich-country investors to invest billions in new productive capacity in Southeast Asia. This exacerbated global supply, producing falling prices and the 1997–8 Asian financial crises. Once more US consumers bridged the gap by borrowing, this time against their houses, in order to absorb excess global production. China and to a lesser extent the oil exporters funded this borrowing by recycling their trade surpluses into mortgage backed securities (MBS) and US public debt. This produced the more visible 2007–9 US debt crisis. Because MBS and derivatives based on them circulated so widely in developed-country banking and financial systems, the deterioration of the US housing market triggered a global financial meltdown, because it simultaneously removed the central source for creating new global demand and crippled financial firms. The astute reader will note that these oscillations correspond to the yo-yoing of the US dollar highlighted in Chapter 10 and the spasmodic expansion of production to ever lower wage zones in Asia noted in Chapter 12.

US hegemony or power thus is not permanent. Each round of crisis has led to more and more new debt. The US international debt position somewhat resembles the children's *slinky* spring toy, which retains its energy as it walks down the steps; ultimately it hits the floor and stops. The periphery reaches unsustainable levels of debt more quickly than the United States, but the current financial crisis is large enough to call into question the dollar's reserve status, and thus the US ability to create new demand in the global economy. Chapter 13 examined the bottom-up issue of whether US productive ability can validate the current overhang of US debt. In principle, as long as the US economy continues to generate domestic growth, the United States can validate its debts. But in practice the alternatives matter, as the current crisis calls into question the long-term US growth trajectory.

This chapter thus looks at the possible decline of US hegemony from the top down to understand the alternatives and the crisis. It focuses on the two most recent iterations of the new debt, new demand, new oversupply, new financial crisis cycle: Asia 1997–8 and the United States 2007–9. It concentrates on two issues: the mechanisms creating and suppressing new demand, and divergent visions for organizing the global economy. The first crisis has causes essentially identical to those of the nineteenth-century debt crises: individually rational but collectively irrational overinvestment in new, largely extensive, production for export back to the central economies of the system (Chapter 6). The second one increasingly resembles that of the 1920s, in that it is demand and finance at the system core that is out of balance (Chapter 7). Every financial asset has a corresponding debt on someone else's balance sheet. Validation of those assets thus rests on debtors' incomes. But the imbalance between supply and demand – the lack of enough income among debtors to validate creditors' assets by absorbing production – caused the notional value of global financial assets to plummet from about $80 trillion in early 2007 to about $60 trillion in early 2009 (IMF, v.d.). Financial assets fell because in the real economy demand fell well short of supply. The fall in US growth and demand in 2007–9 unmasked enormous surplus capacity in the global economy and caused prices to fall. In 2008 – before the even bigger drop in demand in 2009 – the global car industry was already running at only 73 percent of capacity and the global semiconductor industry at 62 percent (Coy, 2009: 25; Welch, 2009).

US power and global financial flows

To understand the basis for US power we need to understand the role the United States plays in the global economy. A curious paradox makes that role clear: although the United States has been a net international debtor since the late 1980s, it has consistently had net positive international investment income. In 2008 the United States had a net foreign debt of roughly $2.5 trillion, the result of 25 years of cumulating trade deficits. Yet the United States also earned about $100 billion in net investment income that year. As Gourinchas and Rey (2005) have shown, from 1960 to 2001, US overseas assets earned an annualized rate of return 2 percentage points higher than US liabilities to foreigners, at 5.6 percent versus 3.6 percent. Furthermore, the gap expanded after 1973, as US overseas assets yielded 6.8 percent while its liabilities to foreigners cost only 3.5 percent. This is one reason why, despite five more years of cumulating trade deficits, US net foreign debt was the same 20 percent of GDP in 2007 as it had been in 2002. It is perfectly plausible that a savvy individual investor might borrow money for investment purposes and reap a positive return. Yet it is implausible that every American investor is systematically savvier than everyone else in the rest of the world.

Instead, the United States has operated a system of global financial arbitrage. At the simplest level, the United States borrows short term at low interest rates from the world, and then turns around and invests long term at higher returns into the world. The similarity to Britain's global financial arbitrage (Chapter 6) is not accidental. Despres, Salant and Kindleberger (1970) argue that this process is simply *intermediation*, and that the United States in effect acts like a giant bank. But it is not clear why European and Japanese investors, who account for half of the US foreign debt, cannot supply their own intermediation services. Moreover, banks' ability to make money on the spread between deposits and loans depends heavily on political management of the maturity mismatch between short-term deposits and long-term investments. Without the political infrastructure of central banks and deposit insurance, 'intermediation' usually ends in bank runs and failures.

Arbitrage also has political roots. Asian central banks and many oil exporters – these countries account for three-quarters of US foreign debt – consciously and conscientiously recycled their trade surpluses with the United States as purchases of low-return investments. The Japanese and Chinese central banks did so in order to keep their exchange rates from rising against the US dollar (Dooley, Folkerts-Landau, and Garber, 2003). A stable and low exchange rate allowed them to continue to grow via exports to the United States. The oil exporters did so to buy military protection, in all senses, from the United States, in addition to funding continued US consumption of oil.

The differences between US outward investment and foreign investment into the United States thus explain the different rates of return. In 2007 approximately 60 percent of the stock of US overseas investment was foreign direct investment (FDI), where firms control production and thus profits, or portfolio holdings of equities, which also have the potential for appreciation

Table 14.1   *International investment into and out of the United States, 2007, $ billions and percent*

$ Billion	FDI[a]	Portfolio equities	Portfolio debt[b]	Loans	Total
United States	5148	5171	1478	5002	16 799
Rest of World	3524	2833	6965	4982	18 304
Of which, Central Banks			2931	406	3337
% shares	FDI[a]	Portfolio equities	Portfolio debt[b]	Loans	Total
United States	30.6	30.8	8.8	29.8	100
Rest of World	19.3	15.5	38.1	27.2	100
Of which, Central Banks			16.0	2.2	18.2

Notes:
[a] Market valuation.
[b] Omits trivial US holdings of currency and foreign holdings of US currency totaling $279 billion.

Source: Based on data from BEA, *International Investment Position*, http://www.bea.gov/international/index.htm#iip, date accessed 1 August 2008.

(Table 14.1). The reverse was true for foreign investment into the United States. Roughly 38 percent of foreign investment was holdings of US public debt, Agency bonds or corporate bonds. Agency bonds are direct borrowings or mortgage-backed securities (MBS) issued by the giant US government-sponsored enterprises Fannie Mae and Freddie Mac. An additional 27 percent was bank loans. Neither has much potential for appreciation, and a large proportion was short-term loans, which have very low interest rates. While US investors earn a higher return on their portfolio investments, the difference in portfolio holdings means that net income still flows out of the United States. The difference in the levels of FDI largely explains the difference in aggregate rates of return, because US direct investment overseas (USDIA) generates return on equity that is 6 percentage points higher than foreign direct investment in the United States (FDIUS) (Mataloni, 2000: 55–6; Gros, 2006a, 2006b).

US arbitrage matters for the global economy because it generates additional demand, helping to reduce global surplus capacity. Financial liberalization in the United States makes it possible for the US economy to generate not only new assets, but more sellable assets than other economies. While the United States, Europe, and Japan had roughly comparable ratios of total assets to GDP, at around 4.5 to 1 in 2006, the United States was at the lower end of the group (IMF, v.d.). But the United States has a much higher level of liquid financial assets, because the bulk of financial assets in Japan and Continental Europe are illiquid bank loans. In 2006 roughly 50 percent of European financial assets were bank loans, as were 32 percent of Japanese assets, but only 18 percent of US assets were. US financial liberalization enabled US banks to turn a vast array of home, car, and personal loans into bonds; this is 'securitization,' turning loans into sellable securities. Adding marketable public and private debt to stock market equity, the ratio of liquid financial assets to GDP in the United States is 3.5, in Japan about 3.1 and in Europe about 2.5. Put simply, the United States funded its chronic trade deficits by using financial deregulation to create and exchange an overabundance of liquid assets for real goods. This exchange soaked up excess global production while creating more debt from the United States to the rest of the world. Moreover, this process created a virtuous – though not permanent – upward growth spiral after 1991. This spiral helped validate those US assets by helping the US economy and productivity grow faster than those of many of its rich-country creditors.

The US economy grew faster because the structure of housing finance in the United States, as well as a handful of other rich countries, created extra aggregate demand and Keynesian multiplier effects as nominal interest rates fell after 1991 (Schwartz, 2009a). Euro-area long-term interest rates fell from 11.2 percent in 1990 to 3.5 percent by 2005; US long-term rates declined less, from 8.7 percent to 4.0 percent during 1990–2003 (OECD, 2008b). The lower nominal cost of borrowing should have stimulated growth everywhere. Indeed, the United States and its OECD competitors all experienced positive effects from the supply chain revolution, the emergence of the internet, and mobile telephony. But the differing structures of housing finance markets account for above OECD average US growth after 1991. The US housing finance system is remarkably liquid, allowing debtors to take out new, lower-interest loans and retire higher-interest debt cheaply and without penalty, to borrow against the equity in their homes, and to deduct mortgage interest from their taxes. Banks permit this because they can sell loans to the two government-sponsored mortgage giants, Fannie Mae and Freddie Mac (now government-owned), which package mortgages together into bonds and sell them into the market. This removes interest-rate risk from banks' balance sheets.

Disinflation (a decline in the rate of inflation) and US arbitrage in global capital markets stimulated the US housing market by providing relatively low interest rates to existing home-owners wishing to refinance their mortgages into (i.e. exchange for) lower interest rate mortgages, and to new homebuyers willing and able to bid up home prices. Such refinancing freed up cash for existing homebuyers. Rising prices created new home equity these buyers could tap via home equity loans and then spend. And spend they did. Meanwhile consumers in less liquid housing markets, like Germany, spent less, inhibiting German growth despite above-average levels of investment in residential construction.

US global financial arbitrage energized this process of housing-driven growth. Foreign purchases of US Treasury and Agency debt helped to drive down interest rates on US mortgages. By December 2006, foreign investors held 52 percent of marketable US Treasury securities and 16.8 percent of outstanding Agency debt (Treasury Department, 2007: 3–5). Interest rates on most US mortgages are referenced against the ten year Treasury bond interest rate. Recycling of Asian trade surpluses during the late 1990s and early 2000s depressed yields on 10-year US Treasury debt by about 90 basis points, or almost 1 percentage point, and as much as 150 basis points in 2005 (Warnock and Warnock, 2006). European and oil exporter acquisitions of dollar-denominated portfolio assets should have had much the same effect in the early to mid-1990s, when those groups primarily funded the US trade deficit. Foreign purchases of Agency debt had an equally direct effect on housing and thus US growth, by allowing banks to originate new mortgages and then sell them onward to Fannie Mae and Freddie Mac.

The United States thus bridged the supply–demand gap by generating low-yielding assets and exchanging them for Asia's and Europe's overproduction. As in the 1920s, debt was an unstable and inadequate tool for resolving the international oversupply problem. It simply created a deeper codependency between European and Asian countries with inadequate domestic demand, and the United States, whose ability to issue dollar-denominated assets enabled it to consume well in excess of local production. Though elites in Europe and Asia (as well as some academics) put on a brave face about their own rising domestic demand, the shocking crash in production and exports subsequent to the 2008 crash in US demand reinforces the numbers. Between 1991 and 2005 the United States and China together accounted for half of global GDP growth and half of global fixed investment growth (Groningen Growth and Development Centre, 2006). The codependence between US debt-financed consumption and excessive investment in productive capacity elsewhere can be seen in the 1997 emerging markets financial crisis and the 2007–9 global financial crisis. The next two sections examine each to show these processes in detail.

Debt and crisis, round one: the 1990s emerging markets crisis

The 1997–8 emerging markets crisis emerged from conflicts between the United States and Japan over the redistribution of global production capacity. In the late 1980s Japanese dominance of manufacturing, based on the three Ks (chapter 13), seemed clear. The United States responded by depreciating the dollar to force Japanese production to shift to the United States. But this ended up creating more excess capacity and the renewed export of US assets as the United States took on the role of buyer of last resort in the 1990s emerging market crises.

The United States in the 1980s

As noted above, the United States tried to stabilize the US dollar and solve the problem of deficient global demand in the 1970s by encouraging the recycling of petro-dollars through US banks to development-minded LDCs (Spiro, 1999). Those late-developing LDCs found themselves in trouble when

Federal Reserve chair Paul Volcker drove interest rates up and thus demand down to cure rich-country inflation woes 1979–82. Indebted LDCs needed export surpluses if they were to make good on their debts. The US policy response imitated that of 1920s Britain, because the same kind of financial interests determined policy. Overseas interest payments ultimately take the form of exported goods, so debtors had to export. To whom could they export, though? Only to the United States, where the same high interest rates that triggered the debt crisis also enabled the United States to import massive volumes of goods with a strong dollar. Reagan's expansive fiscal policy provided people with fistfuls of overvalued dollars to spend on cheap exports from the indebted NICs. Meanwhile the overvalued dollar and a lack of investment in those NICs and NACs depressed US exports.

Alone among the creditor countries, the United States supplied demand to the world economy by consistently running current account deficits. While the United States protected its domestic market (Chapter 12), and indeed set the pattern for protection elsewhere, the US market remained relatively open compared to other developed-country markets. Even in the highly protected and politicized textiles and garment sector, US imports nearly doubled in real terms during the 1980s. The United States thus allowed debtor LDCs to run the current account surpluses they needed. In 1987 the United States absorbed 22 percent of the world's manufactured exports, up from 11 percent in 1975. Moreover, the United States also absorbed over 50 percent of NIC exports of manufactures. In contrast, despite an economy half the size of the United States, Japan in 1987 absorbed only 4 percent of world manufactured exports, up from 2 percent in 1975 (OECD, 1987: 70–1). By 2000, despite much deeper Asian industrialization and integration, the United States still absorbed 17.5 percent of global manufactured exports and 24 percent of NIC manufactured exports. Japan's share of global imports dropped during the 2000s and despite its central position in Asian commodity chains, Japan absorbed only 5.3 percent of LDC exports (WTO, 2008).

Deficits with LDCs accounted for 47 percent of the cumulative US current account deficit of nearly $1 trillion from 1980 to 1989, and the same proportion of the $5 trillion from 1990 to 2005. The bilateral deficit with Japan accounted for only 38 percent in the first period and then fell to 20 percent in the second. These deficits overlapped in some sense – Japanese willingness to recycle their trade surplus kept the dollar strong, enabling the US to turn around and buy from debtor LDCs. But this process reached its political limits in the mid-1980s when US manufacturers threatened to desert the Republican Party, and its economic limits, when foreign investors began to back away from US dollar-denominated assets (Henning, 1994: 277–84). While the dollar comprised nearly 75 percent of official reserves in 1978, by 1989 it had fallen below 50 percent as central banks diversified into deutschemarks and yen. Various Euro-currencies peaked at 40 percent of holdings in 1990, and the yen at 10 percent (Wooldridge, 2006). Meanwhile, Japan alone accounted for 21 percent of foreign-held US assets. The United States appeared unable to continue acting as the global buyer of last resort. As their currencies

Table 14.2   *Outstanding bank lending to Emerging Markets, June 1997, $ billion*

	US	Japan	EU
Asian Emerging Markets	43.3	271.4	353.3
of which:			
5 Crisis Countries[a]	23.8	97.2	98.1
China	2.9	18.7	28.1
Taiwan	2.5	3.0	14.4
Singapore and Hong Kong	14.1	152.4	212.8
Eastern Europe and Turkey	7.4	5.2	47.1
Russia	7.5	0.8	45.5
Latin America	60.3	14.5	125.7
Total Emerging Markets	118.5	291.9	571.6

Note: [a] Korea, Indonesia, Malaysia, Thailand, and the Philippines.
Source: Based on data from OECD (1998a: 21).

strengthened, why didn't Japan or Europe replace it? Why did they instead choose to invest in Southeast Asia and other emerging markets, as Table 14.2 shows?

Europe and Japan in the 1980s

Why didn't Europe and Japan open themselves to more imports in the 1990s and thus respectively cement Eastern Europe and emerging Asia more firmly to their economies? Both continued to suppress domestic demand, on the one hand to prevent inflation, and on the other as a disguised, albeit ineffective, welfare state. Domestic political considerations determined both responses, and helped set the stage for the 1990s emerging markets crisis that originated in Thailand, as well as exacerbating the supply–demand imbalance that created the 2007–9 crisis.

Europe first: The European response to US exchange rate manipulation was an effort to insulate their economies by recreating Bretton Woods at a regional level (recall Chapter 9). European elites intended that monetary and economic unification would create a zone of safety for European-style capitalism, a zone in which a single strong currency could substitute for the dollar (or yen), a zone in which Europe's mostly would-be multinationals could consolidate their control over their regional market, a zone in which social protection through the formal welfare state of taxes, transfers and public services could prevent the barbarity and excess of American and Asian capitalism. However, the political compromises needed to attain monetary unification suppressed European domestic demand, particularly in Continental Europe.

Monetary unification aimed to create a miniature Bretton Woods in Europe. Locking European exchange rates to a pool of local currencies would permit firms to plan without exchange rate risks. But unification could not work without the Germans, and the Bundesbank's strict anti-inflation policy was thus carried into the design of the European Central Bank (ECB) and the Maastricht Treaty eligibility criteria. These required countries qualifying for the euro to have public debt levels below 60 percent of GDP, a fiscal deficit less than 3 percent of GDP, convergence on the three lowest inflation rates in the Union (effectively, less than 3 percent inflation), and convergence within two percentage points of the three lowest nominal long-term interest rates in the EU.

While the original European exchange rate mechanism (ERM) and Maastricht seemed to privilege no single country, the weight of the German economy and deutschemark made the deutschemark the *de facto* anchor currency. The Bundesbank was thus able to export its monetary policy to the rest of Europe. And the Bundesbank has been consistently hawkish on inflation, particularly in the aftermath of German reunification. Consequently, German wage bargains have tended to exchange wage restraint for promises of investment. Jean-Claude Trichet, head of the ECB, expressed the purpose of restraint clearly in April 2007:

> [We are] calling upon [the] social partners to show a high level of responsibility. ... [I]t is clear that if one is not satisfied with the present level of unemployment, wage moderation should remain of the essence. ... [I]f you are in a position where there are doubts about your present level of cost competitiveness, then of course wage moderation remains absolutely of the essence.

Wage restraint is intended to increase exports, and thus provide non-inflationary growth. But as the rest of Europe also has to practice wage restraint to stay competitive against Germany, the result is a continent-wide deficiency of demand. If everyone restrains wage growth, domestic demand cannot grow.

While wage restraint lets firms accrue profits, they quite rationally invest those profits overseas, rather than locally, because overseas markets are growing faster. This further slows domestic growth and raises unemployment, while exacerbating the reliance on external demand. This left Continental European economies with lower labor force participation, lower employment rates and higher open unemployment than those of the United States or Japan in the 1990s and 2000s. The attitude that price stability should prevail at any cost to growth lasted all the way into the 2007–9 financial crisis. As late as August 2008, with major financial firms falling like infantry in Flanders, Trichet was grandly declaring that 'We have only one needle in our compass. That needle is price stability.'

Now Japan: Japan also could not find a political path to increased domestic demand and imports in the 1980s and even more so after its 1990 crash. While Japan possessed a set of highly competitive firms based on the three Ks (see Chapter 13), productivity in the bulk of Japan's economy was well below rich-world norms. Japanese manufacturing productivity was between 65 percent and 80 percent of the US level in 1987–90; in transport and communication only 31 percent; economy-wide only 62 percent (Pilat, 1996; van Ark, Monnikhof, and Mulder, 1999: 483). By 2005, overall Japanese productivity was still only 71 percent of the US level, down from the 1991 highwater mark of 78 percent (Groningen Growth and Development Centre, 2006). Cozy cartels protected firms from external competition; import quotas shielded Japan's agriculture. The political and economic costs of opening these protected markets were high.

Japan could have opened its economy, and used the purchasing power liberated by falling import prices to generate consumer-based, domestic-oriented growth, as the Maekawa Report (MITI, 1986) suggested and as the United States did in the 1990s. But opening markets to NIC and NAC imports would have caused massive labor shedding among small and medium-sized firms. Opening food markets would cause a sudden fall in the value of land. Small and medium-sized firms and farmers constituted the biggest donors to and voters for the then incumbent Liberal Democratic Party. Moreover, any liberalization would also hurt big firms, so they could not constitute an opposition political bloc pressing for trade liberalization the way that British exporters and US TNCs did in the 1840s and 1940s. Although Japan's successful exporters knew that agricultural liberalization could be exchanged for less protection in their target export markets, it would hurt their ability to raise investment capital. Agricultural liberalization would drive Japanese land values down. Because both banks and firms used unrealized gains based on high land values to capitalize themselves, and because about 40 percent of lending in Japan is directly collateralized by property, falling land prices would inhibit investment.

Instead, Japan's political and economic elite reacted to protectionist threats from the United States and a falling dollar after 1986 in very familiar but self-defeating ways: they channeled money to firms for investment in new capacity, shifted old industrial processes offshore, and hoped that US consumers would continue to borrow to acquire the new goods produced by the new capacity. This status quo decision set the scene for the 1990s crisis by creating massive overcapacity in basic goods. How? The falling dollar made exporting from Japan harder and threatened growth. The Bank of Japan tried to promote domestic growth by lowering interest rates to 2 percent. Low interest rates and lots of liquidity set off the stock and land market bubbles of the late 1990s, as asset prices zoomed up from 300 percent to 400 percent in response to falling interest rates.

Domestic firms took advantage of rising equity and property values to use them as collateral. They borrowed to engage in an orgy of on- and offshore investment. This investment created three new production zones. First, responding to US VERs on cars and electronics, they built new production complexes in North America. Second, having shifted basic car production to the United States, Japanese firms re-equipped or built entirely new factories in Japan to produce their new luxury cars and high-end electronics, investing roughly $3 trillion in new plant from 1986 to 1991. Table 14.3 gives an indication of the degree of excess capacity ultimately created in the car industry. In

Table 14.3   *Excess capacity in the global car industry, 2008, millions of units and percent*

	Total capacity	Share of global capacity	Surplus capacity	Surplus as % of capacity
North America	17.3	18.4%	7.2	41.6%
Europe (incl. Russia, Turkey)	27.3	29.0%	9.5	34.8%
Japan and Korea	17.3	18.4%	3.4	19.7%
China and Taiwan	15.8	16.8%	8.0	50.6%
South Asia, SEA, and Australia	8.3	8.8%	3.6	43.4%
South America	5.5	5.9%	1.8	32.7%
Mid-East and North Africa	2.5	2.7%	0.8	32.0%
Global	94.0	100.0%	34.3	36.5%

Source: Welch (2009: 42–3).

the semiconductor industry, which occupied roughly the same place in Japan as the car industry did in the United States in 1929, the investment boom in 1988–90 created excess capacity equal to between 30 percent and 50 percent of projected consumption at that time. The last new production zone was in Southeast Asia, understood here as also encompassing south China. Just as they had shifted production offshore to Asia in response to US protectionism in the 1960s and 1970s (Chapter 12), Japanese firms again shifted production outward, sending $50 billion in new direct foreign investment to Asia.

This made sense because the currencies of these countries were largely tied to the US dollar, so they could continue to export to the United States even when the dollar fell against the yen. As sectors like low-end consumer electronics, basic steel and car assembly shifted to Korea and Taiwan, those countries shifted labor-intense production of textiles, toys and trash outward to new production sites in the 'MIT' economies – Malaysia, Indonesia, and Thailand – and, somewhat later, to China. In the short run, this expansion of capacity did not produce overcapacity. Japanese and American consumers continued their spending spree until 1990. Investment in Southeast Asia produced rising incomes that absorbed some of the new production there. And, of course, it took some time for the new production complexes to get up to full speed. Thus by the mid-1990s, Asian governments were committing a huge share of GDP to fixed capital formation: 45 percent in Malaysia and Thailand; 36 percent in Singapore, Indonesia, and Korea. These states used both overt and covert forms of protection to steer local business groups' and MNCs' investment into targeted sectors.

From overcapacity to crisis

In 1990, the Bank of Japan significantly tightened monetary policy to deflate the speculative bubble, dropping money supply growth to zero in 1992.

Japan's central bank succeeded in deflating the boom, perhaps too much so. The Nikkei stock index lost half its value and land about 30 percent, obliterating the collateral backing much bank lending. Because Japanese banks rely on unrealized gains on property to meet capital adequacy standards, and because so much lending was collateralized by property, banks drastically curtailed lending. US policy aggravated this. As Chapter 9 noted, the Clinton administration, abetted by the Federal Reserve, allowed the dollar to fall to historically low levels against the yen. By 1995 the dollar bought between 80 and 90 yen, rather than the 150 it had bought in 1990. This second *endaka* (high yen shock) certainly had its intended effect on Japan's exports of cars, home electronics, cameras and precision machinery. These fell by roughly half, between 1992 and 1996 after rising by 16 percent in the prior three years (Toshitomi, 1996: 66). Japanese firms could have shut down some of this capacity. But lifetime employment was a crucial component of Japan's postwar domestic political economy, so this proved politically unpalatable until 1999. Instead, Japanese firms doubled down on their Southeast Asian production bet.

This shift involved both a transfer of physical machinery and the export of Japan's growth model to Asia. Japanese elites used a revisionist World Bank publication arguing that state coordination of investment and protection for domestic industry (read: resolution of Gerschenkronian collective problems) along with state mediation of the relationship between foreign capital and the local economy, export surges, and targeting of high-value-added sectors (read: resolution of Kaldorian collective problems) would produce Japanese-style miracle growth (World Bank, 1993). But just as wage restraint could only produce growth for one country, export surges also could not all succeed at the same time. Trade surpluses had to be recycled as new lending to overseas consumers to prevent the exchange rate from rising, but eventually these consumers would be over-borrowed. Second, if all of Asia tried this strategy, they would create so much overcapacity that profits would disappear everywhere just as in the nineteenth century.

The Clinton administration meanwhile was pursuing its Big Emerging Markets strategy (Garten, 1997). This called for opening up the domestic markets of the ten BEMs to service-sector exports, like finance, telecommunications, and air transport, along with the capital goods that these services required, like switching systems, massive construction projects, aircraft, computers, earth-moving equipment. These public-sector capital goods constitute about one-third of US merchandise exports. The BEM strategy reflected US efforts to liberalize public-sector procurement and service-sector trade via the WTO and conflicted with Japan's vision. The US project also had its own internal contradiction: free movement of capital would naturally lead to overheated economies and a potential for the very financial panics the United States hoped to avoid.

In the short run this clash of titans was remarkably peaceful, because both economies could have their relationship with Southeast Asia without getting in each other's way, rather like a bigamist wife enjoying two husbands on different shifts. As Japan's bilateral trade surplus with the United States fell from $60 billion to $30 billion, the United States somehow overlooked the concurrent increase in its deficit with Southeast Asia by the same $30 billion. Southeast Asian growth meanwhile generated enormous demand for US exports of the kinds of public-sector capital goods the Clinton BEM policy promoted.

But this success prompted ever more investment in export capacity. Asian fixed investment, net of that in Japan, went from 6 percent of total world investment to 18 percent 1990 to 1996. One quarter – $420 billion – of this investment came from foreign sources, often as short-term lending (Table 14.2 above). This investment had a second problem. While Southeast Asian states largely agreed with the principles of the Japanese growth model, they deviated from its practices. States proved unable to *consistently* direct investment into productive capacity and to *consistently* discipline local firms into upgrading production. They could resolve their Gerschenkronian collective action problems but not their Kaldorian problems. Thus, much of this investment produced extensive growth. That is, the Southeast Asian economies, and to a lesser extent Korea, simply generated massive overcapacity in basic industries, turning not only textiles, toys and trash into cheap commodities, but also low-end electronics and car parts.

As with nineteenth-century food agricultural exporters whose resolution of their Gerschenkronian problems flooded world markets, Southeast Asia's successes undermined ability to repay its loans. As production ramped up across Southeast Asia and especially China after 1990, terms of trade apparently fell for all but Singapore and Taiwan. China appears to have depressed terms of trade by 20 percent for the MIT economies when it devalued its yuan by 32 percent in 1994 (Kaplinsky, 1999). Like their nineteenth-century NAC cousins, these brave new NICs needed to export greater and greater volumes of goods to pay back a given volume of debt, but greater export volumes only drove prices further down. This helped US consumers, who saw import prices for consumer non-durables continuously dropping in the 1990s (Broda and Romalis, 2008).

Devaluation increased China's exports and Japan's direct exports, but at the expense of the MIT economies. Japanese firms, faced with a fratricidal choice between producing at home or producing abroad, naturally favored home production. China's emergence as the largest exporter of clothing and toys (a third of global markets for each) displaced exports from the MIT economies. Thus after racking up successive years of double-digit export growth after 1990, MIT export growth fell to virtually nothing by 1997, and their current account deficits expanded. Meanwhile the bilateral US trade deficit with China doubled to $30 billion as China won the competitive struggle for export market shares between itself and the MIT economies.

The MIT economies meanwhile were faced with difficult choices whose parameters were set by the Mundell-Fleming model (see Chapter 9). Recall that they could have only two of the following three policy choices: monetary policy autonomy, free capital flows, and fixed exchange rates. Their policy stance in 1995 was free capital flows and fixed exchange rates (the peg to the dollar). From 1995 to 1997, the rising US dollar and the inflationary effects of capital inflows combined to price their exports out of world markets. Doing nothing would simply erode export competitiveness as local wage and land costs rose, and cause foreign capital to shift to cheaper locations. If they raised interest rates to damp down inflation, and thus kept their export prices in line with China's, they would also have to impose capital controls to prevent even more inflationary inflows of capital attracted by high interest rates. But capital controls would slow investment, and make highly indebted firms go bust, particularly in the property sector. Slower investment would also disadvantage them in what was essentially a race to expand production before anyone else did. Finally, they could devalue, matching China's devaluation. But doing this would certainly push local firms with foreign currency debts into bankruptcy, because their borrowing was premised on the ability to exchange local currency earning into foreign exchange at fixed parities. Either way, MIT states would have had to hurt powerful local interests to change their policy stance. Consequently they dithered, allowing currency speculators to force devaluations when it became apparent that current account deficits were depleting Thailand's foreign exchange reserves.

The crisis temporarily resolved these problems. Massive capital flight and IMF interventions decreased growth and investment, curing the inflation problem. Currency devaluations and cheaper petrol from Asia's smaller call on global oil supplies put more cash in US consumers' hands, enabling them to import more. And US dominance increased. The quid pro quo for bailouts from the IMF and US banks was financial and trade liberalization along with privatization. Financial liberalization included sales of local banks to OECD financial firms (read: US firms, since Japanese and European banks were too overextended, as Table 14.2 shows), and a shift to OECD accounting conventions and loan practices. Similarly trade liberalization and privatization opened markets for US sellers of public sector capital goods. But these sales and changes destroyed the ability of Asian and other would-be industrializers to use their financial systems to overcome Gerschenkronian and Kaldorian problems using strategies akin to the Japanese model. These states understood this, and resisted such sales. Nevertheless, US banks accounted for 20 percent of Korean banking assets by 2005 and foreign investors owned 50 percent of the outstanding shares of Korean commercial banks, giving them effective control over much of the banking sector (Korea Federation of Banks, 2006: 24–5).

The Emerging Markets crisis of 1997–8 thus consolidated US dominance by reinforcing a global division of labor in which the emerging markets remain industrial peripheries, producing low-value, commodity-type goods, with low levels of domestic demand in relation to their productive capacity. This outcome led directly to the housing-based global financial crisis of 2007–9. As in the 1980s, the United States became the market of last resort for NICs that needed export surpluses to make debt payments; the US share of global imports rose from 15 percent to 19.5 percent during 1995–2000. These NICs consciously (and conscientiously) built up enormous holdings of US assets in order to insure against currency speculation, and to hold their exchange rates stable – and low – against the US dollar (McKinnon, 2005).

Debt and crisis, round two: housing boom, housing bust

All the macroeconomic imbalances of the 1990s re-emerged full force in the 2000s. The 1990s Clinton boom had produced modest real wage growth in the United States. Falling interest rates and cheaper imports enhanced this in a self-sustaining way, creating a virtuous cycle of rising employment, rising real wages, rising domestic and import demand. After the internet stock market bubble burst, the subsequent Bush administration tax opted for tax cuts for the rich and the Federal Reserve opted for very low interest rates. These led to an exaggerated re-run of the 1990s, in which the cumulative $3.3 trillion trade deficit of 2004–7 overmatched the $3 trillion accrued in 1992–2003. Americans consumed more while China expanded production and exports. The circle was closed by Chinese purchases of US Treasury and Agency debt, and, after oil prices rose in 2004, by oil exporter purchases. With wages stagnating, Americans borrowed more against their homes to raise consumption by 5 percentage points of GDP; Chinese consumption fell by the same 5 percentage points as businesses poured cash into infrastructure and export production and the central bank hoovered up bank reserves to keep the yuan low against the dollar. Using this level of borrowing to bridge the international gap between supply and demand could not go on for ever. And it didn't.

As noted above, Asian central bank and oil exporter recycling of US trade deficits energized the US economy after 1990 and even more so after 2002. Falling interest rates led to rising house prices. America's liquid mortgage market allowed homeowners to tap into those rising prices via mortgage equity withdrawal (MEW). The US Federal Reserve Bank estimates that 80 percent of the increase in US mortgage debt in the 1990s–2000s can be accounted for by MEW, and that MEW ran at roughly $0.3 trillion annually during 1991–2000 and then at roughly $1 trillion annually during 2001–5 (or $530 billion on average). MEW generated a huge increase in US purchasing power. But MEW could only occur if willing buyers for that mortgage paper existed. China and the oil exporters were those buyers, as foreign holdings of Agency MBS rose by $1 trillion, 2000–07 (Treasury Department, 2008: 11).

US and Chinese codependence had wonderful short-run consequences for elites in each. China attained consistently high growth, most of which was captured by a new generation of millionaires connected to the ruling Communist Party. The top 1 percent of the American population by income, which owns 40 percent of all personal wealth, and the whole top 20 percent, which owns 90 percent, saw their stock portfolios and home equity soar back to internet bubble heights. And, if we can believe the data, China shifted from extensive growth to intensive growth, with large increases in productivity

(Holz, 2006). The rest of Asia, as well as Latin American commodity exporters, rode China's coat-tails to unprecedented trade surpluses. But everything depended on American consumption, which in turn required continuous increases in housing prices and continuous foreign lending to the United States.

The same dynamics driving the housing boom in the United States and elsewhere also drove the boom off the rails, producing the current global financial crisis. As in all booms, the bubble burst when the boom used up its fuel. Global disinflation, the recycling of US trade deficits, and a ready supply of new buyers at the bottom of the US housing ladder powered the boom. When these gave out, so did the boom. During the 1990s, US multinational and retail firms offshored more and more labor-intense production to low-cost Asia, particularly China, producing a flood of ever cheaper non-durable goods imports. Net, this lowered official inflation rates and thus the corresponding interest rates for mortgages. Simultaneously, European and Asian recycling of trade surpluses allowed US arbitrage in global financial markets – the United States was able to borrow short term at low interest rates while investing overseas long term at higher return. This also lowered interest rates for mortgages. Cheap mortgages lured millions of aspiring US homebuyers onto the bottom rungs of the housing ladder. These new housing market entrants generated trillions of dollars of fictitious capital gains for incumbent home-owners, freeing them to move up the housing ladder and spend freely.

The exhaustion of growth was an endogenous feature of growth itself. One of the most powerful fuels for disinflation was the reduction of prices for consumer non-durables through the offshoring of labor-intense production to Asia. This reduced cumulative non-durables inflation by 10 percentage points relative to services (Broda and Romalis, 2008; Broda and Weinstein, 2008). But on net, new homebuyers by definition tended to be lower-income, lower-skilled workers. The more that labor-intense production moved offshore, the fewer potential housing market entrants there could be as incomes stagnated at the bottom. Initially the relatively high proportion of non-durable goods in the consumption package of those unskilled workers offset their falling real wages, as did falling interest rates on mortgages. Yet eventually the two blades of the scissors of falling wages and rising house prices had to meet, cutting one fuel line to the housing boom machine. Real wages stagnated for the bottom 80 percent of the US population after 2000.

Second, successful offshoring of low-wage manufacturing to China and other developing countries produced multiplier effects there, powering their economic growth but also creating new inflationary pressures. Given their initial low level of development, economic growth necessarily involved greater and greater calls on global raw material supplies, including, most importantly, oil. Development meant creating an entirely new infrastructure – roads, buildings, power generation, telecommunications – and thus huge energy-intense inputs of cement, steel, and copper. All told, Chinese imports of oil, soybeans, and copper were about 30 times higher in 2008 than they were in 1995 (Jen and Bindelli, 2007). Developing nations' calls on global resources reversed the 1990s disinflation, forcing developed-country central banks to raise interest rates in 2005. This cut a second fuel line.

Third, the very nature of housing and credit markets meant that the last entrants into the market would be the least creditworthy, making loans to them a risky proposition. From 1995 to 2005, the US home-ownership rate rose by roughly 5 percentage points, pushing the home-ownership frontier out into the *terra incognita* of the un-creditworthy. In 2004 subprime loans rose from about 7 percent of new mortgages to nearly 20 percent, while 'Alt-A' loans (to borrowers with good credit but excessive debt) accounted for another 20 percent (Harvard University Joint Center, 2008). These loans generally had variable interest rates, making debtors vulnerable to any up-tick in the reference rate for mortgages. Everyone understood that these buyers could not survive an increase in their mortgage interest rate. Thus these loans were designed to be refinanced into lower, fixed-rate loans after a few years of house price appreciation gave owners enough home equity to qualify for those loans. But what if prices failed to rise?

By 2006, the housing boom had exhausted its inputs of new homebuyers, disinflation, and low interest rates. The housing-led differential growth machine then began to run backward, slowing the US economy. Why did this produce a global financial crisis? The macroeconomic phenomena above were not disembodied, abstract flows. Instead they were channeled through a relatively small set of financial intermediaries who transformed global capital flows into mortgages and then back out into global financial markets as MBS and collateralized debt obligations (CDOs), derivatives largely based on MBS. Global financial firms devised what they thought was a relatively simple system for profiting from these trillion dollar flows. They created a carry trade in which they borrowed billions in short-term money to buy their own apparently long term CDOs, profiting from the difference in interest rates. This carry trade was safe and profitable only if housing prices continued to rise. But when Chinese growth turned disinflation to inflation, and the housing boom absorbed all the creditworthy buyers, housing prices turned and began a self-sustaining fall mirroring the earlier self-sustaining rise.

Falling home prices threw financial institutions running the deceptively simple but extremely risky carry trade into crisis. In some sense, the last US subprime buyer was buying a house in Modesto, California, 100 miles from her job in Silicon Valley, and thus contributing to the increased oil prices that caused her mortgage interest rate to rise. Increased inflation indirectly contributed to rising mortgage defaults by draining cash from stressed homeowners, and directly contributed by causing interest rates to rise on their mortgages. Delinquency on all US mortgages made in 2007 ran at three times the level for 2005 vintage mortgages, with 15 percent of 2007 subprime mortgages and 7 percent of Alt-A mortgages delinquent (Simon, 2008). With $1.6 trillion outstanding in MBS built on subprime and Alt-A mortgages, and 56 percent of the global total of $1.3 trillion CDOs backed by US residential mortgages, this threw highly leveraged financial firms into a crisis of their own making (Schwartz, 2009a). I will not discuss the events of the crisis, except to note that unlike crises in the 1980s and 1990s it involved nearly the entire global financial system, that it started in core countries rather than the periphery, and that state responses to the crisis reversed three decades of deregulation and privatization. This reversal also potentially threw the current round of globalization into reverse, which is the subject of the final section.

The future of globalization

For many observers, the financial crisis of 2007–9 definitively reversed the core dynamics of the prior 40 years of globalization. States *de facto* or *de jure* renationalized the banking industry and 'finance' as an organized group lost significant political power. Rising oil prices called into question business models built on trans-Pacific supply chains. In turn this cast doubt on the viability of export-led growth in Asia and elsewhere. And the centrality of the US dollar seemed in doubt as the Federal Reserve and ECB created trillions of dollars and euros in liquidity to prevent a second Great Depression. Surely all this heralded a return to the halcyon days of the Bretton Woods-era Keynesian welfare state, when economies were semi-closed and capital was controlled.

But as the very first edition of this book stressed, globalization was not some novel or unusual phenomenon that suddenly emerged from the regulated economies of the Bretton Woods period. Rather, Bretton Woods was historically unusual. 'Globalization' after the 1970s was a return to the patterns characterizing the nineteenth century. These patterns include periodic crises and a relentless global expansion of capitalist production. Markets force capitalists to lower costs, which at the broadest historical level induces a search for ways to overcome the limiting factor, the scarcest and thus most expensive factor, in production. In the pre- and early industrial era that limiting factor was scarce and thus expensive land in Europe, because industry largely transformed agricultural products. The first half of this book analyzed how the search for cheaper land brought more and more areas outside Europe into commodity chains centered on Europe. We can understand the second half of the book as capital's search for ways to overcome the scarce and thus expensive factor of labor in rich countries after the diffusion of the assembly line. This search dynamized growth in Asia and has set off a process of partially endogenous growth in Asia – but only partially, as China's rapid slowdown in 2008 demonstrates.

Asian growth has three major consequences. First, access to a few billion low-wage workers in Asia has kept wage growth low in rich countries, just as access to non-European land brought down land rents in Europe. Reasonably sober economists have argued that much of the rising income inequality in the OECD is driven by the *availability* of low-wage workers with a basic education, even if production never actually moves to those workers (Williamson, 1997). What John Hobson (1938 [1902]) said one century ago seems roughly correct:

Once encompass China with a network of railroads and steamer services, the size of the labour market to be tapped is so stupendous that it might well absorb in its development all the spare capital and business energy that the advanced European countries and the United States can supply for generation. Such an experiment may revolutionize the methods of Imperialism; the pressure on the working-class movements in politics and industry in the West can be met by a flood of China goods, so as to keep down wages and compel [labor discipline].

(1938 [1902]: 313)

Second, the relentless shift of production towards Asia has created a third new and giant Thünen world city to match the earlier ones in Europe and North America. The North American production zone began absorbing more of its own production as it matured. So too may the Asian one, as elites begin pondering the political costs of maintaining export-oriented economies that can no longer find export markets. China in particular needs to shift from investment towards domestic consumption, and towards some dis-saving of its roughly $1.9 trillion in foreign exchange reserves. This would go some way towards helping to bring global supply and demand back in balance. Given that China's incremental capital output ratio (ICOR – the number of dollars of investment needed to produce one additional dollar of output) has gone from 3.3 before 1995 to 4.9 in 2001, the limits of further investment in export production are obvious (McKinsey Global Institute, 2006: 11).

Third, China's rise has both abetted and undermined US global dominance or hegemony. Above-OECD average economic growth in the US after 1991 was central to US power, US financial arbitrage was central to that growth, and Chinese acquiescence in recycling its trade surpluses was central to that arbitrage. At the same time, China's own growth and the rise of a new Thünen town threatens the relatively huge domestic market and equally huge share of global economic activity that is essential for US dominance. While US dominance will surely falter if growth does not resume in the United States, as the prior paragraph notes it is not certain that China can grow without the United States. And a China that cannot grow will not be a challenger. The two giants may continue to prop each other up as they stumble towards more viable growth models. The record of great power cooperation in the 1920s is not reassuring, but the lingering historical memory of that record surely will help.

Finally, it is well to remember Karl Polanyi's two important conclusions about the end of the long nineteenth century. For Polanyi (1957) the 'Great Transformation' was not simply the fact that markets had become more global, that trade had risen, and that capital flowed across borders. For Polanyi the significant transformation was the exposure of virtually all life chances and income streams to the logic and volatility of the market. This transformation was as destructive of the market as it was of human values. Polanyi's counter-movement against the market and for 'social protection' was about sheltering people's (and firms') incomes and life chances from market outcomes and market volatility, much of which was 'domestic' in the sense in which debunkers of 'globalization' have labeled most economic activity domestic. In that counter-movement states ended up saving the market from itself. After a period in which they tried to contain markets, states in the post-Bretton Woods period actively re-created markets for the very specific reasons outlined in the prior six chapters. This process delinked wage growth and productivity growth, forcing an ever greater reliance on debt to expand consumption.

Just as in the decades before the first Great Depression, markets left to rule themselves proved incapable of doing so, as Polanyi pointed out. Markets need the state as much as the state needs the market. States consciously created markets in the first place from 1500 through 1914; states have consciously re-created markets today. From 1500 to around 1800 those states made markets in agricultural goods and tried to extend those markets into all agricultural production. In the long nineteenth century they made markets in industrial goods and this finally did facilitate the extension of markets into agriculture, producing the 1930s disaster Polanyi analyzed. In the past two decades states made markets in the service sectors which they had regulated and sheltered from the market since the Depression. As in the nineteenth century, the (re-)emergence of markets was planned by market actors and states that stood to benefit from the destruction or reconfiguration of the various forms of social protection created in the 'golden era' of the Keynesian welfare state.

This pervasive expansion of the market, and the subjugation of life chances to market logics, is what constitutes 'globalization.' Ironically, globalization, the extension of market logics into new spheres, has created larger and larger domestic markets, given that services often are consumed locally. But the driving force is still conflict between states worried about global market shares, states reacting to shifts in their relative ability to generate export streams and attract capital investment. Those states are hardly likely to totally suppress markets. And should we be shocked to find markets relentlessly expanding once they are unleashed? Hardly. In this sense the critiques of popular notions of globalization are correct. As Marx, Weber and Simmel observed at the turn of the century, once started, capitalist markets are extremely difficult to suppress.

The current crisis is hardly likely to return us to the historical oddity that the post-World War II interregnum constituted, where social protection prevailed over markets. But it does present an opportunity to tame financial capital enough to permit markets to survive. For it is obvious that each expansion of mass consumption and social protection has benefited capital as a whole as much as it has benefited those groups able to claim protection and some degree of income stability. Yet in the absence of the kind of mass social movements that produced the Depression-era reaction against markets, we are unlikely to see social protection and regulation of the market on the scale that post-Depression politics produced.

Bibliography

Abe, T. (2005) 'The Chinese Market for Japanese Cotton Textile Goods', in Sugihara, K. (ed.), *Japan, China, and the Growth of the Asian International Economy, 1850–1949*. New York: Oxford University Press.

Abel, W. (1980) *Agricultural Fluctuations in Europe: From the Thirteenth to the Twentieth Centuries*, trans. O. Ordisk. London: Methuen.

Abernathy, W., Cole, K. and Kantrow, A. (1983) *Industrial Renaissance*. New York: Basic Books.

Aboulafia, R. (2007) 'Airbus Reinvests to Reinvent', *Aerospace America* (May), 18–20.

Abu-Lughod, J. (1990) *Before European Hegemony*. Cambridge: Cambridge University Press.

Altschuler, A., Anderson, M., Jones, D., Roos, D. and Womack, J. (1984) *Future of the Automobile*. Cambridge, Mass.: MIT Press.

Amiti, M. and Stiroh, K. (2007) 'Is the US Losing its Productivity Edge?', *Current Issues in Economics and Finance* 13(8), 1–7, New York Federal Reserve Bank.

Amsden, A. (1989) *Asia's Next Giant: South Korea and Late Industrialization*. New York: Oxford University Press.

Amsden, A. (2001) *The Rise of 'The Rest'*. New York: Oxford University Press.

Anderson, K. (1990) 'China and the MultiFibre Arrangement', in Hamilton, C. (ed.), *Textiles Trade and the Developing Countries*. Washington, DC: World Bank.

Anderson, P. (1974) *Passages from Antiquity*. London: Verso.

Anderson, P. (1979) *Lineages of the Absolutist State*. London: Verso.

Arista, J. D' and Griffith-Jones, S. (2006) 'The Dilemmas and Dangers of the Build-up of US Debt', in Teunissen, J.J. and Akerman, A. (eds.), *Global Imbalances and the US Debt Problem*. The Hague: Fondad.

Ardant, G. (1975) 'Financial Policy and Economic Infrastructure of Modern States and Nations', in Tilly, C. (ed.), *The Formation of National States in Western Europe*. Princeton, N.J.: Princeton University Press.

Arrighi, G. (1970) 'Labor Supplies in Historical Perspective: Proletarianisation of the Rhodesian African Peasantry', *Journal of Development Studies* no. 3, 180–234.

Arrighi, G. (1994) *The Long Twentieth Century: Money, Power, and the Origins of our Times*. London: Verso.

Arrighi, G., Hui, P.-K., Hung, H.-F. and Selden, M. (2003) 'Historical Capitalism, East and West', in Arrighi, G., Hamashita, T. and Selden, M. (eds.), *The Resurgence of East Asia: 500, 150 and 50 Year Perspectives*. London: Routledge.

Athukorala, P. (2007) 'The Rise of China and East Asian Export Performance: Is the Crowding-out Fear Warranted?', unpublished paper. Canberra: Australian National University.

Athukorala, P. (2005) 'Product Fragmentation and Trade Patterns in East Asia', *Asian Economic Papers* 4(3), 1–27.

Audet, D. and Safadi, R. (2004) *A New World Map in Textiles and Clothing: Adjusting to Change*. Paris: OECD.

Baily, M., Do, C., Kim, Y., Lewis, W., Nam, V., Palmade, V., and Zitzewitz, E. (1998) 'The Roots of Korea's Crisis', *McKinsey Quarterly* (2), 76–83.

Baldwin, R. (1956) 'Patterns of Development in Newly Settled Regions', *The Manchester School Journal of Economic and Social Studies* 24, 161–79.

Baer, W., da Fonseca, M., and Guilhoto, J., (1987) 'Structural Changes in Brazil's Industrial Economy 1960–1980', *World Development* 15(2), 275–86.

Bairoch, P. (1976) 'Europe's Gross National Product, 1800–1975', *Journal of European Economic History* 5(2), 273–340.

Bairoch, P. (1982) 'International Industrialization Levels from 1750–1980', *Journal of European Economic History* 11: 269–334.

Bairoch, P. (1991) 'Economic Inequalities between 1800 and 1913' in Batou, J. (ed.), *Between Development and Underdevelopment, 1800–1870*. Geneva: Librairie Droz.

Bassino, J.-P. and van der Eng, P. (2006) 'The First East Asian Economic Miracle: A Comparison of Nominal Wages and Welfare of Urban Workers in East Asia and Europe, 1880–1938', unpublished paper. Canberra: Australian National University.

Bates, R. (1981) *Markets and States in Tropical Africa*. Berkeley: University of California Press.

Becker, W.H. (1982) *The Dynamics of Business-Government Relations: Industry and Exports, 1893–1921*. Chicago: University of Chicago Press.

Bennett, D. and Sharpe, K. (1985) *Transnational Corporations versus the State: The Political Economy of the Mexican Auto Industry*. Princeton, NJ: Princeton University Press.

Bensel, R. (1990) *Yankee Leviathan*. Cambridge: Cambridge University Press.

Berend, I. and Ranki, G. (1982) *The European Periphery and Industrialization, 1780–1914*. Cambridge: Cambridge University Press.

Bernard, M. and Ravenhill, J. (1995) 'Beyond Product Cycles and Flying Geese: Regionalization, Hierarchy, and the Industrialization of East Asia', *World Politics* 47(2), 171–209.

Berry, B. (1991) *Long Wave Rhythms in Economic Development and Political Behavior*. Baltimore: Johns Hopkins University Press.

Bin Wong, R. (1998) *China Transformed: Historical Change and the Limits of European Experience*. Ithaca, NY: Cornell University Press.

Bloom, N. and Van Reenen, J. (2006) *Measuring and Explaining Management Practices across Firms and Countries*, Center for Economic Performance (CEP) discussion paper 0716, March. London: London School of Economics.

Bloom, N., Sadun, R. and Van Reenen, J. (2007) *Americans Do IT Better: US Multinationals and the Productivity Miracle*, CEP discussion paper 788. London: London School of Economics.

Borchardt, K. (1972–77) 'The Industrial Revolution in Germany 1700–1914', in Cipolla, C. (ed.), *Fontana Economic History of Europe*, vol. 4. London: Collins/Fontana.

Bosworth, B. and Trippett, J. (2007) 'The Early 21st Century U.S. Productivity Growth is *Still* in Services', *Brookings Institution International Productivity Monitor* 14, 1–19.

Braudel, F. (1981) *Civilization and Capitalism, Fifteenth–Eighteenth Century*, vol. I, *The Structures of Everyday Life*, trans. Sian Reynolds. New York: Harper and Row.

Braudel, F. (1982) *Civilization and Capitalism*. Baltimore, Md.: Johns Hopkins University Press.

Braudel, F. (1984) *Civilization and Capitalism, Fifteenth-Eighteenth Century*, vol. III, *The Perspective of the World*, trans. Sian Reynolds. New York: Harper and Row.

Brenner, R. (1977) 'The Origins of Capitalist Development: A Critique of Neo-Smithian Marxism', *New Left Review* no. 104, 25–93.

Brenner, R. (1985) 'Agrarian Class Structure and Economic Development in Pre-Industrial Europe', in Aston, T. and Philpin, C. (eds.), *The Brenner Debate: Agrarian Class Structure and Economic Development in Pre-Industrial Europe*. Cambridge: Cambridge University Press.

Brenner, R. (1998) 'The Economics of Global Turbulence', *New Left Review* no. 229.

Brewer, J. (1988) *The Sinews of Power: War, Money and the English State, 1688–1783*. Cambridge, Mass.: Harvard University Press.

Brinley, T. (1973) *Migration and Economic Growth*. Cambridge: Cambridge University Press.

Broadberry, S.N. (1994) 'Technological Leadership and Productivity Leadership since the Industrial Revolution: Implications for the Convergence Debate', *Economic Journal* 104(423), 291–302.

Broadberry, S. (1998) 'How did the United States and Germany Overtake Britain? Comparative Productivity Levels, 1870–1990' *Journal of Economic History* 58(2), 375–407.

Broadberry, S. and Gupta, B. (2006) 'The Early Modern Great Divergence: Wages, Prices and Economic Development in Europe and Asia, 1500–1800', *Economic History Review* 59(1), 2–31.

Broda, C. and Romalis, J. (2008) 'Inequality and Prices: Does China Benefit the Poor in America?', unpublished paper. University of Chicago.

Broda, C. and Weinstein, D. (2008) 'Exporting Deflation? Chinese Exports and Japanese Prices', unpublished paper. University of Chicago.

Bureau of Economic Analysis (2007) 'An Ownership Based Framework of the US Current Account, 1995–2005', *Survey of Current Business*, http://www.bea.gov/scb/pdf/2007/01%20January/0107_current_acct.pdf accessed 25 September 2007.

Bureau of Economic Analysis (2008) *International Economic Accounts*, http://www.bea.gov/International/Index.htm, accessed 1 July 2008.

Butlin, N. (1972) *Investment in Australian Economic Development, 1861–1890*. Canberra: Australian National University Press.

Callaghy, T. (1984) *State–Society Struggle: Zaire in Comparative Perspective*. New York: Columbia University Press.

Callendar, G. (1902) 'The Early Transportation and Banking Enterprises of the States in Relation to the Growth of Corporations', *Quarterly Journal of Economics* 17(1), 111–62.

Calleo, D. (1982) *Imperious Economy*. Cambridge, Mass.: Harvard University Press.

Caves, R., Frankel, J. and Jones, R. (1990) *World Trade and Payments*. Glenview, Ill.: Scott Foresman.

Chandler, A. (1962) *Strategy and Structure*. Cambridge, Mass.: MIT Press.

Chandler, A. (1977) *Visible Hand*. Cambridge, Mass.: Harvard University Press.

Chandler, A. (1984) 'The Emergence of Managerial Capitalism', *Business History Review* 58 (4, Winter), 473–503.

Chandler, A. (1990) *Scale and Scope: The Dynamics of Industrial Change*. Cambridge, Mass.: Belknap Press.

Chaudhuri, K.N. (1985) *Trade and Civilisation in the Indian Ocean*. Cambridge: Cambridge University Press.

Chaudhuri, K.N. (1990) *Asia before Europe*. Cambridge: Cambridge University Press.

Christaller, W. (1966 [1933]) *Central Places in Southern Germany*. Englewood Cliffs, NJ: Prentice Hall.

Cole, D. (1971) *Japanese Blue Collar*. Berkeley: University of California Press.

Costigliola, F. (1984) *Awkward Dominion*. Ithaca, N.Y.: Cornell University Press.

Cowhey, P. and Aronson, J. (1993) *Managing the World Economy*. New York: Council on Foreign Relations.

Cox, R. (1988) *Power, Production and World Order*. New York: Columbia University Press.

Coy, P. (2009) 'What Falling Prices Tell Us', *Business Week* 16 February, 24–6.

Craig, J.E. (1970) 'Ceylon', in Lewis, W.A. (ed.), *Tropical Development 1880–1914*. Evanston, Ill.: Northwestern University Press.

Crouzet, F. (1996) 'France', in Teich, M. and Porter, R. (eds.), *The Industrial Revolution in National Context*. Cambridge: Cambridge University Press.

Crosby, A. (1986) *Ecological Imperialism: The Biological Expansion of Europe 900–1900*. Cambridge: Cambridge University Press.

Cusumano, M. (1985) *Japanese Automobile Industry*. Cambridge, Mass.: Harvard University Press.

Dassbach, C. (1993) 'Enterprises and B Phases: The Overseas Expansion of U.S. Auto Companies in the 1920s and Japanese Auto Companies in the 1980s', *Sociological Perspectives* 36(4), 359–75.

de Cecco, M. (1984) *The International Gold Standard: Money and Empire*. New York: St Martin's Press.

de Cecco, M. (1986) 'Choice of a Monetary Standard: National Dilemmas and National and Supranational Solutions 1890–1914', in Fischer, W., McInnes, M. and Schneider, J. (eds.), *Emergence of a World Economy 1500–1913*, vol. II. Wiesbaden: F. Steiner.

de Hevesy, P. (1940) *World Wheat Planning and Economic Planning in General*. New York: Oxford University Press.

Denemark, R. and Thomas, K. (1988) 'The Brenner-Wallerstein Debate', *International Studies Quarterly* 32, 47–65.

Denoon, D. (1983) *Settler Capitalism*. Oxford: Oxford University Press.

Despres, E., Kindleberger, C. and Salant, W. (1970) 'The Dollar and World Liquidity: A Minority View', in Balassa, B. (ed.), *Changing Patterns in Foreign Trade and Payments*. New York: W.W. Norton.

Destler, I.M. (1992) *American Trade Policy*. Washington, DC: Institute for International Economics.

Dohse, K. (1985) 'From Fordism to Toyotism? Social Organization of the Labor Process in the Japanese Automobile Industry', *Politics & Society* 14(2), 115–45.

Dooley, M.P., Folkerts-Landau, D. and Garber, P. (2003) *An Essay on the Revived Bretton Woods System*, NBER Working Paper 9971. Cambridge, Mass.: National Bureau of Economic Research.

Doremus, P., Keller, W., Pauly, L. and Reich, S. (1998) *Myth of the Global Corporation*. Princeton, N.J.: Princeton University Press.

Duncan-Baretta, S. and Markoff, J. (1978) 'Civilization and Barbarism: Cattle Frontiers in Latin America', *Comparative Studies in Society and History* 20(4), 587–620.

Dunkerley, J. (1988) *Power in the Isthmus*. London: Verso.

Dunlavy, C. (1991) 'Mirror Images: Political Structures and Early Railroad Policy in the United States and Prussia', *Studies in American Political Development* 5(1), 1–35.

Dunn, J. (1987) 'Automobiles in International Trade: Regime Change or Persistence?', *International Organization* 41(2), 225–52.

Dunstan, H. (2006) *State or Merchant? Political Economy and Political Process in 1740s China*. Cambridge, Mass.: Harvard University Press.

Edelstein, M. (1982) *Overseas Investment in the Age of High Imperialism*. New York: Columbia University Press.

Eden, L. (1984) 'Capitalist Conflict and the State: The Making of United States Military Policy in 1948', in Bright, C. and Harding, S. (eds.), *Statemaking and Social Movements*. Ann Arbor: University of Michigan Press.

Edwards, R. (1979) *Contested Terrain*. New York: Basic Books.

EEC (European Economic Community) (1991) *The Agricultural Situation in the Community*. Brussels: EEC.

Eichengreen, B. (ed.) (1985) *Gold Standard in Theory and History*. New York: Methuen.

Eichengreen, B. and Portes, R. (1986) 'Debt and Default in the 1930s: Causes and Consequences', *European Economic Review* 30, 599–640.

Eichengreen, B. (1992) *Golden Fetters: The Gold Standard and the Great Depression*. New York: Oxford University Press.

Elbaum, B. (1986) 'The Steel Industry before World War I', in Elbaum, B. and Lazonick, W. (eds.), *Decline of the British Economy*. Oxford: Oxford University Press.

Ellman, M. (1975) 'Did the Agricultural Surplus Provide the Resources for the Increase in Investment during the First Five Year Plan?', *Economic Journal* 85, 844–64.

Ellsworth, P.T. (1950) *The International Economy: Structure and Operation*. New York: Macmillan.

Emmanuel, A. (1972) *Unequal Exchange: A Study of the Imperialism of Trade*. New York: Monthly Review Press.

Ernst, D. (1997) *From Partial to Systemic Globalization: International Production Networks in the Electronics Industry*, BRIE Working Paper no. 98. Berkeley, Calif.: Berkeley Roundtable on the International Economy, University of California at Berkeley.

Evans, P. (1979) *Dependent Development: The Alliance of State, Multinational and Local Capital in Brazil*. Princeton, NJ: Princeton University Press.

Falkus, M.E. (1972a) *The Industrialization of Russia 1700–1914*. London: Macmillan.

Falkus, M.E. (1972b) 'United States Economic Policy and the "Dollar Gap" in the 1920s', *Economic History Review* 24, 599–623.

Fatton, R. (1992) *Predatory States*. Boulder, Colo.: Westview.

Feis, H. (1930) *Europe: The World's Banker*. New Haven, Conn.: Yale University Press.

Fishlow, A. (1985) 'Lessons from the Past: Capital Markets during the 19th Century and the Interwar Period', *International Organization* 39(3), 383–439.

Flandreau, M. and Zumer, F. (2004) *The Making of Global Finance 1880–1913*. Paris: OECD.

Florida, R. and Kenney, M. (1988) 'Beyond Mass Production: Production and the Labor Process in Japan', *Politics and Society* 16(1), 121–58.

Foreman-Peck, J. and Michie, R. (1986) 'Performance of the Nineteenth Century International Gold Standard', in Fischer, W., McInnis, R. and Schneider, J. (eds.), *The Emergence of a World Economy 1500–1914*, vol. II. Wiesbaden: Franz Steiner.

Fox, E.W. (1966) *History in Geographic Perspective*. New York: Norton.

Frieden, J. (1988) 'Sectoral Conflict and US Foreign Economic Policy 1914–1940', *International Organization* 42(1), 59–90.

Frieden, J. (1991) 'Invested Interests: The Politics of National Economic Policies in a World of Global Finance', *International Organization* 45(4), 425–51.

Friedland, W. (1994) 'The Global Fresh Fruit and Vegetable System: An Industrial Organization Analysis', in McMichael, P. (ed.), *The Global Restructuring of Agro-Food Systems*. Ithaca: Cornell University Press, pp.173–89.

Friedmann, H. (1978) 'World Market, State and Family Farm', *Comparative Studies in Society and History* 20(3), 545–86.

Friman, H.R. (1990) *Patchwork Protectionism*. Ithaca, NY: Cornell University Press.

Fritsch, W. and Franco, G. (1991) *FDI in Brazil: Its Impact on Industrial Restructuring*. Paris: OECD.

Froebel, F., Heinrichs, J. and Kreye, O. (1980) *New International Division of Labour*. New York: Cambridge University Press.

Furber, H. (1976) *Rival Empires of Trade in the Orient*. Minneapolis: University of Minnesota Press.

Furnivall, J. (1956) *Colonial Policy and Practice: Burma and the Netherlands East Indies*. New York: New York University Press.

Gardner, R. (1969) *Sterling-Dollar Diplomacy*. New York: McGraw-Hill.

Garten, J. (1997) *The Big Ten: The Big Emerging Markets and How they Will Change our Lives*. New York: Basic Books.

Germain, R. (1998) *The International Organization of Credit*. Cambridge: Cambridge University Press.

Gerschenkron, A. (1966) *Economic Backwardness in Historical Perspective*. Cambridge, Mass.: Harvard University Press.

Gilpin, R. (1975) *US Power and the Multinational Corporation*. New York: Basic Books.

Glamann, K. (1974) 'European Trade 1500–1700', in Cipolla, C. (ed.), *Fontana Economic History of Europe: The Sixteenth and Seventeenth Centuries*. Glasgow: William Collins.

Goldstein, J. (1988) *Long Cycles: War and Prosperity in the Modern Age*. New Haven, Conn.: Yale University Press.

Gordon, A. (1985) *The Evolution of Labor Relations in Japanese Heavy Industry, 1853–1945*. Cambridge, Mass.: Harvard University Press.

Gourevitch, P. (1985) *Politics in Hard Times*. Ithaca, NY: Cornell University Press.

Gourinchas, P.-O. and Rey, H. (2005) *From World Banker to World Venture Capitalist: US External Adjustment and the Exorbitant Privilege*, NBER Working Paper 11563. Chicago: NBER.

Gowa, J. (1983) *Closing the Gold Window*. Ithaca, NY: Cornell University Press.

Gowan, P. (1999) *The Global Gamble: Washington's Faustian Bid for World Dominance*. London: Verso.

Greenspan, A. and Kennedy, J. (2007) *Sources and Uses of Equity Extracted from Homes*, Federal Reserve Bank, FEDS research paper 2007–20, http://www.federalreserve.gov/pubs/feds/2007/200720/200720pap.pdf.

Gregory, P. (1994). *Before Command: An Economic History of Russia from Emancipation to the First Five-Year Plan*. Princeton, NJ: Princeton University Press.

Grieco, J. (1990) *Cooperation among Nations: Europe, America and Non-Tariff Barriers to Trade*. Ithaca, N.Y.: Cornell University Press.

Groningen Growth and Development Centre (2006) *Groningen Growth and Development Centre and the Conference Board, Total Economy Database*, September 2006, http://www.ggdc.net.

Gros, D. (2006a) *Foreign Investment in the US (I), Disappearing in a Black Hole?*, Center for European Policy Studies Working Document 242. Brussels: Center for European Policy Studies.

Gros, D. (2006b) *Foreign Investment in the US (II), Being Taken to the Cleaners?*, Center for European Policy Studies Working Document 243. Brussels: Center for European Policy Studies.

Grotewold, A. (1971) 'The Growth of Industrial Core Areas and Patterns of World Trade', *Annals of the Association of American Geographers* 612, 361–70.

Hall, P. and Soskice, D. (2001) *Varieties of Capitalism: The Institutional Foundations of Comparative Advantage*. New York: Oxford University Press.

Hamilton, G. and Chang, W.-A. (2003) 'China's Late Imperial Economy', in Arrighi, G., Hamashita, T. and Selden, M. (eds.), *The Resurgence of East Asia: 500, 150 and 50 Year Perspectives*. London: Routledge.

Hamper, B. (1992) *Rivethead*. New York: Warner Books.

Harvard University Joint Center for Housing Studies (2008) *The State of the Nation's Housing, 2008*. Cambridge, Mass.: Harvard University.

Hathaway, D. (1987) *Agriculture and the GATT: Rewriting the Rules*. Washington, DC: Institute for International Economics.

Helleiner, E. (1994) *States and the Reemergence of Global Finance*. Ithaca, N.Y.: Cornell University Press.

Henning, C.R. (1994) *Currencies and Politics in the United States, Germany, and Japan*. Washington, DC: Institute for International Economics.

Higgott, R. and Cooper, A. (1990) 'Middle Power Leadership and Coalition Building: Australia, the Cairns Groups and the Uruguay Round of Trade Negotiations', *International Organization* 44(4), 589–632.

Hilferding, R. ([1910] 1981) *Finance Capital*, trans. Tom Bottomore. London: Routledge & Kegan Paul.

Hilgert, F. (1943) 'The Case for Multilateral Trade', *American Economic Review* 33(1), 393–407.

Hirschman, A. (1980) *National Power and the Structure of Foreign Trade*. Berkeley: University of California Press.

Hobsbawm, E. (1969) *Industry and Empire*. London: Weidenfeld.

Hobsbawm, E. (1975) *Age of Capital, 1848–1875*. New York: Scribner.

Hobson, J.A. (1938 [1902]) *Imperialism: A Study*. London: Allen and Unwin.

Hobson, J.M. (1997) *The Wealth of States*. Cambridge: Cambridge University Press.

Hochberg, L. (1984) 'The English Civil War in Geographic Perspective', *Journal of Interdisciplinary History* 14(4), 729–50.

Holz, C. (2006) 'Measuring China's productivity Growth, 1952–2005', unpublished paper. Hong Kong: University of Science and Technology.

Howard, M. (1976) *War in European History*. Oxford: Oxford University Press.

Hummels, D. (2007) 'Transportation Costs and International Trade in the Second Era of Globalization', *Journal of Economic Perspectives* 21(3), 131–54.

Hurt, S. (2009) 'Science, Power, and the State: U.S. Foreign Policy, Intellectual Property Law, and the Origins of Agricultural Biotechnology, 1969–1994', unpublished PhD dissertation. New York: New School for Social Research.

Huang, Y. (2008) *Capitalism with Chinese Characteristics*. Cambridge: Cambridge University Press.

Hymer, S. (1972) 'The Multinational Corporation and the Law of Uneven Development', in Bhagwati, J. (ed.), *Economics and World Order*. New York: Macmillan.

IMF (International Monetary Fund) (various dates) *Global Financial Stability Report, April and September*. Washington, DC: IMF.

Inklaar, R., Timmer, M.P., and van Ark, B. (2007) 'The End of Convergence: Market Services Productivity in Europe', unpublished paper. University of Groningen, March.

Innis, H. (1930) *The Fur Trade: An Introduction to Canadian Economic History*. New Haven, Conn.: Yale University Press.

Intracen (International Trade Centre) (2008) *International Trade Center on-line database*, http://www.intracen.org, accessed October 2008.

Islam, N. (1990) *Horticultural Exports of Developing Countries*. Washington, DC: International Food Policy Research Institute.

Israel, J. (1989) *Dutch Primacy in World Trade 1585–1740*. Oxford: Oxford University Press.

Jacks, D., Meissner, C. and Novy, D. (2008) 'Trade Costs, 1870–2000', *American Economic Review* 98(2), 529–34.

Janos, A. (1989) 'The Politics of Backwardness in Continental Europe, 1780–1945', *Comparative Politics* 41(3), 325–58.

Jen, S. and Bindelli, L. (2007) 'AXJ as a Source of Global Disinflation and Inflation', *Morgan Stanley Global Economic Forum 30 November 2007*, at http://www.morganstanley.com/views/gef/archive/2007/20071130-Fri.html.

Jenkins, R. (1984) *Transnational Corporations and Industrial Transformation in Latin America*. London: Macmillan.

Johansen, H.C. (1986) 'How to Pay for Baltic Products?', in Fischer, W., McInnis, R. and Schneider, J. (eds.), *The Emergence of a World Economy 1500–1914*, vol. II. Wiesbaden: Franz Steiner.

Ka, C. and Selden, M. (1986) 'Original Accumulation, Equity and Late Industrialization: The Cases of Socialist China and Capitalist Taiwan', *World Development* 14(10), 1293–310.

Kalecki, M. (1943) 'Political Aspects of Full Employment', *Political Quarterly* 14, 322–31.

Kamen, H. (2003) *Empire: How Spain Became a World Power, 1492–1763*. New York: HarperCollins.

Kaplinsky, R. (1999) 'If You Want to Get Somewhere Else, You Must Run at Least Twice as Fast as That!', *Competition and Change* 4(1), 1–30.

Katznelson, I. and Pietrykowski, B. (1991) 'Rebuilding the American State: Evidence from the 1940s', *Studies in American Political Development* 5, 301–39.

Kawakatsu, H. (1986) 'International Competition in Cotton Goods in the Late Nineteenth Century: Britain versus India and East Asia', in Fischer, W., McInnis, R. and Schneider, J. (eds.), *The Emergence of a World Economy 1500–1914*, vol. II. Wiesbaden: Franz Steiner.

Kindleberger, C. (1966) 'A Theory of Direct Foreign Investment', in C. Kindleberger (ed.), *American Business Abroad: Six Lectures on Direct Foreign Investment*. New Haven, Conn.: Yale University Press.

Kindleberger, C. (1973) *World in Depression*. Berkeley: University of California Press.

Kindleberger, C. (1975) 'The Rise of Free Trade in Western Europe 1820–1875', *Journal of Economic History* 35(1), 22–55.

Kitschelt, H. (1991) 'Industrial Governance Structures, Innovation Strategies and the Case of Japan', *International Organization* 45(4), 454–93.

Kocka, J. (1978) 'Entrepreneurs and Managers in German Industrialization', in Mathias, P. (ed.), *Cambridge Economic History of Europe*, vol. 7, Part I. Cambridge: Cambridge University Press.

Kondratieff, N. (1935) 'Long Waves in Economic Life', *Review of Economic Statistics* 17: 105–15, trans. E. Stolper.

Korea Federation of Banks (2006) *Annual Report*. Seoul: Korea Federation of Banks.

Kronish, R. and Mericle, K. (eds.) (1984) *The Political Economy of the Latin American Motor Vehicle Industry*. Cambridge, Mass.: MIT Press.

Krasner, S. (1978) *Defending the National Interest*. Princeton, N.J.: Princeton University Press.

Kriedte, P. (1983) *Peasants, Landlords, and Merchant Capitalists: Europe and the World Economy, 1500–1800*. Cambridge: Cambridge University Press.

Krugman, P. (1991a) 'Increasing Returns and Economic Geography', *Journal of Political Economy* 99(3), 483–99.

Krugman, P. (1991b) *Geography and Trade*. Cambridge, Mass.: MIT Press.

Krugman, P. (1994) 'The Myth of Asia's Miracle', *Foreign Affairs* 73, 62–4.

Krugman, P. and Venables, A. (1995) 'Globalization and the Inequality of Nations', *Quarterly Journal of Economics* 110(4), 857–80.

Kurth, J. (1979) 'Political Consequences of the Product Cycle', *International Organization* 33(1), 1–34.

Kuznets, S. (1967) *Secular Movements in Production and Prices*. New York: Augustus Kelly.

Lake, D. (1988) *Power, Protection and Free Trade*. Ithaca, NY: Cornell University Press.

Lane, F. (1958) 'The Economic Consequences of Organized Violence', *Journal of Economic History* 18(4), 401–17.

Latham, R. (1997) *The Liberal Moment: Modernity, Security, and the Making of Postwar International Order*. New York: Columbia University Press.

Laux, J.M. (1982) *The Automobile Revolution*. Chapel Hill, NC: University of North Carolina Press.

Lazonick, W. and Williamson, F. (1979) 'Industrial Relations and Uneven Development: A Comparative Study of the American and British Steel Industries', *Cambridge Journal of Economics* 3(3), 275–303.

Lazonick, W. (1990) *Competitive Advantage on the Shop Floor*. Cambridge, Mass.: Harvard University Press.

Lazonick, W. (1991) *Business Organization and the Myth of the Market Economy*. Cambridge, Mass.: Harvard University Press.

Lee, J. (1997) 'The Maturation and Growth of Infant Industries: The Case of Korea', *World Development* 25(8), 1271–81.

Levi, M. (1988) *Of Rule and Revenue*. Berkeley: University of California Press.

Lewis, W.A. (1954) 'Economic Development with Unlimited Supplies of Labour', *The Manchester School Journal* 22(2), 134–91.

Lewis, W.A. (ed.) (1970) *Tropical Development 1880–1914*. Evanston, Ill.: Northwestern University Press.

Lewis, W.A. (1978) *Growth and Fluctuations 1870–1913*. Boston, Mass.: Allen and Unwin.

Linden, G., Kraemer, K. and Dedrick, J. (2007) 'Who Captures value in a Global Innovation System: The Case of Apple's iPod', unpublished paper. Irvine: University of California.

Lynch, J. (1981) *Argentine Dictator: Juan Manuel de Rosas*. Oxford: Oxford University Press.

Maddison, A. (1985) *Two Crises*. Paris: OECD.

Maddison, A. (2007) *Chinese Economic Performance in the Long Run*. Paris: OECD.

Ministry for International Trade and Industry (Tokyo) (1986) *Maekawa Report (Report of the Advisory Group on Economic Structural Adjustment for International Harmony)*. Toyko: MITI.

Maier, C. (1975) *Recasting Bourgeois Europe*. Princeton, N.J.: Princeton University Press.

Maier, C. (1976) 'The Politics of Productivity', in Katzenstein, P. (ed.), *Between Power and Plenty*. Madison: University of Wisconsin Press.

Maier, C. (2006) *Among Empires: American Ascendancy and Its Predecessors*. Cambridge, Mass.: Harvard University Press.

Malenbaum, W. (1953) *The World Wheat Economy, 1885–1939*. Cambridge, Mass.: Harvard University Press.

Mandel, E. (1975) *Late Capitalism*. London: New Left Books.

Mandel, E. (1980) *Long Waves of Capitalist Development: The Marxist Interpretation*. Cambridge: Cambridge University Press.

Mann, M. (1986) *The Sources of Social Power*, vol. I. Cambridge: Cambridge University Press.

Mataloni, R., Jr. (2000) 'An Examination of the Low Rates of Return of Foreign Owned U.S. Companies', *Survey of Current Business*. Washington, DC: Department of Commerce.

McKeown, T. (1983) 'Hegemonic Stability and Nineteenth-Century Tariff Levels', *International Organization* 37(1), 73–91.

McKeown, T. (1991) 'A Liberal Trade Order? The Long Run Pattern of Imports to the Advanced Capitalist States', *International Studies Quarterly* 35, 151–72.

McKinnon, R. (2005) *Exchange Rates under the East Asian Dollar Standard: Living with Conflicted Virtue*. Cambridge, Mass.: MIT Press.

McKinsey Global Institute (2006) *From 'Made in China' to 'Sold in China': The Rise of the Chinese Urban Consumer*. New York: McKinsey and Company.

McMichael, P. (1984) *Settlers and the Agrarian Question*. Cambridge: Cambridge University Press.

McNeil, W. (1986) *American Money and the Weimar Republic*. New York: Columbia University Press.

Mintz, S. (1985) *Sweetness and Power: The Place of Sugar in Modern History*. London: Penguin.

Mitchell, B.R. (1988) *British Historical Statistics*. Cambridge: Cambridge University Press.

Mitchell, B.R. (1992) *International Historical Statistics, Europe: 1750–1988*. New York: Stockton Press.

Mitchell, B.R. (2000) *International Historical Statistics, Asia, Africa and Oceania, 1750–1993*. London: Palgrave Macmillan.

Mitchell, B.R. and Deane, P. (1962) *Abstract of British Historical Statistics*. Cambridge: Cambridge University Press.

Modelski, G. (1987) *Long Waves in World Politics*. London: Macmillan.

Modelski, G. and Thompson, W.R. (1990) *Seapower in Global Politics 1494–1993*. Seattle: University of Washington Press.

Moran, T. (1973) 'Foreign Expansion as an Institutional Necessity', *World Politics* 25(3), 369–86.

Moulton, H. and Pasvolsky, L. (1932) *War Debts and World Prosperity*. Washington, DC: Brookings Institution.

Muller, P. (1973) 'Trend Surfaces of American Agricultural Patterns: A Macro-Thünian Analysis', *Economic Geography* 493, 228–42.

National Science Foundation (2007) *Asia's Rising Science and Technology Strength: Comparative Indicators for Asia, the European Union, and the United States*. Washington, DC: National Science Foundation.

Naughton, B. (2007) *China's Economy: Transition and Growth*. Cambridge, Mass: MIT Press.

Newhouse, J. (2007) *Boeing versus Airbus*. New York: Knopf.

Nitzan, J. (1998) 'Differential Accumulation: Towards a New Political Economy of Capital', *Review of International Political Economy* 5(2), 169–216.

Nivola, P. (1993) *Regulating Unfair Trade*. Washington, DC: Brookings Institution.

Norman, E.H. (1975) *Origins of the Modern Japanese State*, ed. J. Dower. New York: Pantheon.

North, D.C. and Thomas, R. (1973) *Rise of the Western World*. Cambridge: Cambridge University Press.

Nye, J.V. (1991) 'Revisionist Tariff History and the Theory of Hegemonic Stability', *Politics and Society* 19(2), 209–32.

OECD (1987) *Economic Outlook No. 42*. Paris: OECD.

OECD (1998a) *Economic Outlook No. 64*. Paris: OECD.

OECD (1998b) *Economic Outlook No. 65*. Paris: OECD.

OECD (1998c) *Economic Survey: Australia, 1998*. Paris: OECD.

OECD (1999) 'Recent Trends in Direct Foreign Investment', *Financial Market Trends no. 73, June 1999*. Paris: OECD.

OECD (2006) *Agricultural Policy in OECD Countries*. Paris: OECD.

OECD (2008a) *Measuring Globalization: Activities of Multinationals, volume II, Services*. Paris: OECD.

OECD (2008b) *Economic Outlook No. 83*. Paris: OECD.

OECD (2008c) *OECD online database*, at http://www.SourceOECD.org, date accessed 5 September 2008.

Offer, A. (1989) *The First World War: An Agrarian Interpretation*. Oxford: Clarendon Press.

Okimoto, D. (1989) *Between MITI and Market*. Stanford, Calif.: Stanford University Press.

Orde, A. (1990) *British Policy and European Reconstruction after the First World War*. Cambridge: Cambridge University Press.

O'Rourke, K. and Williamson, J. (1999) *Globalization and History: The Evolution of a Nineteenth-Century Atlantic Economy*. Cambridge, Mass.: MIT Press.

O'Rourke, K. and Williamson, J. (2002) 'After Columbus: Explaining Europe's Overseas Trade Boom, 1500–1800', *Journal of Economic History* 62(2), 417–456.

Ozawa, T. (1979) *Multinationalism, Japanese Style*. Princeton, NJ: Princeton University Press.

Page, B. and Walker, R. (1991) 'From Settlement to Fordism: The Agro-Industrial Revolution in the American Midwest', *Economic Geography* 67(4), 294–5.

Palloix, C. (1977) 'Self Expansion of Capital on a World Scale', *Review of Radical Political Economy* 9(2), 3–17.

Parboni, R. (1981) *The Dollar and its Rivals*. London: Verso.

Parker, G. (1972) *The Army of Flanders and the Spanish Road 1567–1699*. Cambridge: Cambridge University Press.

Parker, G. (1988) *The Military Revolution*. Cambridge: Cambridge University Press.

Pearson, M.N. (1991) 'States and Merchants', in Tracy, J. (ed.), *Political Economy of Merchant Empires*. Cambridge: Cambridge University Press.

Peet, J.R. (1969) 'The Spatial Expansion of Commercial Agriculture in the Nineteenth Century: A von Thünen Interpretation', *Economic Geography* 45(4), 283–301.

Peet, J.R. (1972) 'The British Market and European Agriculture, c. 1700–1860', *Transactions of the Institute of British Geographers* 56.

Pilat, D. (1996) 'Competition, Productivity and Efficiency', *OECD Economic Studies* no.27: 107–46.

Piore, M. and Sabel, C. (1985) *Second Industrial Divide*. New York: Basic Books.

Platt, D.C.M. (1973) *Latin America and British Trade*. New York: Barnes and Noble.

Platt, D.C.M. and Di Tella, G. (1985) *Argentina, Australia, and Canada: Studies in Comparative Development 1870–1965*. New York: St Martin's Press.

Polanyi, K. (1957) *The Great Transformation*. Boston, Mass.: Beacon Press.

Pollard, S. (1981) *Peaceful Conquest: The Industrialization of Europe 1760–1970*. New York: Oxford University Press.

Pomeranz, K. (2000) *The Great Divergence: Europe, China, and the Making of the Modern World Economy*. Princeton, NJ: Princeton University Press.

Prebisch, R. (1950) *The Economic Development of Latin America and its Principal Problems*. New York: United Nations.

Price, R. (1981) *An Economic History of Modern France 1730–1914*. London: Macmillan.

PriceWaterhouseCoopers (2005) *China's Impact on the Semiconductor Industry, 2005 Update*, http://www.pwc.com/techforecast/pdfs/ChinaSemis2005_x.pdf.

Pucik, V. (1984) 'White Collar Human Resource Management: A Comparison of the US and Japanese Automobile Industries', *Columbia Journal of World Business* 19(3), 87–94.

Pullen, W. (1987) *World War Debts and United States Foreign Policy 1919–1929*. New York: Columbia University Press.

Putnam, R. and Bayne, N. (1987) *Hanging Together: Cooperation and Conflict in the Seven-Power Summits*. Cambridge, Mass.: Harvard University Press.

Reich, S. (1989) 'Roads to Follow: Regulating Direct Foreign Investment', *International Organization* 43(4), 543–84

Reid, A. (1990) *Southeast Asia in the Age of Commerce, 1450–1680: The Land beneath the Winds*. New Haven, Conn.: Yale University Press.

Reynolds, L. (1985) *Economic Growth in the Third World*. New Haven, Conn.: Yale University Press.

Reynolds, S. (1994) *Fiefs and Vassals: The Medieval Evidence Reinterpreted*. New York: Oxford University Press.

Rogowski, R. (1991) *Commerce and Coalitions*. Princeton, NJ: Princeton University Press.

Rostow, W.W. (1978) *The World Economy*. Austin: University of Texas.

Ruggie, J.G. (1982) 'International Regimes, Transactions and Change: Embedded Liberalism in the Post-War International Economic Order', *International Organization* 36(2), 379–415.

Ruoen, R. (1997) *China's Economic Performance in an International Perspective*. Paris: OECD.

Rupert, M. (1995) *Producing Hegemony: The Politics of Mass Production and American Global Power*. Cambridge: Cambridge University Press.

Salaman, R. (1949) *The History and Social Influence of the Potato*. Cambridge: Cambridge University Press.

Sandholtz, W. and Zysman, J. (1989) '1992: Recasting the European Bargain', *World Politics* 42(1), 1–30.

Saul, S. (1985) *Myth of the Great Depression 1873–1896*. London: Macmillan.

Schlebecker, J. (1960) 'The World Metropolis and the History of American Agriculture', *Journal of Economic History* 202: 187–208.

Schuker, S. (1988) *American 'Reparations' to Germany*, Princeton Studies in International Finance No. 61. Princeton, NJ: International Finance Section, Dept. of Economics, Princeton University.

Schumpeter, J. (1939) *Business Cycles: A Theoretical, Historical and Statistical Analysis of the Capitalist Process*. Cambridge, Mass.: Harvard University Press.

Schumpeter, J. (1942) *Capitalism, Socialism, Democracy*. New York: Harper and Row.

Schurmann, F. (1974) *Logic of World Power*. New York: Pantheon.

Schwartz, H. (1989) 'Foreign Creditors and the Politics of Development in Australia and Argentina 1880–1913', *International Studies Quarterly* 33(3), 281–301.

Schwartz, H. (2007) 'Dependency or Institutions? Economic Geography, Causal Mechanisms and Logic in Understanding Development', *Studies in Comparative International Development* 42(1), 115–35.

Schwartz, H. (2009a) *Subprime Nation: American Power, Global Finance and the Housing Bubble*. Ithaca, NY: Cornell University Press.

Schwartz, H. (2009b) 'Housing Finance, Growth, and the US Dollar's Past and Future', in Helleiner, E. and Kirshner, J. (eds.), *Future of the US Dollar*. Ithaca, NY: Cornell University Press.

Seguino, S. (2000) 'Gender Inequality and Economic Growth: A Cross-Country Analysis', *World Development* 28(7), 1211–30.

Seidman, J. (1953) *American Labor from Defense to Reconversion*. Chicago: University of Chicago Press.

Senghaas, D. (1985) *The European Experience: A Historical Critique of Development Theory*. Dover, NH: Berg.

Servan-Schreiber, J.-J. (1969) *The American Challenge*. New York: Avon.

Shaiken, H. (1991) 'Universal Motors Assembly and Stamping Plant: Transferring High-Tech Production to Mexico', *Columbia Journal of World Business* 26(2), 124–37.

Shenfeld, A. and Grauman, M. (2008) 'Oil and Growth: That 70s Show Re-Run', *CIBC World Markets* 26 June.

Shonfield, A. (1964) *Modern Capitalism*. New York: Oxford University Press.

Shoup, L. and Minter, W. (1977) *Imperial Brain Trust*. New York: Monthly Review Press.

Simon, R. (2008) 'Mortgages Made in 2007 Go Bad at a Rapid Clip', *Wall Street Journal*, 9 August.

Skinner, G.W. (1964) 'Marketing and Social Structures in Rural China', *Journal of Asian Studies* 24, 3–43.

Slicher van Bath, B.H. (1963) *Agrarian History of Western Europe 500–1850*. New York: St Martin's Press.

Smith, B. (1986) *The War's Long Shadow*. New York: Simon and Schuster.

Spiro, D. (1999) *The Hidden Hand of American Hegemony: Petrodollar Recycling and International Markets*. Ithaca, NY: Cornell University Press.

Spruyt, H. (1994) *The Sovereign State and its Competitors*. Princeton, N.J.: Princeton University Press.

Steensgaard, N. (1974) *The Asian Trade Revolution of the Seventeenth Century*. Chicago: University of Chicago Press.

Steensgaard, N. (1991) 'Trade of England and the Dutch before 1750', in Tracy, J. (ed.), *Political Economy of Merchant Empires*. Cambridge: Cambridge University Press.

Stone, K. (1974) 'Origins of Job Structures in the Steel Industry', *Review of Radical Political Economy* 6: 113–73

Strange, S. and Tooze, R. (1981) *Politics of Surplus Capacity: Competition for Market Shares in the World Recession*. Boston, Mass.: Allen and Unwin.

Strayer, J. (1970) *On the Medieval Origins of the Modern State*. Princeton, NJ: Princeton University Press.

Subrahmanyam, S. and Thomaz, L.F. (1991) 'Evolution of Empire', in Tracy, J. (ed.), *The Political Economy of Merchant Empires*. Cambridge: Cambridge University Press.

Sugihara, K. (1986) 'Patterns of Asia's Integration into the World Economy 1880–1913', in Fischer, W.W., McInnis, R. and Schneider, J. (eds.), *The Emergence of a World Economy 1500–1914*, vol. II. Wiesbaden: F. Steiner.

Sugihara, K. (2003) 'East Asian economic Development: A Long Term View', in Arrighi, G., Hamashita, T. and Selden, M. (eds.), *The Resurgence of East Asia: 500, 150, and 50 Year Perspectives*. London: Routledge.

Suter, C. (1992) *Debt Cycles in the World-Economy*. Boulder, Colo.: Westview.

Teece, D.J. (1977) 'Technology Transfer by Multinational Firms', *Economic Journal* 87: 242–61.

Teece, D.J. (1980) 'Economies of Scope and the Scope of the Enterprise', *Journal of Economic Behavior and Organization* 1(3), 223–45.

Thompson, E.P. (1966) *The Making of the English Working Class*. New York: Vintage.

Thompson, W.R. (1993) 'Dehio, Long Cycles and the Geohistorical Context of Structural Transition', *World Politics* 43: 127–52.

Thompson, W.R. (1990) 'Long Waves, Technological Innovation and Relative Decline', *International Organization* 44(2), 201–34.

Thorne, C. (1978) *Allies of a Kind*. New York: Oxford University Press.

Thünen, J.H. von (1966) *The Isolated State [Der isolierte Staat]*, ed. P. Hall and trans. C.M. Wartenberg. New York: Pergamon Press.

Tilly, C. (1985) 'War Making and State Making as Organized Crime', in Evans, P., Rueschmeyer, D. and Skocpol, T. (eds.), *Bringing the State Back In*. Cambridge: Cambridge University Press.

Tilly, C. (1990) *Coercion, Capital, and European States*. Cambridge, Mass.: Basil Blackwell.

Tomich, D. (1990) *Slavery in the Circuit of Sugar*. Baltimore, Md.: Johns Hopkins University Press.

Thorne, C. (1978) *Allies of a Kind*. New York: Oxford University Press.

Toshitomi, M. (1996) 'On the Changing International Competitiveness of Japanese Manufacturing since 1985', *Oxford Review of Economic Policy* 12(3), 61–73.

Treasury Department (2008) *Foreign Portfolio Holdings of US Securities, June 2007*. Washington, DC: US Treasury Department.

Triffin, R. (1960) *Gold and the Dollar Crisis: The Future of Convertibility*. New Haven, Conn.: Yale University Press.

Triffin, R. (1964) *The Evolution of the International Monetary System: Historical Reappraisal and Future Perspectives*. Princeton, NJ: Princeton University Press.

UNCTAD (United Nations Conference on Trade and Development) (1991) *World Investment Report 1991*. New York: United Nations.

UNCTAD (2002) *World Investment Report 2002*. New York: United Nations.

UNCTAD (2006) *World Investment Report, 2006*. New York: United Nations.

UNCTAD (United Nations Conference on Trade and Development) (2008) *World Investment Report, 2008*. New York: United Nations.

van Ark, B., Monnikhof, E. and Mulder, N. (1999) 'Productivity in Services: An International Comparative Perspective', *Canadian Journal of Economics* 32(2), 471–99.

van Ark, B., O'Mahoney, M. and Timmer, M. (2008) 'The Productivity Gap between Europe and the United States: Trends and Causes', *Journal of Economic Perspectives* 22(1), 25–44.

van der Pijl, K. (1984) *Making of an Atlantic Ruling Class*. London: Verso.

van Valkenburg, S. and Held, C. (1952) *Europe*. New York: John Wiley.

Vernon, R. (1971) *Sovereignty at Bay*. New York: Basic Books.

Vilar, P. (1976) *A History of Gold and Money*. London: New Left Books.

Volland, C. (1987) 'A Comprehensive Theory of Long Wave Cycles', *Technological Forecasting and Social Change* 32: 120–45.

Waldner, D. (1999) *State Building and Late Development*. Ithaca, NY: Cornell University Press.

Wallerstein, I. (1974–89) *Modern World System*, 4 vols. New York: Academic Publishers.

Warnock, F. and Warnock, V.C. (2006) *International Capital Flows and U.S. Interest Rates*, FRB International Finance Discussion Paper No. 840. Washington, DC: Federal Reserve Bank.

Watkins, M. (1963) 'A Staples Theory of Economic Growth', *Canadian Journal of Economics and Political Science* 29(2), 141–58.

Weber, A. (1929 [1909]) *Theory of the Location of Industries*, trans. C. Friedrich. Chicago: University of Chicago Press.

Welch, D. (2009) 'A Hundred Factories too Many', *Business Week* 12 January, 42–3.

Weiss, L. (1993) 'War, the State, and the Origins of the Japanese Employment System', *Politics and Society* 21(3), 325–54.

Weiss, L. and Hobson, J. (1995) *States and Economic Development*. London: Polity Press.

White, L.J. (1982) 'The Automobile Industry', in Adams, W. (ed.), *Structure of American Industry*. New York: Macmillan.

Wilkins, M. (1974) *The Maturing of Multinational Enterprise: American Business Abroad 1914–1970*. Cambridge, Mass.: Harvard University Press.

Williams, K., Haslam, C., Johal, S. and Williams, J. (1994) *Cars: Analysis, History, Cases*. New York: Berghahn Books.

Williamson, J. (1997) 'Globalization and Inequality, Past and Present', *World Bank Research Observer* 12(2), 117–35.

Williamson, O. (1985) *Economic Institutions of Capitalism*. New York: Free Press.

Wolf, E. (1986) *Europe and the People without History*. Berkeley: University of California Press.

Womack, J., Jones, D. and Roos, D. (1992) *The Machine that Changed the World.* New York: Rawson Associates.

Wood, A. (1994) *North-South Trade, Employment, and Inequality.* New York: Oxford University Press.

Wooldridge, P. (2006) 'The Changing Composition of Official Reserves', *Bank for International Settlements Quarterly Review.* September.

World Bank (1993) *The East Asian Miracle.* New York: Oxford University Press.

World Bank (2008) *World Development Indicators, 2008.* Washington, DC: World Bank.

WTO (World Trade Organization) (1998) *International Trade Statistics, 1998.* Geneva: WTO.

WTO (World Trade Organization) (2008) *International Trade Statistics, 2008.* Geneva: WTO.

Wunde, H. (1985) 'Peasant Organization and Class Conflict in Eastern and Western Germany', in Aston, T.H. and Philpin, C. (eds.), *The Brenner Debate: Agrarian Class Structure and Economic Development in Pre-Industrial Europe.* Cambridge: Cambridge University Press.

Yokeno, N. (1956) 'Thünen's Structure in the Agriculture of Japan', *Sophia Economic Review* 3(1), 14–22.

Zimmermann, H. (2002) *Money and Security: Troops, Monetary Policy and West Germany's Relations to the United States and the United Kingdom, 1950–1971.* Cambridge: Cambridge University Press.

Zolberg, A. (1987) 'Wanted but Not Welcome', in Alonso, W. (ed.), *Population in an Interacting World.* Cambridge, Mass.: Harvard University Press.

Index

absolute advantage, 46
absolutism, 23, 30, 36
Aden, 33, 37
Africa, 28, 33–5, 98–9, 108, 126, 135, 238, 267, 313; foreign investment, 137–8, labor supplies, 118–21; slavery, 111, 113–15
Agency bonds, *see* mortgage-backed securities (*under* mortgages)
agglomeration, 22, 44, 56–9, 87, 270, 271; *see also* Krugman model
agriculture, 11–13, 15, 45, 49–51, 55–60, 62, 68, 81, 84–5, 88–90, 92, 96–8, 100–2, 104, 108, 110, 120, 125–7, 129–30, 134, 137, 144–5, 149–50, 153, 168, 181–3, 195, 196, 201, 213, 236–7, 248, 250–1, 255–7, 259, 263–9, 275, 278–9, 284, 312, 322; agricultural revolution, 15, 29, 43, 50, 83
Airbus Industrie, 257, 297–8
Amsden, Alice, 91, 236, 250, 257, 259
Amsterdam, 37–8, 54, 77
andon lights, 289–90
Antwerp, 37
Arabs, 35
Aragon, 27–8
arbitrage, 38, 77, 148, 163, 202, 305–7, 318, 321
Argentina, 43, 67, 106, 108, 114, 116–20, 125–6, 131–3, 135, 137–8, 141–3, 145, 166, 172, 184, 229, 237, 239–40, 244, 265; Buenos Aires, 117–18, 131–2, 141; Cordoba, 132
Arrighi, Giovanni, 14, 24, 65, 113, 120, 160
Asia, 24, 32, 33, 36, 38, 41, 42, 43, 80, 84, 95–101, 105, 108, 111, 113–14, 116, 119, 121, 123, 125–7, 129–30, 134–5, 141, 145, 180, 188, 197, 214, 216, 218, 232, 234, 236, 238, 249–51, 253–4, 260, 262, 271, 274–5, 304, 308, 310, 313–16, 318, 320–1
Asian financial crisis (1997–8), 216, 254, 316

assembly line, 71–3, 170, 177–80, 183–4, 187, 189–91, 203, 219, 229–31, 257, 282–3, 285–6, 288–90, 292, 320
Australia, 43, 67, 82, 106, 108, 111, 114–19, 125, 127, 130–3, 135–7, 143–5, 166, 184, 223, 265, 267, 300, 313
Austria, 27–8, 85, 95, 137, 165, 300

Babbage, Charles, 271
Baltic Sea region, 17, 32–3, 37–9, 42, 51, 77
bananas, 267–8
Bank of England, 162, 164
Bank of Japan, 312–13
bank-led development, 89
banks, 77, 87, 89–90, 92, 94–6, 98, 128, 132–3, 138–9, 141–3, 148, 151, 155, 161–3, 166, 172, 183, 185–6, 198–9, 204–5, 208–13, 217, 240, 249, 254, 258, 260–1, 279, 291, 305, 307–9, 312–16, 319
Barbados, 115, 130
Baring Brothers, 139
Belgium, 27, 50, 84–5, 92, 97, 137, 300
Bengal, 40–1, 100
bills of exchange, 161–4
biotechnology, 182
Bismarck, Otto, 95, 158
blue-collar workers, 286, 290, 293
Boeing, 297–8
Braudel, Fernand, 50
Brazil, 39, 62, 108, 115, 126, 134–5, 177, 180, 229, 255–9, 261, 267, 279; late development in, 237, 239–47
Brenner, Robert, 48, 54
Bretton Woods Agreements, 192–4, 197–209, 213, 217, 219, 223, 227, 234, 262, 265, 302, 310, 320, 322
Britain: Civil War, 31; Corn Laws, 109; declining hegemony, 148–54, 160–6; Glorious Revolution of 1688, 31; imports 103–11; Indian Ocean empire, 39–42; industrial revolution, 80–6; Navigation Acts, 39;

339